Pearls of Algorithm Engineering

There are many textbooks on algorithms that focus on big-O notation and basic design principles. This book offers a unique approach to taking the design and analyses to the level of predictable practical efficiency, discussing core and classic algorithmic problems that arise in the development of big data applications, and presenting elegant solutions of increasing sophistication and efficiency. Solutions are analyzed within the classic RAM model, and the more practically significant external-memory model that allows one to perform I/O complexity evaluations. Chapters cover various data types, including integers, strings, trees, and graphs; algorithmic tools such as sampling, sorting, data compression, and searching in dictionaries and texts; and lastly, recent developments regarding compressed data structures. Algorithmic solutions are accompanied by detailed pseudocode and many running examples, thus enriching the toolboxes of students, researchers, and professionals interested in effective and efficient processing of big data.

Paolo Ferragina is Professor of Algorithms at the University of Pisa, with a postdoc at the Max-Planck Institute for Informatics. He served his university as Vice Rector for ICT (2019–22) and for Applied Research and Innovation (2010–16) and as the Director of the PhD program in Computer Science (2018–20). His research focuses on designing algorithms and data structures for compressing, mining, and retrieving information from big data. The joint recipient of the prestigious 2022 ACM Paris Kanellakis Theory and Practice Award and numerous other international awards, Ferragina has previously collaborated with AT&T, Bloomberg, Google, ST microelectronics, Tiscali, and Yahoo. His research has produced several patents and has featured in over 170 papers published in renowned conferences and journals. He has spent research periods at the Max Planck Institute for Informatics, the University of North Texas, the Courant Institute at New York University, the MGH/Harvard Medical School, AT&T, Google, IBM Research, and Yahoo.

When I joined Google in 2000, algorithmic problems came up every day. Even strong engineers didn't have all the background they needed to design efficient algorithms. Paolo Ferragina's well-written and concise book helps fill that void. A strong software engineer who masters this material will be an asset.

— Martin Farach-Colton, Rutgers University

There are plenty of books on Algorithm Design, but few about Algorithm Engineering. This is one of those rare books on algorithms that pays the necessary attention to the more practical aspects of the process, which become crucial when actual performance matters and render some theoretically appealing algorithms useless in real life. The author is an authority on this challenging path between theory and practice of algorithms, which aims at both conceptually nontrivial and practically relevant solutions. I hope the readers will find the reading as pleasant and inspiring as I did.

— Gonzalo Navarro, University of Chile

Ferragina combines his skills as a coding engineer, an algorithmic mathematician, and a pedagogic innovator to engineer a string of pearls made up of beautiful algorithms. In this, beauty dovetails with computational efficiency. His data structures of Stringomics hold the promise for a better understanding of population of genomes and the history of humanity. It belongs in the library of anyone interested in the beauty of code and the code of beauty.

— Bud Mishra, Courant Institute, New York University

There are many textbooks on algorithms focusing on big-O notation and general design principles. This book offers a completely unique aspect of taking the design and analyses to the level of predictable practical efficiency. No sacrifices in generality are made, but rather a convenient formalism is developed around external memory efficiency and parallelism provided by modern computers. The benefits of randomization are elegantly used for obtaining simple algorithms whose insightful analyses provide the reader with useful tools to be applied to other settings. This book will be invaluable in broadening the computer science curriculum with a course on algorithm engineering.

— Veli Mäkinen, University of Helsinki

Pearls of Algorithm Engineering

PAOLO FERRAGINA

University of Pisa

CAMBRIDGE
UNIVERSITY PRESS

CAMBRIDGE
UNIVERSITY PRESS

Shaftesbury Road, Cambridge CB2 8EA, United Kingdom

One Liberty Plaza, 20th Floor, New York, NY 10006, USA

477 Williamstown Road, Port Melbourne, VIC 3207, Australia

314–321, 3rd Floor, Plot 3, Splendor Forum, Jasola District Centre, New Delhi – 110025, India

103 Penang Road, #05–06/07, Visioncrest Commercial, Singapore 238467

Cambridge University Press is part of Cambridge University Press & Assessment,
a department of the University of Cambridge.

We share the University's mission to contribute to society through the pursuit of
education, learning and research at the highest international levels of excellence.

www.cambridge.org
Information on this title: www.cambridge.org/9781009123280
DOI: 10.1017/9781009128933

© Paolo Ferragina 2023

First published 2023

A catalogue record for this publication is available from the British Library.

A Cataloging-in-Publication data record for this book is available from the Library of Congress.

ISBN 978-1-009-12328-0 Hardback

to Bebe and Franci

Contents

Preface

This book offers advice for programmers and software engineers: no matter how smart you are, in the field of algorithm engineering, the proverbial five-minutes thinking will not be enough to get a reasonable solution for real-life problems. Real-life problems have reached such a large size, machines have become so complicated, users so demanding, applications so resource-hungry, and algorithmic tools so sophisticated that you cannot improvise being an algorithm engineer: you need to be trained to be one.

The following chapters bear witness to this situation by introducing challenging problems together with elegant and efficient algorithmic techniques to solve them. In selecting their topics I was driven by a twofold goal: on the one hand, to provide readers with an *algorithm engineering toolbox* that will help them tackle programming problems involving massive datasets; and, on the other hand, to collect together the scientific material that I would have liked to have been taught when I was a master's/PhD student. Some of the following sections, typically (though not always) at the ends of chapters, have their titles completed by the superscripted symbol ∞; this indicates more advanced contents that the reader can skip without jeopardizing the reading of the book. As a final note for the reader passionate of programming, I point out another specialty of this book related to the fact that array indexes start from 1, instead of the classic 0 usually adopted in coding, because in this way algorithms may be paraphrased more easily and formulas do not become complicated by the presence of ± 1.

The style and content of these chapters is the result of many hours of illuminating, and sometimes hard and fatiguing, discussions with many fellow researchers and students. Some of these lectures comprised the courses on information retrieval and advanced algorithms that I have been teaching at the University of Pisa and in various international PhD schools since 2004. In particular, a preliminary draft of these notes was prepared by the students of the Algorithm Engineering course in the master's degree of Computer Science and Networking in September–December 2009, in a collaboration between the University of Pisa and the Sant'Anna School of Advanced Studies. Some other notes were prepared by the PhD students attending the course on Advanced Algorithms for Massive DataSets that I taught at the Bertinoro International Spring School (BISS), held in March 2010 (Bertinoro, Italy). I used these draft notes as a seed for some of the following chapters. Of course, many changes have been made to these notes in the following years, thanks to the corrections and suggestions made by the many students who attended the Algorithm Engineering courses since 2010.

Special thanks go to Antonio Boffa, Andrea Guerra, Francesco Tosoni, and Giorgio Vinciguerra for carefully reading the latest version of this book, to Gemma Martini for contributing to Chapter 15, and to Riccardo Manetti for the figures in tikz. I also thank my PhD students and colleagues: Jyrki Alakuijala, Ricardo Baeza-Yates, Lorenzo Bellomo, Massi Ciaramita, Marco Cornolti, Martin Farach-Colton, Andrea Farruggia, Raffaele Giancarlo, Roberto Grossi, Antonio Gullì, Luigi Laura, Veli Makinen, Giovanni Manzini, Kurt Mehlhorn, Ulli Meyer, Bud Mishra, S. Muthukrishnan, Gonzalo Navarro, Igor Nitto, Linda Pagli, Francesco Piccinno, Luca Pinello, Marco Ponza, Prabhakar Raghavan, Peter Sanders, and Rossano Venturini, Jeff S. Vitter, for the many hours of fascinating and challenging discussions about these topics over the years. My final and warmest thanks go to Fabrizio Luccio, my mentor, who has continuously stimulated my research passion and instilled in me the desire for and pleasure in teaching and writing as simply and clearly as possible… but not too much simply. You will be the judge of whether I have succeeded in achieving this goal with the present book.

My ultimate hope is that in reading the following pages you will be pervaded by the same pleasure and excitement that filled me when I met these algorithmic solutions for the first time. If this is the case, please read more about algorithms to find inspiration for your academic and professional work. It is still the case that *computer programming is an art*, but you need good tools to express it at the highest level of beauty.

P. F.

1 Introduction

This is rocket science but you don't have
to be a rocket scientist to use it.
Jack Noonan, CEO of SPSS

The main actor in this book is the *algorithm*, so in order to dig into the beauty and challenges that pertain to its ideation and design, we need to start from one of its many possible definitions. The Oxford English Dictionary reports that an algorithm is, informally, *"a process, or set of rules, usually one expressed in algebraic notation, now used esp. in computing, machine translation and linguistics."* The modern meaning of *algorithm* is quite similar to that of *recipe, method, procedure,* or *routine,* but in computer science the word connotes something more precisely described. In fact many authoritative researchers have tried to pin down the term over the past 200 years by proposing definitions that have become more complicated and detailed but, in the minds of their proponents, more precise and elegant.[1] As algorithm designers and engineers we will follow the definition provided by Donald Knuth at the end of the 1960s [7]: an algorithm is *a finite, definite, effective procedure, with some output.* Although these features may be intuitively clear and are widely accepted as requirements for a sequence of steps to be an algorithm, they are so dense in significance that we need to look at them in more detail; this will lead us to the scenarios and challenges posed nowadays by algorithm design and engineering, and to the motivation behind this book.

- Finite: "An algorithm must always terminate after a finite number of steps ... a very finite number, a reasonable number." Clearly, the term "reasonable" is related to the *efficiency* of the algorithm: Knuth [7] states that "In practice, we not only want algorithms, we want good algorithms." The "goodness" of an algorithm is related to the use that the algorithm makes of some precious *computational resources,* such as: time, space, communication, I/Os, energy, or just simplicity and elegance, which both impact on its coding, debugging and maintenance costs.
- Definite: "Each step of an algorithm must be precisely defined; the actions to be carried out must be rigorously and unambiguously specified for each case." Knuth made an effort in this direction by detailing what he called the "machine language"

---

[1] See "algorithm characterizations" at https://en.wikipedia.org/wiki/Algorithm_characterizations.

for his "mythical MIX... the world's first polyunsaturated computer." Today there are many other programming languages, such as C/C++, Java, Python, and so on. They all specify a set of instructions that programmers may use to describe the procedure[s] underlying their algorithm[s] in an unambiguous way: "unambiguity" here is granted by the formal semantics that researchers have attached to each of these instructions. This eventually means that anyone reading that algorithm's description will interpret it in a precise way: nothing will be left to personal choice.

- Effective: "all of the operations to be performed in the algorithm must be sufficiently basic that they can in principle be done exactly and in a finite length of time by a man using paper and pencil." Therefore the notion of "step" invoked in the previous item implies that one has to dig into a complete and deep understanding of the problem to be solved, and then into logical well-defined structuring of a step-by-step solution.
- Procedure: "the sequence of specific steps arranged in a logical order."
- Input: "quantities which are given to it initially before the algorithm begins. These inputs are taken from specified sets of objects." Therefore the behavior of the algorithm is not unique, but it depends on the "sets of objects" given as input to be processed.
- Output: "quantities which have a specified relation to the inputs" given by the problem at hand, and constitute the answer returned by the algorithm for those inputs.

In this book we will not use a formal approach to algorithm description, because we wish to concentrate on the theoretically elegant and practically efficient ideas that underlie the algorithmic solution of some interesting problems, without being lost in the maze of programming technicalities. So, in every chapter, we will take an interesting problem that emerges from a practical/useful application and then propose solutions of increasing sophistication and improved efficiency, taking care that this will not necessarily lead to increasing the complexity of the algorithm's description. Actually, problems were selected to admit surprisingly elegant solutions that can be described in a few lines of code. So we will opt for the current practice of algorithm design and describe our algorithms either colloquially or by using *pseudocode* that mimics, the most well known languages. In all cases the algorithm descriptions will be as rigorous as they need to be to match Knuth's six features.

Elegance will not be the only goal of our algorithm design, of course; we will also aim for *efficiency*, which commonly relates to the *time/space complexity* of the algorithm. Traditionally, time complexity has been evaluated as a function of the input size n by counting the (maximum) number of steps, say $T(n)$, an algorithm takes to complete its computation over an input of n items. Since the maximum is taken over all inputs of that size, the time complexity is termed *worst case* because it concerns the input that induces the worst behavior in time for the algorithm. Of course, the larger n is, the larger $T(n)$ is, which is therefore nondecreasing and positive. In a similar way we can define the (worst-case) space complexity of an algorithm as the maximum number of memory cells it uses for its computation over an input of size n.

This approach to the *design* and *analysis* of algorithms assumes a very simple model of computation, known as the *Von Neumann model* (aka random access machine, or *RAM model*). This model consists of a CPU and a memory of infinite size, and constant-time access to each of its cells. Here we argue that every step takes a fixed amount of time on a PC, which is the same for any operation, be it arithmetic, logical, or just a memory access (read/write). Hence we postulate that it is enough to *count* the number of steps executed by the algorithm in order to have an "accurate" estimate of its execution time on a real PC. Two algorithms can then be compared according to the *asymptotic behavior* of their time-complexity functions as $n \to +\infty$; the faster the time complexity grows over inputs of increasing size, the worse the corresponding algorithm is judged to be. The robustness of this approach has been debated for a long time but, eventually, the RAM model dominated the algorithmic scene for decades (and is still dominating it) because of its simplicity, which impacts on algorithm design and evaluation, and its ability to estimate the algorithm performance "quite accurately" on (old) PCs and small input sizes. Therefore it is not surprising that most introductory books on algorithms deploy the RAM model to evaluate their performance [6].

But in the past ten years things have changed significantly, thus highlighting the need for a shift in algorithm design and analysis. Two main changes occurred: the architecture of modern PCs became more and more sophisticated (not just one CPU and one monolithic memory), and input data has exploded in size ("$n \to +\infty$" does not only belong in the theoretical world), because it is abundantly generated by many sources, such as DNA sequencing, bank transactions, mobile communications, web navigation and searches, auctions, and so on. The first change turned the RAM model into an unsatisfactory abstraction of modern PCs, whereas the second change made the design of asymptotically good algorithms ubiquitous and fruitful not only for theoreticians but also for a much larger professional audience because of their impact on business [2], society [1], and science in general [3]. The net consequence was a revamped scientific interest in algorithmics and the spread of the word "algorithm" to even colloquial speech.

In order to make algorithms effective in this new scenario, researchers needed new models of computation able to abstract in a better way the features of modern computers and applications and, in turn, to derive more accurate estimates of algorithm performance from the analysis of their complexity. Nowadays a modern PC consists of one or more CPUs (multi-cores, GPUs, TPUs, etc.) and a very complex hierarchy of memory levels, all with their own technological peculiarities (see Figure 1.1): L1 and L2 caches, internal memory, one or more mechanical or solid-state disks, and possibly other (hierarchical) memories of multiple hosts distributed over a (possibly geographic) network, the so-called "cloud." Each of these memory levels has its own cost, capacity, latency, bandwidth, and access method. The closer a memory level is to the CPU, the smaller, the faster, and the more expensive it is. Currently, nanoseconds suffice to access the caches, whereas milliseconds are needed to fetch data from disks (aka I/O). This is the so-called *I/O bottleneck*, which amounts to the astonishing factor of $10^5 - 10^6$, nicely illustrated in a quote attributed to Thomas H. Cormen:

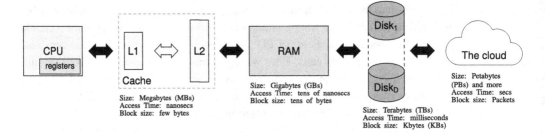

Figure 1.1 An example of memory hierarchy in a modern PC.

"The difference in speed between modern CPU and (mechanical) disk technologies is analogous to the difference in speed in sharpening a pencil using a sharpener on one's desk or by taking an airplane to the other side of the world and using a sharpener on someone else's desk."

Engineering research is trying nowadays to improve input/output subsystems to reduce the impact of the I/O bottleneck on the efficiency of applications managing large datasets; on the other hand, however, the improvements achievable by means of good algorithm design and engineering abundantly surpass the best expected technology advancements. Let us see the why, with a simple example.[2]

Consider three algorithms which have increasing I/O complexity (and thus, time complexity): $C_1(n) = n$, $C_2(n) = n^2$, and $C_3(n) = 2^n$. Here $C_i(n)$ denotes the number of disk accesses executed by the i-th algorithm to process n input data. Notice that the first two algorithms execute a *polynomial* number of I/Os (in the input size n), whereas the last one executes an *exponential* number of I/Os in n. Note that these I/O complexities have a very simple (and thus unrealistic) mathematical form, because we want to simplify the calculations without impairing our final conclusions. Let us now ask how much data each of these algorithms is able to process in a fixed time interval of length t, given that each I/O takes c time. The answer is obtained by solving the equation $C_i(n) \times c = t$ with respect to n: so we get t/c data are processed by the first algorithm in time t, $\sqrt{t/c}$ data are processed by the second algorithm, and only $\log_2(t/c)$ data are processed by the third algorithm in time t. These values are already impressive by themselves, and provide a robust understanding of why polynomial-time algorithms are called *efficient*, whereas exponential-time algorithms are called *inefficient*: a large change in the length t of the time interval induces just a tiny change in the amount of data that exponential-time algorithms can process. Of course, this distinction admits many exceptions when the problem instances have limited input size or have distributions that favor efficient executions. But, on the other hand, these examples are quite rare, and the much more stringent bounds on execution time satisfied by polynomial-time algorithms mean that they are considered *provably* efficient and the preferred way to solve problems. Algorithmically speaking, most exponential-time algorithms are merely implementations of the approach based on exhaustive searches, whereas

---

[2] This is paraphrased from [8]; here we talk about I/Os instead of steps.

polynomial-time algorithms are generally made possible only through gaining some deeper insight into the structure of a problem. So polynomial-time algorithms are the right choice from many points of view.

Let us now assume that we run these algorithms with a better I/O-subsystem, say one that is k times faster, and ask: How much data can be managed by this new computer? To address this question we solve the previous equations with the time interval set to the length $k \times t$, thus implicitly assuming that the algorithms are executed with k times more available running time than the previous computer. We find that the first algorithm perfectly scales by a factor of k, the second algorithm scales by a factor of $\sqrt{k}$, whereas the last algorithm scales *only by an additive term* $\log_2 k$. We can see that the improvement induced by a k-times more powerful computer for an exponential-time algorithm is totally negligible even in the presence of impressive (and thus unrealistic) technology advancements. Super-linear time algorithms, like the second one, are positively affected by technology advancements, but their performance improvement decreases as the degree of the polynomial-time complexity grows: more precisely, if $C(n) = n^\alpha$ then a k-times more powerful computer induces an increase in speed by a factor of $\sqrt[\alpha]{k}$. Overall, it is safe to say that the impact of a good algorithm is far beyond any optimistic forecasting for the performance of future (mechanical or solid-state) disks.[3]

Given this appetizer on the "power" of algorithm design and engineering, let us now turn back to the problem of analyzing the performance of algorithms in modern computers by considering the following simple example: compute the sum of the integers stored in an array $A[1, n]$. The simplest idea is to scan A and accumulate in a temporary variable the sum of the scanned integers. This algorithm executes n sums between two integers, accesses each integer in A once, and thus takes n steps. Let us now generalize this approach by considering a family of algorithms, denoted by $\mathcal{A}_{s,b}$, which differentiate themselves according to the pattern of accesses to A's elements, as driven by the parameters s and b. In particular, $\mathcal{A}_{s,b}$ looks at array A as logically divided into blocks of b elements each, say $A_j = A[j \times b + 1, (j + 1) \times b]$ for $j = 0, 1, 2, \ldots, n/b - 1$.[4] Then it sums all items in one block A_j before moving to the next block A_{j+s}, which occurs s blocks farther on the right. Array A is considered cyclic so that, when the next block lies out of A, the algorithm wraps around it, starting again from its beginning: hence, the index of the next block is actually defined as $(j + s)$ mod (n/b).[5] Clearly, not all values of s allow us to take into account all of A's blocks (and thus sum all of A's integers). And in fact we know that if s is coprime with n/b then the sequence of visited-block indexes, that is, $j = s \times i$ mod (n/b) for $i = 0, 1, \ldots, n/b - 1$, is a permutation of the integers $\{0, 1, \ldots, n/b - 1\}$, and thus $\mathcal{A}_{s,b}$ touches all blocks in A and hence sums all of its integers. But the peculiarity of this parametrization is that by varying s and b we can sum A's integers according to different patterns of memory accesses:

---

[3] See [11] for an extended treatment of this subject.

[4] For the sake of presentation we assume that n and b are powers of two, so b divides n.

[5] The modulo (mod) function is defined as follows: given two positive integers x and $m > 1$, x mod m is the remainder of the division of x by m.

from the sequential scan we have described (setting $s = b = 1$), to sequential-wise blocked access (setting a larger b), or to random-wise blocked access (setting a larger s). Nicely enough, all algorithms $\mathcal{A}_{s,b}$ are equivalent from a computational point of view, because they read and sum exactly n integers and thus take exactly n steps; but from a practical point of view, they have different time performance which becomes more and more different as the array size n grows. The reason for this is that, for a growing n, data will be spread over more and more memory levels, each with its own capacity, latency, bandwidth and access method. So the "equivalence in efficiency" derived by adopting the RAM model, and counting the number of steps executed by $\mathcal{A}_{s,b}$, is not an accurate estimate of the real time required by the algorithms to sum A's elements.

We need a different model that grasps the essence of real computers and is simple enough to not jeopardize the algorithm design and analysis. In a previous example we argued that the number of I/Os is a good estimator for the time complexity of an algorithm, given the large gap between disk- and internal-memory performance. This is indeed captured by the *2-level memory model* (aka disk model, or external-memory model [11]), which abstracts the computer as comprising only *two memory levels*: the internal memory of (bounded) size M, and the (unbounded) disk memory which operates by reading/writing data via blocks of size B (called *disk pages*). Sometimes the model consists of D disks, each of unbounded size, so that each I/O reads or writes a total of $D \times B$ items stored in D pages, each one residing on a different disk. For the sake of clarity we remark that the two-level view must not suggest to the reader that this model is restricted to abstract disk-based computations; in fact, we are actually free to choose any two levels of the memory hierarchy, with their M and B parameters properly set. The algorithm performance is evaluated in this model by counting: (i) the number of accesses to disk pages (hereafter *I/Os*), (ii) the running time (CPU time), and (iii) the number of disk pages used by the algorithm as its working space. This also suggests two golden rules for the design of "good" algorithms operating on large datasets: they must exploit *spatial locality* and *temporal locality*. The former imposes a data organization in the disk(s) that makes each accessed disk page as useful as possible; the latter requires as much useful work as possible over the data fetched in internal memory, before it is written back to disk.

In the light of this new model, let us reanalyze the time complexity of algorithms $\mathcal{A}_{s,b}$ by taking into account I/Os, given that the CPU time is n and the space occupancy is n/B disk pages independently of s and b. We start from the simplest settings for s and b in order to gain some intuitions about the general formulas. The case $s = 1$ is obvious: algorithms $\mathcal{A}_{1,b}$ scan A rightward, summing the items one block at a time, by taking n/B I/Os independently of the value of b. As s and b change, the situation gets complicated, but by not much. As an example, fix $s = 2$ and select some $b < B$ that, for simplicity, is assumed to divide the block-size B. Every block of size B consists of B/b smaller (logical) blocks of size b, and the algorithms $\mathcal{A}_{2,b}$ examine only half of them because of the jump $s = 2$. This actually means that each B-sized page is half utilized in the summing process, thus inducing a total of $2n/B$ I/Os. It is then not difficult to generalize this formula by writing a cost of $\min\{s, B/b\} \times (n/B)$ I/Os, which correctly gives n/b for the case of large jumps over array A. This formula provides a better approximation of the real time complexity of the algorithms $\mathcal{A}_{s,b}$, although it does not capture all features of the disk: all I/Os are evaluated as equal, independently of their distribution. This is clearly not precise, because on real disks *sequential* I/Os are faster than *random* I/Os.[6] As such, referring to the previous example, all algorithms $\mathcal{A}_{s,B}$ have the same I/O complexity n/B, independently of s, although their behavior is rather different if executed on a (mechanical) disk, because of the disk seeks induced by increasing s. Therefore, we can conclude that even the two-level memory model provides an approximation of the behavior of algorithms on real computers, although its results are sufficiently good that it has been widely adopted in the literature to evaluate algorithm performance on massive datasets. So in order to be as precise as possible, we will evaluate algorithms in these pages not only by specifying the number of executed I/Os but also by characterizing their *distribution* (random vs. sequential) over the disk.

At this point one could object that given the impressive technological advancements of recent years, internal-memory size M is so large that most of the working set of an algorithm (roughly speaking, the set of pages it will reference in the near future) can fit into it, thus reducing significantly the number of I/O faults. We will argue that even a small portion of data resident in disk makes the algorithm slower than expected, so that data organization cannot be neglected even in these extremely favorable situations. Let us see why, by means of a "back of the envelope" calculation.

Assume that the input size $n = (1 + \epsilon)M$ is larger than the internal-memory size of a factor $\epsilon > 0$. The question is how much ϵ impacts on the average cost of an algorithm step, given that it may access a datum located either in internal memory or on disk. To simplify our analysis, while still obtaining a meaningful conclusion, we assume that $p(\epsilon)$ is the probability of an I/O fault: hence, if $p(\epsilon) = 1$, the algorithm always accesses data on disk; if $p(\epsilon) = 0$, the algorithm has a working set smaller than the internal-memory size, and thus it always accesses data in internal memory; finally, $p(\epsilon) = \frac{\epsilon M}{(1+\epsilon)M} = \frac{\epsilon}{1+\epsilon}$ when the algorithm has a fully random behavior in accessing its input data. In other words, we can look at $p(\epsilon)$ as a measure of the non-locality of the memory references of the analyzed algorithm.

To complete the notation, let us indicate with c the time cost of one I/O with respect to one internal-memory access (we have in practice $c \approx 10^5 - 10^6$, see above), with f the fraction of steps that induce a memory access in the running algorithm (this is typically 30%–40%, according to [5]), with t_m the average time cost of such memory accesses and the cost of a computation step or an internal-memory access set as 1. To derive t_m we have to distinguish two cases: an in-memory access (occurring with probability $1 - p(\epsilon)$) or a disk access (occurring with probability $p(\epsilon)$). So we have $t_m = 1 \times (1 - p(\epsilon)) + c \times p(\epsilon)$.

---

[6] Conversely, this difference will be almost negligible in an (electronic) memory, such as DRAM or modern solid-state disks, where the distribution of the memory accesses does not significantly impact on the throughput of the memory/SSD.

Now we are ready to estimate the *average time cost of a step* for an algorithm working in this scenario: it is $1 \times (1 - f) + t_m \times f$, since $1 - f$ is the fraction of computing steps and f is the fraction of memory accesses (both in internal memory and on disk). By plugging in the value computed for t_m, we can lower bound that cost by $3 \times 10^4 \times p(\epsilon)$. This formula clearly shows that, even for algorithms exploiting locality of references (i.e. a small $p(\epsilon)$), the slowdown may be significant, resulting in four orders of magnitude larger than what might be expected (i.e. $p(\epsilon)$). As an example, take an algorithm that forces locality of references into its memory accesses: say 1 out of 1000 memory accesses go to data stored on disk (i.e. $p(\epsilon) = 0.001$). Then, its performance gets slowed down by a factor larger than 30 in comparison with the case in which its computation would be fully executed in internal memory.

It goes without saying that this is just the tip of the iceberg, because the larger the amount of data to be processed by an algorithm, the higher is the number of memory levels involved in the storage of this data and, hence, the more varied are the types of "memory faults" that need to be coped with for achieving efficiency. The overall message is that neglecting questions pertaining to the cost of memory references in a hierarchical-memory system may prevent the use of an algorithm for large input data.

Motivated by these premises, this book will provide a few examples of challenging problems that admit elegant algorithmic solutions whose efficiency is crucial to manage the large datasets that occur in many real-world applications. Details of the algorithm design will be accompanied by several comments on the difficulties that underlie the engineering of those algorithms: how to turn a "theoretically efficient" algorithm into a "practically efficient" code. In fact, too many times, as a theoretician, I was told that "your algorithm is far from being amenable to an efficient implementation!" Furthermore, by following the recent surge of investigations in *algorithm engineering* [10] (not to be confused with the "practice of algorithms"), we will also dig into the deep computational features of some algorithms by resorting to a few other successful models of computation – mainly the streaming model [9] and the cache-oblivious model [4]. These models will allow us to capture and highlight some interesting issues of the underlying computation, such as disk passes (streaming model), and universal scalability (cache-oblivious model). We will try our best to describe all these issues in their simplest terms but, nonetheless, we will be unsuccessful in turning this "rocket science for non-boffins" into a "science for dummies" [2]. In fact many more things have to fall into place for algorithms to work: top IT companies (like Amazon, Facebook, Google, IBM, Microsoft, Oracle, Spotify, Twitter, etc.) are perfectly aware of the difficulty of finding people with the right skills for designing and engineering "good" algorithms. This book will only scratch the surface of algorithm design and engineering, with the main goal of inspiring you in your daily job as a software designer and engineer.

References

[1]   Person of the Year. *Time Magazine*, 168:27, December 2006.
[2]   Business by numbers. *The Economist*, September 2007.

[3] Declan Butler. *2020 computing: Everything, everywhere. Nature*, 440(7083): 402–5, 2006.

[4] Rolf Fagerberg. Cache-oblivious model. In Ming-Yang Kao, editor, *Encyclopedia of Algorithms*. Springer, 264–9, 2016.

[5] John L. Hennessy and David A. Patterson. *Computer Architecture: A Quantitative Approach*. Morgan Kaufmann, fourth edition, 2006.

[6] Ming-Yang Kao. *Encyclopedia of Algorithms*. Springer, 2016.

[7] Donald Knuth. *The Art of Computer Programming: Fundamental Algorithms*, Vol. 1. Addison-Wesley, 1973.

[8] Fabrizio Luccio. *La struttura degli algoritmi*. Boringhieri, 1982.

[9] S. Muthukrishnan. Data streams: Algorithms and applications. *Foundations and Trends in Theoretical Computer Science*, 1(2): 117–236, 2005.

[10] Peter Sanders. Algorithm engineering – an attempt at a definition. In Susanne Albers, Helmut Alt, and Stefan Näher, editors, *Efficient Algorithms: Essays Dedicated to Kurt Mehlhorn on the Occasion of His 60th Birthday*. Lecture Notes in Computer Science, 5760, Springer, 321–3, 2009.

[11] Jeffrey S. Vitter. External memory algorithms and data structures. *ACM Computing Surveys*, 33(2): 209–71, 2001.

2   A Warm-up

Everything should be made as simple as
possible, but not simpler.
Attributed to Albert Einstein

Let us consider the following problem, which is on the face of it simple, but for which
the design of its optimal solution is much less straightforward.

> **Problem.** We are given the performance of a stock at the New York Stock
> Exchange (NYSE) expressed as a sequence of day-by-day differences of its
> quotations. We wish to determine the best buy-and-sell strategy for that stock,
> namely the pair of days $\langle b, s \rangle$ that would have maximized our revenues if we had
> bought the stock at (the beginning of) day b and sold it at (the end of) day s.

The specialty of this problem is that it has a simple formulation, which has many other
useful variations and applications. We will comment on some of these at the end of
this chapter; for now we content ourselves by mentioning that we are interested in this
problem because it admits of a sequence of algorithmic solutions of increasing sophistication and elegance, which imply a significant reduction in their time complexity.
The ultimate result will be a linear-time algorithm, that is, linear in the number n of
stock quotations. This algorithm is *optimal* in terms of the number of executed steps,
because all day-by-day differences must be looked at in order to determine whether
they need to be included or not in the optimal solution – one single difference could
provide a one-day period worth of investment. Surprisingly, the optimal algorithm will
exhibit the simplest pattern of memory accesses – it will execute a single scan of the
available stock quotations – and thus it utilizes a *streaming behavior*, which is particularly useful in a scenario in which the granularity of the buy-and-sell actions is not
restricted to full days, and we may need to compute the optimal time-window on the fly
as quotations oscillate. Moreover, as we commented in the Chapter 1, this algorithmic
scheme is optimal in terms of I/Os and *uniformly* over all levels of the memory hierarchy. In fact, because of its streaming behavior, it will execute n/B I/Os independently
of the disk-page size B, which may thus be unknown to the underlying algorithm. This
is the typical feature of the *cache-oblivious algorithms* [4], which we will therefore
introduce in this chapter (Section 2.3).

This chapter is the prototype of what you will find in the following chapters: a problem that is simple to state, with a few elegant solutions and challenging techniques to teach and learn, together with several intriguing extensions that can be posed as exercises to students or as puzzles to tempt your mathematical skills.

Let us now dig into the technicalities, and consider the following example. Take the case of 11 days of exchange for a given stock, and let $D[1, 11] = [+4, -6, +3, +1, +3, -2, +3, -4, +1, -9, +6]$ denote the day-by-day differences of quotations for that stock. It is not difficult to convince yourself that the gain of buying the stock at the beginning of day x and selling it at the end of day y is equal to the sum of the values in the subarray $D[x, y]$, namely the sum of all its fluctuations. As an example, take $x = 1$ and $y = 2$: the gain is $+4 - 6 = -2$, and indeed we would lose two dollars in buying at the morning of the first day and selling the stock at the end of the second day. Note that the starting value of the stock is not crucial for determining the best time interval of our investment; what is important are its variations. In the literature this problem is indeed known as the *maximum subarray sum* problem.

> **Problem abstraction.** Given an array $D[1, n]$ of positive and negative numbers, we want to find the subarray $D[b, s]$ that maximizes the sum of its elements.

It is clear that if all numbers are positive, then the optimal subarray is the entire D: this is the case of an always increasing stock price, and there is no reason to sell it before the last day. Conversely, if all numbers are negative, then we can select the element window containing the largest negative value: if you have to buy this poor stock, then do it on the day it loses the smallest value and sell it quickly. In all other cases, it is not at all clear where the optimum subarray is located. In the example, the optimum spans $D[3, 7] = [+3, +1, +3, -2, +3]$ and has a gain of eight dollars. This shows that the optimum neither includes the day with the greatest gain (i.e. $+6$), nor does it consist of positive values only. Determining the optimal subarray is not simple but, surprisingly enough, also not very complicated.

2.1   A Cubic-Time Algorithm

We start by considering an inefficient solution which just translates in pseudocode the formulation of the problem we have described. Algorithm 2.1 uses the pair of variables $\langle b_o, s_o \rangle$ to identify the current subarray with the maximum sum, whose value is stored in *MaxSum*. Initially *MaxSum* is set to the dummy value $-\infty$, so that it is immediately changed whenever the algorithm executes Step 8 for the first time. The core of the algorithm consists of the two nested for-loops (Steps 2–3), which examine all possible subarrays $D[b, s]$, computing for each of them the sum of their elements (Steps 4–7). If a sum larger than the current maximal value is found (Steps 8–9), then *TmpSum* and its corresponding subarray extremes are stored in *MaxSum* and $\langle b_o, s_o \rangle$, respectively.

The correctness of the algorithm is immediate, since it checks all possible subarrays of $D[1, n]$ and selects the one whose sum of elements is the largest (Step 8). The time

---

Algorithm 2.1 The cubic-time algorithm

1: $MaxSum = -\infty$;
2: **for** $(b = 1; b \leq n; b{+}{+})$ **do**
3:      **for** $(s = b; s \leq n; s{+}{+})$ **do**
4:          $TmpSum = 0$;
5:          **for** $(i = b; i \leq s; i{+}{+})$ **do**
6:              $TmpSum{+} = D[i]$;
7:          **end for**
8:          **if** $MaxSum < TmpSum$ **then**
9:              $MaxSum = TmpSum$; $b_o = b$; $s_o = s$;
10:         **end if**
11:     **end for**
12: **end for**
13: **return** $\langle MaxSum, b_o, s_o \rangle$;

---

complexity is cubic, that is, $\Theta(n^3)$, and can be evaluated as follows. Clearly the time complexity is upper bounded by $O(n^3)$, because we can form no more than $\frac{n^2}{2}$ pairs $\langle b, s \rangle$ out of n elements, and n is an upper bound to the cost of computing the sum of the elements of each subarray.[1] Let us now show that the time cost is also $\Omega(n^3)$, so concluding that the time complexity is strictly cubic. To show this lower bound, we observe that $D[1, n]$ contains $(n - L + 1)$ subarrays of length L, and thus the cost of computing the sum for all of their elements is $(n - L + 1) \times L$. Summing over all values of L would give us the exact time complexity. But here we are interested in a lower bound, so we can evaluate that cost just for the subset of subarrays whose length L is in the range $[n/4, n/2]$. For each such L, $L \geq n/4$ and thus $n - L + 1 > n/2$, so the cost is $(n - L + 1) \times L > n^2/8$. Since we have $\frac{n}{2} - \frac{n}{4} + 1 > n/4$ of those Ls, the total cost for analyzing that subset of subarrays is lower bounded by $n^3/32 = \Omega(n^3)$.

It is natural now to ask ourselves how fast Algorithm 2.1 is in practice: It is too slow if we wish to scale to very large sequences (of stock quotations), as we are aiming for here.

2.2   A Quadratic-Time Algorithm

The key inefficiency of the cubic-time Algorithm 2.1 resides in the execution of Steps 4–7, which recompute from scratch the sum of the elements in the subarray $D[b, s]$ each time its extremes change in Steps 2–3. Now, if we look carefully at the for-loop at Step 3 we note that the size s is incremented by one unit at a time from the value b (one-element subarray) to the value n (the longest possible subarray that starts at b). Therefore, from one iteration to the next of that for-loop, the subarray to be summed changes from $D[b, s]$ to $D[b, s + 1]$. It can thus be concluded that the new sum for $D[b, s+1]$ does not need to be recomputed from scratch, but can be computed

---

[1] For each pair $\langle b, s \rangle$, with $b \leq s$, $D[b, s]$ is a possible subarray, but $D[s, b]$ is not.

Algorithm 2.2 The quadratic-time algorithm

1: $MaxSum = -\infty$;
2: **for** $(b = 1; b \leq n; b{+}{+})$ **do**
3:     $TmpSum = 0$;
4:     **for** $(s = b; s \leq n; s{+}{+})$ **do**
5:         $TmpSum \mathrel{+}= D[s]$;
6:         **if** $MaxSum < TmpSum$ **then**
7:             $MaxSum = TmpSum$; $b_o = b$; $s_o = s$;
8:         **end if**
9:     **end for**
10: **end for**
11: **return** $\langle MaxSum, b_o, s_o \rangle$;

---

incrementally just by adding the value of the new element $D[s + 1]$ to the current value of *TmpSum* (which inductively stores the sum of $D[b, s]$). This is exactly what the pseudocode of Algorithm 2.2 implements: its two main changes with respect to Algorithm 2.1 are in Step 3, which nulls *TmpSum* every time b is changed (because the subarray starts again from length 1, namely $D[b, b]$), and in Step 5, which implements the incremental update of the current sum. Such small changes are worth a saving of $\Theta(n)$ additions per execution of Step 2, thus making the new algorithm have quadratic-time complexity, namely $\Theta(n^2)$.

More precisely, let us concentrate on counting the number of additions executed by Algorithm 2.2; this is the prominent operation of this algorithm, whose evaluation will give us an estimate of its total number of steps. This number is[2]

$$\sum_{b=1}^{n}\left(1+\sum_{s=b}^{n}1\right) = \sum_{b=1}^{n}(1+(n-b+1)) = n\times(n+2) - \sum_{b=1}^{n}b = n^2+2n-\frac{n(n-1)}{2} = O(n^2).$$

This improvement is effective also in practice. Consider an array D of size $n = 10^3$; Algorithm 2.1 implemented in Python takes about 17 seconds on a commodity PC with an Intel i5 processor, whereas Algorithm 2.2 takes less than 1 second on the same machine. This means an arguably "small" difference, which actually becomes "significant" if the size of the array D becomes $n = 10^4$. In this case, Algorithm 2.1 takes about 17,000 seconds (pretty much 10^3 times more), whereas Algorithm 2.2 takes about 7 seconds. This means that the quadratic-time algorithm is able to manage more elements in a "reasonable" time than the previous cubic-time algorithm. Clearly, these figures change if we use a different programming language (Python, in the present example), operating system (MacOS), or processor (Intel Core i5). Nevertheless, they are interesting anyway because they provide a concrete picture of what asymptotic improvement like the one described here means in a real-life situation. It goes without saying that the life of a coder is typically not easy, because theoretically

---

[2] We use here the famous formula, discovered by the young Gauss, to compute the sum of the first n positive integers.

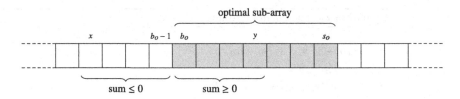

Figure 2.1 An illustrative example of Properties 1 and 2.

good algorithms often conceal so many details that their engineering is difficult, and big-O notation often turns out to be not very "realistic." Do not worry – we will have time in these chapters to look at these issues in more detail.

2.3   A Linear-Time Algorithm

The final step of this chapter is to show that the maximum subarray sum problem admits of an elegant algorithm that processes the elements of $D[1, n]$ in a streaming fashion and takes the *optimal* $O(n)$ time. We cannot aim for more, as we have noted.

To design this algorithm we need to dig into the structural properties of the optimal subarray. For the purpose of clarity, we refer the reader to Figure 2.1, where the optimal subarray is assumed to be located between two positions $b_o \leq s_o$ in the range $[1, n]$.

Let us now take a subarray that starts before b_o and ends at position $b_o - 1$, say $D[x, b_o - 1]$, with $x < b_o$. The sum of the elements in this subarray cannot be positive because, otherwise, we could merge it with the (adjacent) optimal subarray and thus get a longer subarray, $D[x, s_o]$, whose sum is *larger than* the one obtained with the (claimed) optimal $D[b_o, s_o]$. So we can state the following:

Property 1: The sum of the elements in a subarray $D[x, b_o - 1]$, with $x < b_o$, cannot be (strictly) positive.

Via a similar argument, we can consider a subarray that prefixes the optimal $D[b_o, s_o]$, and thus has the form $D[b_o, y]$ with $y \leq s_o$. This subarray cannot have a negative sum because, otherwise, we could drop it from the optimal solution and get a shorter array, namely $D[y + 1, s_o]$, whose sum is *larger than* the one obtained by the (claimed) optimal $D[b_o, s_o]$. So we can state the following second property:

Property 2: The sum of the elements in a subarray $D[b_o, y]$, with $y \leq s_o$, cannot be (strictly) negative.

Any one of the subarrays considered in these properties might have a sum equal to zero. This would not affect the optimality of $D[b_o, s_o]$; rather it could only introduce other optimal solutions either longer or shorter than $D[b_o, s_o]$.

Let us illustrate these two properties in the array $D[1, 11]$ used as example at the beginning of this chapter: hence $D = [+4, -6, +3, +1, +3, -2, +3, -4, +1, -9, +6]$. Recall that the optimum subarray is $D[3, 7] = [+3, +1, +3, -2, +3]$. Note that $D[x, 2]$ is always negative (as stated in Property 1); in fact for $x = 1$ the sum is $+4 - 6 = -2$, and for $x = 2$ the sum is -6. On the other hand, the sum of all elements in $D[3, y]$ is positive for all prefixes of the optimum subarray (as stated in Property 2), namely

---

Algorithm 2.3 The linear-time algorithm

1: $MaxSum = -\infty$;

2: $TmpSum = 0; b = 1$;

3: **for** $(s = 1; s \leq n; s{+}{+})$ **do**

4:     $TmpSum \mathrel{+}= D[s]$;

5:     **if** $MaxSum < TmpSum$ **then**

6:         $MaxSum = TmpSum; b_o = b; s_o = s$;

7:     **end if**

8:     **if** $TmpSum < 0$ **then**

9:         $TmpSum = 0; b = s + 1$;

10:    **end if**

11: **end for**

12: **return** $\langle MaxSum, b_o, s_o \rangle$;

$y \leq 7$. Note also that the sum of $D[3, y]$ is positive even for some $y > 7$; take, for example, $D[3, 8]$, for which the sum is 4, and $D[3, 9]$, for which the sum is 5, which does not contradict Property 2.

These two properties lead to the simple linear-time Algorithm 2.3. It consists of one unique for-loop (Step 3) which keeps in $TmpSum$ the sum of a subarray starting at some position b and ending at the currently examined position s, where $b \leq s$. At any step of the for-loop, the candidate subarray is extended one position to the right (i.e. $s{+}{+}$), and its sum $TmpSum$ is increased by the value of the current element $D[s]$ (Step 4). Since the current subarray is a candidate to be the optimal one, its sum is compared with the current optimal value (Step 5). Then, according to Property 1, if the subarray sum is negative, the current subarray is discarded and the process "restarts" with a new subarray beginning at the next position $b = s + 1$ (Steps 8–9). Otherwise, the current subarray is extended to the right, by incrementing s. The tricky issue here is to show that the optimal subarray is checked in Step 5, and thus stored in $\langle b_o, s_o \rangle$. This is not intuitive at all, because the algorithm is checking n subarrays out of the $\Theta(n^2)$ possible ones, and we want to show that this (minimal) subset of candidates actually contains the optimal solution. This subset is *minimal* because these subarrays form a *partition* of $D[1, n]$ so that every element belongs to one, and only one, checked subarray. Moreover, since every element must be analyzed, we cannot discard any subarray of this partition without checking its sum.

Before digging into the formal proof of correctness, let us follow the execution of the algorithm over the array $D[1, 11] = [+4, -6, +3, +1, +3, -2, +3, -4, +1, -9, +6]$. Remember that the optimal subarray is $D[3, 7] = [+3, +1, +3, -2, +3]$. Since $D[x, 2]$ is negative for $x = 1, 2$, the algorithm zeroes the variable $TmpSum$ when $s = 2$ in Steps 8–9. At that time, b is set to 3 and $TmpSum$ is set to 0. The subsequent scanning of the elements $s = 3, \ldots, 7$ will add their values to $TmpSum$, which is always positive (as commented above). When $s = 7$, the examined subarray coincides with the optimal one, we thus have $TmpSum = 8$, and so Step 5 stores the optimum subarray locations in $\langle b_o, s_o \rangle$. It is interesting to note that, in this example, the algorithm does not restart the value of *TmpSum* at the next position $s = 8$ because it is still positive (namely, `TmpSum` $= 4$); hence, the algorithm will examine subarrays longer than the optimal one, but all having a smaller sum. The next restarting will occur at position $s = 10$, where *TmpSum* $= -4$.

It is easy to see that the time complexity of the algorithm is $O(n)$, because every element is examined just once. More tricky is to show formally that the algorithm is correct, which actually means that Steps 4–5 eventually compute and check the optimal subarray sum. To show this, it suffices to prove the following two facts: (i) when $s = b_o - 1$, Step 8 resets b to b_o; (ii) for all subsequent positions $s = b_o, \ldots, s_o$, Step 8 never resets b, so it will eventually compute in *TmpSum* the sum of all elements in $D[b_o, s_o]$, whenever $s = s_o$. It is not difficult to see that (i) derives from Property 1, and (ii) derives from Property 2.

This algorithm is very fast in the experimental scenario mentioned in Section 2.2; it takes less than one second to process millions of stock quotations: a truly scalable algorithm, indeed, with many nice features that also make it appealing in a hierarchical-memory setting. In fact this algorithm scans the array D from left to right and examines each of its elements just once. If D is stored on disk, these elements are fetched into internal memory one page at a time. Hence the algorithm executes n/B I/Os, which is *optimal*. It is interesting also to note that the design of the algorithm does not depend on B (which indeed does not appear in the pseudocode), but we can still evaluate its I/O complexity in terms of B. Hence the algorithm takes n/B optimal I/Os independently of the page size B, and thus subtly independently of the characteristics of the memory levels involved in the algorithm execution. Decoupling the use of the parameter B in algorithm design and algorithm analysis is the key issue of the *cache-oblivious algorithms*. This feature is achieved here in a basic way simply by adopting a scan-based approach. The literature offers more sophisticated results regarding the design of cache-oblivious algorithms and data structures [4].

2.4   Another Linear-Time Algorithm

There is another optimal solution to the maximum subarray sum problem, which hinges on a different algorithm design. For simplicity of exposition, let us denote by $\text{Sum}_D[y', y'']$ the sum of the elements in the subarray $D[y', y'']$. Take now a selling time s and consider all subarrays that end at s: namely, we are interested in subarrays that have the form $D[x, s]$, with $x \leq s$. The value $\text{Sum}_D[x, s]$ can be expressed as the difference between $\text{Sum}_D[1, s]$ and $\text{Sum}_D[1, x - 1]$. Both of these sums are indeed *prefix* sums over the array D and can be computed in linear time. As a result, we can rephrase our maximization problem as follows:

$$\max_s \max_{b \leq s} \text{Sum}_D[b, s] = \max_s \max_{b \leq s} (\text{Sum}_D[1, s] - \text{Sum}_D[1, b - 1]).$$

If $b = 1$ the second term refers to the empty subarray $D[1, 0]$, so we can assume that $\text{Sum}_D[1, 0] = 0$. This is the case in which $D[1, s]$ is the subarray of maximum sum among all the subarrays ending at s (so no prefix subarray $D[1, b - 1]$ is dropped from it).

The next step is to precompute all prefix sums $P[i] = \text{Sum}_D[1, i]$ in $O(n)$ time and $O(n)$ space via a scan of the array D: just note that $P[i] = P[i - 1] + D[i]$, where we set $P[0] = 0$ in order to manage the special case considered here. Hence we can rewrite the maximization problem in terms of the array P, rather than Sum_D: namely, write $\text{Sum}_D[1, s] - \text{Sum}_D[1, b - 1]$ as $P[s] - P[b - 1]$. We can now decompose the $\max_s \max_{b \leq s}$ computation into a min/max calculation as follows:

$$\max_s \max_{b \leq s}(P[s] - P[b - 1]) = \max_s(P[s] - \min_{b \leq s} P[b - 1]).$$

In fact we can move $P[s]$ outside the inner max-calculation because it does not depend on the variable b, and then change a max into a min because of the negative sign. The final step is then to precompute the minimum $\min_{b \leq s} P[b - 1]$ for all positions s, and store it in an array $M[0, n - 1]$. Note that, in this case also, the computation of $M[i]$ can be performed via a single scan of P in $O(n)$ time and space: set $M[0] = 0$ and then derive $M[i]$ as $\min\{M[i - 1], P[i]\}$. Finally, we can rewrite the previous formula as:

$$\max_s(P[s] - \min_{b \leq s} P[b - 1]) = \max_s(P[s] - M[s - 1]),$$

which can be clearly computed in $O(n)$ time given the two arrays P and M. Overall, this new approach takes $O(n)$ time, as in Algorithm 2.3, but it needs $\Theta(n)$ extra space.

As an example, consider again the array $D[1, 11] = [+4, -6, +3, +1, +3, -2, +3, -4, +1, -9, +6]$. We compute the prefix-sum array $P[0, 11] = [0, +4, -2, +1, +2, +5, +3, +6, +2, +3, -6, 0]$ and the minimum array $M[0, 10] = [0, 0, -2, -2, -2, -2, -2, -2, -2, -2, -6]$. If we compute the difference $P[s] - M[s-1]$ for all $s = 1, \ldots, n$, we obtain the sequence of values $[+4, -2, +3, +4, +7, +5, +8, +4, +5, -4, +6]$, whose maximum is $+8$, which has the (correct) ending position $s = 7$. It is interesting to note that the left-extreme b_o of the optimal subarray could be derived by finding the position $b_o - 1$ where $P[b_o - 1]$ is the minimum: in the example, $P[2] = -2$ and thus $b_o = 3$.

Algorithm 2.4 implements these algorithmic ideas, but with a nice *coding trick* that turns it into a one-pass approach using only $O(1)$ extra space, as for Algorithm 2.3. It deploys the associativity of the min/max functions, and uses two variables that inductively keep the values of $P[s]$ (i.e. *TmpSum*) and $M[s - 1]$ (i.e. *MinTmpSum*) as the array D is scanned from left to right. This way the formula $\max_s(P[s] - M[s - 1])$ is evaluated incrementally for $s = 1, \ldots, n$.

2.5   A Few Interesting Variants$^\infty$

As promised at the beginning of this chapter, we discuss now a few interesting variants of the maximum subarray sum problem. For further algorithmic details and formulations, we refer the interested reader to [1, 2]. Note that this is a challenging section, because it proposes an algorithm whose design and analysis are sophisticated,

---

Algorithm 2.4 Another linear-time algorithm

1: $MaxSum = -\infty$; $b_{tmp} = 1$;
2: $TmpSum = 0$; $MinTmpSum = 0$;
3: **for** ($s = 1$; $s \leq n$; s++) **do**
4:     $TmpSum$ += $D[s]$;
5:     **if** $MaxSum < TmpSum - MinTmpSum$ **then**
6:         $MaxSum = TmpSum - MinTmpSum$; $s_o = s$; $b_o = b_{tmp}$;
7:     **end if**
8:     **if** $TmpSum < MinTmpSum$ **then**
9:         $MinTmpSum = TmpSum$; $b_{tmp} = s + 1$;
10:     **end if**
11: **end for**
12: **return** $\langle MaxSum, b_o, s_o \rangle$;

---

so we label it with the symbol ∞. We adopt this notation to denote such challenging sections in the rest of this book.

Sometimes in the bioinformatics literature the term "subarray" is substituted by "segment," and the problem takes the name of "maximum-sum segment problem." Here the goal is to identify segments that occur inside DNA sequences (i.e. strings drawn from a four-letters alphabet {A, T, G, C}) and are *rich* in G and C nucleotides. In biology it is believed that these segments are significant since they predominantly contain genes. The mapping from DNA sequences to *arrays of numbers*, and thus to our problem abstraction, can be obtained in several ways depending on the objective function that models the *GC-richness* of a segment. Two interesting mappings to identify C- and G-rich sequences are the following ones:

- Assign a penalty $-p$ to the nucleotides A and T in the sequence, and a reward $1 - p$ to the nucleotides C and G. Given this assignment, the sum of a segment of length l containing x occurrences of C or G is equal to $x - p \times l$. Interestingly enough, all algorithms described in the previous sections can be used to identify the CG-rich segments of a DNA sequence in linear time according to this objective function. Often, biologists prefer to define a cut-off range on the length of the segments for which the maximum sum needs to be searched, in order to avoid the reporting of extremely short or extremely long segments. In this new scenario the algorithms of the previous sections cannot be applied, but there are linear-time optimal solutions for them (see, e.g., [2]).
- Assign a value 0 to the nucleotides A and T of the sequence, and a value 1 to the nucleotides C and G. Given this assignment, the *density* of C and G nucleotides in a segment of length l containing x occurrences of C and G is x/l. Clearly, $0 \leq x/l \leq 1$ and every single occurrence of a nucleotide C or G provides a segment with maximum density 1. Biologists consider this to be an interesting measure of CG-richness for a segment, provided that a cut-off on the length of the searched segments is imposed. This problem is more difficult than the one stated in the previous bullet

point, nevertheless it posses optimal (quasi-)linear time solutions which are very sophisticated and for which we refer the interested reader to the pertinent literature (e.g. [1, 3, 5]).

These examples are useful to highlight a *dangerous trap* that often occurs when abstracting a real-life problem: apparently small changes in the problem formulation lead to big jumps in the complexity of designing efficient algorithms for them. Think, for example, of the density function introduced in the second item above; we needed to introduce a cut-off lower bound to the segment length in order to avoid the trivial solution consisting of *single* nucleotides C or G. With this "small" change, the problem becomes more challenging and its solutions need to be more sophisticated.

Other subtle traps are more difficult to discover. Assume that we decide to circumvent the single-nucleotide outcome by searching for the *longest* segment whose density x/l is *not smaller than* a fixed value t. This is, in some sense, complementary to the problem stated in the second item above, because maximization is here on the segment length and a cut-off is imposed on the density value. Surprisingly, it is possible to *reduce* this density-based problem to a sum-based problem, in the spirit of the one stated in the first item above, and those solved in the previous sections. Algorithmic reductions are often employed by researchers to reuse known solutions and thus not need to reinventing the wheel again and again.

To prove this reduction it is enough to note that, for any subarray $D[a, b]$,

$$\frac{\text{Sum}_D[a, b]}{b - a + 1} = \sum_{k=a}^{b} \frac{D[k]}{b - a + 1} \geq t \iff \sum_{k=a}^{b} (D[k] - t) \geq 0.$$

Therefore, subtracting the density threshold t from all elements in D, we can turn the density-based problem into one that asks for the *longest segment that has a sum larger than or equal to 0*.

> **Problem.** Given an array $D[1, n]$ of positive and negative numbers, we want to find the *longest* segment in D whose density is *larger than or equal to* a fixed threshold t.

Be aware that if you change the request from the *longest segment* to the *shortest one* whose density is larger than a threshold t, then the problem becomes trivial again: just take the single occurrence of a nucleotide C or G. Similarly, if we fix an upper bound u to the segment's sum (instead of a lower bound), then we can change the sign of all D's elements and thus turn the problem again into a problem with a lower bound $t = -u$. We finally note that this formulation is in some sense a complement of the one given in the first item. Here we maximize the segment length and force a lower bound on the sum of its elements; there, we maximized the sum of the segment's elements provided that its length was within a given range. It is nice to observe that the structure of the algorithmic solution for both problems is similar, so we detail only the former one and refer the reader to the literature for the latter.

The algorithm to solve this problem proceeds inductively by assuming that, at step $i = 1, 2, \ldots, n$, it has computed the longest subarray that has a sum larger than t

and occurs within $D[1, i - 1]$. Let us denote the solution available at the beginning of step i by $D[l_{i-1}, r_{i-1}]$. Initially we have $i = 1$, and thus the inductive solution is the empty one, hence it has a length equal to 0. To move from step i to step $i + 1$, we need to compute $D[l_i, r_i]$, possibly by taking advantage of the currently known solution.

It is clear that the new segment either is inside $D[1, i - 1]$ (namely, $r_i < i$) or ends at $D[i]$ (namely, $r_i = i$). The former case admits as a solution the one of the previous iteration, namely $D[l_{i-1}, r_{i-1}]$, and so nothing has to be done: just set $r_i = r_{i-1}$ and $l_i = l_{i-1}$. The latter case is more involved and requires the use of some special data structures and a tricky analysis to show that the total complexity of the proposed algorithm is $O(n)$ in space and time, thus turning out to be asymptotically optimal.

We start by making a simple, yet effective, observation:

Fact 2.1 If $r_i = i$ then the segment $D[l_i, r_i]$ must be strictly longer than the segment $D[l_{i-1}, r_{i-1}]$. This means in particular that l_i occurs to the left of position $L_i = i - (r_{i-1} - l_{i-1})$.

The proof of this fact follows immediately by the observation that, if $r_i = i$, then the current step i has found a segment that is "longer" than the previously known one. This is the reason why we can discard all positions within the range $[L_i, i]$, because they generate segments of length shorter than or equal to the previous solution $D[l_{i-1}, r_{i-1}]$.

> **Reformulated problem.** Given an array $D[1, n]$ of positive and negative numbers, we want to find at every step the *smallest* index $l_i \in [1, L_i)$ such that $\text{Sum}_D[l_i, i] \geq t$.

There could be many indexes l_i such that $\text{Sum}_D[l_i, i] \geq t$; here we wish to find the *smallest* one, because we aim to determine the *longest* segment.

At this point it is useful to recall that $\text{Sum}_D[l_i, i]$ can be rewritten in terms of prefix sums of array D, namely $\text{Sum}_D[1, i] - \text{Sum}_D[1, l_i - 1] = P[i] - P[l_i - 1]$, where the array P was introduced in Section 2.4 and precomputed in linear time and space. So we need to find the smallest index $l_i \in [1, L_i)$ such that $P[i] - P[l_i - 1] \geq t$.

It is worth observing that the computation of l_i could be done by scanning $P[1, L_i - 1]$ and searching for the *leftmost* index x such that $P[i] - P[x] \geq t$ or, equivalently, $P[x] \leq P[i] - t$. We could then set $l_i = x + 1$ and be done. Unfortunately, this is inefficient because it requires us to repeatedly scan the same positions of P as i increases, thus leading to a quadratic-time algorithm. Since we are aiming for a linear-time algorithm, we need to spend constant time "amortized" per step i.

In order to achieve this performance we first need to show that we can avoid scanning the whole prefix $P[1, L_i - 1]$ by identifying a *subset* of *candidate positions* for x. Call $C_{i,j}$ the candidate positions for iteration i, where $j = 0, 1, \ldots$. They are defined as follows: $C_{i,0} = L_i$ (it is a dummy value), and $C_{i,j}$ is defined inductively as the *leftmost minimum* of the subarray $P[1, C_{i,j-1} - 1]$ (i.e. the subarray to the left of the current minimum and to the left of L_i). We denote by $c(i)$ the number of these

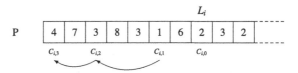

Figure 2.2 An illustrative example for the $c(i)$ candidate positions $C_{i,j}$ relative to the position L_i, given an array P of prefix sums.

candidate positions for the step i, where clearly $c(i) \leq L_i$ (equality holds when $P[1, L_i]$ is decreasing).

For an illustrative example see Figure 2.2, where $c(i) = 3$ and the candidate positions are connected via left-pointing arrows.

Looking at Figure 2.2, we derive three key properties whose proof is left to the reader because it immediately comes from the definition of $C_{i,j}$:

- **Property a:** The sequence of candidate positions $C_{i,j}$ occurs within $[1, L_i)$ and moves leftward, namely $C_{i,j} < C_{i,j-1} < \ldots < C_{i,1} < C_{i,0} = L_i$, where $j = c(i)$.

- **Property b:** At each iteration i, the sequence of candidate values $P[C_{i,j}]$ is increasing with $j = 1, 2, \ldots, c(i)$. More precisely, we have $P[C_{i,j}] > P[C_{i,j-1}]$ and $C_{i,j} < C_{i,j-1}$, so values increase as the positions $C_{i,j}$ move leftward.

- **Property c:** The value $P[C_{i,j}]$ is smaller than any other value on its left in P, because it is the leftmost minimum of the prefix $P[1, C_{i,j-1} - 1]$.

It is crucial now to show that the index we are searching for, namely l_i, can be derived by looking only at these candidate positions $C_{i,j}$ and corresponding prefix-sum values $P[C_{i,j}]$. From Fact 2.1 we are interested in segments that have the form $D[x, i]$ with $x < L_i$ and sum $\text{Sum}_D[x, i] \geq t$, and among those x we search for the smallest one (i.e. l_i). Since $\text{Sum}_D[x, i] = P[i] - P[x - 1]$, Property c allows us to conclude that if we have $\text{Sum}_D[C_{i,j} + 1, i] < t$ then all longer segments will have a sum smaller than t. Therefore we can conclude that:

Fact 2.2 At each iteration i, the largest index j^* such that $\text{Sum}_D[C_{i,j^*} + 1, i] \geq t$ (if any) provides us with the longest segment we are searching for.

There are two main problems in deploying the candidate positions $C_{i,j}$ for the efficient computation of l_i: (i) How do we compute the $C_{i,j}$s as i increases, and (ii) How do we search for the index j^*. To address (i) we note that the computation of $C_{i,j}$ depends only on the position of the previous $C_{i,j-1}$ and *not* on the indices i or j. So we can define an auxiliary array $LMin[1, n]$ such that $LMin[i]$ is the leftmost position of the minimum within $P[1, i - 1]$. It is not difficult to see that $C_{i,1} = LMin[L_i]$, and that according to the definition of Cs it is $C_{i,2} = LMin[\, LMin[L_i]\,]$, which we write as $LMin^2[L_i]$. In general, it is $C_{i,k} = LMin^k[L_i]$. This allows an incremental computation:

$$LMin[x] = \begin{cases} 0 & \text{if } x = 0 \\ x - 1 & \text{if } P[x-1] < P[\,LMin[x-1]\,] \\ LMin[x-1] & \text{otherwise} \end{cases}$$

This formula has an easy explanation using *induction*. Initially we set $LMin[0]$ to the dummy value 0. To compute $LMin[x]$ we need to determine the leftmost minimum in $P[1, x-1]$: this is either located in $x-1$ (with value $P[x-1]$) or is the one determined for $P[1, x-2]$ in position $LMin[x-1]$ (with value $P[LMin[x-1]]$). Therefore, by comparing these two values we can compute $LMin[x]$ in constant time. Hence the computation of all candidate positions $LMin[1, n]$ takes $O(n)$ time.

We are left with the problem of determining j^* efficiently. We will not be able to compute j^* in constant time at each iteration i but we will show that, if at step i we execute $s_i > 1$ steps, then we are extending the length of the current solution by $\Theta(s_i)$ units. Given that the longest segment cannot be longer than n, the sum of these extra costs cannot be larger than $O(n)$, and thus we are done. This is called the *amortized argument*, because we are, in some sense, charging the cost of the expensive iterations to the cheapest ones. The computation of j^* at iteration i requires checking the positions $LMin^k[L_i]$ for $k = 1, 2, \ldots$ until the condition in Fact 2.2 is satisfied; in fact, we know that all the other $j > j^*$ do not satisfy Fact 2.2. This search takes j^* steps and finds a new segment whose length is *increased* by at least j^* units, given Property a. Since a segment cannot be longer than the entire sequence $D[1, n]$, we can conclude that the total extra time incurred by the search for j^* cannot be larger than $O(n)$.

We leave to the diligent reader to work out the details of the pseudocode of this algorithm; the techniques underlying its elegant design and analysis should be clear enough that it can be approached without any difficulties.

References

[1] Kun-Mao Chao. Maximum-density segment. In Ming-Yang Kao, editor, *Encyclopedia of Algorithms*. Springer, 502–4, 2008.

[2] Kun-Mao Chao. Maximum-scoring segment with length restrictions. In Ming-Yang Kao, editor, *Encyclopedia of Algorithms*. Springer, 506–7, 2008.

[3] Chih-Huai Cheng, Hsiao-Fei Liu, and Kun-Mao Chao. Optimal algorithms for the average-constrained maximum-sum segment problem. *Information Processing Letters*, 109(3): 171–4, 2009.

[4] Rolf Fagerberg. Cache-oblivious model. In Ming-Yang Kao, editor, *Encyclopedia of Algorithms*. Springer, 264–9, 2016.

[5] Takeshi Fukuda, Yasuhiko Morimoto, Shinichi Morishita, and Takeshi Tokuyama. Mining optimized association rules for numeric attributes. *Journal of Computer System Sciences*, 58(1): 1–12, 1999.

3 Random Sampling

So much of life, it seems to me, is
determined by pure randomness.
Sidney Poitier

This chapter addressses a problem that is simple to state, is the backbone of many randomized algorithms, and admits of solutions that are algorithmically challenging to design and analyze.

> **Problem.** Given a sequence of n items $S = (i_1, i_2, \ldots, i_n)$ and a positive integer $m \leq n$, the goal is to select a subset of m items from S uniformly at random.

"Uniformly" here means that any item in S has to be sampled with probability $1/n$. Items can be numbers, strings, or complex objects, either stored in a file located on disk or streamed through a channel. In the former scenario, the input size n is known and items occupy a contiguous sequence of pages; in the latter scenario, the input size may be unknown, yet the *uniformity* of the sampling process must be guaranteed. In this chapter we will address both scenarios, aiming at efficiency in terms of I/Os, extra space required for the computation (in addition to the input), and amount of randomness deployed (expressed as number of randomly generated integers). Hereafter, we will make use of a built-in procedure RAND(a,b) that randomly selects a number within the range $(a, b]$. Whether the number is a real or an integer will be clear from the context. The design of a good RAND function is a challenging task; however, we will not go into detail here because we wish to concentrate only on the sampling process, rather than on the generation of random numbers for which the interested reader can refer to the wide literature on (pseudo-)random number generators.

Finally, we note that it is desirable to have the positions of the sampled items in *sorted* order, because this speeds up their extraction from S both in the disk setting (less seek time) and in the stream-based setting (fewer passes over the data). Moreover, it reduces the working space because it enables the efficient extraction of the items via a scan, rather than using an auxiliary array of pointers to the sampled items. We do not want to detail further the sorting issue here, which gets complicated whenever $m > M$ and thus these positions cannot fit into internal memory. In this case we would need a disk-based sorter, which is an advanced topic, and is dealt with in Chapter 5. If, instead, $m \leq M$ we can deploy the fact that positions are integers in a fixed range, and thus use radix sort or any other fast internal-memory sorting routine available in the literature.

3.1 Disk Model and Known Sequence Length

We start by assuming that the input size n is known and that $S[1, n]$ is stored in a contiguous set of pages on disk. These pages cannot be modified because they may be the input of a more complicated problem that includes the current one as a sub-task. Algorithm 3.1 is the first solution we propose for the sampling problem we have described; it is very simple and allows us to raise some issues that will be addressed in the subsequent solutions.

Algorithm 3.1 Drawing from unsampled positions

1: Initialize the auxiliary array $S'[1, n] = S[1, n]$;
2: **for** $s = 0, 1, \ldots, m - 1$ **do**
3:     $p = \text{RAND}(1, n - s)$;
4:     select the item (pointed to by) $S'[p]$;
5:     swap $S'[p]$ with $S'[n - s]$;
6: **end for**

At each step s the algorithm maintains the following invariant: *the subarray $S'[n - s + 1, n]$ contains the items that have already been sampled, and the unsampled items of S are contained in $S'[1, n - s]$*. Initially (i.e. $s = 0$) this invariant holds because $S'[n - s + 1, n] = S'[n + 1, n]$ is the empty array. At a generic step s, the algorithm selects uniformly at random one item from $S'[1, n - s]$, and replaces it with the last item of that sequence (namely, $S'[n - s]$). This preserves the invariant for $s + 1$. At the end (i.e. $s = m$), the sampled items are contained in $S'[n - m + 1, n]$.

S' cannot be a *pure* copy of S, but it must be implemented as an *array of pointers* to S's items. The reason for this is that these items may have variable length (e.g. strings or complex objects), so their retrieval in constant time could not be obtained via arithmetic operations; also, the replacement step might be impossible due to a difference in length between the item at $S'[p]$ and the item at $S'[n - s]$. Pointers avoid these issues but occupy $\Theta(n \log n)$ bits of extra space, which might be nonnegligible when n gets large and might turn out even larger than S's space if the average length of its items is shorter than $\log n$ bits. Another drawback of this approach is given by its pattern of memory accesses, which act over $\Theta(n)$ cells in a purely random way, thus taking $\Theta(m)$ I/Os. This may be too slow when $m \approx n$, because in this case we would like to obtain $O(n/B)$ I/Os, which is the cost of scanning the whole S.

Let us approach these issues by proposing a series of algorithms that incrementally improve the I/Os and the space resources of the previous solution, up to the final result, which will achieve $O(m)$ extra space, $O(m)$ expected time, and $O(\min\{m, n/B\})$ I/Os. We start by observing that the swap of the items in Step 5 of Algorithm 3.1 guarantees that every step generates one distinct item, but forces to duplicate S. Algorithm 3.2 improves the I/O and space complexities by avoiding the item swapping via the use of an auxiliary data structure that keeps track of the selected positions in sorted order and needs only $O(m)$ space.

Algorithm 3.2 Dictionary of sampled positions

1: Initialize a dictionary $\mathcal{D} = \emptyset$;
2: **while** $|\mathcal{D}| < m$ **do**
3:      $p = \text{RAND}(1, n)$;
4:      if $p \notin \mathcal{D}$ insert it;
5: **end while**

Algorithm 3.2 stops when $\mathcal{D}$ contains m (distinct) integers which constitute the positions of the items to be sampled. The efficiency of the algorithm mainly depends on the implementation of the dictionary $\mathcal{D}$, which allows us to detect the presence of duplicate positions (and thus duplicate items). The literature offers many data structures that efficiently support membership and insert operations, based either on hashing or on trees. Here we consider only a hash-based solution, which consists of implementing $\mathcal{D}$ via a hash table of size $\Theta(m)$ with collisions managed via chaining, and a universal hash function for table access (see Chapter 8 for details on hashing). This way each membership query and insertion operation over $\mathcal{D}$ takes $O(1)$ expected time (the load factor of this table is $O(1)$), and total space $O(m)$. Time complexity could be improved by using more sophisticated data structures, such as dynamic perfect hashing or cuckoo hashing, but the final time bounds would always be *in expectation* because of the underlying resampling process. In fact, this algorithm may generate *duplicate* positions, which must be discarded and *resampled*. Bounding the cost of the resampling is the main drawback of this approach, which induces a constant-factor slowdown in expectation, thus making this solution very appealing in practice for small m. The reason for this is that the probability of having extracted an item already present in $\mathcal{D}$ is $|\mathcal{D}|/n \le m/n < 1/2$ because, without loss of generality, we can assume that $m < n/2$; if that isn't the case, we can solve the *complement* of the current problem and thus randomly select the positions of the items that are *not* sampled from S. So we need an expected constant number of resamplings in order to obtain a new item for $\mathcal{D}$, and thus advance in our selection process. Overall we have proved:

Fact 3.1 Algorithm 3.2 based on hashing with chaining requires $O(m)$ expected time and $O(m)$ additional space to select uniformly at random m positions in $[1, n]$. An additional sorting step is needed if we wish to extract the sampled items of S in a streaming-like fashion. In this case, the overall sampling process takes $O(\min\{m, n/B\})$ I/Os.

If we substitute hashing with a (balanced) search tree and assume we are working in the RAM model (hence we assume $m < M$), then we can avoid the sorting step by performing an *in-visit* of the search tree in $O(m)$ time. However, Algorithm 3.2 would still require $O(m \log m)$ time because each insertion/membership operation would take $O(\log m)$ time. We could do better by deploying an *integer*-based dictionary data structure, such as a van Emde Boas tree [1], and thus take $O(\log \log n)$ time for each dictionary operation (which is executed on integer keys of $\Theta(\log n)$ bits each). Note that the two bounds are incomparable, because of the relative magnitudes of m and n. Many other trade-offs are possible by changing the underlying dictionary data structure; we leave this exercise to the reader. As a final point we observe that, if $m \leq M$, the random generation and the management of $\mathcal{D}$ can occur within main memory without incurring any I/Os. Sometimes this is useful because the randomized algorithm that invokes the random-sampling subroutine does not need the corresponding items, but rather it needs only their positions in S.

3.2   Streaming Model and Known Sequence Length

We turn next to the case in which S is flowing through a channel and the input size n is known and large (e.g. internet traffic or query logs). This stream-based model requires that no preprocessing is possible (as instead done in Section 3.1 items' positions were resampled and/or sorted), every item of S is considered once, and the algorithm must immediately and irrevocably take a decision whether that item should be included or not in the set of sampled items. Later items may possibly kick that one out of the sampled set, but no discarded item can be reconsidered again in the future. Even in this case the algorithms are simple in their design, but their probabilistic analysis is a little more involved than before. The algorithms of the previous section offer an *expected* time complexity because they are faced with the resampling problem: some samples may have to be eliminated because they are duplicated. In order to avoid resampling, we need to ensure that each item is not considered more than once. So the algorithms that follow implement this idea in the simplest possible way: they scan the input sequence S and consider each item once. This approach brings with it two main difficulties that are related to the two requirements: uniformly sampling from the range $[1, n]$, and returning a sample of size m.

We start by designing an algorithm that draws just one item from S (hence $m = 1$), and then we generalize it to the case of a subset of $m > 1$ items. This algorithm proceeds by selecting the item $S[j]$ with probability $\mathcal{P}(j)$, which is properly defined in order to guarantee the selection of just one item uniformly at random.[1] In particular, we set $\mathcal{P}(1) = 1/n$, $\mathcal{P}(2) = 1/(n-1)$, $\mathcal{P}(3) = 1/(n-2)$, and so on, so the algorithm selects the item j with probability $\mathcal{P}(j) = \frac{1}{n-j+1}$, and if this occurs it stops. Eventually the item $S[n]$ is selected because its probability of being drawn is $\mathcal{P}(n) = 1$.

So the proposed algorithm guarantees the condition on the sample size $m = 1$, but that the probability of sampling any item $S[j]$ is $1/n$ is more difficult to be proved,

---

[1] In order to draw an item with probability P, it suffices to draw a random real $p = \text{RAND}(0, 1) \in (0, 1]$ and then compare it against P. If $p \leq P$ then the item is selected, otherwise it is not. Hence, for any p, an item will never be selected if $P = 0$ and it will always be selected if $P = 1$.

independently of j, given that we defined $\mathcal{P}(j) = 1/(n - j + 1)$. The reason for this derives from a simple probabilistic argument because $n - j + 1$ is the number of remaining elements in the sequence and all of them have to be drawn uniformly at random. By induction, the first $j - 1$ items of the sequence have uniform probability $1/n$ to be sampled; so the probability of not selecting any one of them is $1 - \frac{j-1}{n}$. As a result,

$$\mathcal{P}(\text{Sampling } i_j) = \mathcal{P}(\text{Not sampling } i_1 \cdots i_{j-1}) \times \mathcal{P}(\text{Selecting } i_j)$$

$$= \left(1 - \frac{j-1}{n}\right) \times \frac{1}{n-j+1} = \frac{1}{n}.$$

Algorithm 3.3 details the pseudocode for this approach, here generalized to work for an arbitrarily large sample $m \geq 1$.

Algorithm 3.3 Scanning and selecting

1: $s = 0$;
2: **for** $(j = 1; (j \leq n)$ **and** $(s < m); j\text{++})$ **do**
3:     $p = \text{RAND}(0, 1)$;
4:     **if** $p \leq \frac{m-s}{n-j+1}$ **then**
5:         select $S[j]$;
6:         $s\text{++}$;
7:     **end if**
8: **end for**

The difference with the previously described algorithm, which sets $m = 1$, lies in the probability $\mathcal{P}(j)$ of sampling $S[j]$, which is now $\mathcal{P}(j) = \frac{m-s}{n-j+1}$, where s is the number of items already selected before $S[j]$. Notice that if we have already got all samples, it is $s = m$ and thus $\mathcal{P}(j) = 0$, which means that Algorithm 3.3 does not generate more than m samples. On the other hand, Algorithm 3.3 cannot generate less than m samples, say y samples with $y < m$, because the last $m - y$ items of S would have probability 1 of being selected and thus they would be included in the final sample (according to Step 4 and Footnote 1). As far as the uniformity of the sample is concerned, we show that $\mathcal{P}(j)$ is equal to the probability that $S[j]$ is included in a random sample of size m given that s samples lie within $S[1, j - 1]$. We can rephrase this as the probability that $S[j]$ is included in a random sample of size $m - s$ taken from $S[j, n]$, and thus from $n - j + 1$ items. This probability is obtained by counting how many such combinations include $S[j]$, that is, $\binom{n-j}{m-s-1}$, and dividing by the number of combinations that either include or do not include $S[j]$, that is, $\binom{n-j+1}{m-s}$. Since $\binom{b}{a} = \frac{b!}{a! \, (b-a)!}$, we get the formula for $\mathcal{P}(j)$.

Fact 3.2 Algorithm 3.3 takes $O(n/B)$ I/Os and $O(n)$ time, generates n random numbers, and takes $O(m)$ additional space to sample uniformly m items from the sequence $S[1, n]$ in a streaming-like way.

We conclude this section by mentioning a solution proposed by Jeffrey Vitter [4] that reduces the amount of randomly generated numbers from n to m, and thus speeds up the solution to $O(m)$ time and I/Os. This solution could also be fit into the framework of the previous section (random access to input data), and in that case its specialty would be the avoidance of resampling. Its key idea is not to generate random *indicators*, which specify whether or not an item $S[j]$ should be selected, but rather generate random *jumps* that count the number of items to skip over before selecting the next item of S. Vitter introduces a random variable $G(v, V)$, where v is the number of items remaining to be selected, and V is the total number of items left to be examined in S. According to our previous notation, at step j we have that $v = m - s$ and $V = n - j + 1$. The item $S[G(v, V) + 1]$ is the next one selected to form the uniform sample from the *remaining* ones. It goes without saying that this approach avoids the generation of duplicate samples, but it does incur an expected time bound because of the cost of generating the jumps G according to the following distribution:

$$P(G = g) = \binom{V - g - 1}{v - 1} / \binom{V}{v}.$$

The key difficulty here is that we cannot tabulate (and store) the values of all binomial coefficients in advance, because this would need too much time and space, since $V \leq n$ and $v \leq m$. Surprisingly, Vitter solved this problem in $O(1)$ expected time, by adapting in an elegant way von Neumann's rejection-acceptance method to the discrete case induced by G's jumps. We refer the reader to [4] for further details.

3.3   Streaming Model and Unknown Sequence Length

It goes without saying that the knowledge of n was crucial to compute $P(j)$ in Algorithm 3.3. If n is unknown we need to proceed differently, and so the rest of this chapter is dedicated to detailing two possible solutions for this scenario.

The first solution is fairly simple and deploys a min-heap $\mathcal{H}$ of size m plus the random number generator RAND$(0,1)$. The key idea is to associate a random priority r_j to each item $S[j]$ and then use the min-heap $\mathcal{H}$ to select the items that have the top-m priorities. The pseudocode in Algorithm 3.4 implements this idea, by comparing the minimum priority among the top-m ones currently stored in the the min-heap $\mathcal{H}$ (and located in its root) with priority r_j associated to the currently examined item $S[j]$. If r_j is larger than that minimum priority, then $S[j]$ is inserted in $\mathcal{H}$ and the minimum priority is deleted from $\mathcal{H}$, thus updating the set of top-m priorities (and their associated items).

Since the heap $\mathcal{H}$ has size m, the final sample will consist of m items. Each priority takes $O(\log m)$ time to be inserted in or deleted from $\mathcal{H}$. The randomness of the priorities ensures that every item has the same probability of being included in the top-m set. So we have proved:

Fact 3.3 Algorithm 3.4 takes $O(n/B)$ I/Os and $O(n \log m)$ time, generates n random numbers, and uses $O(m)$ additional space to sample uniformly at random m items from the sequence $S[1, n]$ in a streaming-like way and without the knowledge of n.

Algorithm 3.4 Heap and random keys

1: Initialize a min-heap $\mathcal{H}$ with m dummy items having priority $-\infty$;
2: **for** each item $S[j]$ **do**
3:   $r_j = \text{RAND}(0, 1)$;
4:   $y =$ the minimum priority in $\mathcal{H}$;
5:   **if** $r_j > y$ **then**
6:     extract the item with priority y from $\mathcal{H}$;
7:     insert item $S[j]$ in $\mathcal{H}$, assigning priority r_j;
8:   **end if**
9: **end for**
10: **return** the m items contained in $\mathcal{H}$;

We conclude this chapter by introducing the elegant *reservoir sampling* algorithm, attributed to Alan Waterman according to [5], which improves Algorithm 3.4 both in time and space complexity. The idea is similar to the one adopted for Algorithm 3.3 and consists of properly defining the probability with which an item is selected. But the key issue here is that we cannot take an irrevocable decision on $S[j]$ because we do not know how long the sequence S is, so we need some freedom to *change* what we have decided so far as the scanning of S goes on.

Algorithm 3.5 Reservoir sampling

1: Initialize array $R[1, m] = S[1, m]$;
2: **for** each item $S[j]$ **do**
3:   $h = \text{RAND}(1, j)$;
4:   **if** $h \leq m$ **then**
5:     set $R[h] = S[j]$;
6:   **end if**
7: **end for**
8: **return** array R;

The pseudocode of Algorithm 3.5 uses a "reservoir" array $R[1, m]$ to keep the candidate samples. Initially R is set to contain the first m items of the input sequence. At any subsequent step j, the algorithm makes a choice whether $S[j]$ has to be included or not in the current sample. This choice occurs with probability $\mathcal{P}(j) = m/j$, in which case some previously selected item has to be kicked out of R. This item is chosen at random in R, hence with probability $1/m$. This *double choice* is implemented in Algorithm 3.5 by choosing an integer h in the range $[1, j]$, and making the substitution only if $h \leq m$. This event has probability m/j: exactly what we wished to set for $\mathcal{P}(j)$.

For the correctness of the algorithm, it is clear that Algorithm 3.5 selects m items; it is less clear that these items are drawn uniformly at random from S, which actually means that they are drawn with probability m/n. Let us see why this is the case, by induction on the (unknown) sequence length n. The base case in which $n = m$ is obvious: every item has to be selected with probability $m/n = 1$, and indeed this is what Step 1 does by writing the first m items of S in the reservoir R. To prove the inductive step (from $n-1$ to n items), we note that the uniform-sampling property holds for $S[n]$ since by definition that item is inserted in R with probability $\mathcal{P}(n) = m/n$ (Step 4). Computing the probability of being sampled for the previous items in $S[1, n-1]$ is more difficult. An item $S[j]$, with $j < n$, belongs to the reservoir R at the n-th step of Algorithm 3.5 if and only if it was in the reservoir at the $(n-1)$-th step and it is not kicked out at the n-th step. This latter may occur either if $S[n]$ is not selected (and thus R is untouched) or if $S[n]$ is selected and $S[j]$ is not kicked out of R (as these two events are independent of each other). Expressed as a formula, the probability at the n-th step is

$$\mathcal{P}(S[j] \in R) \times [\mathcal{P}(S[n] \text{ is not selected}) + \mathcal{P}(S[n] \text{ is selected})$$
$$\times \mathcal{P}(S[j] \text{ is not kicked out of } R)] .$$

By induction, each item $S[j]$ preceding $S[n]$ has probability $m/(n-1)$ of being in the reservoir R before that $S[n]$ is processed. Moreover, item $S[j]$ remains in the reservoir either if $S[n]$ is not selected (which occurs with probability $1 - \frac{m}{n}$) or if it is not kicked out by the selected $S[n]$ (which occurs with probability $\frac{m-1}{m}$). Summing up these terms we get:

$$\mathcal{P}(\text{item } S[j] \in R \text{ after } n \text{ items, and } j < n) = \frac{m}{n-1} \times \left[\left(1 - \frac{m}{n}\right) + \left(\frac{m}{n} \times \frac{m-1}{m}\right) \right]$$
$$= \frac{m}{n-1} \times \frac{n-1}{n} = \frac{m}{n} .$$

To understand this formula, assume that we have a reservoir of 10 items, so the first 10 items of S are inserted in R by Step 1. Then item $S[11]$ is inserted in the reservoir with probability $10/11$, item $S[12]$ with probability $10/12$, and so on. Each time an item is inserted in the reservoir, a random element is kicked out of it, hence with probability $1/10$. After n steps the reservoir R contains 10 items, each sampled from S with probability $10/n$.

Fact 3.4 Algorithm 3.5 takes $O(n/B)$ I/Os, $O(n)$ time, and exactly m additional space, and generates n random numbers to sample uniformly at random m items from the sequence $S[1, n]$ in a streaming-like way and without the knowledge of n. Hence it is time, space, and I/O optimal in this model of computation.

A drawback of this approach is the number of times Step 3 is executed, which needs the generation of a random integer of increasing size for each processed item $S[j]$. Researchers have investigated the problem of reducing this number; here we mention an asymptotically optimal solution called Algorithm L in [3]. This algorithm requires $O(m(1 + \log(n/m)))$ expected time and random number generations, which is optimal up to a constant factor. We refer the reader to [3] for the in-depth algorithmic details; here we content ourselves with a few important observations.

The first concerns the expected number of insertions in the reservoir R. Given that the first m items are always inserted in the reservoir and each subsequent item $S[j]$

executes Step 5 with probability m/j, with $j > m$, the expected number of insertions in R can be estimated as

$$m + \sum_{j=m+1}^{n} (m/j) = m + \left(\sum_{j=1}^{n} (m/j) - \sum_{j=1}^{m} (m/j) \right) = m\,(1 + H_n - H_m),$$

where $H_n = \sum_{j=1}^{n}(1/j)$ is the n-th harmonic number which can be asymptotically bounded by $O(\log n)$. This proves also to be the bound on the expected number of times Step 5 of Algorithm 3.5 is executed. This is exactly the number of steps Algorithm L executes provided that the generation of the "jumps" takes constant time.

The second key idea underlying Algorithm L is to compute how many items in S are discarded before the next item enters the reservoir R, and thus Step 5 is executed. This is implemented by simulating the approach of Algorithm 3.4, which associates a random priority in $(0, 1)$ to each item $S[j]$ and then selects the items corresponding to the top-m priorities. Here, however, we cannot generate these priorities explicitly for all items but need to do this just for the checked ones. It can be shown that the number of skipped items follows a geometric distribution and can therefore be computed in constant time [2].

References

[1] Thomas H. Cormen, Charles E. Leiserson, Ronald L. Rivest, and Clifford Stein. Hashing, Chapter 11 in *Introduction to Algorithms*. Chapter 11, "Hash tables", 253–83, The MIT Press, third edition, 2009.

[2] Luc Devroye. Random sampling, in *Non-uniform Random Variate Generation*. Chapter 12, "Random Sampling," 611–41, Springer, 611–41, 1986.

[3] Kim-Hung Li. Reservoir-sampling algorithms of time Complexity $O(n(1 + \log(N/n)))$. *ACM Transactions on Mathematical Software*, 20(4): 481–93, 1994.

[4] Jeffrey Scott Vitter. Faster methods for random sampling. *ACM Computing Surveys*, 27(7): 703–18, 1984.

[5] Jeffrey Scott Vitter. Random sampling with a reservoir. *ACM Transactions on Mathematical Software*, 11(1): 37–57, 1985.

4 List Ranking

Pointers are dangerous in disks!

This chapter addresses a simple problem related to lists: the basic data structure underlying the design of many algorithms that manage interconnected items. We start with an easy to state but inefficient solution derived from the optimal one designed for the RAM model; then we discuss increasingly sophisticated solutions that are elegant and efficient or optimal, but still simple enough to be implemented with a few lines of code. The treatment of this problem will also allow us to highlight a subtle relation between *parallel computation* and *external memory computation*, which can be deployed to derive efficient disk-aware algorithms from efficient parallel algorithms.

> **Problem.** Given a (unidirectional) list $\mathcal{L}$ of n items, the goal is to compute the distance of each of those items from the tail of $\mathcal{L}$.

Items are represented via their ids, which are integers from 1 to n. The list is encoded by means of an array $\texttt{Succ}[1, n]$, which stores in entry $\texttt{Succ}[i]$ the id j if item i points to item j. If t is the id of the tail of the list $\mathcal{L}$, then we have $\texttt{Succ}[t] = t$, and thus the link outgoing from t forms a *self-loop*. Figure 4.1 exemplifies these ideas by showing a graphical representation of a list (left), its encoding via the array $\texttt{Succ}$ (right), and the output required by the list-ranking problem, hereafter stored in the array $\texttt{Rank}[1, n]$.

This problem can be solved easily in the RAM model by exploiting the constant-time access to its internal memory. Actually, we can foresee three simple algorithmic

id	Succ	Rank
1	3	1
2	5	5
3	3	0
4	6	3
5	4	4
6	1	2

Figure 4.1 An example of input and output for the list-ranking problem, defined over a list $\mathcal{L}$ of $n = 6$ items. The head of the list is the only item h in $\{1, \ldots, 6\}$ not occurring in $\texttt{Succ}$ (in the example, $h = 2$); the tail of the list is the only item t in $\{1, \ldots, 6\}$ for which $\texttt{Succ}[t] = t$ (in the example, $t = 3$). It is $\texttt{Rank}[t] = 0$ and $\texttt{Rank}[h] = n - 1 = 5$.

solutions, each requiring optimal $O(n)$ time. This time complexity is optimal because all items in $\mathcal{L}$ must be visited to set their Rank's values.

The first solution scans the list from its head and computes the number n of its items, then re-scans the list by assigning to its head the rank $n - 1$ and to every subsequent element in the list a rank decremented by one at every step. The second solution computes the array of predecessors as Pred[Succ[i]] $= i$, and then scans the list backward, starting from its tail t and setting Rank[t] $= 0$, and then incrementing the Rank's value for each item as the traversal proceeds from t. The third way to solve the problem is *recursively*, defining the function ListRank(i), which works as follows: Rank[i] $= 0$ if Succ[i] $= i$ (and hence $i = t$), else it sets Rank[i] $=$ ListRank(Succ[i]) $+ 1$.

If we execute these algorithms over a list stored on disk (via its array Succ), then they could elicit $\Theta(n)$ I/Os because of the arbitrary distribution of links, which might induce an irregular pattern of disk accesses to the entries of arrays Rank and Succ. This I/O cost is significantly far from the obvious lower bound $\Omega(n/B)$, which can be derived by the same argument we used for the RAM model. Although this lower bound seems very low, in this chapter we will come very close to it by introducing a bunch of sophisticated techniques that are general enough to find applications in many other, apparently dissimilar, scenarios.

The moral is that, in order to achieve I/O-efficiency on *linked* data structures, you need to avoid the traversal of pointers as much as possible and dig into the wide parallel-algorithm literature (see, e.g., [2], where the parallel-RAM (PRAM) model is also defined) because efficient parallelism can, surprisingly, be turned into I/O-efficiency.

4.1   The Pointer-Jumping Technique

There is a well-known technique for solving the list-ranking problem in parallel settings, based on the *pointer-jumping* technique. The algorithmic idea is quite simple, it takes n processors, each dealing with one item of $\mathcal{L}$. Processor i initializes Rank[i] $= 0$ if $i = t$, otherwise it sets Rank[i] $= 1$. Then it executes the following two instructions: Rank[i] $=$ Rank[i] $+$ Rank[Succ[i]] and Succ[i] $=$ Succ[Succ[i]]. This double update actually maintains the following invariant: Rank[i] *measures the distance (i.e. the number of items) in the original list between i and the item currently stored in* Succ[i]. We will skip the formal proof that can be derived by induction, and refer the reader to the illustrative example in Figure 4.2. In the figure the dashed arrows indicate the new links computed by one pointer-jumping step, and the table on the right of each list specifies the values of the array Rank[$1, n$] as they are recomputed after this step. The values in bold are the final/correct values. Note that distances do not grow linearly (i.e. $1, 2, 3, \ldots$), but they grow as a power of two (i.e. $1, 2, 4, \ldots$), up to the step in which the next jump reaches t, the tail of the list. This means that the total number of times the parallel algorithm executes these two steps is $O(\log n)$, thus resulting in an exponential improvement compared to the time required by the sequential algorithm.

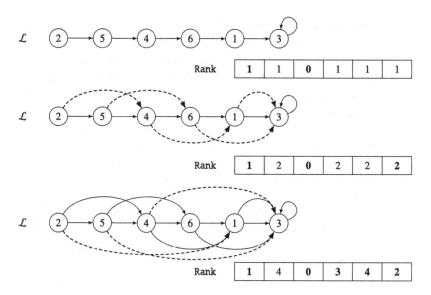

Figure 4.2 An example of pointer jumping applied to the list $\mathcal{L}$ of Figure 4.1. The dashed arrows indicate the result of executing one pointer-jumping step applied to the solid black arrows, which represent the current configuration of the list. Rank's values in bold are correct and correspond to dashed arrows pointing to the tail t of the list.

If n processors are involved, pointer jumping executes a total of $O(n \log n)$ operations, which is inefficient if we compare it to the number $O(n)$ of operations executed by the optimal RAM algorithm.

Lemma 4.1 *The parallel algorithm, using n processors and the pointer-jumping technique, takes $O(\log n)$ time and $O(n \log n)$ operations to solve the list-ranking problem.*

Optimizations are possible to further improve the previous result and come close to the optimal number of operations; for example, turning off processors as their corresponding items reach the end of the list could be an idea. We will not dig into these details as this topic is covered elsewhere in the literature (see, e.g., [2]). Here we are interested in simulating the pointer-jumping technique in our setting, which consists of one single processor and a two-level memory, and show that deriving an I/O-efficient algorithm is very simple whenever an efficient parallel algorithm is available. The simplicity hinges on an algorithmic scheme which deploys two basic primitives – Scan and Sort a set of tuples – nowadays available in almost every distributed platform, such as Apache Hadoop.

4.2   Parallel Algorithm Simulation in a Two-Level Memory

The key difficulty in using the pointer-jumping technique within the two-level memory framework is the arbitrary layout of the list on disk, and the consequent arbitrary pattern of memory accesses to update Succ-pointers and Rank-values, which might induce many "random" I/Os. To circumvent this problem we will describe how the two key steps of the pointer-jumping technique can be simulated via a constant number of Sort and Scan primitives over n triples of integers. Sorting is a basic primitive, which is very complicated to implement I/O-efficiently, and indeed, it will be the subject of Chapter 5. For the sake of presentation, we will denote in this chapter its I/O complexity as $\widetilde{O}(n/B)$ which means that we have a hidden logarithmic factor depending on the main parameters of the model, namely M, n, and B. This factor is negligible in practice, since we can safely upper bound it with a very small constant, such as 4 or less. So we prefer now to *hide it*, in order to simplify the discussion. On the other hand, Scan is easy and takes $O(n/B)$ I/Os to process a contiguous disk portion occupied by the n triples.

We can identify a common algorithmic structure in the two steps of the pointer-jumping technique: they both consist of an operation (either copy or sum) between two entries of an array (either Succ or Rank). For the sake of presentation, we will refer to a generic array A, and model the parallel operation to be simulated on disk as follows:

> Assume that a parallel step has the following form: $A[a_i]$ op $A[b_i]$, where op is the operation executed in parallel over the two array entries $A[a_i]$ and $A[b_i]$ by all processors $i = 1, 2, \ldots, n$ which actually read $A[b_i]$ and use this value to update the content of $A[a_i]$.

The operation op is a sum and an assignment for the update of the Rank-array (here $A = $ Rank), whereas it is a copy for the update of the Succ-array (here $A = $ Succ). As far as the array indices are concerned, for both steps they are $a_i = i$ and $b_i = $ Succ[i]. The key issue is to show that $A[a_i]$ op $A[b_i]$ can be implemented, simultaneously over all $i = 1, 2, 3, \ldots, n$, by using a constant number of Sort and Scan primitives, thus taking a total of $\widetilde{O}(n/B)$ I/Os. This implementation consists of five steps:

1. Scan the disk and create a sequence of triples with the form $\langle a_i, b_i, 0 \rangle$. Every triple carries information about the source address of the array entry involved in op (i.e., b_i), its destination address (i.e. a_i), and the value that we are moving (the third component, initialized to 0).
2. Sort the triples according to their second component (i.e. the source address b_i). Here we are "aligning" each triple $\langle a_i, b_i, 0 \rangle$ with the memory cell $A[b_i]$.
3. Scan the triples and the array A using two iterators, one over the triples and one over the array A. Because the triples are sorted according to their second component (i.e. b_i), we can efficiently create the new triples $\langle a_i, b_i, A[b_i] \rangle$ during the Scan. Note that not all memory cells of A are necessarily present as second component of a triple; nevertheless, their coordinated order allows $A[b_i]$ to be copied into the triple for b_i within the coordinated Scan.
4. Sort the triples according to their first component (i.e. the destination address a_i). This way, we are "aligning" the triple $\langle a_i, b_i, A[b_i] \rangle$ with the memory cell $A[a_i]$.

5. Scan the triples and the array A, again using two iterators, one over the triples and one over the array A. For every triple $\langle a_i, b_i, A[b_i]\rangle$, update the content of the memory cell $A[a_i]$ according to the semantics of op and the value $A[b_i]$. This update can be done efficiently within the coordinated Scan.

The I/O complexity is easy to derive since the previous algorithm is executing two Sorts and three Scans which involve n triples. Therefore we can state:

Theorem 4.1 *The parallel execution of n operations $A[a_i]$ op $A[b_i]$ can be simulated in a two-level memory model by using a constant number of Sort and Scan primitives, thus taking a total of $\widetilde{O}(n/B)$ I/Os.*

In the case of the parallel pointer-jumping algorithm, the parallel pointer-jumps are executed $O(\log n)$ times, so we have:

Theorem 4.2 *The parallel pointer-jumping algorithm can be simulated in a two-level memory model taking $\widetilde{O}((n/B)\log n)$ I/Os.*

This bound turns out to be $o(n)$, and thus better than the direct execution of the RAM algorithm on disk, whenever $B = \omega(\log n)$. This condition is trivially satisfied in practice because $B \approx 10^4$ bytes and $\log n \le 80$ for any real dataset size 2^{80} (being the estimated number of atoms in the Universe[1]).

Figure 4.3 illustrates a running example of this simulation. The table on the left indicates the content of the arrays Rank and Succ encoding the list of $n = 6$ items depicted at the top of the figure with black solid arrows; the table on the right indicates the content of these two arrays after one step of the pointer-jumping technique and encoding the dashed arrows. The four columns of triples correspond to the application of the five Scan/Sort phases described earlier in this section. More precisely, the first column of triples is created via the first Scan as $\langle i, \text{Succ}[i], 0\rangle$, since $a_i = i$ and $b_i = \text{Succ}[i]$. The second column of triples is obtained via the first Sort executed according to their second component. The third column of triples can thus be computed via a coordinated Scan of the triples and the array Rank, thus creating the new triples $\langle i, \text{Succ}[i], \text{Rank}[\text{Succ}[i]]\rangle$. The fourth column of triples is Sorted by their first component, namely i, so that the final coordinated Scan of the array Rank and the third component of those triples can compute correctly $\text{Rank}[i] = \text{Rank}[i] + \text{Rank}[\text{Succ}[i]]$.

This simulation demonstrates the updating of the array Rank; array Succ can be updated similarly. Nonetheless, note that the update of the two arrays Rank and Succ can be done simultaneously by using a quadruple, instead of a triple, which carries both values of $\text{Rank}[\text{Succ}[i]]$ and $\text{Succ}[\text{Succ}[i]]$. This is possible because both values refer to the same source and destination addresses (namely, i and $\text{Succ}[i]$).

---

[1] See, e.g., http://en.wikipedia.org/wiki/Large_numbers.

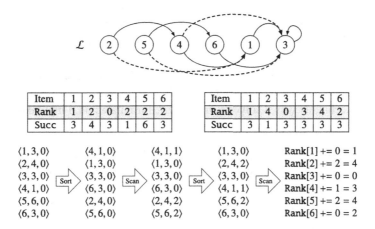

Figure 4.3 An example of simulation of the basic parallel step via Scan and Sort primitives, relative to the computation of the array Rank, with the configuration specified in the diagram and tables. Black solid arrows indicate the pointers encoded in the table on the left; the dashed arrows indicate the updated pointers after one step of pointer-jumping, and they are encoded in the table on the right.

The simulation scheme introduced in this section can actually be generalized to every parallel algorithm, thus leading to the following important, and useful, result (see [1]):

Theorem 4.3 *Every parallel algorithm using n processors and taking T steps can be simulated in a two-level memory by a disk-aware sequential algorithm taking $\widetilde{O}((n/B)\,T)$ I/Os and $O(n)$ space.*

This simulation is advantageous whenever $T = o(B)$, which implies a sublinear number of I/Os, namely $o(n)$. This occurs in all cases in which the parallel algorithm takes a low *polylogarithmic* time complexity. Such a situation is typical of the parallel algorithms developed for the so-called P-RAM model of computation, which assumes that all processors work independently of each other and can access in constant time an unbounded shared memory. It is an ideal model which was very famous in the 1980s–1990s [2], and led to the design of many powerful parallel techniques, which were applied to distributed as well as disk-aware algorithms. Its main limitation was that it did not account for conflicts among the many processors accessing the shared memory, and a simplified communication framework among them. Nevertheless, the simplicity of P-RAM allowed researchers to concentrate on the algorithmic aspects of parallel computation and thus design parallel schemes such as the pointer-jumping one and the others described in the remainder of this chapter.

4.3   A Divide-and-Conquer Approach

The goal of this section is to show that the list-ranking problem can be solved more efficiently than what can be achieved with the pointer-jumping technique. The algorithmic solution we describe in this section relies on an interesting application of the *divide-and-conquer paradigm*, here specialized to work on a (uni-directional) list of items.

Before going into the technicalities of this application, let us briefly recall the main ideas underlying the design of an algorithm, say $\mathcal{A}_{dc}$, based on the divide-and-conquer technique which solves a problem $\mathcal{P}$, formulated on n input data [3]. $\mathcal{A}_{dc}$ consists of three main phases:

- **Divide:** $\mathcal{A}_{dc}$ creates a set of k *subproblems*, say $\mathcal{P}_1, \mathcal{P}_2, \dots, \mathcal{P}_k$, having sizes $n_1, n_2, \dots, n_k$, respectively. They are identical to the original problem $\mathcal{P}$ but formulated on smaller inputs, that is, $n_i < n$.
- **Conquer:** $\mathcal{A}_{dc}$ is invoked *recursively* on the subproblems $\mathcal{P}_i$, thus obtaining the solutions s_i.
- **Recombine:** $\mathcal{A}_{dc}$ recombines the solutions s_i to obtain the solution s for the original problem $\mathcal{P}$. s is returned as the output of $\mathcal{A}_{dc}$.

It is clear that the divide-and-conquer technique generates a recursive algorithm $\mathcal{A}_{dc}$, which needs a base case to terminate. Typically, the base case consists of stopping $\mathcal{A}_{dc}$ whenever the input consists of a few items, that is, $n \leq 1$. For small inputs, the solution can be computed easily and directly, possibly by enumeration, within constant time.

The time complexity $T(n)$ of $\mathcal{A}_{dc}$ can be described by a recurrence relation, in which the base condition is $T(n) = O(1)$ for $n \leq 1$, and for the other cases it is

$$T(n) = D(n) + R(n) + \sum_{i=1,\dots,k} T(n_i),$$

where $D(n)$ is the cost of the Divide step, $R(n)$ is the cost of the Recombine step, and the final term accounts for the cost of all k recursive calls. These observations are sufficient here; we refer the reader to Chapter 4 in [3] for a deeper discussion on the divide-and-conquer technique and the master theorem, which provides a mathematical solution for most recurrence relations, such as the one here.

We are ready now to adapt the divide-and-conquer technique to the list-ranking problem. The algorithm we propose is quite simple and starts by setting $\text{Rank}[t] = 0$ and $\text{Rank}[i] = 1$, for all items $i \neq t$. Then it executes three main steps:

- **Divide:** Identify a set of items $I = \{i_1, i_2, \dots, i_h\}$ drawn from the input list $\mathcal{L}$. Set I must be an *independent set*, which means that the successor of each item in $\mathcal{L}$ that is added to I is not itself added to I. This condition clearly guarantees that $|I| \leq n/2$, because at most one item out of two consecutive items may be selected. The algorithm will also guarantee that $|I| \geq n/c$, where $c > 2$, in order to make the approach efficient in time.
- **Conquer:** Form the list $\mathcal{L}^* = \mathcal{L} - I$, by removing the items in I from the list $\mathcal{L}$. This is implemented by applying the pointer-jumping technique only to the predecessors of the removed items: for every item $x \in \mathcal{L}^*$ such that $\text{Succ}[x] \in I$, we set $\text{Rank}[x] = \text{Rank}[x] + \text{Rank}[\text{Succ}[x]]$ and $\text{Succ}[x] = \text{Succ}[\text{Succ}[x]]$.

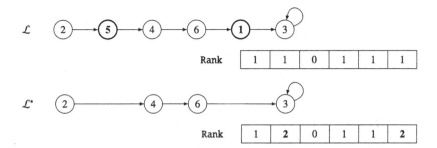

Figure 4.4 Reduction of a list by the removal of the items belonging to an independent set, here specified by the bold nodes. This results in the lower list in the figure; the Rank-array is recomputed accordingly to reflect the missing items. The updated ranks, namely those of items 2 and 6 (because of the removal of items 5 and 1, respectively), are shown in bold.

This means that, at any recursive call, Rank[x] accounts for the number of items of the original input list that lie between x (included) and the current Succ[x]. Then we solve recursively the list-ranking problem over $\mathcal{L}^*$. Note that $n/2 \leq |\mathcal{L}^*| \leq (1 - 1/c)\,n$, so the recursion acts on a sublist $\mathcal{L}^*$ whose size is a fractional part of $\mathcal{L}$. This is crucial for the efficiency of the recursive calls.

- **Recombine:** At this point, the recursive call has computed correctly the list rank-ing of all items in $\mathcal{L}^*$. So, we derive the rank of each item $x \in I$ as Rank[x] = Rank[x] + Rank[Succ[x]], thus adopting an updating rule which reminds us of the one used in pointer jumping. The correctness of this computation is given by two facts: (i) the independent-set property of I ensures that Succ[x] $\notin I$, thus Succ[x] $\in \mathcal{L}^*$ and its Rank is available; (ii) by induction, Rank[Succ[x]] accounts for the distance of Succ[x] from the tail of $\mathcal{L}$, and Rank[x] accounts for the number of items between x (included) and Succ[x] in the original input list (as observed in the Conquer step). In fact, the removal of x (because of its selection in I) may occur at any recursive step, so x may be far from the current Succ[x] when considering them in the original list; this means that it might be the case of Rank[x] $\gg 1$, which the previous summation step will correctly take into account. As a result, all items in $\mathcal{L} = \mathcal{L}^* \cup I$ will have their Rank-value correctly computed and, hence, induction is preserved and the algorithm may return to its invoking caller.

Figure 4.4 illustrates how an independent set (denoted by bold nodes) is removed from the list $\mathcal{L}$ and how the Succ-links are updated. Note that we are indeed *pointer jumping* only on the predecessors of the removed items (that is, the predecessors of the items in I), and that the Succ-pointers for others are unchanged. It is clear that, if the next recursive step selects $I = \{6\}$, the final list will be constituted by three items $\mathcal{L} = (2, 4, 3)$ whose final ranks are $(5, 3, 0)$, respectively. The Recombination-step will reinsert 6 in $\mathcal{L} = (2, 4, 3)$, just after 4, and compute Rank[6] = Rank[6] + Rank[3] = 2 + 0 = 2, because Succ[6] = 3 in the current list. Conversely, if one did not take into account the fact that item 6 may be far from Succ[6] = 3 in the original list and summed 1, the calculation for Rank[6] would be wrong.

It is clear that the I/O-efficiency of this algorithm depends on the Divide step. In fact, the Conquer step is recursive and thus its cost can be estimated as $T\left(\left(1 - \frac{1}{c}\right) n\right)$ I/Os; the Recombine step executes all reinsertions at once, given that the removed items are not contiguous (by the definition of independent set), and hence it can be implemented in $\widetilde{O}(n/B)$ I/Os (see Theorem 4.1).

Theorem 4.4 *The list-ranking problem formulated over a list $\mathcal{L}$ of length n can be solved via the divide-and-conquer paradigm in $T(n) = I(n) + \widetilde{O}(n/B) + T\left(\left(1 - \frac{1}{c}\right) n\right)$ I/Os, where $I(n)$ is the I/O cost of selecting an independent set from $\mathcal{L}$ of size at least n/c (and, of course, at most $n/2$).*

Deriving a large independent set is trivial if we can sequentially traverse the list $\mathcal{L}$: just pick one of every two items. But in our disk context the sequential list traversal is I/O-inefficient, and this is exactly what we want to avoid: otherwise we would have solved the list-ranking problem.

In what follows we will therefore concentrate on the problem of identifying a *large* independent set within the list $\mathcal{L}$ in an I/O-efficient manner, thus deploying only local information within the list. We will solve this issue in two ways: one is simple and randomized, the other one is deterministic and more involved. It is surprising that the latter solution (called *deterministic coin tossing*) has found applications in many other contexts, such as data compression, text similarity, and string-equality testing. It is a very general and powerful technique that definitely deserves some attention in here.

4.3.1   A Randomized Solution

The algorithmic idea is simple: toss a fair coin for each item in $\mathcal{L}$, and then select those items i such that $\text{coin}(i) = \text{H}$ but $\text{coin}(\text{Succ}[i]) = \text{T}$.[2]

The probability that the item i is selected is 1/4, because this happens for one configuration (HT) out of the four possible configurations. So the expected number of items selected for I is $n/4$. By using sophisticated probabilistic tools, such as Chernoff bounds,[3] it is possible to prove that the number of selected items is strongly concentrated around $n/4$. This means that the algorithm can repeat the coin tossing until $|I| \geq n/c$, for some $c > 4$. The strong concentration guarantees that this repetition is executed a (small) constant number of times.

We finally note that the check on the values of coin, for selecting I's items, can be simulated by Theorem 4.1 via few Sort and Scan primitives, thus taking $I(n) = \widetilde{O}(n/B)$ expected I/Os. So by substituting this value in Theorem 4.4, we get the following recurrence relation for the I/O-complexity of the proposed algorithm:

---

[2] The algorithm also works if we exchange the role of head (H) and tail (T), but it does not work if we choose the configurations HH or TT. Why?

[3] See https://en.wikipedia.org/wiki/Chernoff_bound.

$T(n) = \tilde{O}(n/B) + T\left(\frac{(c-1)n}{c}\right)$, with $c > 4$. Using the master theorem (see Chapter 4 in [3]), we can prove the following result.

Theorem 4.5 *There exists a randomized algorithm that solves the list-ranking problem, formulated over a list of length n, in $\tilde{O}(n/B)$ expected I/Os.*

4.3.2   Deterministic Coin-Tossing$^\infty$

The key property of the randomized algorithm, described in Section 4.3.1, was the *locality* of I's construction, which allowed it to pick an item i just by looking at the results of the coins tossed for i itself and for its successor Succ[i]. In this section we simulate *deterministically* this process by introducing the so-called *deterministic coin-tossing* technique that, instead of assigning two coin values to each item (i.e. H or T), starts by assigning n coin values (hereafter indicated by the integers $0, 1, \ldots, n-1$) and eventually reduces them to *three* coin values (namely $0, 1, 2$). The final selection process for I will then pick the items whose coin value is minimum among their adjacent items in $\mathcal{L}$. This means that the algorithm will have to compare three items adjacent in $\mathcal{L}$, and this still needs the execution of a constant number of Sort and Scan primitives. Let us provide more algorithmic details about this approach.

- **Initialization:** Assign to each item i the value $\text{coin}(i) = i - 1$. This way all items take a different coin value, which is smaller than n. We represent these values in $b = \lceil \log n \rceil$ bits, and we denote by $\text{bit}_b(i)$ the binary representation of $\text{coin}(i)$ using b bits.
- **Get six coin values:** Repeat the following steps until $\text{coin}(i) < 6$, for all items $i \in \mathcal{L}$:

  - Compute the first position $\pi(i)$ from the right where $\text{bit}_b(i)$ and $\text{bit}_b(\text{Succ}[i])$ differ, and denote by $z(i)$ the bit value of $\text{bit}_b(i)$ at that position, for all items i that are not the tail of the list.
  - Compute the new coin value for i as $\text{coin}(i) = 2\,\pi(i) + z(i)$ and represent it by using $\lceil \log b \rceil + 1$ bits. If i is the last item in the list, and hence has no successor, we define $\text{coin}(i)$ as the minimum value that is different from all the other assigned coins.

- **Get just three coin values:** For each value $v \in \{3, 4, 5\}$, take all items i such that $\text{coin}(i) = v$, and change their value to $\{0, 1, 2\} \setminus \{\text{coin}(\text{Succ}[i]), \text{coin}(\text{Pred}[i])\}$.
- **Select I:** Select those items i such that $\text{coin}(i)$ is a local minimum, that is, it is smaller than $\text{coin}(\text{Pred}[i])$ and $\text{coin}(\text{Succ}[i])$.

Let us first discuss the correctness of this algorithm. At the beginning all coin values are distinct, and in the range $\{0, 1, \ldots, n-1\}$. By distinctness, the computation of $\pi(i)$ is sound and $2\pi(i) + z(i) \leq 2(b-1) + 1 = 2b - 1$ since $\text{coin}(i)$ was represented with b bits and hence $\pi(i) \leq b - 1$ (counting from 0). Therefore, the new value

$\mathtt{coin}(i)$ can be represented by $\lceil \log b \rceil + 1$ bits, and thus the updating of b is correct too.

A key observation is that the new value of $\mathtt{coin}(i)$ is still different to the coin value of its adjacent items in $\mathcal{L}$, namely $\mathtt{coin}(\mathtt{Succ}[i])$ and $\mathtt{coin}(\mathtt{Pred}[i])$. We prove this by contradiction. Let us assume that $\mathtt{coin}(i) = \mathtt{coin}(\mathtt{Succ}[i])$ (the other case is similar); then $2\pi(i) + z(i) = 2\pi(\mathtt{Succ}[i]) + z(\mathtt{Succ}[i])$. Since z denotes a bit value, the two coin values are equal if and only if it is both $\pi(i) = \pi(\mathtt{Succ}[i])$ and $z(i) = z(\mathtt{Succ}[i])$. But if this condition holds, then the two-bit sequences $\mathtt{bit}_b(i)$ and $\mathtt{bit}_b(\mathtt{Succ}[i])$ cannot differ at the bit-position $\pi(i)$, as we had assumed.

This clearly demonstrates the correctness of the step that allows us to go from n coin values to six coin values, and then in turn get three coin values. It is also obvious that the selected items form an independent set because of the minimality of $\mathtt{coin}(i)$ and the distinctness of adjacent coin values.

As far as the I/O complexity is concerned, we start by introducing the function $\log^* n$ defined as $\min\{j \mid \log^{(j)} n \le 1\}$, where $\log^{(j)} n$ is the repeated application of the logarithm function for j times to n.[4] As an example, take $n = 16$ and compute $\log^{(0)} 16 = 16, \log^{(1)} 16 = 4, \log^{(2)} 16 = 2, \log^{(3)} 16 = 1$; thus $\log^* 16 = 3$. It is not difficult to convince yourselves that $\log^* n$ grows very slowly, and indeed its value is 5 for $n = 2^{65536}$.

Now, in order to estimate the I/O complexity of the proposed algorithm, we need to bound the number of iterations it needs to reduce the coin values to $\{0, 1, \dots, 5\}$. This number is $\log^* n$, because at each step the number of bits used to represent the coin values reduces logarithmically (from b to $\lceil \log b \rceil + 1$). All single steps can be implemented by Theorem 4.1 via a few $\mathtt{Sort}$ and $\mathtt{Scan}$ primitives, thus taking $\widetilde{O}(n/B)$ I/Os. So the construction of the independent set takes $I(n) = \widetilde{O}((n/B) \log^* n) = \widetilde{O}(n/B)$ I/Os, by definition of $\widetilde{O}()$. The size of I can be lower bounded as $|I| \ge n/4$, because the distance between two consecutive selected items (local minima) is maximized when the coin values form a *bitonic sequence* of the form $\dots, 0, 1, 2, 1, 0, 1, 2, 1, 0, \dots$.

By substituting this value in Theorem 4.4, we get the same recurrence relation of the randomized algorithm presented in Section 4.3.1, with the exception that now the algorithm is deterministic and its I/O-bound is worst case.

Theorem 4.6 *There exists a deterministic algorithm that solves the list-ranking problem, formulated over a list of length n, in $\widetilde{O}(n/B)$ worst-case I/Os.*

A comment is in order to conclude this chapter. The logarithmic term hidden in the $\widetilde{O}()$-notation has the form $(\log^* n)(\log_{M/B} n)$, as will be shown in Chapter 5. This term can be safely assumed to be smaller than 15 because, in practice, $\log_{M/B} n \le 3$ and $\log^* n \le 5$ for n up to 1 petabyte and using a commodity machine with a few gigabytes of internal memory.

---

[4] Recall that logarithms are all in base 2, unless otherwise stated.

References

[1] Yi-Jen Chiang, Michael T. Goodrich, Edward F. Grove, *et al.* External-memory graph algorithms. *Proceedings of the 6th ACM–SIAM Symposium on Algorithms (SODA)*, 139–49, 1995.

[2] Joseph JaJa. *An Introduction to Parallel Algorithms*. Addison-Wesley, 1992.

[3] Tomas H. Cormen, Charles E. Leiserson, Ron L. Rivest, and Clifford Stein. *Introduction to Algorithms*. The MIT Press, third edition, 2009.

5 Sorting Atomic Items

> We adore chaos because we love to
> produce order.
> *Attributed to M. C. Escher*

This chapter focuses on the very well known problem of sorting a set of *atomic* items; the case of *variable-length* items (aka strings) will be addressed in the following chapter. *Atomic* means that the items occupy a constant fixed number of memory cells. Typically they are integers or reals represented with a fixed number of bytes, say four (32 bits) or eight (64 bits) bytes each.

> **The sorting problem.** Given a sequence of n atomic items $S[1, n]$ and a total ordering $\leq$ between each pair, sort S into increasing order.

We will consider two complementary sorting paradigms: the *merge-based* paradigm, which underlies the design of MERGESORT, and the *distribution-based* paradigm, which underlies the design of QUICKSORT. We will adapt them to work in the two-level memory model, analyze their I/O complexity, and propose some useful algorithmic tools that allow us to speed up their execution in practice, such as the Snow-Plow technique and data compression. We will also demonstrate that these disk-based adaptations are I/O-optimal by proving a sophisticated lower bound on the number of I/Os that any external-memory sorter must execute in order to produce an ordered sequence of S. In this context we will relate the sorting problem to the so-called *permuting* problem, which is typically neglected when dealing with sorting in the RAM model, and then argue an interesting I/O-complexity equivalence between them which will allow us to provide a mathematical ground to the ubiquitous use of sorters when designing I/O-efficient solutions for problems involving large datasets.

> **The permuting problem.** Given a sequence of n atomic items $S[1, n]$ and a permutation $\pi[1, n]$ of the integers $\{1, 2, \ldots, n\}$, permute S according to π and thus obtain the new sequence $S[\pi[1]], S[\pi[2]], \ldots, S[\pi[n]]$.

Clearly, sorting includes permuting as a subtask: to order the sequence S we need to determine its sorted permutation and then implement it (these two phases may be intricately intermingled). So sorting should be more difficult than permuting. And indeed, in the RAM model, we know that comparison-based sorting n atomic items takes $\Theta(n \log n)$ time (via MERGESORT or HEAPSORT [3]) whereas permuting them takes $\Theta(n)$ time. The latter time bound can be obtained by just moving one item at a time according to what the array π indicates. We will show that, surprisingly, this complexity gap does not exist in the disk model, because these two problems exhibit the same I/O-complexity under some reasonable conditions on the input and model parameters n, M, B. This elegant and profound result was obtained by Aggarwal and Vitter in 1988 [1], and it is surely the result that spurred the huge amount of algorithmic literature on the I/O subject. Philosophically speaking, this result formally proves the intuition that *moving* items in the disk is the real bottleneck, rather than *finding* the sorted permutation. And indeed, researchers and software engineers typically speak about the *I/O bottleneck* to characterize this issue in their (slow) algorithms.

We will conclude this section by briefly mentioning two solutions for the problem of sorting items on D disks: the disk-striping technique, which is at the base of RAID ('redundant array of independent disks') systems and turns any efficient/optimal 1-disk algorithm into an efficient D-disk algorithm (typically losing its optimality, if any), and the GREEDSORT algorithm, which is specifically tailored for the sorting problem on D disks and achieves I/O optimality.

5.1 The Merge-Based Sorting Paradigm

We recall the main features of the external-memory model introduced in Chapter 1: it consists of an internal memory of size M and allows blocked access to disk by reading/writing B items at once (the *disk page*).

Algorithm 5.1 Binary Merge-Sort: MERGESORT(S, i, j)

1: **if** $i < j$ **then**
2:     $m = (i + j)/2$;
3:     MERGESORT($S, i, m - 1$);
4:     MERGESORT(S, m, j);
5:     MERGE(S, i, m, j);
6: **end if**

MERGESORT is one of the most well known sorting algorithms, and it is based on the divide-and-conquer paradigm [3]. Its pseudocode is given in Algorithm 5.1. Step 1 checks if the array to be sorted consists of at least two items; otherwise it is already ordered and nothing has to be done. If there are at least two items, it splits the input array S into two halves, and then recurses on each part. As recursion ends, the two halves $S[i, m - 1]$ and $S[m, j]$ are ordered so that Step 5 fuses them in $S[i, j]$ by invoking the MERGE procedure. This merging step needs an auxiliary array of size n, so that MERGESORT is not an *in-place* sorting algorithm (unlike HEAPSORT and, somewhat, QUICKSORT), but needs $\Theta(n)$ extra working space.

Given that at each recursive call we halve the size of the input array to be sorted, the total number of recursive calls is $O(\log n)$. The MERGE procedure can be implemented in $O(j - i + 1)$ time by using two pointers, say x and y, that start at the beginning of the two halves $S[i, m - 1]$ and $S[m, j]$. Then $S[x]$ is compared with $S[y]$, the smaller one is written out in the merged sequence, and its pointer is advanced. Given that each comparison advances one pointer, the total number of steps is bounded above by the total number of the pointer's advancements, which is upper bounded by the length of $S[i, j]$. So the time complexity of MERGESORT($S, 1, n$) can be modeled via the recurrence relation $T(n) = 2T(n/2) + O(n) = O(n \log n)$, as is well known from any basic algorithm course (see, e.g., [3]).[1]

Let us assume now that $n > M$, so that S must be stored on disk and I/Os become the most important computational resource to be analyzed and minimized. In practice every I/O takes 5 ms on average, so one could think that every item comparison takes one I/O and thus one could estimate the running time of MERGESORT on a massive S as: 5 ms $\times (n \log n)$, rounding up the big-O notation a little. If n is of the order of few gigabytes, say $n \approx 2^{30}$, which is actually not that massive for the current memory size of commodity PCs, the previous time estimate would be at least $5 \times (2^{30} \times 30) > 10^8$ ms, which is more than one day of computation. However, if we run MERGESORT on a commodity PC it completes in less than one hour. This is not surprising, because the previous evaluation totally neglects the existence of the internal memory, of size M, and the sequential pattern of memory accesses induced by MERGESORT. Let us therefore analyze the MERGESORT algorithm in a more precise way within the two-level memory model.

First of all, we note that $O(z/B)$ I/Os is the cost of merging two ordered sequences of z items in total. This holds if $M \geq 3B$, because the MERGE procedure in Algorithm 5.1 keeps in internal memory the two disk pages that contain the two items pointed to by the two pointers scanning $S[i, j]$, where $z = j - i + 1$, and one disk page to write the sorted output sequence (which is flushed to disk every time it gets full). Every time a pointer advances onto another disk page, an I/O fault occurs, that disk page is fetched into internal memory, and the merging continues. Given that S is stored contiguously on disk, $S[i, j]$ occupies $O(z/B)$ disk pages, and this is the I/O bound for merging two subsequences of total size z. Similarly, the I/O cost of writing the merged sequence is $O(z/B)$, because it occurs sequentially from the smallest to the largest item of $S[i, j]$, by exploiting an auxiliary array of size z. As a result, the recurrent relation for the I/O complexity of MERGESORT can be written as $T(n) = 2T(n/2) + O(n/B) = O(\frac{n}{B} \log n)$ I/Os.

But this formula does not explain completely the good behavior of MERGESORT in practice, because it does not yet account for the memory hierarchy. In fact, as MERGESORT recursively splits the sequence S, smaller and smaller subsequences are generated that have to be sorted. So when a subsequence of length z fits in internal memory, namely $z = O(M)$, then it is entirely cached by the underlying operating system using $O(z/B)$ I/Os, and thus the subsequent sorting steps do not incur any I/Os. The net result of this simple observation is that the I/O cost of sorting a subsequence of $z = O(M)$ items is no longer $\Theta(\frac{z}{B} \log z)$, as accounted for in the previous recurrence relation, but it is $O(z/B)$ I/Os, which only accounts for the cost of loading the subsequence in internal memory. This saving applies to all S's subsequences of size $\Theta(M)$

---

[1] Throughtout the book, when the base of the logarithm is not indicated, it should be taken to be 2.

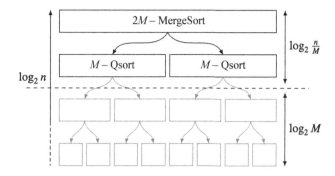

Figure 5.1 The recursive call of MERGESORT over a subarray of size $2M$. This is split into two subarrays of size M on which it is suggested to apply `qsort`, an efficient internal-memory implementation of QUICKSORT. Below the horizontal dotted line are depicted the recursive calls over subarrays shorter than M. They do not elicit I/Os because they are executed in internal memory. On the left side, the total number of recursive calls executed by MERGESORT is indicated (i.e. $O(\log n)$; big-O notation is hidden for simplicity); on the right side, that number is divided between the ones executed on disk (i.e. $O(\log(n/M))$) and the ones executed in internal memory (i.e. $O(\log M)$).

on which MERGESORT is recursively run, which are $\Theta(n/M)$ in total. So the overall saving is $\Theta(\frac{n}{B} \log M)$, which leads us to reformulate the MERGESORT's complexity as $\Theta(\frac{n}{B} \log \frac{n}{M})$ I/Os.

This bound is particularly interesting because it relates the I/O complexity of MERGESORT not only to the disk-page size B but also to the internal-memory size M, and thus to the *caching* feature made available to the sorter by the underlying operating system. Moreover, this bound suggests three immediate optimizations to the classic pseudocode of Algorithm 5.1, which we discuss in the following Sections 5.1.1–5.1.3.

5.1.1 Stopping Recursion

The first optimization consists of introducing a threshold on the subsequence size, say $j - i < cM$, where $c \le 1$, which triggers the stop of the recursion, the fetching of that subsequence entirely into internal memory, and the application of an internal-memory sorter on this subsequence (see Figure 5.1). The value of the parameter c depends on the space occupancy of the sorter, which must be guaranteed to work entirely in internal memory. As an example, c is 1 for in-place sorters such as INSERTIONSORT and HEAPSORT; it is close to 1 for QUICKSORT (because of the use of the *call stack* during its recursion; see Section 5.3.3), and it is less than 0.5 for MERGESORT (because of the extra array used by MERGE). As a result, we should write cM instead of M in the I/O bound above, because recursion is stopped at cM items, thus obtaining $\Theta(\frac{n}{B} \log \frac{n}{cM})$. This substitution is useless when dealing with asymptotic analysis, given that c is a constant, but it is important when considering the real performance of algorithms in the external-memory scenario, since c is smaller than 1. Hence it is desirable to make c as close as possible to 1, in order to reduce the impact of the logarithmic factor on the I/O complexity, thus preferring in-place sorters such as HEAPSORT.

We finally remark that INSERTIONSORT could also be a good choice (and indeed it is) whenever M is small, as it occurs when the n items fit in internal memory and thus M denotes the size of the two caches, L1 and L2. In this case M is a few megabytes.

5.1.2 The Snow-Plow Technique$^\infty$

Looking at the I/O complexity of (binary) MERGESORT, that is, $\Theta(\frac{n}{B} \log \frac{n}{M})$, it is clear that the larger M is, the smaller is the number of merge-passes over the data. These passes are clearly the bottleneck to the efficient execution of the algorithm, especially in the presence of disks with low bandwidth. In order to circumvent this problem we can either buy a larger memory, or try to deploy as much as possible the one we have available. As algorithm engineers we opt for the second option, and thus propose two techniques that can be combined together in order to enlarge (virtually) M.

The first technique is based on data compression and builds upon the observation that the runs are increasingly sorted. So, instead of representing items via fixed-length codes (e.g. four or eight bytes), we can use *integer compression* techniques that squeeze those items into fewer bits, thus allowing us to pack more of them in internal memory or in a disk page. Chapter 11 will describe in detail several approaches to this problem; here we content ourselves with mentioning the names of some of these approaches: γ-code, δ-code, Rice coding, Golomb coding, and so on. In addition, since the smaller an integer is, the fewer bits are used for its encoding, we can enforce the presence of small integers in the sorted runs by encoding not just their absolute value but the *difference* between one integer and the previous one in the sorted run (*gap* coding). This difference is surely nonnegative, and smaller than the item to be encoded. This is the typical approach to the encoding of integer sequences used in modern search engines, which we will also discuss in Chapter 11.

The second technique is based on an elegant idea, called Snow-Plow and attributed to Donald Knuth [5], that allows one to *virtually* increase the memory size by a factor of two *on average*. This technique scans the input sequence S and generates sorted runs whose length have variable size which is never smaller than M, and proved to be $2M$ on average. Its use needs to change the sorting scheme because it first creates these sorted runs, now of variable length, and then applies repeatedly over these sorted runs the MERGE procedure. Although runs will have different lengths, the MERGE will operate as usual, requiring an optimal number of I/Os for their merging. Hence $O(n/B)$ I/Os will suffice to halve the number of runs to be merged, what ever their length is, and thus a total of $O(\frac{n}{B} \log \frac{n}{2M})$ I/Os will be used on average to produce the totally ordered sequence. This corresponds to a saving of one pass over the data, which is nonnegligible if the sequence S is very long.

For ease of description, let us assume that items are transferred one at a time from disk to memory, rather than block-wise. Eventually, since the algorithm scans the input items, it will be apparent that the number of I/Os required by this process is still the optimal $O(n/B)$ I/Os.

The algorithm proceeds in phases, each phase generating a sorted run. See Figure 5.2 for a pictorial description of a phase, and Algorithm 5.2 for its pseudocode. A

 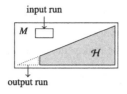 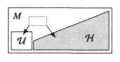 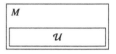

Figure 5.2 The four main steps of a phase in Snow-Plow. The leftmost picture shows the starting step, in which M unsorted items present in memory are heapified in the min-heap $\mathcal{H}$. The second picture shows the basic I/O step in which the minimum item in $\mathcal{H}$ is written to disk and a new item is fetched from S. The third picture shows the two possible cases occurring at the fetching of an item from S: it is either inserted in $\mathcal{U}$ or in $\mathcal{H}$, depending on the current heap-minimum. The rightmost picture shows the stopping condition of a phase, namely the one in which $\mathcal{H}$ is empty and $\mathcal{U}$ entirely fills the internal memory.

phase starts with the internal memory filled with M (unsorted) items, stored in a min-heap data structure called $\mathcal{H}$. Since the array-based implementation of heaps requires no additional space, in addition to the indexed items, we can fit in $\mathcal{H}$ as many items as we have memory cells available. The phase scans the input sequence S (which is unsorted) and, at each step, it writes to the output the minimum item within $\mathcal{H}$, say min, and loads in memory the next item from S, say next. Since we want to generate a sorted output, we cannot store next in $\mathcal{H}$ if next $<$ min, because it would be the new heap-minimum and thus it would be written out at the next step, thus destroying the property of ordered run. So in this case next is stored in an auxiliary array, called $\mathcal{U}$, which stays unsorted and is kept in internal memory too. Of course, the total size of $\mathcal{H}$ and $\mathcal{U}$ is M over the whole execution of a phase. A phase ends whenever $\mathcal{H}$ is empty, and thus $\mathcal{U}$ consists of M unsorted items. At this point, the next phase can start by moving the M items in $\mathcal{U}$ to form a new min-heap for $\mathcal{H}$ (in this way $\mathcal{U}$ ends up empty).

Algorithm 5.2 A phase of the Snow-Plow technique

Require: $\mathcal{U}$ is an unsorted array of M items
 1: Build $\mathcal{H}$ as a min-heap over $\mathcal{U}$'s items;
 2: Set $\mathcal{U} = \emptyset$;
 3: **while** $\mathcal{H} \neq \emptyset$ **do**
 4:     min $=$ Extract minimum from $\mathcal{H}$;
 5:     Write min to the output run;
 6:     next $=$ Read the next item from the input sequence;
 7:     **if** next $<$ min **then**
 8:         insert next in $\mathcal{U}$;
 9:     **else**
10:         insert next in $\mathcal{H}$;
11:     **end if**
12: **end while**

Two observations are in order: (i) during the phase execution, the minimum of $\mathcal{H}$ is nondecreasing, and so it is also nondecreasing the output run; (ii) the items stored in $\mathcal{H}$ at the beginning of the phase are eventually output before the phase ends. Observation (i) implies the correctness, observation (ii) implies that this approach forms sorted runs longer than M, and thus its use makes the final algorithm not less efficient than MERGESORT.

Actually, the resulting algorithm is more efficient than MERGESORT on average. Suppose that a phase reads τ items in total from S. By the while-guard in Step 3, we know that a phase starts with M items in $\mathcal{U}$, which are then heapified and moved to the min-heap $\mathcal{H}$ (Step 1 in Algorithm 5.2), and then ends when the min-heap is empty and $|\mathcal{U}| = M$ again. We know that the next τ items read from S go in part to $\mathcal{H}$ and in part to $\mathcal{U}$. But since items are added to $\mathcal{U}$ and never removed from it during a phase, since $|\mathcal{U}| \leq M$ we can conclude that M of the τ items end up in $\mathcal{U}$. Consequently $(\tau - M)$ items are inserted in $\mathcal{H}$ and eventually written to the output (sorted) run. So the length of the sorted run at the end of the phase is $M + (\tau - M) = \tau$, where the first addendum accounts for the items in $\mathcal{H}$ at the beginning of a phase, whereas the second addendum accounts for the items read from S and inserted in $\mathcal{H}$ during the phase. The key issue now is to compute the average of τ, which is easy if we assume a random distribution of the input items. In this case we have probability $1/2$ that next is smaller than min, and thus we have equal probability that a read item is inserted either in $\mathcal{H}$ or in $\mathcal{U}$. Overall it follows that, on average, $\tau/2$ items go to $\mathcal{H}$ and $\tau/2$ items go to $\mathcal{U}$. But we already know that the items inserted in $\mathcal{U}$ are M, so we can set $M = \tau/2$ and thus we get $\tau = 2M$.

Fact 5.1 Snow-Plow builds $O(n/M)$ sorted runs, each longer than M and actually of length $2M$ on average. Using Snow-Plow for the formation of sorted runs, MERGESORT takes an average I/O complexity of $O\left(\frac{n}{B} \log \frac{n}{2M}\right)$.

5.1.3   From Binary to Multi-way MERGESORT

Previous optimizations deployed the internal-memory size M to reduce the number of recursion levels by increasing the size of the initial (sorted) runs. But then the merging was *binary*, in that it processed two input runs at a time. This binary merge impacted on the base 2 of the logarithm of the I/O complexity of MERGESORT. Here we wish to increase that base to a much larger value, and in order to achieve this goal we need to deploy the memory M also in the merging phase by enlarging the number of runs that are processed at a time. In fact, merging two runs uses only three blocks of size B in internal memory: two blocks are used to cache the current disk pages that contain the compared items, namely $S[x]$ and $S[y]$ from the notation of the previous sections, and one block is used to cache the output items, which are flushed when the block is full (to allow a block-wise writing to disk of the merged run). But the internal memory contains a much larger number of blocks, that is, $M/B \gg 3$, which remain unused over the whole merging process.

In light of this observation, we propose a third optimization, which consists in deploying all those internal-memory blocks by designing a k-way merging algorithm that processes k runs at a time, with $k \gg 2$. In particular, we will set $k = (M/B) - 1$,

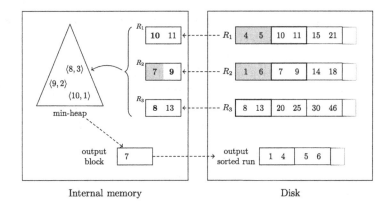

Figure 5.3 An illustration of the k-way merging algorithm over $k = 3$ sorted runs stored on disk, whose pages contain $B = 2$ items. The gray blocks on disk have already been processed and their items have been written to the output sorted run on disk. The disk pages in bold rectangles are the ones under processing by the three-way merging algorithm, and in fact they have been fetched in internal memory. Actually, the first item of R_2's page, namely item 7, has already been written to the output block in internal memory and not yet flushed to disk because that page is not yet full. As explained in the text, the min-heap stores the first item of each run in internal memory that has been not yet processed (shown in bold), and it is indexed as a pair $\langle item, run\_index \rangle$. Given the content of the min-heap, the next item to be written to the internal-memory output block is 8, so that the item replacing it in the min-heap will be the next one from its same run, namely 13 (hence, the pair inserted in the min-heap will be $\langle 13, 3 \rangle$).

so that k blocks are available to read block-wise k input sorted runs, and one block is reserved for a block-wise writing of the merged sorted run to disk. This scheme poses a challenging algorithmic problem because, at each step, we have to select the minimum among k candidate items coming from k distinct sorted runs, and this cannot be done by brute force in $\Theta(k)$ time by iterating among them. We need a smarter solution that hinges on the use of a min-heap data structure, and takes $O(\log k)$ time per item written to the output block. The min-heap contains k pairs (one per input run), each consisting of two components: one denoting an item to be compared and the other denoting the index of its run. Initially the items are the minimum items of the k runs, and so the pairs have the form $\langle R_i[1], i \rangle$, where $R_i[1]$ denotes the first item of the i-th sorted run and $i = 1, 2, \ldots, k$.

Figure 5.3 shows an example of the k-way merge algorithm, and its caption explains it in detail. At each step, the k-way merge algorithm extracts the pair containing the current smallest item in $\mathcal{H}$ (given by the first component of its pairs), writes that item to the output block, and inserts in the heap the next item of its run. As an example, if the minimum pair is $\langle R_m[x], m \rangle$, then the algorithm writes $R_m[x]$ to the output block in internal memory, and inserts in $\mathcal{H}$ the next pair $\langle R_m[x + 1], m \rangle$ from the same run R_m, provided that it is not exhausted. In this latter case no pair replaces the extracted one. If the disk page containing $R_m[x + 1]$ is not cached in internal memory, an I/O fault occurs and that page is fetched, thus guaranteeing that the next B reads from run R_m will not elicit any further I/Os. It should be clear that this merging process takes $O(\log_2 k)$ time per item, and again $O(z/B)$ I/Os to merge k runs of total length z.

As a result, the k-way merging scheme recalls a k-way tree with $O(n/M)$ leaves (i.e. sorted runs of length at least M) which have been formed, possibly using Snow-Plow. Hence the total number of merging levels is now $O(\log_{M/B} \frac{n}{M})$ for a total volume of I/Os equal to $O(\frac{n}{B} \log_{M/B} \frac{n}{M})$. We observe that sometimes we also write the formula as $O(\frac{n}{B} \log_{M/B} \frac{n}{B})$, as it typically occurs in the literature, because $\log_{M/B} M$ can be written as $\log_{M/B}(B \times (M/B)) = (\log_{M/B} B) + 1 = \Theta(\log_{M/B} B)$. This makes no difference asymptotically, hence $\log_{M/B} \frac{n}{M} = \Theta(\log_{M/B} \frac{n}{B})$.

Theorem 5.1 *Multi-way* MERGESORT *takes* $O(\frac{n}{B} \log_{M/B} \frac{n}{M})$ *I/Os and* $O(n \log n)$ *comparisons and time to sort n atomic items in a two-level memory model in which the internal memory has size M and the disk page has size B.*

In practice the number of merging levels will be very small: assuming a block size $B = 4$ KB and a memory size $M = 4$ GB, we get $M/B = 2^{32}/2^{12} = 2^{20}$ so that the number of passes is $(1/20)$-th smaller than the ones needed by binary MERGESORT. Probably more interesting is the observation that one pass is able to individually sort runs of M items, but two passes are able to individually sort runs of $(M/B) \times M = M^2/B$ items, because of the (M/B)-way merge, which is already a large number. It goes without saying that in practice the internal-memory space that can be dedicated to sorting is smaller than the *physical* memory available (typically MBs versus GBs). Nevertheless, it is evident that M^2/B is already of the order of terabytes for $M = 128$ MB and $B = 4$ KB. Furthermore, we note that the use of Snow-Plow or integer compressors could virtually increase the value of M with a *twofold advantage* in the final I/O complexity, because M occurs twice in the I/O bound.

5.2   Lower Bounds

At the beginning of this chapter we commented on the relation between the sorting and the permuting problems, concluding that the former is more difficult than the latter in the RAM model. The gap in time complexity is given by a logarithmic factor. The question we address in this section is whether this gap also exists when measuring I/Os. We will show that, surprisingly, sorting is *equivalent* to permuting in terms of I/O volume, for most reasonable situations for the setting of the parameters N, M, and B. This result is amazing because it can be read as saying that the I/O cost for sorting is not in the *computation* of the sorted permutation but rather in the *movement* of the data on the disk to realize it. This result offers a mathematical proof and quantification of the popular expression "I/O-bottleneck".

Before digging into the proof of this lower bound, let us briefly show how a sorter can be used to permute a sequence of items $S[1, n]$ in accordance with a given permutation $\pi[1, n]$. This will allow us to derive an upper bound to the number of I/Os that suffice to solve the permuting problem for any instance of $\langle S, \pi \rangle$. Recall that this means generating the sequence $S[\pi[1]], S[\pi[2]], \ldots, S[\pi[n]]$. In the RAM model we can jump among S's items according to the permutation π and create the new sequence $S[\pi[i]]$, for $i = 1, 2, \ldots, n$, thus taking $\Theta(n)$ optimal time. On disk we have actually two different algorithms which induce two incomparable I/O bounds. The

Table 5.1 Time and I/O complexities of the permuting and sorting problems in a two-level memory model in which M is the internal-memory size, B is the disk-page size, and $D = 1$ is the number of available disks. The case of multi-disks presents the multiplicative term n/D in place of n.

	Time complexity (RAM model)	I/O complexity (two-level memory model)
Permuting	$O(n)$	$O(\min\{n, \frac{n}{B} \log_{M/B} \frac{n}{M}\})$
Sorting	$O(n \log_2 n)$	$O(\frac{n}{B} \log_{\frac{M}{B}} \frac{n}{M})$

first algorithm consists of mimicking what is done in RAM, paying one I/O per moved item and thus taking $\Theta(n)$ I/Os in the worst case. The second algorithm consists of generating a proper set of tuples and then sorting them. Precisely, the algorithm creates the sequence $\mathcal{P}$ of pairs $\langle i, \pi[i]\rangle$ where the first component indicates the position i where the item $S[\pi[i]]$, stored in the position specified by the second component, must be stored. Then it sorts these pairs according to the π-component, and via a parallel scan of S and $\mathcal{P}$ substitutes $\pi[i]$ with the item $S[\pi[i]]$, thus creating the new pairs $\langle i, S[\pi[i]]\rangle$. Finally, another sort is executed according to the first component of these pairs, so that another parallel scan of S and $\mathcal{P}$ can be used to write $S[\pi[i]]$ into $S[i]$, thus obtaining the sequence of items correctly permuted. Overall, this second algorithm uses two scans and two sorts of the data, so it needs $O(\frac{n}{B} \log_{M/B} \frac{n}{M})$ I/Os, according to Theorem 5.1.

This means that a user can choose the algorithm that requires the minimum number of I/Os depending on the parameter setting of N, M, and B. Table 5.1 summarizes these algorithmic considerations.

Theorem 5.2 *Permuting n items takes $O(\min\{n, \frac{n}{B} \log_{M/B} \frac{n}{M}\})$ I/Os in a two-level memory model in which the internal memory has size M and the disk page has size B.*

In what follows we will show that this approach, in its simplicity, is I/O-optimal. The two upper bounds for sorting and permuting asymptotically equal each other whenever $n = \Omega(\frac{n}{B} \log_{M/B} \frac{n}{M})$. This occurs when $B = \Omega(\log_{M/B} \frac{n}{M})$, which always holds in practice because that logarithm term is a very small constant for input sizes n up to exabytes. So programmers don't need to find sophisticated strategies, but can simply sort as described here.

5.2.1 A Lower-Bound for Sorting

There are some subtle issues here that we do not wish to investigate too much, so we will here give just a brief description of what underlies the I/O lower bounds for both sorting and permuting.[2] We start by recalling the use of the *decision tree* technique

---

[2] There are two assumptions that are typically introduced in those arguments. One concerns *item indivisibility*, so items cannot be broken up into pieces (hence hashing is not allowed), and the other

for proving comparison-based lower bounds in the RAM model [3]. An algorithm corresponds to a family of such trees, one per input size (so infinite in number). Every node is a comparison between two items, generating two possible results, so the fan-out of each internal node is two and the tree is binary. Each leaf of the tree corresponds to a solution of the underlying problem to be solved: so in the case of sorting n items, the tree has one leaf per possible permutation of the input, hence $n!$ leaves.[3] Every root-to-leaf path in the decision tree corresponds to a computation, so the longest path corresponds to the worst-case number of comparisons executed by the algorithm to solve the problem at hand for a specific input size n. In order to derive a lower bound, it is therefore enough to compute the depth of the shallowest binary tree having that number of leaves. The shallowest binary tree with ℓ leaves is the (quasi-)perfectly balanced tree, for which the height h is such that $2^h \geq \ell$; hence $h \geq \log_2 \ell$. In the case of sorting, we have $\ell = n!$, so the classic lower bound $h = \Omega(n \log_2 n)$ can be easily derived by applying logarithms to both sides of the equation and using Stirling's approximation for the factorial function (see Footnote 3).

In the two-level memory model the use of such decision trees is more sophisticated. Here we wish to account for I/Os, and exploit the fact that the information available in the internal memory can be used for free. As a result, every node of the decision tree now corresponds to one I/O, and the number of leaves still equals $n!$, but the fan-out of each internal node equals the *number of distinct comparison-based results* that a single I/O can generate among the items it reads from disk (i.e. B) and the items available in internal memory (i.e. $M - B$). These B items can be distributed in at most $\binom{M}{B}$ ways among the other $M - B$ items present in internal memory.[4] Hence, one I/O can generate no more than $\binom{M}{B}$ different results for those comparisons.

But this is an incomplete answer because we are not considering the permutations among those items. In fact, some of these permutations have been already counted by some previous I/Os, and thus we should not recount them. These permutations are the ones concerning items that have already passed through internal memory, and thus have been fetched by some previous I/Os. So we need to count only the permutations among the *new* items, namely the ones residing in the input pages that have not yet been fetched. There are n/B input pages, and thus n/B I/Os accessing new items. So these I/Os may generate $\binom{M}{B}(B!)$ distinct results by comparing those new B items (to be sorted) with the $M - B$ ones in internal memory.

Let us now consider a computation with t I/Os, and thus a path in the decision tree with t nodes. A total of n/B of those nodes must access the input items, which must

---

concerns the possibility of *only moving items* and not creating/destroying/copying them, which actually implies that exactly one copy of each item does exist during their sorting or permuting process.

[3] Recall that the factorial function is defined as $n! = n \times (n-1) \times (n-2) \cdots \times 2 \times 1$. It is well known that $n! = \Theta\left(\left(\frac{n}{e}\right)^n \sqrt{2\pi n}\right)$; this is the *Stirling's approximation* of large factorials.

[4] To convince yourself about this binomial coefficient, just observe that the $M - B$ items already present in internal memory can be assumed to be sorted. Now the read B items are distributed among the $M - B$ sorted items so as to generate a sequence of M sorted items. To count in how many ways this may occur, it is enough to consider the fact that this corresponds to selecting B positions out of the M available ones where the B read items will be stored.

be read to generate the final permutation. The other $t - \frac{n}{B}$ nodes read pages containing already processed items. Any root-to-leaf path has this form, so we can look at the decision tree as having the nodes for the new I/Os at the top and the other nodes at its bottom. Hence, if the tree has depth t, its number of leaves is at least $\left(\frac{M}{B}\right)^t \times (B!)^{n/B}$. By imposing that this number is $\geq n!$, and applying logarithms to both sides of the inequality, we derive $t = \Omega(\frac{n}{B} \log_{M/B} \frac{n}{M})$. It is not difficult to extend this argument to the case of D disks, thus obtaining Theorem 5.3.

Theorem 5.3 *In a two-level memory model with internal memory of size M, disk-page size B and D disks, a comparison-based sorting algorithm must execute $\Omega(\frac{n}{DB} \log_{M/B} \frac{n}{DB})$ I/Os.*

It is interesting to observe that the number of available disks D does not appear in the denominator of the base of the logarithm, although it appears in the denominator of all other terms. If this was the case, D would somewhat penalize the sorting algorithms, making the lower bound larger and thus increasing the needed I/O complexity, because it would reduce the logarithm's base. In the light of Theorem 5.1, multi-way MERGESORT is I/O and time optimal on one disk. But, according to Theorem 5.3, MERGESORT is no longer optimal on multi-disks because the simultaneous merging of $k > 2$ runs should take $O(n/DB)$ I/Os in order to be optimal. This means that the k-way merge algorithm should be able to fetch D pages per I/O, hence one per disk. This cannot be guaranteed at every step by the current merging scheme because whatever the distribution of the k runs among the D disks is, even if we know which are the next DB items to be loaded in the heap $\mathcal{H}$, it could be the case that more than B of these items reside on the same disk, thus requiring more than one I/O from that disk, hence preventing the D-way parallelism in the read operation.

In Section 5.4 we will address this issue by proposing the *disk-striping* technique, which comes close to the I/O-optimal bound via a simple data layout on disks, and the GREEDSORT algorithm, which achieves full optimality by devising an elegant and sophisticated merging scheme.

5.2.2 A Lower-Bound for Permuting

Let us assume that at any time the global memory of our model, hence the internal memory of size M and the unbounded disk, contains a permutation of the input items possibly interspersed by empty cells. No more than n blocks will be non-empty during the execution of the algorithm, because n steps (and thus I/Os) is an obvious upper bound to the I/O complexity of permuting (obtained by mimicking on disk the permuting algorithm for the RAM model, as observed at the beginning of this chapter). We denote by P_t the maximum number of permutations generated by any algorithm with t I/Os. Given the previous observation, we can state that $t \leq n$ and $P_0 = 1$, since at the beginning we have the input order as initial permutation. In what follows we estimate P_t and then set $P_t \geq n!$ in order to derive the minimum number of steps *t* that any algorithm needs to realize any possible permutation of *n* items given in input.

Recall that permuting is different from sorting because the permutation to be realized is provided in input, and thus we do not need any computation. So in this case we distinguish three types of I/Os, which contribute differently to the number of generated permutations:

- **Read I/O of an untouched page:** If the page was an input page never read before, the read operation requires accounting for the permutations among the read items, hence $B!$ in number, and also for the permutations that these B items can realize by distributing them among the $M - B$ items present in internal memory (as was similarly done for sorting). So this read I/O can increase P_t by a factor $O(\binom{M}{B}(B!))$. The number of input (hence "untouched") pages is n/B. After a read I/O, they become "touched."
- **Read I/O on a touched page:** If the page has already been read or written, P_t has already accounted for the permutations among its items, so this read I/O can only increase P_t by a factor $O(\binom{M}{B})$ due to the shuffling of the B read items with the $M - B$ ones present in internal memory. The number of touched pages is at most n, as this is an upper bound to the number of steps executed by the permuting algorithm.
- **Write I/O:** When a page is flushed from internal memory to disk, it can be written in at most $n + 1$ possible ways among the at most n non-empty pages available on disk. Therefore, a write I/O may increase P_t by a factor of $O(n)$. We say that any written page is "touched," and recall that they are no more than n in number at any instant of the permuting process.

If t_r is the number of read I/Os and t_w is the number of write I/Os executed by a permuting algorithm, where $t = t_r + t_w$, then we can bound P_t as follows (here "big-O" has been dropped to ease the reading of the formulas):

$$P_t \leq \left(\frac{n}{B}\binom{M}{B}(B!)\right)^{n/B} \times \left(n\binom{M}{B}\right)^{t_r - n/B} \times n^{t_w} \leq \left(n\binom{M}{B}\right)^t (B!)^{n/B}. \quad (5.1)$$

In this formula we have multiplied every factor by the number of possible ways that a page may participate in a read or a write I/O: this number is n/B for reads of untouched pages, while, as we have stated, it is at most n for writes and reads of touched pages.

In order to generate every possible permutation of the n input items, we need $P_t \geq n!$. From equation (5.1), this means that it should be $\left(n\binom{M}{B}\right)^t (B!)^{n/B} \geq n!$. Resolving with respect to t, we get

$$t = \Omega\left(\frac{n \log \frac{n}{B}}{B \log \frac{M}{B} + \log n}\right).$$

We distinguish two cases. If $B \log \frac{M}{B} \leq \log n$, then this equation becomes $t = \Omega\left(\frac{n \log \frac{n}{B}}{\log n}\right) = \Omega(n)$; otherwise it is $t = \Omega\left(\frac{n \log \frac{n}{B}}{B \log \frac{M}{B}}\right) = \Omega\left(\frac{n}{B} \log_{\frac{M}{B}} \frac{n}{M}\right)$. As for sorting, it is not difficult to extend this proof to the case of D disks. Overall this means that we have proved the following result:

Theorem 5.4 *In a two-level memory model with internal memory of size M, disk-page size B and D disks, permuting n items requires $\Omega\left(\min\left\{\frac{n}{D}, \frac{n}{DB}\log_{M/B}\frac{n}{DB}\right\}\right)$ I/Os.*

Theorems 5.2–5.4 prove that the I/O upper bounds provided in Table 5.1 for the sorting and permuting problems are asymptotically optimal. Actually, we have already noted that they are asymptotically equivalent when $B = \Omega\left(\log_{M/B}\frac{n}{M}\right)$. Given the current values for B and M in modern computers, respectively tens of KBs and at least tens of GBs, this equality holds for any practical (even very large) values of n. It is therefore not surprising that researchers and algorithm engineers typically assume computationally that Sorting = Permuting in the I/O setting.

5.3 The Distribution-Based Sorting Paradigm

Like MERGESORT, QUICKSORT is based on the divide-and-conquer paradigm, so it proceeds by dividing the array to be sorted into two parts, which are then sorted recursively. But unlike MERGESORT, QUICKSORT does not explicitly allocate extra working space, its *combine* step is absent, and its *divide* step is sophisticated and impacts on its overall efficiency. Algorithm 5.3 gives the pseudocode of QUICKSORT; this will be used to comment on its complexity and argue for some optimizations and tricky issues that arise when implementing it over hierarchical memories.

Algorithm 5.3 Binary QuickSort: QUICKSORT(S, i, j)

1: **if** $i < j$ **then**
2:     $r = $ select the position of a "good pivot";
3:     swap $S[r]$ with $S[i]$;
4:     $p = $ PARTITION(S, i, j);
5:     QUICKSORT($S, i, p - 1$);
6:     QUICKSORT($S, p + 1, j$);
7: **end if**

The key idea is to partition the input array $S[i, j]$ into two parts such that one contains items that are *smaller* than the items contained in the latter part. This partition is order-preserving because no subsequent steps are necessary to recombine the ordered parts after the two recursive calls. Partitioning is typically obtained by selecting one input item as a pivot, and by distributing all the other input items into two subarrays according to whether they are smaller/greater than the pivot (Step 4). Items equal to the pivot can be stored anywhere. In the pseudocode the pivot is forced to occur in the first position $S[i]$ of the array to be sorted (Steps 2–3); this is obtained by swapping the chosen pivot $S[r]$ with $S[i]$ before the procedure PARTITION(S, i, j) is invoked. Step 2 does not detail the selection of the pivot, because this will be the topic of Section 5.3.2.

We notice that the execution of procedure PARTITION(S, i, j) returns the position p occupied by the pivot after the partitioning of the items in $S[i,j]$; this position will drive the two following recursive calls.

There are two issues for achieving efficiency in the execution of QUICKSORT: one concerns the implementation of PARTITION(S, i, j), and the other the relationship between the size of the two formed parts, because the more *balanced* they are, the more QUICKSORT comes closer to MERGESORT and thus to the optimal time complexity of $\Theta(n \log n)$. In the case of a totally unbalanced partition, in which one part is possibly empty (i.e. $p = i$ or $p = j$), the time complexity of QUICKSORT is $\Theta(n^2)$, thus incurring a time complexity similar to that of INSERTIONSORT. We will comment on these two issues in detail in the following subsections.

5.3.1   From Two- to Three-Way Partitioning

The goal of PARTITION(S, i, j) is to divide the input array into two parts, one containing items that are smaller than the pivot, and the other containing items that are larger than the pivot. Items equal to the pivot can be arbitrarily distributed between the two parts. The input array is therefore permuted so that the smaller items are located before the pivot, which in turn precedes the larger items. At the end of PARTITION(S, i, j), the pivot is located at $S[p]$, the smaller items are stored in $S[i, p-1]$, and the larger items are stored in $S[p+1, j]$. This partition can be implemented in many ways, taking $O(n)$ optimal time, but each way offers a different cache usage and thus different performance in practice. We present in Algorithm 5.4 a tricky algorithm that actually implements a *three-way* distribution and takes into account the presence of items equal to the pivot. They are detected and stored aside in a "special" subarray which is located between the two smaller/larger parts.

It is clear that the central subarray, which contains items equal to the pivot, can be discarded from the subsequent recursive calls, similarly to how we discard the pivot. This reduces the number of items to be sorted recursively, but needs a change in

---

Algorithm 5.4 Three-way partitioning: PARTITION(S, i, j)

```
 1: P = S[i]; l = i; r = i + 1;
 2: for (c = r; c ≤ j; c++) do
 3:        if S[c] = P then
 4:                swap S[c] with S[r];
 5:                r++;
 6:        else if S[c] < P then
 7:                swap S[c] with S[l];
 8:                swap S[c] with S[r];
 9:                r++; l++;
10:        end if
11: end for
12: return ⟨l, r − 1⟩;
```

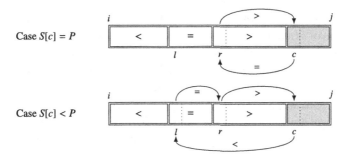

Figure 5.4 The two cases and the corresponding swapping operations. The arrows specify the ordered relations between the moved items and the pivot.

the (classic) pseudocode of Algorithm 5.3, because PARTITION must now return the pair of indices which delimit the central subarray instead of just the position p of the pivot.

Algorithm 5.4 details an implementation for the three-way partitioning of $S[i,j]$ which uses three pointers that move rightward over this array and maintain the following invariant: *P is the pivot driving the three-way distribution, $S[c]$ is the item currently compared against P, and $S[i, c - 1]$ is the part of the input array already processed and three-way partitioned in its items.* In particular, $S[i, c - 1]$ consists of three parts: $S[i, l - 1]$ contains items smaller than P, $S[l, r - 1]$ contains items equal to P, and $S[r, c - 1]$ contains items larger than P. It may be the case that any one of these subarrays is empty. Referring to the pseudocode of Algorithm 5.4, Step 1 initializes P to the first item of the array to be partitioned (which is the pivot), l and r are set to guarantee that the smaller/greater parts are empty, whereas the part containing items equal to the pivot consists only of item P. Next, the algorithm scans $S[i,j]$, trying to maintain the invariant. This is easy if $S[c] > P$, because it suffices to extend the part of the larger items by advancing r. In the other two cases (i.e. $S[c] \leq P$) we have to insert $S[c]$ in its correct position among the items of $S[i, r - 1]$, in order to preserve the invariant on the three-way partition of $S[i, c]$. The neat idea is that this can be implemented in constant time by means of at most two swaps, as described graphically in Figure 5.4 and coded in Steps 3–9 of Algorithm 5.4.

The three-way partitioning algorithm takes $O(n)$ time and offers two positive properties: (i) stream-like access to the array S, which allows the processor to prefetch the items to be read; (ii) the items equal to the pivot, residing in the subarray $S[l, r - 1]$, can then be eliminated from the following recursive calls because they are in their final correct position.

5.3.2   Pivot Selection

The selection of the pivot is crucial to get balanced partitions, reduce the number of recursive calls, and achieve optimal $O(n \log n)$ time complexity. The pseudocode of Algorithm 5.3 does not detail the way the pivot is selected because this may occur in many different ways, each offering pros and cons. As an example, if we choose the pivot as the first item of the input array (namely $r = i$), the selection is fast, but it is easy to instantiate the input array in order to induce unbalanced partitions: we can just take S to be an increasing or decreasing ordered sequence of items. However, any deterministic choice may incur in this drawback.

One way to prevent the case that a given input is bad for QUICKSORT is to select the pivot *randomly* among the items in $S[i, j]$. But this makes the behavior of the algorithm unpredictable in advance and dependant on the random selection of the pivot. We can show that the *expected* time complexity is the optimal $O(n \log_2 n)$, with a hidden constant smaller than 2. This fact, together with the space efficiency of QUICKSORT (see Section 5.3.3), makes this approach very appealing in practice (cf. qsort, mentioned in Section 5.3.3).

Theorem 5.5 *The random selection of the pivot drives* QUICKSORT *to compare no more than* $2n \ln n$ *items, in expectation.*

Proof The proof of this theorem is deceptively simple if approached from the correct angle. We wish to compute the number of comparisons executed by PARTITION over the input sequence S. Let $X_{u,v}$ be the random binary variable that indicates whether $S[u]$ and $S[v]$ are compared by PARTITION, and denote by $p_{u,v}$ the probability that this event occurs. The expected number of comparisons executed by QUICKSORT can then be computed as

$$E[\sum_{u,v} X_{u,v}] = \sum_{u=1}^{n} \sum_{v=u+1}^{n} E[X_{u,v}] = \sum_{u} \sum_{v>u} 1 \times p_{u,v} + 0 \times (1 - p_{u,v}) = \sum_{u=1}^{n} \sum_{v=u+1}^{n} p_{u,v}$$

by linearity of expectation.

To estimate $p_{u,v}$ we concentrate on the random choice of the pivot $S[r]$, because two items are compared by PARTITION only if one of them is the pivot. So we distinguish three cases. If $S[r]$ is smaller or larger than both $S[u]$ and $S[v]$, then the two items $S[u]$ and $S[v]$ are not compared to each other and they are passed to the same recursive call of QUICKSORT. In this case, the problem presents itself again on a smaller subset of items containing both $S[u]$ and $S[v]$. Therefore it is not interesting for estimating $p_{u,v}$, because we cannot conclude anything at this recursive point about the execution or not of the comparison between $S[u]$ and $S[v]$. In the other case where either $S[u]$ or $S[v]$ is the pivot, then they are surely compared by PARTITION. In all remaining cases, the pivot is taken among the items of S whose value is strictly between $S[u]$ and $S[v]$; so these two items go to two different partitions (hence two different recursive calls of QUICKSORT) and they will never be compared.

As a result, to compute $p_{u,v}$ we have to consider as interesting pivot selections the previous last two situations. In those situations, two selections provide the "good" cases (i.e. $S[u]$ and $S[v]$ are compared), and b selections provide the "bad" cases, where b is the number of items in S whose value is strictly between $S[u]$ and $S[v]$ (i.e. $S[u]$ and $S[v]$ are not compared). In order to estimate b we consider the sorted version of S, denoted by S'. There is an obvious bijection between pairs of items in S' and pairs of items in S. Let us assume that $S[u]$ is mapped to $S'[u']$ and $S[v]$ is mapped to $S'[v']$; it is then easy to derive b as $v' - u' - 1$. So the probability that $S[u]$ and $S[v]$ are compared is $p_{u,v} = 2/(b+2) = 2/(v' - u' + 1)$.

This formula may appear complicated, because we have on the left u, v and on the right u', v'. Given the bijection between S and S', we can rephrase the statement "considering all pairs (u, v) in S" as "considering all pairs (u', v') in S'," and thus write the previous summation as

$$\sum_{u=1}^{n} \sum_{v=u+1}^{n} p_{u,v} = \sum_{u'=1}^{n} \sum_{v'>u'}^{n} \frac{2}{v' - u' + 1} = 2 \sum_{u'=1}^{n} \sum_{k=2}^{n-u'+1} \frac{1}{k} \le 2 \sum_{u'=1}^{n} \sum_{k=2}^{n} \frac{1}{k} \le 2n \ln n,$$

where the final inequality comes from the properties of the n-th harmonic number. ∎

The next question is how we can "enforce" the expected behavior. The natural answer is to sample more than one pivot. Typically, three pivots are randomly sampled from S and the median is taken, thus requiring just two comparisons. Taking more than three pivots makes the selection of a "good one" more robust [2], as proved in Theorem 5.6.

Theorem 5.6 *If* QUICKSORT *partitions around the median of* $2s + 1$ *randomly selected items, it sorts n distinct items in* $\frac{2n H_n}{H_{2s+2} - H_{s+1}} + O(n)$ *expected comparisons, where* H_z *is the z-th harmonic number* $\sum_{i=1}^{z} \frac{1}{i}$.

By increasing s, we can push the expected number of comparisons close to $n \log n + O(n)$, however the selection of the median incurs a higher cost. In fact this can be implemented either by sorting the s samples in $O(s \log s)$ time and taking the one in the middle position $s + 1$ of the ordered sequence; or in $O(s)$ worst-case time via a sophisticated algorithm (not detailed here; see [3]). Randomization helps in simplifying the selection and still guarantees $O(s)$ expected time performance. We detail this approach here because its analysis is elegant and its algorithmic structure is general enough to be applied not only for the selection of the median of an unordered sequence, but also for selecting the item of any rank k.

Algorithm 5.5 is randomized and selects the item of the unordered S having rank k. It is interesting to see that the algorithmic scheme mimics the one used in the Partitioning phase of QUICKSORT: here the selected item $S[r]$ plays the same role of the pivot in QUICKSORT, because it is used to partition the input sequence S in three parts consisting of items smaller/equal/larger than $S[r]$. But unlike QUICKSORT, RANDSELECT recurses only in one of these three parts, namely the one containing the k-th ranked item, which can be determined by just looking at the sizes of those parts, as done in Steps 6 and 8. There are two specific issues that deserve a comment. First, we do not need to recurse on $S_=$ because it consists of items all equal to $S[r]$, so the k-th ranked item has value $S[r]$. Second, if recursion occurs on $S_>$, we need to update the searched rank k because we are dropping from the original sequence the items belonging to the set $S_< \cup S_=$. Correctness is immediate, so we are left with computing the expected time complexity of this algorithm, which turns out to be the optimal $O(n)$,

---

Algorithm 5.5 Selecting the k-th ranked item: RANDSELECT(S, k)

1: $r =$ random position in $\{1, 2, \ldots, n\}$;
2: $S_< =$ items of S which are smaller than $S[r]$;
3: $S_> =$ items of S which are larger than $S[r]$;
4: $n_< = |S_<|$;
5: $n_= = |S| - (|S_<| + |S_>|)$;
6: **if** $k \leq n_<$ **then**
7:     **return** RANDSELECT($S_<, k$);
8: **else if** $k \leq n_< + n_=$ **then**
9:     **return** $S[r]$;
10: **else**
11:     **return** RANDSELECT($S_>, k - n_< - n_=$);
12: **end if**

---

given that S is unsorted and thus all of its n items have to be examined to find the one having rank k among them.

Theorem 5.7 *Selecting the k-th ranked item in an unordered sequence of size n takes $O(n)$ expected time in the RAM model, and $O(n/B)$ expected I/Os in the two-level memory model.*

Proof Let us call "good selection" the one that induces a partition in which $n_<$ and $n_>$ are not larger than $2n/3$. We do not care about the size of $S_=$ since, if it contains the searched item, that item is returned immediately as $S[r]$. It is not difficult to observe that $S[r]$ must have a rank in the range $[n/3, 2n/3]$ in order to ensure that $n_< \leq 2n/3$ and $n_> \leq 2n/3$. This occurs with probability $1/3$, given that $S[r]$ is drawn uniformly at random from S (Step 1). So let us denote by $\hat{T}(n)$ the expected time complexity of RANDSELECT when run on an array $S[1, n]$. We can write

$$\hat{T}(n) \leq O(n) + \frac{1}{3} \times \hat{T}(2n/3) + \frac{2}{3} \times \hat{T}(n),$$

where the first linear term accounts for the time complexity of Steps 2–5, the second term accounts for the expected time complexity of a recursive call on a "good pivot selection," and the third term is a crude upper bound to the expected time complexity of a recursive call on a "bad pivot-selection" (that is actually referring to the case of a recursion on the entire S again). This is a special recurrence relation because the term $\hat{T}(n)$ occurs on both sides of the inequality; nevertheless, we observe that this term occurs with different constants in the front. Thus we can simplify the relation by subtracting those terms and get $\frac{1}{3}\hat{T}(n) \leq O(n) + \frac{1}{3}\hat{T}(2n/3)$, which gives $\hat{T}(n) \leq O(n) + \hat{T}(2n/3) = O(n)$. If this algorithm is executed in the two-level memory model, the equation becomes $\hat{T}(n) \leq O(n/B) + \hat{T}(2n/3) = O(n/B)$ given that the construction of the three subsets can be done via a single pass over the n input items, thus eliciting $O(n/B)$ I/Os. ∎

We can use RANDSELECT in many different ways within QUICKSORT. For example, we can select the pivot as the median of the entire array S (setting $k = n/2$) or the median among an oversampled set of $2s + 1$ pivots (setting $k = s + 1$, where $s \ll n/2$), or finally, it could be subtly used to select a pivot that generates a balanced partition in which the two parts have different sizes both being a fraction of n, say αn and $(1 - \alpha)n$ with $\alpha < 0.5$. This last choice $k = \lfloor \alpha n \rfloor$ seems useless because the three-way partitioning still takes $O(n)$ time, but it increases the number of recursive calls from $\log_2 n$ to $\log_{\frac{1}{1-\alpha}} n$. On the other hand, this observation neglects the sophistication of modern CPUs, which implement pipeline or instruction-level parallelism provided that there are no events that *break* the instruction flow, thus significantly slowing down the computation. Particularly slow are *branch mispredictions*, which might occur in the execution of PARTITION(S, i, j) whenever an item smaller than or equal to the pivot is encountered. If we reduce their number, then we increase the full instruction-level parallelism of modern CPUs [4].

Starting from these considerations, a new QUICKSORT variant was chosen in 2012 as the standard sorting method for Oracle's Java 7 runtime library. The decision for the change was based on empirical studies showing that, on average, this new algorithm was faster than the formerly used classic QUICKSORT. The improvement was achieved by means of a new three-way partitioning strategy based on a *pair of pivots properly moved* over the input sequence S. Researchers showed that this change reduced in expectation the number of comparisons at the expenses of an increase in the number of swaps [9]. Despite this trade-off, this dual-pivot strategy was more than 10 percent faster than classic QUICKSORT implementation, and the researchers argued that this was due to the fact that branch mispredictions were more costly than memory accesses at that time.

This example is illustrative of the fact that classic algorithms and problems, known for decades and considered antiquated, may be harbingers of innovation and deep-/novel theoretical analysis. So do not ever lose the curiosity to explore and analyze new algorithmic schemes!

5.3.3 Bounding the Extra-Working Space

QUICKSORT is frequently referred to as an *in-place* sorter, because it does not use extra space for ordering the array S. This is true if we limit ourself to the pseudocode of Algorithm 5.3, but it is no longer true if we consider the cost of managing the recursive calls. In fact, at each recursive call, the operating system must allocate space to save the local variables of the caller, in order to retrieve them whenever the recursive call ends. Each recursive call has a space cost of $\Theta(1)$, which has to be multiplied by the number of nested calls QUICKSORT can issue on an array $S[1, n]$. This number can be $\Theta(n)$ in the worst case, thus making the extra working space $\Theta(n)$ on some bad inputs (such as the already sorted ones, which induce totally unbalanced partitions).

We can circumvent this behavior by restructuring the pseudocode of Algorithm 5.3 as specified in Algorithm 5.6. This algorithm is cryptic at a first glance, but the

---

Algorithm 5.6 Binary QuickSort with bounded recursion: BOUNDEDQS(S, i, j)

1: **while** $j - i > n_0$ **do**
2:       $r =$ select the position of a "good pivot";
3:       swap $S[r]$ with $S[i]$;
4:       $p = $ PARTITION(S, i, j);
5:       **if** $p \leq \frac{i+j}{2}$ **then**
6:             BOUNDEDQS$(S, i, p - 1)$;
7:             $i = p + 1$;
8:       **else**
9:             BOUNDEDQS$(S, p + 1, j)$;
10:           $j = p - 1$;
11:       **end if**
12: **end while**
13: INSERTIONSORT(S, i, j);

---

underlying design principle is pretty smart and elegant. First, we note that the while-body is executed only if the input array is longer than n_0, otherwise INSERTIONSORT is called in Step 13, thus deploying the well-known efficiency of this sorter over very short sequences. The value of n_0 is typically set at a few tens of items. If the input array is longer than n_0, a modified version of the classic binary QUICKSORT is executed that mixes one single recursive call with an iterative while-loop. The rationale underlying this code refactoring is that the correctness of classic QUICKSORT does not depend on the order of the two recursive calls, so we can reshuffle them in such a way that the first call is always executed on the smaller part of the two/three-way partition. This is exactly what the if-statement in Step 5 guarantees. In addition, the pseudocode drops the recursive call in the longer part of the partition in favor of another execution of the body of the while-loop in which we changed the parameters i and j to reflect the new extremes of that longer part. This "change" is well known in the literature of compilers, and is termed *eliminating the tail recursion*. The net result is that the recursive call is executed on a subarray whose size is no more than half of the input array. This guarantees an upper bound of $O(\log n)$ on the number of recursive calls, and thus on the size of the extra space needed to manage them.

Theorem 5.8 BOUNDEDQS *sorts n atomic items in the RAM model taking* $O(n \log n)$ *expected time, and using* $O(\log n)$ *additional working space.*

We conclude this section by observing that the C89 and C99 ANSI standards define a sorting algorithm called `qsort`, whose implementation encapsulates most of the algorithmic tricks detailed in the previous sections.[5] This demonstrates further the

---

[5] Actually, `qsort` is based on a different two-way partitioning scheme that uses two iterators. One moves forward and the other moves backward over S; a swap occurs whenever two unsorted items are encountered. The asymptotic time complexity does not change, but practical efficiency derives from the fact that the number of swaps is reduced, since equal items are not moved.

efficiency of the distribution-based sorting scheme over the two-levels: cache and DRAM.

5.3.4 From Binary to Multi-way QUICKSORT

Distribution-based sorting is the opposite of merge-based sorting in that the first proceeds by splitting sequences according to pivots and then ordering them recursively, while the latter merges sequences that have been ordered recursively. Disk efficiency was obtained in multi-way MERGESORT by merging multiple sorted sequences together. The same idea is applied to design the multi-way QUICKSORT, which splits the input sequence into $k = \Theta(M/B)$ subsequences by using $k - 1$ pivots. Given that $k \gg 1$, the selection of those pivots is not a trivial task because it must ensure that the k partitions they form are balanced, and thus contain $\Theta(n/k)$ items each. Section 5.3.2 discussed the difficulties underlying the selection of one pivot, so the case of selecting many pivots is even more involved and needs a sophisticated analysis.

We start by denoting by $s_1, \ldots, s_{k-1}$ the pivots used by the algorithm to split the input sequence $S[1, n]$ into k parts, also called *buckets*. For the sake of clarity we introduce two dummy pivots $s_0 = -\infty$ and $s_k = +\infty$, and denote the i-th bucket by $B_i = \{S[j]: s_{i-1} < S[j] \le s_i\}$. We wish to guarantee that $|B_i| = \Theta(n/k)$ for all the k buckets. This would ensure that $\log_k \frac{n}{M}$ partitioning phases are enough to get subsequences shorter than M, which can thus be sorted in internal memory without any further I/Os. Each partitioning phase can be implemented in $O(n/B)$ I/Os by using a memory organization that is the opposite of the one employed for multi-way MERGESORT: namely, one input block (used to read from the input sequence to be partitioned) and k output blocks (used to write into the k partitions under formation). By requiring that $k = \Theta(M/B)$, we derive that the number of partitioning phases is $\log_k \frac{n}{M} = \Theta(\log_{M/B} \frac{n}{M})$, so the multi-way QUICKSORT takes the optimal I/O bound of $\Theta\left(\frac{n}{B} \log_{M/B} \frac{n}{M}\right)$ in expectation, provided that each partitioning step distributes evenly the input items among the k buckets.

To find efficiently $(k - 1)$ good pivots, we deploy a fast and simple randomized strategy based on *oversampling*, whose pseudocode is given in Algorithm 5.7. Parameter $a \ge 0$ controls the amount of oversampling and thus impacts on the robustness of the selection process as well as on the time efficiency of Step 2. This is $O((ak) \log(ak))$ if we adopt an optimal in-memory sorter, such as HEAPSORT or MERGESORT, over the $\Theta(ak)$ sampled items.

Algorithm 5.7 Selection of $k - 1$ good pivots via oversampling
---
1: Take $(a + 1)k - 1$ samples at random from the input sequence;
2: Sort them into an ordered sequence A;
3: For $i = 1, \ldots, k - 1$, select the pivot $s_i = A[(a + 1)i]$;
4: **return** the pivots s_i;

The main idea, after sorting the $\Theta(ak)$ candidate pivots, is then to select $(k - 1)$ among them, namely the ones that are evenly spaced and thus $(a + 1)$ far apart from

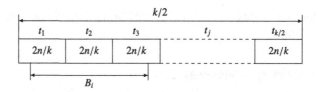

Figure 5.5 Splitting of the sorted sequence S' into segments.

each other. We are arguing that those $\Theta(ak)$ samples provide a faithful picture of the distribution of the items in the entire input sequence, so the balanced selection $s_i = A[(a+1)i]$ should provide us with "good pivots." The larger a is, the closer the size of all buckets will be to $\Theta(n/k)$, but the higher the cost of sorting the samples. At the extreme case of $a = n/k$, the samples could not be sorted in internal memory. On the other hand, the closer a is to zero, the faster the pivot selection, but the higher the likelihood of getting unbalanced partitions. As we will see in Lemma 5.1, choosing $a = \Theta(\log k)$ is enough to obtain balanced partitions with a pivot selection cost of $O(k \log^2 k)$ time. We note that the buckets will be not perfectly balanced, but quasi-balanced, since they include no more than $\frac{4n}{k} = O(n/k)$ items with reasonable probability; the factor of four will nonetheless leave unchanged the aimed asymptotic time and I/O complexity.

Lemma 5.1 *Let $k \geq 2$ and $a + 1 = 12 \ln k$. A sample of size $(a+1)k - 1$ suffices to ensure that all buckets receive less than $4n/k$ items, with probability at least $1/2$.*

Proof We provide an upper bound of $1/2$ to the probability of the complement event stated in the lemma, namely that there exists one bucket whose size is larger than $4n/k$. This corresponds to a *failure* sampling, which induces an unbalanced partition. To get this probability estimate we will introduce a cascade of events that are implied by this one and thus have increasingly large probabilities of occurrence. For the last event in the sequence we will be able to fix an explicit upper bound of $1/2$. Given the implications, this upper bound will also hold for the original event. And so we will be done.

As we did in the proof of Theorem 5.5, let us consider the sorted version of the input sequence S, which hereafter we denote by S'. We logically split S' in $k/2$ segments of length $2n/k$ each. The event we are interested in is that there exists a bucket B_i with at least $4n/k$ items assigned to it, for some index i. As illustrated in Figure 5.5, this large bucket completely spans at least one segment, say t_2 in the figure (but it might be any segment of S'), because the former contains at least $4n/k$ items whereas the latter contains $2n/k$ items.

By the definition of buckets, the pivots s_{i-1} and s_i delimiting B_i fall outside t_2. Hence, by Algorithm 5.7, fewer than $(a+1)$ samples fall into the segment overlapped by B_i. So we have:

$$\mathcal{P}(\exists\, B_i :\ |B_i| \geq 4n/k) \leq \mathcal{P}(\exists t_j :\ t_j \text{ contains less than } (a+1) \text{ samples})$$

$$\leq \frac{k}{2} \times \mathcal{P}(\text{a specific segment contains less than } (a+1) \text{ samples}), \qquad (5.2)$$

where the last inequality comes from the *union bound*, given that $k/2$ is the number of segments constituting S'. So we will hereafter concentrate on proving an upper bound to the last term.

The probability that one sampled item ends in a given segment is equal to $\frac{(2n/k)}{n} = \frac{2}{k}$, because they are assumed to be drawn uniformly at random from S (and thus from S'). Now, let us call X the number of those samples; we are interested in computing $P(X < a + 1)$. We start by observing that, since we take $((a + 1)k - 1)$ samples, it is $E[X] = ((a + 1)k - 1) \times \frac{2}{k} = 2(a + 1) - \frac{2}{k}$. The lemma assumes that $k \geq 2$, so $E[X] \geq 2(a + 1) - 1$, which is at least $\frac{3}{2}(a + 1)$ for all $a \geq 1$. Solving the inequality $E[X] \geq \frac{3}{2}(a+1)$ with respect to $(a+1)$, we get that $a+1 \leq (2/3)E[X] = (1 - \frac{1}{3})E[X]$. This form calls to mind the Chernoff bound:

$$P(X < (1 - \delta)E[X]) \leq e^{-\frac{\delta^2}{2} E[X]}.$$

By setting $\delta = 1/3$, we derive

$$P(X < a + 1) \leq P\left(X < \left(1 - \frac{1}{3}\right)E[X]\right) \leq e^{-(E[X]/2)(1/3)^2} = e^{-E[X]/18}$$

$$\leq e^{-(3/2)(a+1)/18} = e^{-(a+1)/12} = e^{-\ln k} = \frac{1}{k}, \tag{5.3}$$

where we used the inequality $E[X] \geq (3/2)(a + 1)$ and the lemma's assumption that $a + 1 = 12 \ln k$. By plugging the result of equation (5.3) into equation (5.2), we get $P(\exists B_i : |B_i| \geq 4n/k) \leq (k/2) * (1/k) = 1/2$, and thus the statement of the lemma follows. ∎

5.4 Sorting With Multi-Disks$^{\infty}$

The bottleneck in disk-based sorting is the time needed to perform an I/O operation. In order to mitigate this problem, we can use D disks working in parallel so as to transfer DB items per I/O. On the one hand this increases the bandwidth of the I/O subsystem, but on the other hand, it makes the design of I/O-efficient algorithms particularly difficult. Let's see why in the context of sorting n atomic items.

The simplest approach to managing parallel disks is called *disk striping* and consists of looking at the D disks as *one single* disk whose page size is $B' = DB$. This way, on the one hand, we gain simplicity in algorithm design by just using "as-is" any algorithm designed for one disk, now with a disk page of size B'. But, on the other hand, we lose the independence among the D disks, and this comes at some price in terms of I/O complexity, when applied to the sorting algorithms:

$$O\left(\frac{n}{B'} \log_{M/B'} \frac{n}{M}\right) = O\left(\frac{n}{DB} \log_{M/DB} \frac{n}{M}\right).$$

This bound is not optimal, because the base of the logarithm is D times smaller than that indicated by the lower bound proved in Theorem 5.3. Looking at the ratio

	Block 1	Block 2	Block 3	Block 4	Block 5	
Disk 1	1	9	17	25	33	...
	2	10	18	26	34	
Disk 2	3	11	19	27	35	...
	4	12	20	28	36	
Disk 3	5	13	21	29	37	...
	6	14	22	30	38	
Disk 4	7	15	23	31	39	...
	8	16	24	32	40	

Figure 5.6 An example of striping a sequence of items among $D = 4$ disks, with $B = 2$.

between the optimal bound and the bound achieved via disk striping, we find that it is $1 - \log_{M/B} D$. This shows that disk striping is less and less efficient as the number of disks increases: namely, $D \longrightarrow M/B$.

Leveraging the *independence* among the D disks is tricky, and it took several years to develop fully optimal algorithms running over multi-disks and achieve the bounds stated in Theorem 5.3. The key problem is guaranteeing that every time we access the disk subsystem, we are able to read or write D pages, each one coming from or going to a different disk. This is to guarantee a throughput of DB items per I/O. In the case of sorting, such a difficulty arises both in the case of distributed-based and merge-based sorters, each with its own specialty, given the differences between these two approaches.

In particular, let us consider the multi-way QUICKSORT. In order to guarantee a D-way throughput in reading the input items, these must be distributed evenly among the D disks. For example, they could be striped circularly as indicated in Figure 5.6. This ensures that a scan of the input items takes $O(n/DB)$ optimal I/Os. The subsequent distribution phase can then read the input sequence at that I/O speed. Nonetheless, problems occur when writing the output subsequences produced by the partitioning process. In fact, that writing should guarantee that each of these subsequences is circularly striped among the disks in order to maintain the invariant for the next distribution phase (to be executed independently over those subsequences). In the case of D disks, we have D output blocks that are filled by the partitioning phase. So when these D blocks are full, they must be written to D distinct disks to ensure full I/O parallelism, and thus one I/O. Given the striping of the runs, if all these output blocks belong to the same run, then they can be written in one I/O. But, in general, they belong to different runs, so conflicts may arise in the writing process because blocks of different runs could have to be written onto the same disks.

An example is given in Figure 5.7 that illustrates a situation in which we have three runs under formation by the partitioning phase of QUICKSORT, and three disks. Runs are striped circularly among the three disks, and shadowed blocks correspond to the prefixes of the runs that have been already written on those disks. Arrows point to the next *free blocks* of each run that all reside on the same disk D_2. This is an unfortunate situation because, if the partitioning phase of multi-way QUICKSORT needs to write one block per run, then an I/O conflict arises and the I/O subsystem must *serialize* the

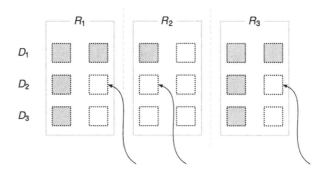

Figure 5.7 An I/O conflict in writing $D = 3$ blocks belonging to three distinct runs.

write operation in $D = 3$ distinct I/Os, hence losing all the I/O parallelism of the D disks.

In order to avoid this inefficiency, researchers have proposed *randomized* and *deterministic* sorters that execute an optimal number of I/Os [8]. In what follows, we sketch a deterministic multi-disk sorter, known as GREEDSORT [7], which solves these difficulties via an elegant merge-based approach consisting of two stages: first, items are *approximately* sorted via an I/O-efficient multi-way merger that deals with $R = \Theta(\sqrt{M/B})$ sorted runs in an independent way (thus deploying disks in parallel), and then it completes the sorting of the input sequence by using an algorithm (aka COLUMNSORT, designed by T. Leighton in 1985) that takes a linear number of I/Os when executed over *short* sequences of length $O(M^{3/2})$. Correctness comes from the fact that the distance of the unsorted items from their correct sorted position, after the first stage, is smaller than the size of the sequences manageable by COLUMNSORT. Hence the second stage can correctly turn the approximately sorted sequence into a totally sorted sequence via a single (I/O-optimal) pass.

How to get the approximately sorted runs in an I/O-efficient way is the elegant algorithmic contribution of GREEDSORT. We sketch its main ideas here, and refer the interested reader to the corresponding paper for further details [7]. We assume that the sorted runs are stored in a striped way among the D disks (see Figure 5.6), so reading D consecutive blocks from each run takes just one I/O. As we discussed for QUICKSORT, in this merge-based approach we could also incur I/O conflicts when reading the striped runs. GREEDSORT avoids this problem by operating independently on each disk and fetching its two *best* available blocks. Here "best" means that these two blocks contain the *smallest minimum item*, say m_1, and the *smallest maximum item*, say m_2, currently present in blocks stored on that disk (these two blocks may be the same). It is evident that this selection can proceed independently over the D disks, and it needs a proper data structure that keeps track of minimum/maximum items in disk blocks. Actually, [7] shows that this data structure can fit in internal memory, thus not incurring any further I/Os for this selection operations.

Figure 5.8 shows an example for the disk j, which contains the blocks of several runs because of the striping-based storage. The figure assumes that Run 1 contains the block with the smallest minimum item (i.e. 1) and Run 2 contains the block with the

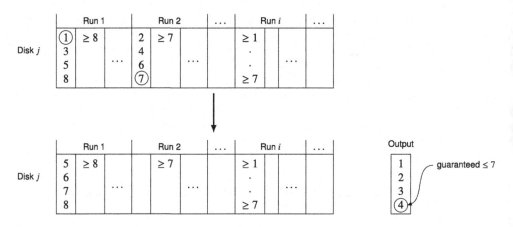

Figure 5.8 Example taken from [7]. Top figure: The disk j contains the blocks of several runs, and its best two blocks are the ones in Run 1 (that block contains the smallest minimum item) and Run 2 (that block contains the smallest maximum item). Bottom figure: The best two blocks of disk j have been merged, and the resulting first block is written to the next free block of the output run residing on disk j, whereas the resulting second block is written to Run 1 of disk j.

smallest maximum item (i.e. 7). Clearly, all the other blocks that come from Run 1 and Run 2 contain items larger than 7, and all blocks coming from the other runs have minimum larger than 1 and maximum larger than 7. GREEDSORT then merges these two best blocks of disk j and creates two new sorted blocks: the first one is written to the next free block of the output run residing on disk j (it contains the items $\{1, 2, 3, 4\}$), and the second one is written back to the run of the smallest minimum m_1, namely run 1 (it contains the items $\{5, 6, 7, 8\}$). This last write back into Run 1 does not disrupt that ordered sub-sequence, because this second-best block contains items which are smaller than the maximum of the original block of m_1.

The selection of the "two best blocks" proceeds independently over all disks until all input runs have been examined and their blocks written to the output run in a striped way among the D disks. But looking at this example, we note that the items written in output to disk j are not necessarily the four smallest items of all blocks residing on that disk. In fact, there could be a block in another run (different from Runs 1 and 2, but still residing on disk j) that contains an item within $[1, 4]$, say 2.5, and whose minimum is larger than 1 and whose maximum is larger than 7. So this block is compatible with the selection of the two best blocks, but it contains items that should be stored in the first block of the sorted sequence. The final sequence produced by this merging process is therefore *not* sorted, but if we read it in a striped way along all D disks, then it is *approximately* sorted, as stated in the following lemma (proved in [7]).

Lemma 5.2 *A sequence is called L-regressive if any pair of unsorted records, say* $\dots y \dots x \dots$ *with* $y > x$, *has distance less than L in the sequence. The previous sorting algorithm creates an output that is L-regressive, with* $L = RDB = D\sqrt{MB}$.

Since $L = D\sqrt{MB} < DB\sqrt{M} \leq M^{3/2}$, the application of COLUMNSORT over a sliding window of $2L$ items, which moves L steps forward at each phase, produces a fully sorted sequence striped along the D disks. Hence the invariant for the next merging phase is preserved, taking $O(n/DB)$ I/Os. Since the number of sorted runs has been reduced by a factor $R = \Theta(\sqrt{M/B})$, the total number of merging phases is $O\left(\log_R \frac{n}{M}\right) = O\left(\log_{M/B} \frac{n}{M}\right)$, and thus the optimal I/O bound for D disks follows.

References

[1] Alok Aggarwal and Jeffrey S. Vitter. The input/output complexity of sorting and related problems. *Communications of the ACM*, 31(9): 1116–27, 1988.

[2] Jon L. Bentley and Robert Sedgewick. Fast algorithms for sorting and searching strings. In *Proceedings of the 8th ACM–SIAM Symposium on Discrete Algorithms (SODA)*, 360–9, 1997.

[3] Tomas H. Cormen, Charles E. Leiserson, Ron L. Rivest, and Clifford Stein. *Introduction to Algorithms*. The MIT Press, third edition, 2009.

[4] Kanela Kaligosi and Peter Sanders. How branch mispredictions affect quicksort. In *Proceedings of the 14th European Symposium on Algorithms (ESA)*, Lecture Notes in Computer Science 4168, Springer, 780–91, 2006.

[5] Donald E. Knuth. *The Art of Computer Programming*, Vol. 3. Addison-Wesley, second edition, 1998.

[6] Frank Thomson Leighton. Tight bounds on the complexity of parallel sorting. *IEEE Transactions on Computers*, C-34(4), Special Issue on Sorting, 1985.

[7] Mark H. Nodine and Jeffrey S. Vitter. Greed sort: Optimal deterministic sorting on parallel disks. *Journal of the ACM*, 42(4): 919–33, 1995.

[8] Jeffrey S. Vitter. External memory algorithms and data structures. *ACM Computing Surveys*, 33(2): 209–71, 2001.

[9] Sebastian Wild and Markus E. Nebel. Average case analysis of Java 7's Dual Pivot Quick-Sort. In *Proceedings of the 20th European Symposium on Algorithms (ESA)*, Lecture Notes in Computer Science 7501, Springer, 826–36, 2012.

6 Set Intersection

Sharing is caring!

This chapter tackles a simple problem related to sets, which constitutes the backbone of every query resolver in a (web) search engine. A search engine is a well-known tool designed to search for information in a collection $\mathcal{D}$ of documents. We restrict our attention to search engines for *textual* documents, meaning that a document $d_i \in \mathcal{D}$ is a book, a news item, a tweet, or any file containing a sequence of linguistic tokens (aka *words*). Along with many other auxiliary data structures, a search engine builds an *index* to answer efficiently the queries posed by users. A query Q is commonly structured as a *bag of words*, say $w_1 w_2 \cdots w_k$, and the goal of the search engine is to retrieve efficiently the *most relevant* documents in $\mathcal{D}$ which contain all the query words. People skilled in this art know that this is a very simplistic definition, because modern search engines look for documents that contain *most* of the words in Q (which may be exact, or include a few typos, or refer to *synonyms or related words*), and are preferably close to each other, and *relevant* to the user issuing Q. However, "relevance" is a quite subjective and time-varying definition.

In any case, this is not a chapter in a book on information retrieval, so we refer the reader interested in these issues to the information retrieval literature, such as [4, 7]. Here we content ourselves with dealing with the most generic algorithmic step solving the bag-of-words query.

> **Problem.** Given a sequence of words $Q = w_1 w_2 \cdots w_k$ and a document collection $\mathcal{D}$, find the documents in $\mathcal{D}$ that contain all words w_i.

An obvious solution is to scan every document in $\mathcal{D}$, searching for all words specified by Q. This is simple, but it would take a time proportional to the whole length of the document collection, which is clearly too much even for a supercomputer or a data centre, given the size of the (indexed) Web. And, in fact, modern search engines build a very simple, but efficient, data structure called an *inverted index*, which helps in speeding up the flow of billions of daily user queries.

The inverted index consists of three main parts: the dictionary of words w, one list of occurrences per dictionary word (called a *posting list*, which we will designate $\mathcal{L}[w]$), and some additional information indicating the importance of each of

Dictionary	Posting list
...	...
abaco	$50, 23, 10$
abiura	$131, 100, 90, 132$
ball	$20, 21, 90$
mathematics	$15, 1, 3, 23, 30, 7, 10, 18, 40, 70$
zoo	$5, 1000$
...	...

Figure 6.1 An example of inverted index for a part of a dictionary. Posting lists are not sorted, for now.

these occurrences (to be deployed in the subsequent phases where the relevance of a document has to be established, but not discussed in this chapter; see, e.g., [4, 7]). The term "inverted" refers to the fact that word occurrences are not sorted according to their position in the document, but according to the alphabetic ordering of the words to which they refer. So inverted indexes are similar to the classic glossary contained in some books, here extended to represent occurrences of *all* the words present in a collection of documents (not just the most important ones).

Each posting list $\mathcal{L}[w]$ is stored contiguously in a single array, possibly on disk. The names of the indexed documents (actually, their identifying URLs) are placed in another table, where they are identified through unique positive integers known as *docIDs*; these IDs are generally assigned in an arbitrary way by the search engine.[1] The dictionary is stored in a table which contains some satellite information plus the pointers to the posting lists. Figure 6.1 illustrates the main structure of an inverted index.

Now let us assume that the query Q consists of the two words abaco and mathematics. Finding the documents in $\mathcal{D}$ that contain both of the words in Q boils down to finding the docIDs shared by the two inverted lists $\mathcal{L}[\text{abaco}]$ and $\mathcal{L}[\text{mathematics}]$: namely, 10 and 23. This is the *set intersection* problem, the key subject of this chapter.

Given that the integers of the two posting lists are arbitrarily arranged, the computation of the intersection might be executed by comparing each docID $a \in \mathcal{L}[\text{abaco}]$ with all docIDs $b \in \mathcal{L}[\text{mathematics}]$. If $a = b$ then a is inserted in the result set. Assuming that the two lists have length n and m, respectively, this brute-force algorithm takes $n \times m$ steps/comparisons. In the real case that n and m are of the order of millions, as typically occurs for common words in the modern Web, then that number of steps/comparisons is of the order of $10^6 \times 10^6 = 10^{12}$. Even assuming that a modern computer is able to execute one billion comparisons per second (10^9 cmp/sec), this trivial algorithm takes 10^3 seconds to process a bi-word query (so about ten minutes), which is too long even for a patient user!

The good news is that the docIDs occurring in the two posting lists can be rearranged so as to impose some proper structure on them in order to speed up the

---

[1] The docID assignment process is crucial to save space in the storage of those posting lists, but its solution is too sophisticated to be discussed here; see [6].

Dictionary	Posting list
...	...
abaco	$10, 23, 50$
abiura	$90, 100, 131, 132$
ball	$20, 21, 90$
mathematics	$1, 3, 7, 10, 15, 18, 23, 30, 40, 70$
zoo	$5, 1000$
...	...

Figure 6.2 An example of an inverted index for part of a dictionary, with sorted posting lists.

identification of the common integers. The key idea here is to sort the posting lists once for all, as shown in Figure 6.2. We thus reformulate the intersection problem on the two *sorted* sets $A = \mathcal{L}[\texttt{abaco}]$ and $B = \mathcal{L}[\texttt{mathematics}]$, as:

(Sorted) set intersection problem. *Given two sorted integer sequences* $A = a_1 a_2 \cdots a_n$ *and* $B = b_1 b_2 \cdots b_m$, *such that* $a_i < a_{i+1}$ *and* $b_i < b_{i+1}$, *compute the integers common to both sets.*

We remark that the following approaches can be extended to work on sequences of items on which it is defined a total order, thus not only integers. Here we discuss integer sequences for simplicity.

6.1   Merge-Based Approach

The *sortedness* of the two sequences allows us to design a set-intersection algorithm that is deceptively simple, elegant, and fast. It simply scans A and B from left to right and compares at each step a pair of docIDs from the two lists. Say a_i and b_j are the two docIDs currently compared, where initially we have $i = j = 1$. If $a_i < b_j$ the iterator i gets incremented, if $a_i > b_j$ the iterator j gets incremented, otherwise it is $a_i = b_j$ and thus a common docID is found and both iterators get incremented.

The correctness can be proved inductively, exploiting the following observation: if $a_i < b_j$ (the other case is symmetric), then a_i is smaller than all elements following b_j in B (because of its order), so $a_i \notin B$. As far as the time complexity is concerned, we note that at each step the algorithm executes one comparison and advances at least one iterator. Given that $n = |A|$ and $m = |B|$ are the number of elements in the two sequences, we can deduce that i (resp. j) can advance at most n times (resp. m times), and thus we can conclude that this algorithm requires no more than $n + m$ comparisons/steps; we say *no more* because it could be the case that one sequence gets exhausted before the other one, so there is no need to compare the remaining elements of the latter sequence. This time cost is significantly smaller than the one mentioned for the unsorted sequences (namely $n \times m$), and its real advantage in practice is strikingly evident. In fact, by considering our running example with n and m of the order of 10^6 docIDs and a computer performing 10^9 comparisons per second, we derive that this new algorithm takes 10^{-3} seconds to compute $A \cap B$, which is in the order of milliseconds, exactly what occurs today in modern search engines.

An attentive reader may have noticed this algorithm mimics the MERGE procedure used in MERGESORT, here adapted to find the common elements of the two sets A and B rather than merging them.

Theorem 6.1 *The algorithm based upon the merging paradigm solves the sorted set intersection problem in $O(m + n)$ time.*

In the case that $n = \Theta(m)$ this algorithm is optimal, because we need to process the smallest set, so $\Omega(\min\{n, m\})$ is an obvious lower bound. What is more, this scan-based paradigm is also optimal in the disk model, because it takes $O(n/B)$ I/Os. To be more precise, it is optimal whatever the memory hierarchy underlying the computation (the *cache-oblivious model*).

The next question is what we can do when m is very different from n, say $m \ll n$. This is the situation in which one word is much more selective than the other; here, the classic *binary search* can be helpful, in the sense that we can design an algorithm that binary searches every element $b \in B$ (which are just a few) into the (many) sorted elements of A, thus taking $O(m \log n)$ steps/comparisons. This time complexity is better than $O(n + m)$ if $m = o(n/\log n)$, which is actually less stringent and more precise than the condition $m \ll n$ that we imposed at the beginning of this paragraph.

Theorem 6.2 *The algorithm based on the binary-search paradigm solves the sorted set intersection problem in $O(m \log n)$ time.*

At this point it is natural to ask whether an algorithm can be designed that combines the best of both merge-based and search-based paradigms. In fact, there is an inefficiency in the binary-search paradigm which becomes apparent when m is of the order of n: when we search element b_i in A we possibly recheck over and over again the same elements of A. This is surely the case for A's middle element, say $a_{n/2}$, which is the first one checked by any binary search. But if $b_i > a_{n/2}$ then it is useless to compare b_{i+1} with $a_{n/2}$ because it must be larger, since $b_{i+1} > b_i > a_{n/2}$. And the same holds for all the subsequent elements of B. A similar argument may apply to other elements in A checked by the binary search. The next section details a new set-intersection paradigm that avoids these unnecessary comparisons.

6.2   Mutual Partitioning

This approach to set intersection adopts another classic algorithmic paradigm, called *partitioning*, which is the one we used to design QUICKSORT; here we deploy it to split repeatedly and mutually the two sorted sets to be intersected [1]. Formally, let us assume that $m \le n$ and that both are even numbers. We select the median element $b_{m/2}$ of the shortest sequence B as a *pivot* and search for it in the longer sequence A. Two cases may occur: (i) $b_{m/2} \in A$, say $b_{m/2} = a_j$ for some j, and thus $b_{m/2}$ is returned as one of the elements of the intersection $A \cap B$; or (ii) $b_{m/2} \notin A$, say $a_j < b_{m/2} < a_{j+1}$ (where we assume that $a_0 = -\infty$ and $a_{n+1} = +\infty$). In both

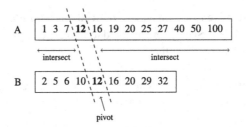

Figure 6.3 The first step of the mutual partitioning paradigm: the pivot is 12, the median element of the shortest sequence B. The pivot splits the sorted sequence A into two parts, one equal to $\{1, 3, 7\}$ and the other equal to $\{16, 19, 20, 25, 27, 40, 50, 100\}$. These two parts are recursively and correspondingly intersected with the two parts of B split by the pivot 12.

cases the intersection algorithm proceeds *recursively* in the two parts in which each sequence A and B has been split according to the choice of the pivot, thus computing recursively $A[1,j] \cap B[1, m/2 - 1]$ and $A[j+1, n] \cap B[m/2+1, m]$. A small optimization consists of discarding from the first recursive call the element $b_{m/2} = a_j$ (in case (i)).

A running example is illustrated in Figure 6.3, and the pseudocode is given in Algorithm 6.1. There, the median element of B is 12 and it is used as the pivot for the mutual partitioning of the two sorted sequences A and B. The pivot splits A into two unbalanced parts (i.e. $A[1, 3]$ and $A[5, 12]$) and B into two almost-halves (i.e. $B[1, 4]$ and $B[6, 9]$) which are recursively and correspondingly intersected; since the pivot occurs both in A and B, it is returned as an element of the intersection. Moreover, we note that the first part of A is shorter than the first part of B, and thus in the recursive call their role will be exchanged.

Algorithm 6.1 Sorted set intersection based on mutual partitioning

---

1: Let $m = |B| \leq n = |A|$, otherwise exchange the role of A and B;
2: Select the median element $p = b_{\lfloor m/2 \rfloor}$ of B;
3: Binary search for the position of p in A, say $a_j \leq p < a_{j+1}$;
4: Compute recursively the intersection $A[1, j] \cap B[1, m/2 - 1]$;
5: **if** $p = a_j$ **then**
6:      print p;
7: **end if**
8: Compute recursively the intersection $A[j + 1, n] \cap B[m/2 + 1, m]$;

Correctness easily follows in this case; for evaluating the time complexity we need to identify the worst case. Let us begin with the simplest situation, in which the pivot falls outside A (i.e. $j = 0$ or $j = n$). This means that one of the two parts in A is empty and thus the corresponding half of B can be discarded from the subsequent recursive calls. So one binary search over A, costing $O(\log n)$ time, has discarded half of B. If this occurs at all recursive calls, the total number of them will be $O(\log m)$, thus inducing an overall cost for the algorithm equal to $O(\log m \, \log n)$ time. That is, an *unbalanced* partitioning of A results in the intersection algorithm performing very well; this is more or less the opposite to what is typical for recursive algorithms, which perform worst on unbalanced partitions. On the other hand, let us assume that the pivot $b_{m/2}$ falls inside the sequence A and consider the case where it coincides with the median element of A, say $a_{n/2}$. In this specific situation the two partitions are balanced in both sequences we are intersecting, so the time complexity can be expressed via the recurrence relation $T(n, m) = O(\log n) + 2T(n/2, m/2)$, with the base case of $T(n, m) = O(1)$ whenever $n, m \leq 1$. It can be proved that this recurrence relation has the solution $T(n, m) = O(m(1 + \log \frac{n}{m}))$ for any $m \leq n$. It is interesting to observe that this time complexity subsumes the ones of the previous two algorithms (namely the one based on merging and the one based on binary searching). In fact, when $m = \Theta(n)$ it is $T(n, m) = O(n)$ (à la merging); when $m \ll n$ it is $T(n, m) = O(m \log n)$ (à la binary searching).

Actually, the time complexity of mutual partitioning is optimal in the comparison model, because this follows from the classic binary decision-tree argument: there exist at least $\binom{n}{m}$ solutions to the set-intersection problem (here we account only for the case in which $B \subseteq A$), and thus every comparison-based algorithm computing any of these solutions must execute $\Omega\left(\log\binom{n}{m}\right)$ steps, which is $\Omega(m \log \frac{n}{m})$ by definition of binomial coefficient.

Theorem 6.3 *The algorithm based on the mutual-partitioning paradigm solves the sorted set intersection problem in $O(m(1 + \log \frac{n}{m}))$ time. The time complexity is optimal in the comparison model.*

6.3 Doubling Search

Despite its optimal time complexity, the mutual-partitioning paradigm is heavily based on recursive calls and binary searching, which are two paradigms that offer poor performance in a disk-based setting when sequences are long and hence there is a large number of recursive calls (thus, dynamic memory allocations) and binary-search steps (thus, random memory accesses). In order to partially deal with these issues we introduce another approach to sorted set intersection which allows us to discuss another interesting algorithmic paradigm: the *doubling search*, or the *galloping search*, also called the *exponential search*. It can be explained most clearly using an inductive argument.

Let us assume that we have already checked the first $j - 1$ elements of B for their appearance in A, and that b_{j-1} is located immediately after a_i in the sorted A. This means that $a_i \leq b_{j-1} < a_{i+1}$. To check the next element of B, namely b_j, it suffices to search for it in $A[i + 1, n]$. However, and this is the bright idea underlying this approach, instead of binary searching this subarray, we execute a *doubling search*, that consists of checking elements of $A[i + 1, n]$ at distances that grow as a power of two (hence the term "doubling"). This means that we compare b_j against the elements $A[i + 2^k]$ for $k = 0, 1, \ldots$ until we find that either $b_j < A[i + 2^k]$, for some k, or we have jumped out of the array A, so that $i + 2^k > n$. Finally, we perform a binary search for b_j in $A[i + 1, \min\{i + 2^k, n\}]$, and we return b_j if the search is successful. We thus determine the position of b_j in that subarray, say $a_{i'} \leq b_j < a_{i'+1}$, so that

---

Algorithm 6.2 Sorted set intersection based on doubling search

---

1: Let $m = |B| \leq n = |A|$, otherwise exchange the role of A and B;
2: $i = 0$;
3: **for** $j = 1, 2, \ldots, m$ **do**
4:     $k = 0$;
5:     **while** $(i + 2^k \leq n)$ **and** $(B[j] > A[i + 2^k])$ **do**
6:         $k = k + 1$;
7:     **end while**
8:     $i' = $ Binary search $B[j]$ into $A[i + 2^{k-1} + 1, \min\{i + 2^k, n\}]$;
9:     **if** $a_{i'} = b_j$ **then**
10:         print b_j;
11:     **end if**
12:     $i = i'$;
13: **end for**

---

the process can be repeated by discarding $A[1, i']$ from the subsequent searches for the next elements of B. Algorithm 6.2 reports the pseudocode of the doubling search algorithm, and Figure 6.4 shows a running example.

Correctness is again immediate, whereas deriving the evaluation of time complexity is more involved. Let us denote with $i_j = i'$ the position where b_j occurs in A and, inductively, denote with i_{j-1} the position of b_{j-1} in A; clearly $i_{j-1} \leq i_j$. For the sake of presentation we set $i_0 = 0$ and denote with $\Delta_j = \min\{2^{k-1}, n\}$ the size of the subarray where the binary search of b_j is executed (according to Step 8 of Algorithm 6.2). From the condition of the while-loop in Step 5, the position of b_j in A is such that $i_j \geq i_{j-1} + 2^{k-1}$ (i.e. b_j is larger than the previously checked element in A) and $i_j < \min\{i_{j-1} + 2^k, n\}$ (i.e. either b_j is smaller than $A[i_{j-1} + 2^k]$ or that checked position is out of A). We can therefore write $2^{k-1} \leq i_j - i_{j-1}$, and combining this inequality with the definition of Δ_j, we get $\Delta_j \leq 2^{k-1} \leq i_j - i_{j-1}$. At this point we have all the mathematical ingredients to estimate the total length of the searched subarrays of A: $\sum_{j=1}^m \Delta_j \leq \sum_{j=1}^m (i_j - i_{j-1}) \leq n$, because the latter is a telescopic sum in which consecutive terms in the summation cancel out except $i_0 = 0$ and $i_m \leq n$. For every j, Algorithm 6.2 executes $O(1 + \log \Delta_j)$ steps because of the while-statement in Steps 5–7 and the binary search in Step 8. Summing for $j = 1, 2, \ldots, m$, we get a total time complexity of $\sum_{j=1}^m O(1 + \log \Delta_j) = O(\sum_{j=1}^m (1 + \log \Delta_j)) = O\left(m + m \log \sum_{j=1}^m \frac{\Delta_j}{m}\right) = O(m\,(1 + \log \frac{n}{m}))$.[2]

Theorem 6.4 *The algorithm based on the doubling-search paradigm solves the sorted set intersection problem in $O(m(1 + \log \frac{n}{m}))$ time. This time complexity is optimal in the comparison model.*

---

[2] We are applying *Jensen's inequality*: https://en.wikipedia.org/wiki/Jensen%27s_inequality.

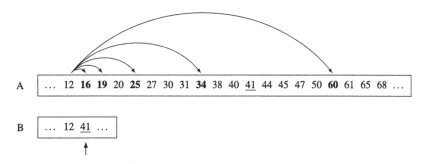

Figure 6.4 An example of the doubling-search paradigm: the two sequences A and B are assumed to have been intersected up to the element $a_i = 12$. The next element in B, that is, $b_j = 41$ (indicated by an upward arrow), is taken to be exponentially searched in the suffix of A following 12. This search checks A's elements at distances that are a power of two – namely $1, 2, 4, 8, 16$ – until it finds the element 60 which is larger than 41 and thus delimits the portion of A within which the binary search for 41 can be confined. We notice that the searched subarray has size 16, whereas the distance of 41 from 12 in A is 11, thus proving, in this example, that the binary search is executed on a subarray whose size is smaller than twice the real distance of the searched element.

We notice that this is the same time complexity of the algorithm based on the mutual-partitioning paradigm (see Theorem 6.3), but the present doubling-search paradigm is iterative and thus it does not execute any recursive calls, as instead occurred for mutual partitioning.

6.4   Two-Level Storage Approach

Although the previous approach avoids some of the pitfalls due to the recursive partitioning of the two sorted sequences A and B, it still needs to jump over the array A because of the doubling scheme; and we know that this is inefficient when executed in a hierarchical memory. In order to avoid this issue, algorithm engineers adopt a *two-level organization of the data*, which is a very common scheme of storing efficient data structures for the two-level memory model. The main idea of this storage scheme, intended to work over a collection of sorted lists in the search-engine scenario, is to preprocess all lists of the collection, *logically* partition each of them into blocks of size L (the final block may be shorter), and copy the first element of each block into an auxiliary sequence. This auxiliary sequence will then be used to speed up the intersection among any pair of sets of the collection that will be involved in a user query composed of two terms. As an example, let us consider a set A, and assume that its length n is a multiple of L (say $n = hL$): the preprocessing of A just described creates h blocks A_i of size L each, and copies the first element of each block (i.e. $A_i[1] = A[(i-1) \times L + 1]$) into an auxiliary sequence A' of size h. This preprocessing is executed over all input sets (see Figure 6.5 for an illustrative example).

At query time, given two sets A and B of the (preprocessed) collection, their intersection proceeds in two main phases. For the sake of presentation, let us assume that A

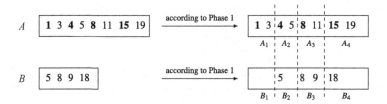

Figure 6.5 An example of the two-level storage approach. The figure on the left shows in bold the elements of A that are copied in the auxiliary sequence $A' = (1, 4, 8, 15)$ given that $L = 2$. Also B is preprocessed, by generating two blocks of length L, thus headed by 5 and 9. However, for the sake of clarity, the blocking of B is not shown, because it is not used in this example, where $|A| > |B|$. The figure on the right graphically shows how the elements of B are partitioned, by merging A' and B into the subsets B_i according to the elements $A_i[1]$ (Phase 1). Block B_1 is empty, because no element in B is between $A_1[1] = 1$ and $A_2[1] = 4$. So Phase 2 does not examine A_1, which is therefore dropped from the computation, without there being any time cost for it. The subsequent intersections executed by Phase 2 between the subset pairs $A_i \cap B_i$, for $i = 2, 3, 4$, will return the correct intersection $A \cap B = \{5, 8\}$.

is longer than B, and thus $n = |A| > |B| = m$. Phase 1 applies the MERGE procedure of MERGESORT to fuse together the two sorted sequences A' and B into one unique sorted sequence (see Section 5.1), which thus consists of elements of B interspersed among elements of A'. This takes $O(n/L + m)$ time. Now, let B_i be the contiguous subsequence of B's elements that fall between two consecutive elements of A', say $A_i[1]$ and $A_{i+1}[1]$. This means that B_i's elements may occur in the block A_i, so that Phase 2 executes the merge-based set-intersection algorithm of Theorem 6.1 to compute $A_i \cap B_i$ in time $O(|A_i| + |B_i|) = O(L + |B_i|)$. This algorithm is indeed executed over all pairs A_i and B_i that involve a non-empty subset B_i. These are no more than m such pairs, and since $B = \cup_i B_i$, the total time taken by Phase 2 is $O(L m + m)$. Summing up the time complexity of the two phases, and observing that sequences are scanned in an I/O-optimal way, we obtain:

Theorem 6.5 *The algorithm based on the two-level storage paradigm solves the sorted set intersection problem in $O(\frac{n}{L} + mL)$ time and $O(\frac{n}{LB} + \frac{mL}{B} + m)$ I/Os, where B is the disk-page size of the two-level memory model.*

We note that the two-level storage approach is suitable for a variant that leverages a compressed storage of the elements in order to save space, and consequently improve the overall performance because of the possibly reduced amount of processed data. There are two main ideas underlying this new proposal. The first one is to represent the increasing elements of every block $A_i = (a'_1, a'_2, \ldots, a'_L)$ by means of a compression scheme that sets $a'_0 = 0$ and then represents a'_j as its difference with the preceding element a'_{j-1}, for $j = 1, 2, \ldots, L$. Each difference is then stored (compressed) by using $\lceil \log_2(1 + \max_j \{a'_j - a'_{j-1}\}) \rceil$ bits, instead of the full representation in four/eight bytes. Since the two-level storage approach proceeds rightward over the sequences, these differences and their corresponding elements can be efficiently decompressed.

The second idea stems from the observation that this compression scheme is advantageous whenever those differences are small. Thus, at preprocessing time, the algorithm may artificially force this situation by shuffling the elements in all sets of the indexed collection via a random permutation, which thus guarantees in expectation the smallest maximum gap between adjacent (shuffled) elements. The permuted sets are eventually preprocessed and queried via the two-level storage approach just described above. For further details on variants of this approach, see [2, 3, 5].

References

[1] Ricardo Baeza-Yates. A fast set intersection algorithm for sorted sequences. In *Proceedings of the 15th Annual Symposium on Combinatorial Pattern Matching (CPM)*, Lecture Notes in Computer Science 3109, Springer, 400–8, 2004.

[2] Jérémy Barbay, Alejandro López-Ortiz, Tyler Lu, and Alejandro Salinger. An experimental investigation of set intersection algorithms for text searching. *ACM Journal of Experimental Algorithmics*, 14(3), 7–24, 2009.

[3] Bolin Ding and Arnd Christian König. Fast set intersection in memory. *Proceedings of the VLDB Endowment (PVLDB)*, 4(4): 255–66, 2011.

[4] Christopher D. Manning, Prabhakar Raghavan, and Hinrich Schütze. *Introduction to Information Retrieval*. Cambridge University Press, 2008.

[5] Peter Sanders and Frederik Transier. Intersection in integer inverted indices. In *Proceedings of the 9th Workshop on Algorithm Engineering and Experiments (ALENEX)*, 71–83, 2007.

[6] Hao Yan, Shuai Ding, and Torsten Suel. Inverted index compression and query processing with optimized document ordering. In *Proceedings of the 18th International Conference on World Wide Web (WWW)*, Association for Computing Machinery, 401–10, 2009.

[7] Ian H. Witten, Alistair Moffat, and Timothy C. Bell. *Managing Gigabytes*. Morgan Kauffman, second edition, 1999.

7 Sorting Strings

In Chapter 5 we dealt with sorting *atomic items*, namely items that either occupy fixed-constant space or have to be managed in their entirety as atomic objects, thus without deploying their constituent parts. In the present chapter we will generalize those algorithms, and introduce new ones, to deal with the case of *variable-length items* (aka *strings*). More formally, we will be interested in solving efficiently the following problem:

> **The string-sorting problem.** Given a sequence $S[1, n]$ of strings, with total length N and drawn from an alphabet of size σ, sort these strings into ascending lexicographic order.

The first idea in approaching this problem consists of deploying the power of *comparison-based* sorting algorithms, such as QUICKSORT or MERGESORT, by implementing a proper comparison function between pairs of strings. The obvious way to do this is to compare the two strings from their beginning, character by character, find their mismatch, and then use it to derive their lexicographic order. Let $L = N/n$ be the average length of the strings in S; an optimal comparison-based sorter would thus take $O(Ln \log n) = O(N \log n)$ average time on RAM, because every string comparison may involve $O(L)$ characters on average.

Apart from the time complexity, which is not optimal (see Section 7.1), the key limitation of this approach in a memory hierarchy is that S is typically implemented as an *array of pointers* to strings that are spread in the internal memory of the computer, or stored on disk if N is very large. Figure 7.1 shows the two situations via a graphical example. Whichever is the allocation an algorithm chooses to adopt, the sorter will *indirectly* order the strings of S by moving their pointers rather than their characters. This situation is typically neglected by programmers, with a consequent slowness of their sorter when executed on large string sets. The motivation is clear; every time a string comparison is executed between two pointers, say $S[i]$ and $S[j]$, they are first resolved by accessing their corresponding strings, and then they are compared character by character. As a result, every string comparison takes two cache misses or I/Os, and the algorithm takes $\Theta(n \log n)$ I/Os overall. As we noted in Chapter 1, the virtual memory of the operating system will help by buffering the most recently compared strings, thus possibly reducing the number of incurred I/Os. Nevertheless, two arrays are here competing for that buffering space – the array of pointers and the array of

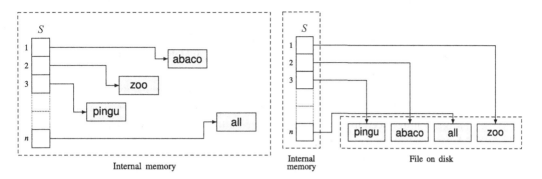

Figure 7.1 Two examples of string allocation, spread in the internal memory (left) and written contiguously in a file on disk (right).

strings – and time is wasted by repeatedly *rescanning* string prefixes that have been already compared.

The rest of this chapter is therefore devoted to proposing algorithms that are *optimal* in the number of executed character comparisons, and offer I/O-conscious patterns of memory accesses, which thus make them efficient in the presence of a memory hierarchy.

7.1   A Lower Bound

Let d_s be the length of the shortest prefix of the string $s \in S$ that distinguishes it from the other strings in the set. The value d_s is called the *distinguishing prefix* of the string s, and the sum of these values over all strings in S is called the distinguishing prefix of the set S, and is denoted by $d = \sum_{s \in S} d_s$. Referring to Figure 7.1, and assuming that S consists of the four strings shown in the figure, the distinguishing prefix of the string all is al because this substring does not prefix any other string in S, whereas a does.

It is evident that any string sorter must compare the initial d_s characters of s, otherwise it would be unable to distinguish s from the other strings in S and thus find its lexicographic position in the sorted set. So $\Omega(d)$ is a term that must appear in the string-sorting lower bound. But this term does not take into account the cost of computing the sorted order among the n strings, which is $\Omega(n \log n)$ string comparisons, and thus at least $\Omega(n \log n)$ character comparisons (because comparing one character per string is surely needed to sort them).

Lemma 7.1 Any *algorithm solving the string-sorting problem must execute $\Omega(d + n \log n)$ character comparisons.*

This formula deserves a few comments. Assume that n is a power of two; the n strings of S are binary, share the initial ℓ bits, and differ for the other $\log n$ bits, so $d_s = \ell + \log n$, and $d = n(\ell + \log n) = N$. The lower bound in this case is $\Omega(N +$

$n \log n) = \Omega(N)$ because $N = n(\ell + \log n) \geq n \log n$. But string sorters based on MERGESORT or QUICKSORT take $\Theta(N \log n)$ time. Thus, for any ℓ, those algorithms may be far from optimality by a factor $\Theta(\log n)$, which gets larger and larger as S grows in cardinality.

One could wonder whether string sorting can be implemented without looking at the entire content of the strings. And indeed, this is the case when $d < N$, which is why we introduced the parameter d, which allows a finer analysis of the algorithms discussed later in this chapter.

7.2 RADIXSORT

The first step to get a more competitive algorithm for string sorting is to look at strings as *sequences of characters* drawn from an integer alphabet $\{0, 1, 2, \ldots, \sigma - 1\}$ (aka *digits*). This condition can be easily enforced by sorting in advance the characters occurring in S, and then assigning to each of them an integer (i.e. its rank) in that range. This is typically called the *naming* process and takes $O(N \log \sigma)$ time because we can use a binary search tree built over at most σ distinct characters occurring in S.

Consequently, we hereafter assume that strings in S have been drawn from an integer alphabet of size σ and keep in mind that, if this is not the case, a term $O(N \log \sigma)$ has to be added to the time complexity of the proposed algorithm. Moreover, we observe that each character can be encoded in $\lceil \log_2 \sigma \rceil$ bits; thus the input size is $\Theta(N \log \sigma)$ whenever it is measured in bits.

We can devise two main variants of RADIXSORT that differentiate each other according to the order in which the digits of the strings are processed: MSD-first processes the strings rightward starting from the most significant digit, LSD-first processes the strings leftward starting from the least significant digit.

7.2.1 MSD-First

This algorithm follows the divide-and-conquer approach in that it processes the strings character by character from their beginning, and distributes them recursively into σ buckets, taking a constant-time per character. Figure 7.2 shows an example in which S consists of seven strings drawn from an alphabet of size $\sigma = 10$. Strings are distributed according to their first (most significant) digit in 10 buckets. Since buckets 1 and 6 consist of one single string each, their ordering is known. Conversely, buckets 0 and 9 have to be sorted recursively according to the second digit of the strings contained in them. At the end, the ordered S is obtained by concatenating all groups of individual strings in left-to-right order.

It is not difficult to notice that distribution-based approaches generate search trees. The classic QUICKSORT generates a binary search tree. The MSD-first RADIXSORT generates a σ-ary tree because of the σ-ary partition of S's strings executed at every distribution step. This tree takes in the literature the name of *trie*, or *digital* search tree, and its main use is in string searching (as we will detail in Chapter 9).

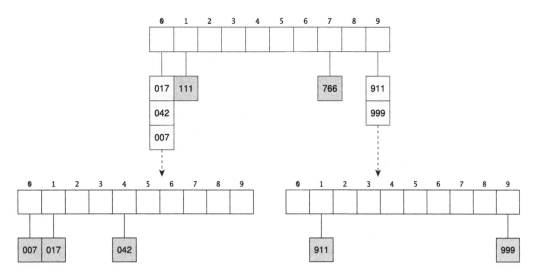

Figure 7.2 (Top) Sorting seven strings according to their first most significant digit. (Bottom) Recursive sort of bucket 0, on top, and bucket 9, below, according to the second most significant digit of their strings.

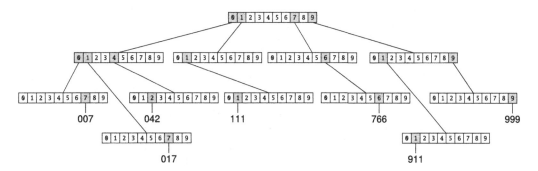

Figure 7.3 The trie-based view of MSD-first RadixSort for the strings in Figure 7.2.

An example of a trie for the string set of Figure 7.2 is given in Figure 7.3. Every node is implemented as a σ-sized array, one entry per possible alphabet character. Strings are stored in the leaves of the trie, hence we have n leaves. Internal nodes are less than N, one per character occurring in the strings of S. Given a node u, the downward path from the root of the trie to u spells out the string, say $s[u]$, that is obtained by concatenating the characters encountered in the path traversal. For example, the path leading to the leaf 017 traverses three nodes, one per possible character of that string. Then, having fixed a node u, all strings that descend from u share the same prefix $s[u]$. For example, $s[root]$ is the empty string, which is obviously shared by all strings of S. The leftmost child of the root spells the string 0 because it is reached from the root by traversing the edge hanging out of the 0-entry of the array.

Notice that the trie may contain *unary* nodes, namely nodes that have one single child, such as the ones on the paths leading to strings 111 and 666, for example.

All the other internal nodes have at least two children, and they are called *branching* nodes. In Figure 7.3 we have nine unary nodes and three branching nodes, with $n = 7$ and $N = 21$. In general the trie can have no more than n branching nodes, and no more than N unary nodes. Actually, the unary nodes that have a descending branching node are at most d. In fact, these unary nodes correspond to characters occurring in the distinguishing prefixes of S's strings, and the lowest descending branching nodes correspond to the characters that end the distinguishing prefixes. On the other hand, the unary paths that start from the lowest branching nodes in the trie and lead to its leaves correspond to the string suffixes that follow those distinguishing prefixes. In algorithmic terms, the unary nodes correspond to buckets formed by items all sharing the same compared characters in the distribution of MSD-first RADIXSORT, while the branching nodes correspond to buckets formed by items with distinct compared characters in the distribution of MSD-first RADIXSORT.

If edge labels are alphabetically sorted, as in Figure 7.3, reading the leaves according to the pre-order visit of the trie gives the sorted S. This suggests a simple trie-based string sorter.

The idea is to start with an empty trie, and then insert one string after another into it. Inserting a string $s \in S$ in the current trie consists of tracing a downward path until s's characters are matched with existing edge labels (i.e. non-empty entries of the σ-sized arrays). As soon as the next character in s cannot be matched with any of the edges leaving the reached node u,[1] then we say that the mismatch for s is found. So a *special* node is appended to the trie at u with that branching character. This special node points to s. The speciality resides in the fact that we have dropped the not-yet-matched suffix of s, but the pointer to the string implicitly keeps track of it for the subsequent insertions. In fact, if while inserting another string s' we encounter the special node u, then we resort to the string s (linked to it) and create a (unary) path for the other characters constituting the common prefix between s and s' which descends from u. The last node in this path branches to s and s', possibly dropping again the two paths corresponding to the not-yet-matched suffixes of these two strings, and introducing for each of them one special node.

Every time a trie node is created, an array of size σ is allocated, thus taking $O(\sigma)$ time and space. So the following theorem can be proved.

Theorem 7.1 *A set of strings over an (integer) alphabet of size σ and distinguishing prefix d can be sorted via the MSD-first* RADIXSORT *with a trie using σ-sized arrays in $O(d \, \sigma)$ time and space.*

Proof Every string s spells out a path of length d_s; before that the special node pointing to s is created. Each node of those paths allocates σ space and takes that amount of time to be allocated. Moreover, $O(1)$ is the time cost for traversing a trie node. Therefore $O(\sigma)$ is the time spent for each traversed/created node. The claim then follows by

---

[1] This actually means that the slot in the σ-sized array of u corresponding to the next character of s is
`null`.

visiting the constructed trie and listing its leaves from left to right, given that they are lexicographically sorted, because the naming of characters is lexicographic and thus reflects their order.   ∎

The space occupancy is significant and should be reduced. An option is to replace the σ-sized array into each node u with a hash table (with chaining) of size proportional to the number of edges leaving u, say e_u, and indexed by the digit associated with that edge label.[2] This guarantees $O(1)$ expected time for searching and inserting one edge in each node. As we have observed, the number of edges can be bounded by the number of internal nodes, that is, $O(d)$, plus the number of special nodes, that is, n leaves, so that $\sum_u e_u = O(d + n) = O(d)$. We can thus derive the construction time, which is $O(d)$ to insert all strings in the trie (here every node access takes constant time), $O(\sum_u e_u \log e_u) = O(\sum_u e_u \log \sigma) = O(d \log \sigma)$ for the sorting of the trie edges over all nodes, and $O(d)$ time to scan the trie leaves rightward via a pre-order visit in order to get the dictionary strings in lexicographic order.

Theorem 7.2 *A set of strings over an (integer) alphabet of size σ and distinguishing prefix d can be sorted via the MSD-first RADIXSORT using a trie with hashing in $O(d \log \sigma)$ expected time and $O(d)$ space.*

When σ is small we cannot conclude that this result is *better than the lower bound* provided in Lemma 7.1, because that applies to comparison-based algorithms and thus it does not apply to hashing or integer sorting.

The space allocated for the trie can be further reduced to $O(n)$, and the construction time to $O(d + n \log \sigma)$, by using *compacted* tries, namely tries in which the unary paths have been compacted into single edges whose length is equal to the number of characters forming the compacted unary path. The discussion of this data structure is deferred to Chapter 9.

7.2.2   LSD-First

The next sorter was discovered by Herman Hollerith more than a century ago, and led to the implementation of a card-sorting machine for the 1890 U Census. Interestingly, he was also the founder of a company that went on to become IBM.[3] The algorithm is counterintuitive because it sorts strings digit by digit, starting from the least significant one and using a *stable* sorter as a black box. We recall that a sorter is *stable* if and only if equal keys maintain in the final sorted order the one they had in the input. We use as stable sorter the *CountingSort* (see, e.g., [3]) and assume that all strings have the same length L; if not, they are *logically* padded at their front with a special digit which

---

[2] More complex hash-based solutions will be presented in Chapter 8. Here we consider hashing with chaining because it is a classic topic of every basic course on algorithms, and it is enough for the teaching purposes of this chapter.

[3] See the entry for Herman Hollerith in Wikipedia: http://en.wikipedia.org/wiki/Herman_Hollerith.

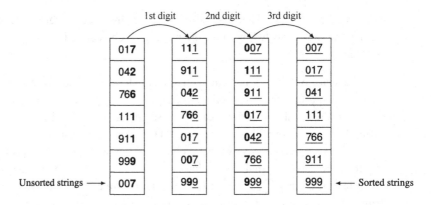

Figure 7.4 A running example for LSD-first RADIXSORT. Plain digits have yet to be processed, underlined digits have already been processed, bold digits are the ones being processed and driving the stable sorter. Since strings consist of three digits, three phases suffice to sort them.

is assumed to be smaller than any other alphabet digit. The logic is that, the LSD-first RADIXSORT will correctly obtain an ordered lexicographic sequence.

The LSD-first RADIXSORT consists of L phases, say $i = 1, 2, \ldots, L$. In each phase we stably sort all strings according to their i-th least significant digit. A running example of LSD-first RADIXSORT is given in Figure 7.4: the bold digits (characters) are the ones that are going to be sorted in the current phase, whereas the underlined digits are the ones already sorted in the previous phases. Each phase produces a new sorted string order which deploys the order in the input sequence, obtained from the previous phases, to resolve the ordering of the strings that show equal digits in the currently compared position i. As an example, let us consider the strings 111 and 017 in the second phase of Figure 7.4. These strings present the same second digit so their ordering in the second phase places 111 before 017, just because this was the ordering after the first sorting step. This is clearly a wrong order, which will be nonetheless correctly adjusted after the final phase, which operates on the third digit, that is 1 versus 0.

The time complexity can be easily estimated as L times the cost of executing COUNTINGSORT over n integer digits drawn from the range $\{0, 1, \ldots, \sigma - 1\}$; hence it is $O(L(n + \sigma))$. A nice property of this sorter is that it is in-place whenever the sorting black box is in-place, namely $\sigma = O(1)$.

Lemma 7.2 *LSD-first Radixsort solves the string-sorting problem in* $O(L(n + \sigma)) = O(N + L\sigma)$ *time and* $O(N)$ *space. The sorter is in-place if and only if an in-place digit sorter is adopted.*

Proof Time and space efficiency follow from the previous observations. Correctness is proved by deploying the stability of COUNTINGSORT. Let α and β be two strings of S, and assume that $\alpha < \beta$ according to their lexicographic order. Since we assumed that S's strings have the same length, we can decompose these two strings into three parts: $\alpha = \gamma a \alpha_1$ and $\beta = \gamma b \beta_1$, where γ is the longest common prefix between α and β (possibly it is empty), $a < b$ are the first mismatch characters, and α_1 and β_1 are the two remaining suffixes (which may be empty).

Let us now look at the history of comparisons between the digits of α and β. We can identify three stages, depending on the position of the compared digit within the three-way decomposition described here. Since the algorithm starts from the least significant digit, it starts comparing digits in α_1 and β_1. We do not care about the ordering after the first $|\alpha_1| = |\beta_1|$ phases, because in the immediately following phase, α and β are sorted in accordance to characters a and b. Since $a < b$, this sorting places α before β. All other $|\gamma|$ sorting steps will compare the digits falling in γ, which are equal in both strings, so their order will not change because of the stability of COUNTINGSORT. At the end we will correctly have $\alpha < \beta$. Since this holds for any pair of strings in S, the final sequence produced by LSD-first RADIXSORT will be lexicographically ordered. ∎

The previous time bound deserves few comments. LSD-first RADIXSORT processes all digits of all strings, so it doesn't seem appealing when $d \ll N$ with respect to MSD-first RADIXSORT. But the efficiency of LSD-first RADIXSORT hinges on the observation that nothing prevents a phase from sorting *groups of digits* rather than a single digit at a time. Clearly the longer this group is, the larger the time complexity of a phase is, but the smaller the number of phases is. We are in the presence of a trade-off that can be tuned by investigating deeply the relation that exists between these two parameters. Without loss of generality, we simplify our discussion by assuming that the strings in S are binary and have an equal length of b bits, so $N \log \sigma = bn$. Of course, this is not a limitation in practice because any string is encoded in memory as a bit sequence, taking $\log \sigma$ bits per digit.

Lemma 7.3 LSD-*first* RADIXSORT *takes* $\Theta\left(\frac{b}{r}(n + 2^r)\right)$ *time and* $O(nb) = O(N \log \sigma)$ *space to sort n strings of b bits each. Here $r \le b$ is a positive integer fixed in advance.*

Proof We decompose each string into $g = \frac{b}{r}$ groups of r bits each. Each phase will order the strings according to a group of r bits. Hence COUNTINGSORT is asked to order n integers between 0 and $2^r - 1$ (extremes included), so it takes $O(n + 2^r)$ time. As there are g phases, the total time is $O(g(n + 2^r)) = O\left(\left(\frac{b}{r}\right)(n + 2^r)\right)$. ∎

Given n and b, we need to choose a proper value for r such that the time complexity is minimized. We could derive this minimum via analytic calculus (i.e. first-order derivatives) but, instead, we argue for the minimum as follows. Since the COUNTINGSORT uses $O(n + 2^r)$ time to sort each group of r digits, it is useless to use groups shorter than $\log n$, given that $O(n)$ time has to be paid in any case. So we have to choose r in the interval $[\log n, b]$. As r grows larger than $\log n$, the time complexity in

Lemma 7.3 also increases because of the ratio $2^r/r$. So the best choice is $r = \Theta(\log n)$ for which the time complexity is $O\left(\frac{bn}{\log n}\right)$.

Theorem 7.3 *LSD-first Radixsort sorts n strings of b bits each in* $O\left(\frac{bn}{\log n}\right)$ *time and* $O(bn)$ *space, by using* COUNTINGSORT *on groups of* $\Theta(\log n)$ *bits. The algorithm is not in-place because it needs* $\Theta(n)$ *space for the* COUNTINGSORT.

We finally observe that bn is the total length in bits of the strings in S, so we can express that number also as $N \log \sigma$ since each character takes $\log \sigma$ bits to be represented.

Corollary 7.1 *LSD-first Radixsort solves the string-sorting problem on n strings drawn from a σ-sized alphabet in* $O\left(\frac{N \log \sigma}{\log n}\right)$ *time and* $O(N \log \sigma)$ *bits of space.*

If $d = \Theta(N)$ and σ is a constant (hence $N = \Omega(n \log n)$ because of string distinctness), the comparison-based lower bound (Lemma 7.1) becomes $\Omega(N)$. So LSD-first RADIXSORT beats that lower bound, and this is not surprising, because this sorter operates on an *integer* alphabet and uses COUNTINGSORT, so it is *not* a comparison-based string sorter.

Comparing the trie-based construction of the MSD-first RADIXSORT algorithm (Theorems 7.1–7.2) against the LSD-first RADIXSORT algorithm, we conclude that the former is always better than the latter for $d = O\left(\frac{N}{\log n}\right)$, which is true for most practical cases. In fact, LSD-first RADIXSORT needs to scan the whole string set whatever the string compositions, whereas the trie construction may skip some string suffixes whenever $d \ll N$. However, the LSD-first approach avoids the dynamic memory allocation incurred by the construction of the trie, and the extra space due to the storage of the trie structure. This additional space and work is nonnegligible in practice and could impact unfavorably on the real-life performance of the MSD-first RADIXSORT, or even prevent its use over large string sets because the internal memory has bounded size M.

7.3   Multi-key QUICKSORT

This is a variant of the well-known QUICKSORT algorithm extended to manage items of variable length, it is a comparison-based string sorter matching the lower bound of $\Omega(d + n \log n)$ stated in Lemma 7.1. For a recap of QUICKSORT we refer the reader to Chapter 5. Here it is enough to recall that QUICKSORT hinges on two main ingredients: the pivot-selection procedure and the algorithm to partition the input array according to the selected pivot. For the present section we restrict ourselves to a pivot selection based on a *random* choice and to a *three-way* partitioning of the input array. All other variants discussed in Chapter 5 can be easily adapted to work in the string setting too.

The key here is that items are not considered to be atomic, but as strings to be split into their constituent characters. Now the pivot is a character, and the partitioning

---

Algorithm 7.1 MULTIKEYQS(R, i)

1: **if** $|R| \leq 1$ **then**
2:      **return** R;
3: **else**
4:      choose a pivot-string $p \in R$;
5:      $R_< = \{s \in R \mid s[i] < p[i]\}$;
6:      $R_= = \{s \in R \mid s[i] = p[i]\}$;
7:      $R_> = \{s \in R \mid s[i] > p[i]\}$;
8:      $A = $ MULTIKEYQS($R_<, i$);
9:      $B = $ MULTIKEYQS($R_=, i + 1$);
10:      $C = $ MULTIKEYQS($R_>, i$);
11:      **return** the concatenated sequence A, B, C;
12: **end if**

---

of the input strings is done according to the single character that occupies a given position within them. Algorithm 7.1 details the pseudocode of multi-key QUICKSORT, in which it is assumed that the input string set R is *prefix free*, so no string in R prefixes any other string in the set. This condition can be easily guaranteed by assuming that strings in R are distinct and logically padded with a dummy character that is smaller than any other character in the alphabet. This guarantees that any pair of strings in R admits a bounded *longest common prefix* (LCP), and that the mismatch character following the LCP exists in both strings.

Algorithm 7.1 receives in input a sequence R of strings to be sorted and an integer parameter $i \geq 0$ that denotes the offset of the character driving the three-way partitioning of R. The pivot character is $p[i]$, where p is a randomly chosen string within R. The real-life implementation of this three-way partitioning can follow the PARTITION procedure of Chapter 5. MULTIKEYQS(R, i) assumes that the following invariant holds on its input parameters: *All strings in R are lexicographically sorted up to their length-$(i - 1)$ prefix*. So the sorting of the input string set $S[1, n]$ is obtained by invoking MULTIKEYQS($S, 1$), which ensures that the invariant trivially holds for the initial sequence S. Steps 5–7 partition the generic string sequence R in three subsets whose notation is explicative of their content. All three subsets are recursively sorted and their ordered sequences are eventually concatenated in order to obtain the ordered R. The tricky issue here is the definition of the parameters passed to the three recursive calls:

- the sorting of the strings in $R_<$ and $R_>$ still has to reconsider the i-th character, because we just checked that it is smaller/greater than $p[i]$ (and this is not sufficient to order those strings). So recursion does not advance i, and it hinges on the current validity of the invariant.
- the sorting of the strings in $R_=$ can advance i because, by the invariant, these strings are sorted up to their length-$(i - 1)$ prefixes and, by construction of $R_=$, they share the i-th character. This character is actually equal to $p[i]$, so $p \in R_=$ too.

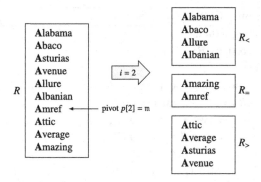

Figure 7.5 A running example for MULTIKEYQS(R, 2). In bold we have the length-1 prefix shared by all strings in R, according to the invariant to be guaranteed. The pivot string chosen at random is $p = $ Amref, and the character thus adopted to three-way partition the string set R is $p[2] = $ m.

Figure 7.5 shows a running example, where readers can also convince themselves about the correctness, which is indeed immediate from the discussion here. We are therefore left with the problem of computing the expected time complexity of MUL-TIKEYQS. Let us concentrate on a single string, say $s \in R$, and count the number of comparisons that involve one of its characters during the sequence of recursive calls. There are two cases at a generic recursive call MULTIKEYQS(R, i): either $s \in R_< \cup R_>$ or $s \in R_=$. In the first case, character $s[i]$ is compared with the corresponding character of the pivot string $p[i]$, and then s included in a smaller set $R_< \cup R_> \subset R$ with the offset i unchanged. In the other case, $s[i]$ is compared with $p[i]$ but, since they are found to be equal, s is included in $R_=$ *and* offset i is advanced. If the pivot selection is good (see Chapter 5), the three-way partitions are balanced and thus $|R_< \cup R_>| \le \alpha n$, for a proper constant $\alpha < 1$. As a result both cases cost $O(1)$ time, but one reduces the string set by a constant factor, while the other increases i. Since the initial set $R = S$ has size n, and i is bounded above by the string length $|s|$, we have that the number of comparisons involving s is $O(|s| + \log n)$. Summing up over all strings in S, we get the time bound $O(N + n \log n)$. A closer look at the second case shows that i can be bounded above by the number d_s of characters that belong to s's distinguishing prefix, because these characters will lead s to be located in a singleton set.

Theorem 7.4 MULTIKEYQS *solves the string-sorting problem by performing* $O(d + n \log n)$ *character comparisons in expectation. This is optimal in the comparison-based model. The bound can be turned into a worst-case bound by adopting a worst-case linear-time algorithm to select the pivot as the median of* R.

Compared to the trie-based sorters of the previous sections, multi-key QUICKSORT is very appealing in practice because it is much simpler, it does not use additional data structures (i.e. hash tables or σ-sized arrays), and the constants hidden in the big-O notation are very small.

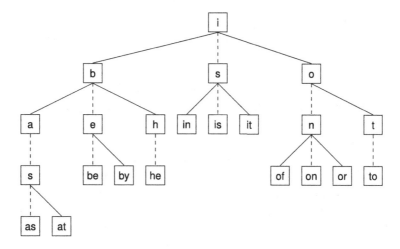

Figure 7.6 A ternary search tree for 12 two-letter strings. The low and high pointers are shown as solid lines, while the pointers to the equal split-character child are shown as dashed lines. The split character is indicated within the internal nodes.

We conclude this section by noting an interesting parallel between multi-key QUICKSORT and *ternary* search trees [4]. These are search data structures in which each node contains a *split character*, and three types of pointers: low, equal, and high (or left, middle, and right). In some sense a ternary search tree is obtained from a trie by collapsing together the children whose first character on their leading edges is smaller/greater than the split character. The elegance and practical efficiency of ternary search trees come from this three-way branching, which is a clear simplification of the σ-ary branching of classic tries and also reduces the cache misses at each node branching.

If a given node splits on the character in position i, say c, the strings descending from the left (resp. right) child are the ones whose i-th character is smaller (resp. larger) than c. Instead, the middle child points to strings that have the i-th character equal to c. In addition, and similarly to multi-key QUICKSORT, the iterator i does not advance when descending in the left/right children, whereas it advances when descending in the middle child.

Ternary search trees may be balanced either by inserting strings in random order or by applying a variety of known schemes. Searching proceeds by following edges according to the split character of the encountered nodes. Figure 7.6 shows an example of a ternary search tree. The search for the pattern $P =$ "ir" starts at the root, which is labeled with the character i, and initializes the iterator $i = 1$. Since $P[1] = $ i, the search proceeds down to the middle child, increments i to 2, and thus reaches the node with split character s. Here $P[2] = $ r $<$ s, so the search goes to the left child and keeps i unchanged. At that node the search stops, because it is a leaf pointing to string in. So the search concludes that P does not belong to the string set indexed by the ternary search tree, and it could actually also determine the lexicographic position of P just to the right of in.

Theorem 7.5 *A search for a pattern $P[1,p]$ in a balanced ternary search tree representing n strings takes $O(p + \log n)$ character comparisons. This is optimal in the comparison-based model.*

7.4   Some Observations on the Two-Level Memory Model$^\infty$

Sorting strings on disk is not nearly as simple as it is in internal memory, and a bunch of sophisticated string-sorting algorithms have been introduced in the literature which achieve I/O-efficiency (see, e.g., [1, 2]). The difficulty is that strings have variable length and their brute-force comparison over the sorting process may induce a lot of I/Os. In the following we will use the notation: n_s is the number of strings shorter than the disk-page size B, whose total length is N_s, and n_l is the number of strings longer than B, whose total length is N_l. Clearly $n = n_s + n_l$ and $N = N_s + N_l$.

The known algorithms can be classified according to the way strings are managed in their sorting process. We can devise three main models of computations [1]:

- Model A: Strings are considered *indivisible* (i.e. they are moved in their entirety and cannot be broken into characters), with the exception that long strings can be divided into blocks of size B.
- Model B: Relaxes the indivisibility assumption of Model A by allowing strings to be divided into single characters, but this may happen *only in internal memory*.
- Model C: Waives the indivisibility assumption by allowing division of strings *in both internal and external memory*.

Model A forces the use of MERGE-based sorters that achieve the following I/O bounds, which can be proved to be optimal:

Theorem 7.6 *In Model A, string sorting takes $\Theta\left(\frac{N_s}{B}\log_{M/B}\frac{N_s}{B} + n_l\log_{M/B} n_l + \frac{N_s+N_l}{B}\right)$ I/Os.*

The first term in the bound is the cost of sorting the short strings, the second term is the cost of sorting the long strings, and the final term accounts for the cost of reading the whole input. The result shows that sorting short strings is as difficult as sorting their individual characters, which are N_s, while sorting long strings is as difficult as sorting their first B characters. The lower bound for small strings in Theorem 7.6 is proved by extending the technique used in Chapter 5 and considering the special case where all n_s small strings have the same length N_s/n_s. The lower bound for the long strings is proved by considering the n_l small strings obtained by looking at their first B characters. The upper bounds in Theorem 7.6 are obtained by using a special multiway MERGESORT that takes advantage of a *lazy trie* stored in internal memory to guide the merge passes among the strings.

Model B presents a more complex situation, and leads to long and short strings being handled separately.

Theorem 7.7 *In Model B, sorting short strings takes* $O\left(\min\left\{n_s \log_M n_s, \frac{N_s}{B}\right.\right.$ $\left.\left.\log_{M/B}\frac{N_s}{B}\right\}\right)$ *I/Os, whereas sorting long strings takes* $\Theta\left(n_l \log_M n_l + \frac{N_l}{B}\right)$ *I/Os.*

The bound for long strings is optimal, whereas the bound for short strings is not known to be optimal. Comparing the optimal bound for long strings with the corresponding bound in Theorem 7.6, we note that they differ in terms of the base of the logarithm: the base is M rather than M/B. This shows that breaking up long strings in internal memory is provably helpful for external string sorting. The upper bound is obtained by combining the String B-tree data structure (described in Chapter 9) with a proper buffering technique. As far as short strings are concerned, we note that the I/O bound is the same as the cost of sorting all the characters in the strings when the average length N_s/n_s is $O\left(\frac{B}{\log_{M/B} M}\right)$. For the (in practice) narrow range $\frac{B}{\log_{M/B} M} < \frac{N_s}{n_s} < B$, the cost of sorting short strings becomes $O(n_s \log_M n_s)$. In this range, the sorting complexity for Model B is lower than the one for Model A, which shows that breaking up short strings in internal memory is provably helpful.

Surprisingly enough, the best deterministic algorithm for Model C is derived from the one designed for Model B. However, since Model C allows the splitting of strings on disk too, we can use randomization and hashing. The main idea is to shrink strings by hashing some of their pieces. Since hashing does not preserve the lexicographic order, these algorithms must orchestrate the selection of the string pieces to be hashed with a carefully designed sorting process so that the correct sorted order may be eventually computed. In [2] the following result was proved (which can be extended to the more powerful cache-oblivious model too):

Theorem 7.8 *In Model C, the string-sorting problem can be solved by a randomized algorithm using* $O\left(\frac{n}{B}\left(\log_{M/B}\frac{n}{M}\right)\left(\log\frac{N}{n}\right) + \frac{N}{B}\right)$ *I/Os, with arbitrarily high probability.*

References

[1] Lars Arge, Paolo Ferragina, Roberto Grossi, and Jeff S. Vitter. On sorting strings in external memory. In *Proceedings of the 29th ACM Symposium on Theory of Computing (STOC)*, pp. 540–8, 1997.

[2] Rolf Fagerberg, Anna Pagh, and Rasmus Pagh. External string sorting: Faster and cache-oblivious. In *Proceedings of the 23rd Symposium on Theoretical Aspects of Computer Science (STACS)*, Lecture Notes in Computer Science 3884, Springer, 68–79, 2006.

[3] Tomas H. Cormen, Charles E. Leiserson, Ron L. Rivest, and Cliff Stein. *Introduction to Algorithms*. The MIT Press, third edition, 2009.

[4] Robert Sedgewick and Jon L. Bentley. Fast algorithms for sorting and searching strings. *Proceedings of the 8th Annual ACM-SIAM Symposium on Discrete Algorithms (SODA)*, 360–9, 1997.

8 The Dictionary Problem

Impossible is a word to be found only in the
dictionary of fools.
Attributed to Napoleone Bonaparte

In this chapter we present *randomized* and simple, yet smart, data structures that solve
efficiently the classic *dictionary problem*, formally defined in the following box. These
solutions will allow us to propose algorithmic fixes for some issues that are typically
left untouched or only addressed via "hand waving" in basic courses on algorithms.

> **Problem.** Let $\mathcal{D}$ be a set of n objects, called the *dictionary*, uniquely identified
> by keys drawn from a *universe* U. The dictionary problem consists of designing
> a data structure that efficiently supports the following three basic operations:
>
> - Search(k) : Check whether $\mathcal{D}$ contains an object x with key $k = \text{key}[x]$,
>   and then return true or false, accordingly. In some cases, the goal is to
>   return the object associated with this key, if any, otherwise return null.
> - Insert(x) : Insert in $\mathcal{D}$ the object x indexed by the key $k = \text{key}[x]$. Typ-
>   ically it is assumed that no object in $\mathcal{D}$ has key k before the insertion takes
>   place; a condition that may be easily checked by executing a preliminary query
>   Search(k).
> - Delete(k) : Delete from $\mathcal{D}$ the object indexed by the key k, if any.

In the case that all three operations have to be supported, the problem and the corresponding data structure that solves it are termed *dynamic*; otherwise, if only the query
operation has to be supported, they are termed *static*.

Note that in several applications the structure of an object x typically consists of a
pair $\langle k, d \rangle$, where $k \in U$ is the key indexing x in $\mathcal{D}$, and d is the so-called *satellite data*
featuring x. For the sake of presentation, in the rest of this chapter, we will drop the
satellite data and the notation $\mathcal{D}$ in favor of just the key set $S \subseteq U$, which consists of all
keys indexing objects in $\mathcal{D}$. In this way, we will simplify the discussion by considering
dictionary search and update operations only on those keys rather than on (whole)
objects. But when the context requires satellite data as well, we will again talk about
objects and their implementing pairs. Moreover, without any loss of generality, since
keys are represented in our computers as binary strings, we will set $U = \{0, 1, 2, ...\}$
as the universe of nonnegative integers. See Figure 8.1 for a graphical representation.

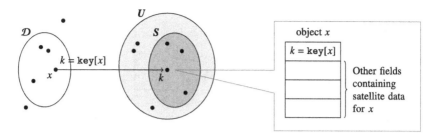

Figure 8.1 Illustrative example for a dictionary $\mathcal{D}$ of objects (left) and their keys $k = \texttt{key}[x]$ forming a subset S of a large universe U (middle), and a rectangle (right) illustrating graphically the satellite data featuring the object x.

In the following sections, we will analyze three main data structures: direct-address tables (or arrays), hash tables (and some of their sophisticated variants), and the Bloom filter. Direct-access tables are introduced for teaching purposes, because the dictionary problem can often be solved very efficiently without resorting to complicated data structures. The subsequent discussion on hash tables will allow us, first, to fix some issues concerning the design of a *good* hash function (typically sketched in basic algorithms courses) and then to design the so-called *perfect* hash tables, which address *optimally and in the worst case* the static dictionary problem; we will lastly move to the elegant cuckoo hash tables, which manage dictionary updates efficiently, still guaranteeing constant query time in the worst case. The chapter concludes with the Bloom filter, one of the most used data structures in the context of large dictionaries and Web/networking applications. Its surprising feature is that it guarantees query and update operations up to constant time, and, more surprisingly, its space requirements depend on the number of keys n, but not on their lengths. The reason for this impressive "compression" is that only a *fingerprint* of a few bits for each key is stored; the incurred limitation is a *one-sided error* when executing $\texttt{Search}(k)$: namely, the data structure answers in a correct way when $k \in S$, but it may answer incorrectly if k is not in the dictionary (a so-called *false positive*). Despite that, we will show that the probability of this error can be mathematically bounded by a function that exponentially decreases with the space m reserved for the Bloom filter or, equivalently, with the number of bits allocated per each key (i.e. its fingerprint). The nice aspect of this formula is that it is enough to take m to be a constant factor slightly more than n and reach a negligible probability of error. This makes the Bloom filter very appealing in several interesting applications: crawlers of search engines, storage systems, P2P systems and so on.

8.1   Direct-Address Tables

The simplest data structure to support all dictionary operations is the one based on a binary table T, of size $u = |U|$ bits. There is a one-to-one mapping between keys and table entries, so entry $T[k]$ is set to 1 if and only if the key $k \in S$. If some satellite data for k has to be stored, then T is implemented as a table of pointers to these satellite data. In this case we have that $T[k] \neq \texttt{NULL}$ if and only if $k \in S$ and $T[k]$ points to the memory location where the satellite data for k is stored.

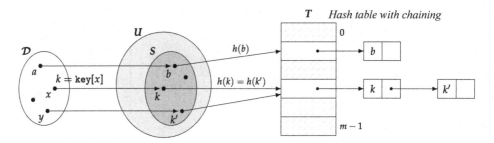

Figure 8.2 Hash table with chaining.

It is quite straightforward to implement dictionary operations upon T in constant (optimal) time in the worst case. The main issue with this solution is that the table's occupancy depends on the universe size u; so if $n = \Theta(u)$, then the approach is optimal. But if the dictionary is small compared to the universe, the approach wastes a lot of space an becomes unacceptable. Take the case of a university which stores the data of its students indexed by their IDs: there could be millions of students, and if the IDs are encoded with integers (e.g., 4 bytes) then the universe size is 2^{32}, and thus of the order of billions. Smarter solutions have therefore been designed to reduce the sparseness of the table with respect to the universe size, still guaranteeing the efficiency of the dictionary operations: among all proposals, hash tables and their many variations provide an excellent choice.

8.2   Hash Tables

The simplest data structures for implementing a dictionary are arrays and lists. Arrays offer constant-time access to their entries, but linear-time updates; lists offer the opposite: linear-time access to their elements, but constant-time updates whenever the position where they have to occur is given. Hash tables combine the best of these two approaches. Their simplest implementation is *hashing with chaining*, which consists of an *array of lists*. The array T of size m points to lists of dictionary objects, or keys, as in our simplified assumption of the previous section. The mapping of keys to array entries is implemented via a *hash function* $h \colon U \to \{0, 1, 2 \ldots, m-1\}$, so that a key k is mapped to the list pointed to by $T[h(k)]$. Figure 8.2 shows a graphical example of a hash table with chaining.

Forget for a moment the implementation of the function h, and just assume that its computation takes constant time. We will dedicate to this issue a significant part of this chapter, because the overall efficiency of the proposed scheme strongly depends on the efficiency and efficacy of h to distribute items evenly among the table entries.

Given a good hash function, dictionary operations are easy to implement over the hash table because they are just turned into operations on the array T and on the lists that are linked to its entries. Searching for a key k (and its associated object) boils down to searching this key in the list $T[h(k)]$. Inserting an object with key k consists of appending it at the front of the list pointed to by $T[h(k)]$. Deleting an object with key k consists of first searching for k in the list $T[h(k)]$, and then removing it. The running time of dictionary operations is constant for `Insert`, provided that the computation of $h(k)$ takes constant time, and it is linear in the length of the list pointed to by $T[h(k)]$ for both the `Search` and `Delete` operations. Therefore, the efficiency of hashing with chaining depends on the ability of the hash function h to *evenly distribute* the dictionary keys among the m entries of table T; the more evenly distributed they are, the shorter the list to scan. The worst situation is when all dictionary keys are hashed to the same entry of T, thus creating a list of length n. In this case, the hash table boils down to a single linked list, so that the cost of searching is $\Theta(n)$.

This is the reason why we are interested in *good* hash functions, namely ones that distribute keys among table entries uniformly at random (aka *simple uniform hashing* [6]). This means that, for such hash functions, every key $k \in S$ is *equally likely* to be hashed to any of the m slots in T, *independently* of where the other dictionary keys are hashed. If h guarantees this strong property, then the following result can be easily proved.

Theorem 8.1 *Under the hypothesis of simple uniform hashing, there exists a hash table with chaining, of size m, in which the operation* `Search(k)` *over a dictionary of n objects takes* $\Theta(1 + n/m)$ *expected time. The value* $\alpha = n/m$ *is often called the* load factor *of the hash table.*

Proof In the case of an unsuccessful search (i.e. $k \notin S$), the time for executing `Search(k)` equals the time to perform a full scan of the list $T[h(k)]$, and thus it equals its length. Given the uniform distribution of the dictionary keys induced by the hash function h, the expected length of a generic list $T[i]$ is $\sum_{k \in S} \mathcal{P}(h(k) = i) = |S| \times \frac{1}{m} = n/m = \alpha$. We add "plus 1" in the time complexity because of the constant-time computation of $h(k)$.

In the case of a successful search (i.e. $k \in S$), the proof is less straightforward. Assume k is the j-th key inserted in the dictionary S, and let the insertion be executed at the tail of the list $\mathcal{L}(k) = T[h(k)]$: we need just one additional pointer per list to keep track of it. The number of elements examined during `Search(k)` equals the number of items that were present in $\mathcal{L}(k)$ plus k itself. Now, the expected length of $\mathcal{L}(k)$ can be estimated as $(j - 1)/m$ (given that k is the j-th key to be inserted), so the expected time taken by a successful search is

$$\frac{1}{n} \sum_{j=1}^{n} \left(1 + \frac{j-1}{m}\right) = 1 + \frac{\alpha}{2} - \frac{1}{2m}.$$

And this can be rewritten as $O\left(1 + \frac{\alpha}{2} - \frac{1}{2m}\right) = O(1 + \alpha)$. ∎

It is fairly easy to estimate the space taken by the hash table by observing that each list pointer takes $\Theta(\log n)$ bits, because it has to index one out of n items, and each dictionary key takes $\Theta(\log u)$ bits, because it is drawn from a universe U of size u. It is interesting to note that the key storage can dominate the overall space occupancy of the table as the universe size increases (think, e.g., of URLs as keys, which require on average hundreds of bytes to be represented). This subtle observation will motivate the discussion of the design of Bloom filters in Section 8.7.

Corollary 8.1 *Hash table with chaining occupies* $O((m + n) \log_2 n + n \log_2 u)$ *bits. Constants hidden in the big-O notation are very small and close to 1.*

It is evident that if the dictionary size n is known, the table can be designed to consist of $m = \Theta(n)$ cells (hence, $\alpha = \Theta(1)$), and thus obtain an expected constant-time performance for all dictionary operations. If n is unknown, one can *resize* the table whenever the dictionary gets too small (many deletions), or too large (many insertions). The idea is to start with a table size $m = 2n_0$, where n_0 is the initial number of dictionary keys. Then, we keep track of the current number n of dictionary keys present in S (and thus in the table T). If the dictionary gets too small, that is, $n < n_0/2$, then we halve the table size m and rebuild T; if the dictionary gets too large, that is, $n > 2n_0$, then we double the table size m and rebuild T. Table *rebuilding* consists of inserting the current dictionary keys in the new table of proper size m, and drop the old one.

This scheme guarantees that, at any time, the dictionary size n is proportional to the table size m: more precisely, $n_0/2 = m/4 \leq n \leq m = 2n_0$. This implies that $\alpha = m/n = \Theta(1)$. Since insertion takes $O(1)$ time per key, and the rebuilding affects n items to be deleted from the current table and then inserted in the resized table, the total rebuilding cost is $\Theta(n)$. But this cost is paid at least every $n_0/2 = \Theta(n)$ operations, the worst case being the one in which these operations consist of all insertions or all deletions between consecutive table reconstructions. So the $\Theta(n)$ rebuilding cost can be *amortized* over the $\Omega(n)$ operations forming this update sequence, thus adding a $O(1)$ *amortized cost* at the actual cost of each update operation. Overall this means that:

Corollary 8.2 *Under the hypothesis of simple uniform hashing, there exists a dynamic hash table with chaining that takes expected constant time for the search operation, expected amortized constant time for the insert and delete operations, and uses $O(n)$ space.*

8.2.1 How Do We Design a "Good" Hash Function?

Simple uniform hashing is difficult to guarantee from a computational point of view, because one rarely knows the probability distribution according to which the dictionary keys are drawn and, in addition, it could be the case that they are not even drawn independently of each other. Since h maps keys from a universe of size u to an integer range of size m, it induces a partition of those keys in m subsets $U_i = \{k \in U : h(k) = i\}$. By the *pigeonhole principle* there does exist at least one of these subsets whose size is larger than the average load factor u/m. Now, if we reasonably assume that the universe is sufficiently large to guarantee that $u/m \geq n$, then an adversary could choose the dictionary S as that subset U_i of keys such that $|U_i| \geq u/m$, and thus force the hash table to offer its worst behavior, by boiling down to a single linked list of length n.

This argument is independent of the hash function h, so we can conclude that no hash function is robust enough to *always* guarantee a "good" behavior. In practice, heuristics are used to create hash functions that perform well *sufficiently often*: the design principle is to compute the hash value in a way that it is expected to be independent of any regular pattern that might exist among the dictionary keys. The two most simple and famous hashing schemes are based on division and multiplication (for more details we refer the reader to any classic text on algorithms, such as [6]):

- **Hashing by division:** The hash value is computed as the remainder of the division of the key k by the table size m, that is, $h(k) = k \bmod m$. This is quite fast and behaves well as long as $h(k)$ depends on most of k's bits. So power-of-two values for m should be avoided, whereas prime numbers not too close to a power of two should be chosen. For the selection of large prime numbers there are both simple, but slow (exponential in time) algorithms (such as the famous sieve of Eratosthenes method), and fast algorithms based on some (randomized or deterministic) *primality test*.[1] In general, the cost of prime selection is negligible in relation to the cost of building the hash table.

- **Hashing by multiplication:** The hash value is computed in two steps: first, the key k is multiplied by a constant A, with $0 < A < 1$; then, the fractional part of kA is multiplied by m and the integral part of the result is taken as the index for the hash table T. An advantage of this method is that the choice of m is not critical, and indeed it is usually set as a power of 2, thus simplifying the multiplication step. For the value of A, it is often suggested to take $A = (\sqrt{5} - 1)/2 \cong 0.618$.

It goes without saying that none of these practical hashing schemes guarantees a "good" mapping behavior: it is always possible to select a dictionary of keys that makes the hash table boil down to a single linked list; for example, just take integer keys that are multiples of m to disrupt the hashing-by-division method. In the next section, we propose a hashing scheme that is robust enough to guarantee a "good" behavior in expectation, whatever is the input dictionary.

8.3 Universal Hashing

Let us first demonstrate, using a counting argument, why the uniformity property we required for *good* hash functions is computationally hard to guarantee. Recall that we are interested in hash functions that map keys in U to integers in $\{0, 1, ..., m - 1\}$. The

---

[1] The most famous, and randomized, primality test is the one by Miller and Rabin; more recently, a deterministic test has been proposed which allows to prove that this problem is solvable in (deterministic) polynomial time. See http://en.wikipedia.org/wiki/Prime_number.

total number of such hash functions is m^u, given that each key among the $u = |U|$ ones can be mapped into any one of the m slots of the hash table. In order to guarantee a uniform distribution of the keys and independence among them, our hash function should be any one of these mappings. But, in this case, its representation would need $\Omega(\log_2 m^u) = \Omega(u \log m)$ bits, which is really too much in terms of space occupancy and computing time: take the case of a computer with a memory word of 64 bits, so that $u = 2^{64}$; we would need a space of the order of zettabytes for storing the encoding of the hash function.

Practical hash functions, on the other hand, suffer from several weaknesses, some of which have already been mentioned. In this section we introduce the powerful universal hashing paradigm, which overcomes these drawbacks by means of a proper design of the *class* of possible hash functions and the use of *randomization* to select one of them, thus proceeding similarly to how we make the pivot selection in the QUICKSORT procedure more robust (see Chapter 5). There, instead of taking the pivot from a fixed position, it was chosen *uniformly at random* from the underlying array to be sorted. This way no input was *in principle* bad for the pivot selection strategy because, this selection being randomized, it allowed the risk to be spread over the many pivot choices, thus guaranteeing that most of them would lead to a well-balanced partitioning.

Universal hashing mimics this algorithmic approach in the context of hash functions. Informally, we do not set the hash function in advance (cf. fix the pivot position), but we will choose the hash function *uniformly at random* from a *properly defined* set of hash functions (cf. random pivot selection) which is defined in a way that makes it very likely to select a good hash for the current input set of keys S (cf. the partitioning is balanced). A good hash function is one that can be computed in constant time and minimizes the number of *collisions* among pairs of dictionary keys. Because of the randomization, even if S is fixed, the algorithm will behave differently on various executions, but the nice property of universal hashing be that, on average, the performance will be the expected one. It is now time to formalize these ideas.

Definition 8.1 Let $\mathcal{H}$ be a finite collection of hash functions that map a given universe U of keys into integers in $\{0, 1, ..., m-1\}$. $\mathcal{H}$ is said to be a *universal class* of hash functions if, and only if, for any fixed pair of distinct keys $x, y \in U$ it is

$$|\{h \in \mathcal{H} : h(x) = h(y)\}| \leq \frac{|\mathcal{H}|}{m}.$$

In other words, the class $\mathcal{H}$ is defined in such a way that a randomly chosen hash function h from this set has a chance no more than $1/m$ of making the two fixed distinct keys x and y collide.[2] This is exactly the basic property that we deployed when designing hashing with chaining (see the proof of Theorem 8.1). And indeed, in Theorem 8.2, we will show that Theorem 8.1 and its Corollaries 8.1–8.2 can be rephrased by substituting the *ideal* simple uniform hashing with the *effective* universal

---

[2] This notion can be extended with some slackness $c \geq 1$ into the guarantee of a probability of collision upper bounded by c/m, thus giving rise to the so-called c-universal hashing.

hashing. Effective because, in Section 8.3.1, we will provide a real universal hash class, which will make concrete all these mathematical ruminations.

Theorem 8.2 *Let $T[0, m-1]$ be a hash table with chaining, and suppose that the hash function h is selected uniformly at random from a universal class $\mathcal{H}$. The expected length of the lists in T, whichever is the input dictionary of keys S, is still no more than $1 + \alpha$, where α is the load factor of T.*

Proof We note that the expectation here is over the choices of h in $\mathcal{H}$, and it does not depend on the distribution of the keys in S. For each pair of keys $x, y \in S$, define the indicator random variable I_{xy}, which is 1 if these two keys collide according to a given $h \in \mathcal{H}$, namely $h(x) = h(y)$; otherwise it takes the value 0. By definition of universal class, given the random choice of $h \in \mathcal{H}$, $\mathcal{P}(I_{xy} = 1) = \mathcal{P}(h(x) = h(y)) \leq 1/m$. Therefore we have $E[I_{xy}] = 1 \times \mathcal{P}(I_{xy} = 1) + 0 \times \mathcal{P}(I_{xy} = 0) = \mathcal{P}(I_{xy} = 1) \leq 1/m$, where the expectation is computed over h's random choices.

Now we define, for each key $x \in S$, the random variable N_x that counts the number of keys other than x that hash to the entry $T[h(x)]$, and thus collide with x. We can write $N_x = \sum_{y \in S, y \neq x} I_{xy}$. By linearity of expectation, the expected length of the list pointed to by $T[h(x)]$ is $E[N_x] = \sum_{y \in S, y \neq x} E[I_{xy}] = (n-1)/m < \alpha$. By adding 1, because of x, the theorem follows. ∎

Note that the time bounds given for hashing with chaining are in expectation, so there could be some lists which might be very long, possibly containing up to $\Theta(n)$ items. This satisfies Theorem 8.2, but is of course not a nice situation because the distribution of the searches might privilege keys that belong to these very long lists, thus taking significantly more than the "expected" time bound. In order to circumvent this problem, one should also guarantee a small upper bound on the length of the *longest list* in T; this is what the Theorem 8.3 proves.

Theorem 8.3 *Let $T[0, n-1]$ be a hash table with chaining indexed by a hash function taken uniformly at random from a universal class $\mathcal{H}$. Assume that we insert in T a dictionary S of n keys; the length of the longest list in T is $O\left(\frac{\log n}{\log \log n}\right)$ with high probability, namely at least $1 - \frac{1}{n}$.*

Proof Let h be a hash function selected uniformly at random from $\mathcal{H}$, and let $Q(k)$ be the probability that exactly k keys of S are hashed by h to a particular slot of the table T. Given the universality of h, the probability that a key is assigned to a fixed slot is bounded above by $1/n$, and the expected number of keys per slot is thus 1.

Let X_j be the random variable denoting the number of keys mapped to slot j, for $j = 0, 1, \ldots, n-1$. There are $\binom{n}{k}$ ways to choose k keys from dictionary S, so the probability that a slot gets at least k keys is bounded above by

$$Q(k) = \binom{n}{k}\left(\frac{1}{n}\right)^k \leq \left(\frac{ne}{k}\right)^k \left(\frac{1}{n}\right)^k \leq \left(\frac{e}{k}\right)^k,$$

where we use the well-known upper bound for the binomial coefficient: $\binom{n}{k} \leq (ne/k)^k$.

Since $Q(k)$ is decreasing for $k > e$, we aim at finding a value k_0 such that $Q(k) \leq 1/n^2$ for $k \geq k_0$. We will show that such a value is $k_0 = \frac{c \ln n}{\ln \ln n}$, where c is some constant such that $c \geq 4$. In fact, it is enough to notice that $Q(k) \leq 1/n^2$ iff $(e/k)^k \leq 1/n^2$ iff $(k/e)^k \geq n^2$, and then by applying the logarithm to both sides, we get $k \ln(k/e) \geq \ln n^2$. We find that this inequality holds for k_0, by simple algebraic manipulations.

Finally, we conclude that the theorem's statement holds because we can use the union bound over the n slots of T, and thus show that the probability that any slot gets more than k_0 keys is at most $n \, Q(k_0) \leq n \, (1/n^2) = 1/n$.   ∎

Two observations are in order at this point. First, the bound on the maximum length of a list in T is *with high probability*, but it can be turned into a *worst-case bound* via a simple argument applied to the construction of T. We start by selecting uniformly at random a hash function $h \in \mathcal{H}$; we hash every dictionary key of S into T, and then check whether the condition on the length of the longest list is at most $2 \log n / \log \log n$. If so, we use T for the subsequent search operations, otherwise we resample $h \in \mathcal{H}$ and reinsert all dictionary keys in T. A constant number of trials suffice to satisfy that bound,[3] thus guaranteeing $O(n)$ construction time in expectation and $O(\log n / \log \log n)$ search time in the worst case.

The second observation is that this result can be further improved by using two or more, say d, hash functions h_i and a hash table T in which the slots are buckets holding all dictionary keys hashed to that slot. The speciality of this scheme resides in the way the d hash functions are deployed to fill the table's buckets. Operation `Insert(k)` tests the loading of the d slots $T[h_i(k)]$, and then inserts k in the least filled one. In the case of a tie in the loading of slots, the algorithm chooses $T[h_1(k)]$. Operation `Search(k)` searches all d lists $T[h_i(k)]$, since, if k exists, we cannot know how loaded each slot was at insertion time. For its algorithmic structure this scheme is also known as *d-choice hashing*. The time cost for `Insert(k)` is $O(d)$, whereas the time cost of `Search(k)` is given by the total length of the d searched lists. We can upper bound this length by d times the length of the longest list in T which, surprisingly, has been proved to be $\frac{\log \log n}{\log d} + O(1)$ for $d \geq 2$ (see [5] for details). The literature offers several variants of this idea, one of the most famous and effective being *d-left hashing*. Here d tables of size m/d are used; each of them being indexed by one distinct hash function, ties are managed by inserting the key into the leftmost table.

It is interesting to note that two-choice hashing is preferable to any other d-choice hashing with $d > 2$, because it achieves $O(\log \log n)$ for the length of the longest list in T, and this bound cannot be improved asymptotically whatever constant d is taken but, in turn, a larger d slows down the search operations by a factor d. Moreover, if we compare the bound of two-choice hashing with the bound obtained for the classic case of hashing with chaining (here $d = 1$) in Theorem 8.3, we notice that two-choice hashing achieves an exponential improvement just by using one more hash function. This surprising result is also known in the literature as *the power of two choices*,

---

3 We just use the Markov bound (see https://en.wikipedia.org/wiki/Markov%27s_inequality) to state that the longest list longer than twice the average may occur with probability $\leq 1/2$.

precisely because choosing the least full slot between two randomly selected ones allows the length of the longest list in T to be reduced exponentially.

As a corollary, we note that this result can be used to design a hash table that saves the space of pointers and increases the locality of reference in the search and update operations (hence less cache/IO misses). The idea is to use two-choice hashing over a table of *small and fixed-size* buckets. If we set the bucket size to $\gamma \log \log n$, for some small constant $\gamma > 1$, we will ensure *with high probability* that (i) no buckets will undergo any overflows and (ii) just two cache misses will be taken by any search and update operation.

8.3.1   Do Universal Hash Functions Exist?

The answer to this question is positive and, surprisingly enough, universal hash functions can be easily constructed, as we will show in this section by providing three concrete examples. We assume, without loss of generality, that the table size m is a prime number and keys are integers represented as bit strings of $\log_2 |U|$ bits.[4] We let $r = \frac{\log_2 |U|}{\log_2 m}$ and assume that this is an integer. We decompose each key k into r parts of $\log_2 m$ bits each, so $k = [k_0, k_1, ... k_{r-1}]$. Clearly, each part k_i is an integer smaller than m, because it is represented in $\log_2 m$ bits. We do the same for a generic integer $a = [a_0, a_1, ..., a_{r-1}] \in [1, |U| - 1]$ used as the parameter that defines the universal class of hash functions $\mathcal{H}$ as follows: $h_a(k) = \sum_{i=0}^{r-1} a_i k_i \bmod m$. The size of $\mathcal{H}$ is $|U| - 1$, because we have one function per value of $a > 0$.

Theorem 8.4 *An example of a universal class is the set of hash functions having the form: $h_a(k) = \sum_{i=0}^{r-1} a_i k_i \bmod m$, where m is prime and a is a positive integer smaller than $|U| = m^r$.*

Proof Suppose that x and y are two distinct keys which differ by at least one bit. For simplicity of exposition, we assume that a differing bit falls into their most significant block of $(\log m)$-bits, that is, $x_0 \neq y_0$. According to Definition 8.1, we need to count how many hash functions of the form $h_a(k) = \sum_{i=0}^{r-1} a_i k_i \bmod m$ make these two keys collide; or equivalently, how many $a > 0$ exist for which $h_a(x) = h_a(y)$. Since $x_0 \neq y_0$, and we operate in arithmetic modulo a prime m, the multiplicative inverse of $(x_0 - y_0)$ must exist and be an integer in the range $[1, |U| - 1]$. By abusing a little bit of the notation, we will denote this inverse by $(x_0 - y_0)^{-1}$. So we can write

$$h_a(x) = h_a(y) \Leftrightarrow \sum_{i=0}^{r-1} a_i x_i \equiv \sum_{i=0}^{r-1} a_i y_i \quad \bmod m$$

$$\Leftrightarrow a_0(x_0 - y_0) \equiv -\sum_{i=1}^{r-1} a_i(x_i - y_i) \quad \bmod m$$

$$\Leftrightarrow a_0 \equiv \left(-\sum_{i=1}^{r-1} a_i(x_i - y_i) \right) (x_0 - y_0)^{-1} \quad \bmod m.$$

---

[4] This is possible by pre-padding the key with 0, thus preserving its value.

The final equation actually shows that, whatever the choice for $[a_1, a_2, ..., a_{r-1}]$ (and they are $m^{r-1} - 1$, since we are excluding the null configuration), there exists only one choice for $a_0 \neq 0$ (the one specified in the last line above) that causes x and y to collide. So there are $m^{r-1} - 1$ choices for a that make $x \neq y$ collide, and this number can be written as $m^{r-1} - 1 = (m^r/m) - 1 = (|U|/m) - 1 \leq (|U| - 1)/m = |\mathcal{H}|/m$. So Definition 8.1 of universal hash class for $\mathcal{H}$ is satisfied.   ∎

It is possible to adjust the previous definition in order to hold for any table size m, thus not only for prime values. The key idea is to make a *nested modular computation* by means of a large prime $p > |U|$, and a generic integer $m \ll |U|$ equal to the size of the hash table we wish to set up. We can then define a hash function parametrized by two integer values $a \neq 0$ and $b \geq 0$: $h_{a,b}(k) = ((ak + b) \bmod p) \bmod m$, and then define the set $\mathcal{H}_{p,m} = \bigcup_{a>0,b\geq0}\{h_{a,b}\}$, which can be shown to be universal.

These two examples of universal classes of hash functions require modulo operations over arbitrary integers. There are indeed other universal hash classes that are faster to compute because they rely on modulo operations involving only power-of-two integers, which can be easily implemented via fast register shifts. An interesting and effective example is provided by the *multiply-add-shift scheme* (see [7, 12]). It assumes that $|U| = 2^w$, and takes a table size $m = 2^\ell < |U|$. Then it defines the class $\mathcal{H}_{w,\ell}$ as containing hash functions of the form: $h_{a,b}(k) = (ak + b \bmod 2^w) \operatorname{div} 2^{w-\ell}$, where a is an odd integer smaller than $|U|$ and $b \geq 0$. Note that $h_{a,b}(k)$ selects first the least significant w bits (because of the modulo operation by 2^w), and then selects their most significant ℓ bits (because of the division operation by $2^{w-\ell}$). In some sense, these ℓ bits fall in the "middle" of the integer $(ak+b)$ and correspond to a nonnegative integer that is smaller than $2^\ell (= m)$. It can be proved that the class $\mathcal{H}_{w,\ell}$ is universal, and can be efficiently implemented by avoiding any modulo operation, via register shifts over memory words of $2w$ bits.

8.4   A Simple (Static) Perfect Hash Table

When dealing with hash tables we are usually led to think that they are very efficient in practice but, in theory, their bounds are *in expectation* and depend on the properties of the underlying universal class of hash functions and/or on the distribution of the dictionary keys. This is a false belief, because nowadays there are many hash-table designs that are elegant, simple to implement, and ensure very efficient performance in the worst case for the query and update operations. The design of such effective hash functions will be the subject of the rest of this chapter; this makes such hashing schemes the right choice whenever the search operation is a *lookup*, that is, when we need to assess whether a key in the dictionary S exists or not.

Let us start from the case of a static dictionary S whose keys do not undergo any insertion and deletion operations, and introduce the following key definition.

Definition 8.2 A hash function $h: U \to \{0, 1, \ldots, m - 1\}$ is said to be *perfect* with respect to a dictionary S of n keys if, and only if, for any pair of distinct keys $k', k'' \in S$, it is $h(k') \neq h(k'')$.

A simple counting argument shows that we need $m \geq n$ in order to make perfect hashing possible. In the case that $m = n$, that is, the minimum possible value, the perfect hash function is termed *minimal* (in short, MPHF). A hash table T using an MPHF h guarantees $O(1)$ worst-case search time as well as no waste of storage space, because it has the size of the dictionary S and keys can be directly stored in the table slots. Perfect hashing is thus a sort of "perfect" variant of direct-address tables (see Section 8.1), in the sense that it achieves constant search time (like those tables), but optimal linear space in the size of S (unlike those tables).

A (minimal) perfect hash function is said to be *order preserving* (for short, OP(MP)HF) if and only if, $\forall k' < k'' \in S$, $h(k') < h(k'')$. Clearly, if h is also minimal, and thus $m = n$, then $h(k)$ returns the rank of the key in the ordered dictionary S. It goes without saying that the property OPMPHF strictly depends on the dictionary S upon which h has been built: by changing S we could destroy this property, so it is difficult, to maintain this property under a dynamic scenario.

In the rest of this section we will confine ourselves to the case of *static* dictionaries, and thus a fixed S. Then in Section 8.5 we extend this design to the case of a dynamic dictionary, and finally return in Section 8.6 to the case of a static dictionary by presenting the design of a perfect, static, minimal, and order-preserving hashing scheme.

The key algorithmic method for designing a static perfect hashing scheme is to use a two-level approach that deploys a group of tables and universal hash functions: one for the first level and the others for the second level. More precisely, the first level is a hash table T_1 of size $m = n$, and keys are distributed according to a primary-level universal hash function, say $h_1(k) : U \to \{0, 1, \ldots, n-1\}$. In order to manage the keys colliding into a same slot $T_1[j]$, for $j = 0, 1, \ldots, n - 1$, we design a secondary hash table $T_{2,j}$, which is addressed by another universal hash function $h_{2,j}$, which must be perfect for the keys colliding at $T_1[j]$, and thus not eliciting any collisions in $T_{2,j}$. So overall we will have at most $1 + n$ universal hash functions: h_1 for the first level and the n hash functions $h_{2,j}$ for the secondary level. The key mathematical result to prove is that each $h_{2,j}$ can be designed to guarantee that there are no collisions in $T_{2,j}$ and that the overall space occupancy of all secondary-level hash tables is bounded above by $O(n)$. In terms of query efficiency, the search for a key k consists of two table lookups (hence $O(1)$ time in the worst case): one at $T_1[j]$ with $j = h_1(k)$, and one at the table $T_{2,j}$ (pointed to by $T_1[j]$). The pseudocode for the searching operation is provided in Algorithm 8.1.

The following theorem is crucial for defining the size of the secondary hash tables.

Theorem 8.5 *If we store q keys in a hash table of size $s = q^2$ using a universal hash function, then the expected number of collisions among those keys is less than 1/2. Consequently, the probability of having at least one collision in that table is less than 1/2.*

Algorithm 8.1 Procedure `Search(k)` in a perfect hash table T

1: Let h_1 and $h_{2,j}$ be the universal hash functions defining T;
2: $j = h_1(k)$;
3: **if** $T_1[j] = $ NULL **then**
4:      **return** false; $// k \notin S$
5: **end if**
6: $T_{2,j} = T_1[j]$;
7: $i = h_{2,j}(k)$;
8: **if** $T_{2,j}[i] = $ NULL **or** $T_{2,j}[i] \neq k$ **then**
9:      **return** false; $// k \notin S$
10: **end if**
11: **return** true; $// k \in S$

Proof Since the keys are q, there are $\binom{q}{2} < q^2/2$ pairs of them that may collide. If we choose the hash function h uniformly at random from a universal class, then each given pair collides with probability $1/s$ (by Definition 8.1). Thus setting $s = q^2$, the expected number of collisions is bounded above by $\binom{q}{2} \frac{1}{s} < q^2/(2q^2) = \frac{1}{2}$. To prove the second statement of the theorem it is enough to apply Markov's inequality (i.e. $\mathcal{P}(X \geq 2E[X]) \leq 1/2$), over a random variable X that expresses the total number of collisions in the hash table T.   ∎

Let S_j be the dictionary keys mapped to the entry $T[j]$ by the first-level hash function h_1, and define $n_j = |S_j|$. Theorem 8.5 proves that, by setting the size m_j of the hash table T_j equal to $(n_j)^2$ (the square of the number of keys hashed to $T[j]$), the randomly chosen secondary-level universal hash function $h_{2,j}$ is perfect for S_j's keys with nonnegligible probability, for every $j = 0, 1, \ldots, n - 1$. Hence, we can iterate the random selection of $h_{2,j}$ until this property is guaranteed, and Theorem 8.5 actually ensures that, in expectation, two iterations are enough to guarantee this for each entry.

We are left with proving that the total size of the secondary-level hash tables is bounded above by $O(n)$, so that the overall size of this two-level hashing scheme will be $n + O(n) = \Theta(n)$.

Theorem 8.6 *If we store n keys in a hash table of size $m = n$ using a universal hash function, then $E[\sum_{j=0}^{n-1}(n_j)^2] < 2n$, where the expectation is with respect to the random selection of the hash function in its universal class. In terms of the two-level hashing scheme, this means that the expected total size of all secondary-level hash tables $T_{2,j}$ is less than 2n, given that we have set $m_j = (n_j)^2$ for every $j = 0, 1, \ldots, n - 1$.*

Proof Let us consider the following identity: $a^2 = a + 2\binom{a}{2}$, which holds for any positive integer a, and note that $n = \sum_{j=0}^{m-1} n_j$ because every dictionary key is mapped by h_1 to one table entry. We use these two equalities in the following algebraic steps:

Algorithm 8.2 Creating a perfect hash table

1: Choose uniformly at random a hash function $h_1 : U \to \{0, 1, \ldots, n - 1\}$ from a universal class;
2: Initialize $n_j = 0$, $S_j = \emptyset$, for all $j = 0, 1, \ldots, n - 1$;
3: **for** $k \in S$ **do**
4:      Add k to set S_j, where $j = h_1(k)$;
5:      $n_j = n_j + 1$;
6: **end for**
7: $L = \sum_{j=0}^{n-1} (n_j)^2$;
8: **if** $L \geq 2n$ **then**
9:      Repeat the algorithm from Step 1;
10: **end if**
11: **for** $j = 0, 1, \ldots, n - 1$ **do**
12:      Allocate table $T_{2,j}$ of size $m_j = (n_j)^2$;
13:      Choose uniformly at random $h_{2,j} : U \to \{0, 1, \ldots, m_j - 1\}$ from a universal class;
14:      **for** $k \in S_j$ **do**
15:          $i = h_{2,j}(k)$;
16:          **if** $T_{2,j}[i] \neq$ NULL **then**
17:              Destroy $T_{2,j}$ and repeat from Step 12;
18:          **end if**
19:          $T_{2,j}[i] = k$;
20:      **end for**
21: **end for**

$$E\left[\sum_{j=0}^{n-1}(n_j)^2\right] = E\left[\sum_{j=0}^{n-1}\left(n_j + 2\binom{n_j}{2}\right)\right]$$

$$= E\left[\sum_{j=0}^{n-1}n_j\right] + 2E\left[\sum_{j=0}^{n-1}\binom{n_j}{2}\right]$$

$$= n + 2E\left[\sum_{j=0}^{n-1}\binom{n_j}{2}\right].$$

Since one collision involves a pair of keys, the number of collisions occurring in a slot $T[j]$ equals the number of pairs of dictionary keys mapping to $T[j]$, hence it is $\binom{n_j}{2}$. Consequently, the summation in the last equality accounts for the total number of collisions induced by the primary-level hash function h_1. By repeating the argument adopted in the proof of Theorem 8.5 with $q = n$ keys, and $s = n$ as the size of table T_1, the expected value for this total number of collisions is $\binom{n}{2}\frac{1}{n} = \frac{n(n-1)}{2n} < \frac{n}{2}$. Substituting this upper bound to the summation $\sum_{j=0}^{n-1}\binom{n_j}{2}$, we derive the statement of the theorem.   ∎

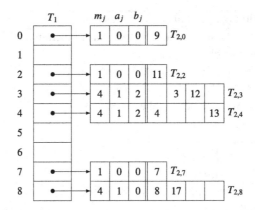

Figure 8.3 A perfect hash table over the dictionary $S = \{3, 4, 7, 8, 9, 11, 12, 13, 17\}$, with universal hash functions having the form $h(k) = (a\,k + b \bmod 19) \bmod s$, where s is the size of the hash table indexed by this hash function. See the text for explanations.

It is important to observe that every secondary-level hash function $h_{2,j}$ is chosen independently of the others, so if it turns out to be not perfect, because it induces some collisions among the n_j keys mapped within $T_{2,j}[0, (n_j)^2 - 1]$, then it can be redrawn from its universal class without influencing the other secondary-level hash functions. The same is true for the primary-level hash function h_1, as we have already observed. Algorithm 8.2 provides the pseudocode for the construction process of this two-level hashing scheme, and Theorems 8.5 and 8.6 ensure that the expected number of redraws is a small constant per hash function, so the overall construction time is $O(n)$, in expectation.

Figure 8.3 shows an example of a two-level hashing scheme for a set S of $n = 9$ integer keys. The example uses universal hash functions with the form $h(k) = (a\,k + b \bmod 19) \bmod s$, where s is the size of the hash table indexed by this hash function. For the primary-level hash table T_1 we set $m = n = 9$, and hash parameters $s = m$, $a = 1$, and $b = 0$; for the secondary-level hash tables $T_{2,j}$ we set $m_j = (n_j)^2$ and show on the left of the figure the three parameters (i.e. $s = m_j, a_j, b_j$) involved in the computation of $h_{2,j}$, and on the right the content of $T_{2,j}[0, m_j - 1]$. In the running example, the condition introduced in Theorem 8.6 for the total size of the secondary-level hash tables is satisfied: in fact, $L = 1 + 1 + 4 + 4 + 1 + 4 = 15 < 2n = 18$.

To search for a key $k = 14$, we follow the pseudocode of Algorithm 8.1, and thus compute $j = h_1(14) = (1 \times 14 + 0 \bmod 19) \bmod 9 = 5$. So we access $T_1[5]$ and find that it is NULL, thus concluding that $14 \notin S$. Let us now assume we search for $k = 13$; we compute $j = h_1(13) = (1 \times 13 + 0 \bmod 19) \bmod 9 = 4$. The entry $T_1[4]$ points to table $T_{2,4}$, and the visited entry is the one at position $h_{2,4}(13) = (1 \times 13 + 2 \bmod 19) \bmod 4 = 3$ that is not NULL: namely, $T_{2,4}[3] = 13$, and thus the algorithm has verified that $13 \in S$. The last case to consider is exemplified by key $k = 18$, which accesses the primary-level hash table at $T_1[0]$, and the secondary-level hash table $T_{2,0}[0] = 9 \neq 18$, so the search algorithm can conclude that $18 \notin S$.

8.5   Cuckoo Hashing

When the dictionary is dynamic a different perfect-hashing scheme has to be devised. Here we describe an efficient and elegant solution called *cuckoo hashing* [10], which achieves expected constant time in updates and worst-case constant time in searches. The only drawback of this approach in its preliminary formulation was that it made use of two hash functions that were $O(\log n)$-independent.[5] However, recent results in the literature have significantly relaxed this requirement to just 2-universal hashing [1], but we stick with the original scheme for its simplicity.

Briefly, cuckoo hashing combines the d-choice hashing of Section 8.3 with the ability to move dictionary keys in a proper way among table entries to avoid their collisions. In its simplest form, cuckoo hashing consists of two hash functions h_1 and h_2 and one table T of size m. Any key k is stored either at $T[h_1(k)]$ or at $T[h_2(k)]$, so searching and deleting operations are trivial: we need to look for k in both those entries and, in the case of a deletion operation, eventually remove it. Inserting a key is a little bit more involved because it can trigger a *cascade* of key moves in the table, and this process is exactly the one that gives the name to this approach, inspired by the behavior of some species of cuckoo which push the other eggs or young out of the nest when they hatch. When inserting a key k, the algorithm looks at positions $h_1(k)$ and $h_2(k)$ in T: if one of them is empty (if both are, $h_1(k)$ is chosen), the key is stored at that position and the insertion process is completed; otherwise, it creates room for k by evicting one of the two keys stored in those two table entries (typically, the key stored in $T[h_1(k)]$ is evicted) and replacing it with k. Then, the evicted key plays the role of k and the insertion process is repeated all over again.

There is a caveat to take into account at this point. If the evicted key, say y, was stored in $T[h_1(k)]$, then $T[h_i(y)] = T[h_1(k)]$ for either $i = 1$ or $i = 2$. This means that, if both positions $T[h_1(y)]$ and $T[h_2(y)]$ are occupied, the key to be evicted at this second step cannot be chosen from the entry that was storing $T[h_1(k)]$, because that key is k, and this would therefore induce a trivial infinite cycle of evictions over this entry between keys k and y. The algorithm therefore is careful to always avoid evicting the previously inserted key. Nevertheless, cycles may arise (e.g. consider the trivial case in which $\{h_1(k), h_2(k)\} = \{h_1(y), h_2(y)\}$), and they can be of arbitrary length, so the algorithm must be careful in defining an *efficient escape condition* which detects this situation, in which case it resamples the two hash functions and rehashes all dictionary keys (similarly to what was done for the perfect hashing of the previous section). The key property, proved in Theorem 8.7, will be that cycles occur with bounded probability, so the $O(n)$ cost of rehashing can be amortized, by charging $O(1)$ time per insertion (as proved in Corollary 8.3).

---

[5] See https://en.wikipedia.org/wiki/K-independent_hashing for a formal yet succinct definition of k-independent hashing. Actually, the universality property we introduced in Section 8.3 may be rephrased as *pairwise independence* or 2-independent hashing, because it holds for pairs of keys, and thus $k = 2$.

Algorithm 8.3 Insert key $k \notin S$ in a dictionary indexed by cuckoo hashing over a table $T[0, m-1]$.

1: **if** $T[h_1(k)] = $ NULL **then**
2:        $T[h_1(k)] = k$; **return**;
3: **end if**
4: **if** $T[h_2(k)] = $ NULL **then**
5:        $T[h_2(k)] = k$; **return**;
6: **end if**
7: $count = 0$;
8: $s = 2$; // *for the inserted key k we use h_1 in Step 10 below*
9: **while** $count < m$ **do**
10:        $d = \{1, 2\} - \{s\}$; // *s is the index of the (source) hash function for k in T*
11:                        // *d is the index of the (destination) hash function for k in T*
12:        $pos = h_d(k)$; // *position in T where k has to be stored*
13:        swap k with $T[pos]$; // *k is the new key to be relocated*
14:        **if** $k = $ NULL **then**
15:                **return**;
16:        **end if**
17:        let s be $h_s(k) = pos$; // *s the (source) hash-function index for k in T*
18:        $count = count + 1$;
19: **end while**
20: rehash the dictionary keys in T by two new hash functions, possibly doubling m;
21: repeat the insertion of k from Step 7.

Algorithm 8.3 gives the pseudocode of the insertion operation, as sketched in the previous paragraph; more compact pseudocodes are possible, but we opt here for a pedantic coding for the sake of teaching purposes. Steps 1–6 check whether at least one of the two candidate table entries for storing k is empty, and in this case the key gets stored therein. Otherwise it starts a while-loop which codes the cascading of evictions described in the previous paragraph. The loop stops either if an empty table entry is met (Steps 14–16), or if it has executed more than m steps (meaning that we ended up in an infinite loop). The coding trick is in Step 10, which ensures that the evicted key is moved to the table entry pointed to by $h_s(k) \rightarrow h_d(k)$, which we will model as a directed edge of a suitably constructed graph (see Figure 8.4).

In fact, in order to analyze this situation it is useful to introduce the *cuckoo graph*, whose nodes are entries of the table T and whose edges are associated to dictionary

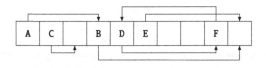

Figure 8.4 Graph-based representation of cuckoo hashing.

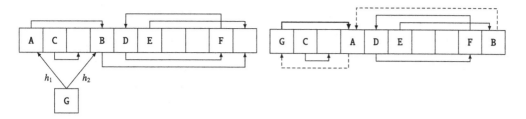

Figure 8.5 Inserting the key G: (left) the two entry options, (right) the final configuration for the table. Note that the edges associated with the moved keys, namely A and B, are dashed and swapped in order to reflect the final positions of these two keys.

keys and connect the two table entries where a key could be stored by the two universal hash functions h_1 and h_2. Edges are directed to keep account of where a key is stored (source), and where a key could be alternatively stored (destination). Figure 8.4 depicts a cuckoo graph for a table of 10 entries, and storing 6 keys, namely {A, B, C, D, E, F}.

The directed edges provide a simple way to identify the sequence of table entries (i.e. path of nodes) traversed by a cascade of evictions triggered by a key k and starting from either entry (node) $T[h_1(k)]$ or $T[h_2(k)]$. Let us call this path the *bucket* of k. It reminds the list associated to entry $T[h(k)]$ in hashing with chaining (Section 8.2), but it might have a more complicated structure because the cuckoo graph can have cycles, and thus this path can form loops as it occurs for the cycle formed by keys D and F.

Let us now consider the insertion of a key G into the cuckoo graph depicted in Figure 8.4, by assuming that $h_1(G) = 3$ and $h_2(G) = 0$ (i.e. table entries are counted from 0), so that G evicts either A or B, as shown in Figure 8.5. We put key G in $T[0]$, thereby evicting A, which attempts to be stored in $T[3] = B$ according to the directed edge. Then A evicts B, which is moved to the last location of the table according to its corresponding directed edge. Since such a table entry is NULL, B is stored there and the insertion process is successfully completed.

Let us now consider a more sophisticated case of insertion, involving a key Z, for which we study two possible mappings of the two hashes $h_1(Z)$ and $h_2(Z)$. Figure 8.6 exemplifies these two situations, which allow us to comment on the relation between the existence of a cycle in the directed cuckoo graph and the impossibility of completing an insertion operation.

On the left of Figure 8.6, key Z is mapped either to table entry $T[1]$ or to table entry $T[4]$. These entries are occupied by keys C and D, respectively. Since the insertion procedure prefers evicting the key $T[h_1(Z)] = D$, the key Z replaces D, which moves to replace F (according to its directed edge), which in turn moves to replace Z again. Hence, the algorithm finds a cycle (shown with bold edges in the figure) which nevertheless does not induces an infinite loop, because the eviction of Z leads to the algorithm checking its second possible location, namely $T[h_2(Z)] = T[1] = C$, which is moved to the free table entry $T[2]$. We conclude that the insertion is completed successfully, even in the presence of a (single) cycle.

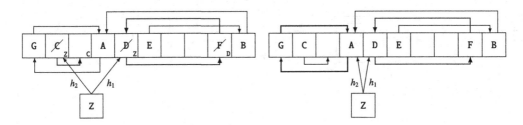

Figure 8.6 Inserting the key Z: (left) successful insertion, (right) unsuccessful insertion. In bold the edges considered by the insertions.

On the right of Figure 8.6, we only change the second mapping of $h_2(Z)$, to the table entry 3 instead of 1. This change makes the insertion unsuccessful because both entries $T[3]$ and $T[4]$ are part of two directed cycles (shown with bold edges in the picture), the former involving entries $\{0, 3\}$ and the latter involving entries $\{4, 8\}$. In this case, the algorithm will end up in an infinite loop of evictions, flowing from one cycle to the other without stopping. This means that the insertion algorithm must be designed to check whether the traversal of the cuckoo graph ends up in such an infinite loop: this is done easily and space efficiently by bounding the number of eviction steps to the table size. If this occurs, as stated in Step 20 of Algorithm 8.3, the table is rebuilt from scratch, eventually using two new hash functions and a larger/smaller size depending on the current load factor of the table.

We are now ready to analyze the time complexity of the insertion operation, which inevitably hinges on the study of some properties of the cuckoo graph. Let us assume that this graph consists of m nodes, one per table entry, and n edges, one per dictionary key. Note that the role of these two parameters is swapped with respect to the classical notation used in the graph literature where, typically, n is the number of nodes and m is the number of edges. The cuckoo graph is a *random* graph because edge endpoints are defined according to the two universal hash functions h_1 and h_2. In the following, to easily bound the event probabilities, we consider the *undirected* version of the cuckoo graph, namely one in which edges are not oriented: this way, we can state that two nodes (i.e. table entries) are involved in an insertion operation if there is an undirected path connecting them in the cuckoo graph. Theorem 8.7 states and proves the key property upon which the efficiency of the insertion operation hinges.

Theorem 8.7 *For any pair of nodes i and j, and any constant $c > 1$, if $m \geq 2cn$, then the probability that in an undirected cuckoo graph of m nodes and n edges there exists a shortest path from i to j of length $L \geq 1$ is at most c^{-L}/m.*

Proof We proceed by induction on the path length $L \geq 1$. The base case $L = 1$ corresponds to the existence of the undirected edge between nodes i and j. Every key can generate that edge with probability no more than $2/m^2$, because edges are undirected and $h_1(k)$ and $h_2(k)$ are uniformly random choices among the m table entries, given the universality of those hash functions. Summing over all n dictionary keys, and recalling that $m \geq 2cn$, we get the bound $\sum_{k \in S} 2/m^2 = 2n/m^2 \leq c^{-1}/m$.

For the inductive step we must bound the probability that there exists a shortest path of length $L > 1$, but no shortest path of length less than L connects i to j (or vice versa). This occurs only if, for some table entry z, the following two conditions hold: (i) there is a shortest path of length $L - 1$ from i to z (that, clearly, does not pass through j); (ii) there is an edge from z to j.

By the inductive hypothesis, the probability that the first condition is true is bounded by $c^{-(L-1)}/m = c^{-L+1}/m$. The probability of the second condition has already been computed for the base case, and it is bounded by c^{-1}/m. So the probability that there exists such a shortest path (passing through z) is at most $(1/cm) \times (c^{-L+1}/m) = c^{-L}/m^2$. Summing over all m table entries z, we get that the probability of a shortest path of length L between i and j is at most c^{-L}/m. ∎

In other words, this theorem states that if the number m of nodes in the cuckoo graph is sufficiently large compared to the number n of edges (i.e. $m \geq 2cn$), there is a low probability that any two nodes i and j are connected by a long path and hence might participate in a long cascade of evictions. Actually, this probability decreases exponentially with L. The case of a constant-length path $L = \Theta(1)$, for which the probability of occurrence is $O(1/m)$, is very significant. This means that, even for this restricted case, the probability of a nonconstant number of evictions is small. We can relate this probability to the *collision probability* in hashing with chaining, by using the notion of "bucket" introduced in Section 8.3, and by including in a bucket all dictionary keys stored in table entries connected by an undirected path of the cuckoo graph.

If the dictionary undergoes many key insertions, the table T eventually gets full and further insertion operations become impossible. Actually, such an impossibility may be met well before T gets full, because Theorem 8.7 holds only for a load factor of the cuckoo hash table equal to $\alpha = n/m \leq 1/2c < 50\%$. Recent results have significantly improved this poor bound, thus making cuckoo hashing a viable, practical, and effective alternative to other hashing schemes. So we conclude this section by focusing on the cost of rehashing the dictionary keys stored in table T and on how much this process impacts on the time complexity of each single insertion operation.

Let us consider a sequence of ϵn key insertions, where ϵ is a small positive constant, and assume that the table size m is sufficiently large to satisfy the conditions imposed in Theorem 8.7 after that sequence of insertions: namely, $m \geq 2cn + 2c(\epsilon n) = 2cn(1 + \epsilon)$. There is a rehashing of T only if some key insertion induces an infinite loop in the cuckoo graph (i.e. Step 20 of Algorithm 8.3). In order to bound this probability we consider the final cuckoo graph in which all ϵn keys have been inserted, and thus consists of m nodes and $n(1 + \epsilon)$ edges. The presence of a cycle in this graph is surely an event that includes the one inducing an infinite loop in the insertion of those keys, so its probability of occurrence provides a simple (yet significant) upper bound to the probability of an unsuccessful insertion. This probability can be easily estimated in two steps. First, we compute the probability that a node in the cuckoo graph is part of a cycle of any length: this is at most $\sum_{L=1}^{\infty} c^{-L}/m = \frac{m^{-1}}{c-1}$, according to Theorem 8.7, because we assumed $m \geq 2cn(1 + \epsilon)$. Second, note that the probability of having a cycle in the cuckoo graph can be bounded by summing the previous bound over all m table entries: namely, $\frac{m}{m(c-1)} = \frac{1}{c-1}$.

Corollary 8.3 *By setting $c = 3$, the insertion of ϵn keys in a dictionary of size n implemented via cuckoo hashing over a table of size $m \geq 6n(1 + \epsilon)$ takes $\Theta(n)$ amortized expected time.*

Proof By setting $c = 3$ in the paragraph preceding this theorem, we derive that the probability of the existence of a cycle in a cuckoo graph of $m \geq 6n(1 + \epsilon)$ nodes and $n(1 + \epsilon)$ keys is at most $1/2$. Therefore a constant number of rehashes are enough to ensure the successful insertion of ϵn keys in that cuckoo hashing table. Given that the expected time for an insertion is $O(1)$, because of the observation about the constant expected size of a bucket, we can derive that one rehashing of $n(1+\epsilon)$ keys takes $O(n)$ expected time. Therefore, we can conclude that the insertion of ϵn keys completes successfully in $O(n)$ expected amortized time.   ∎

In order to make this algorithm work for every n and ϵ, we can adopt the same idea sketched for hashing with chaining at the beginning of this chapter, just after Corollary 8.1, called the *global rebuilding technique*. More precisely, whenever the size of the dictionary becomes too small compared to the size of the hash table, a new, smaller hash table is created; conversely, whenever the hash table becomes too full, a new, larger hash table is created. To make this work efficiently, the size of the hash table is increased or decreased by a constant factor (larger than 1), for example, doubled or halved. The cost of rehashing can be further reduced by using a very small amount (i.e. constant) of extra space, called a *stash*. Once a failure situation is detected during the insertion of a key k (i.e. k incurs an infinite loop), then this key is stored in the stash (without rehashing). This reduces the rehashing probability to $\Theta(1/n^{s+1})$, where s is the size of the stash. The choice of the parameter s is related to some structural properties of the cuckoo graph and of the universal hash functions, which are too involved to be discussed here (for details see [1] and references therein).

8.6   More on Static and Perfect Hashing: Minimal and Ordered

We recall that a minimal ordered perfect hash function is a hash function that avoids collisions between the dictionary keys, maps to a codomain whose size matches the dictionary size (i.e. $m = n$), and preserves in the hash values the key order (i.e. $\forall k' < k'' \in S$, it is $h(k') < h(k'')$). The minimality implies that, given a dictionary key $k \in S$, the integer $h(k)$ corresponds to the *rank* of k in the ordered dictionary S.

The design of h strictly depends on the dictionary S: by changing S we could destroy either the fact that it is "perfect" or the fact that it is "ordered," or both. So it is difficult to maintain this property under a dynamic scenario. Moreover, even if U is ordered, the order-preserving property is guaranteed only for the dictionary keys, so if we select a key $\widehat{k} \notin S$ we cannot say anything about the value $h(\widehat{k})$ and the position of $\widehat{k}$ in the ordered S: we can conclude only that it is a value in $\{0, 1, \ldots, m-1\}$. Nevertheless, for the dictionary keys, we can use h to implement a direct-access table without incurring its space-occupancy limitations mentioned in Section 8.1: just allocate a table of size n and store the dictionary key k, and its satellite information, in $T[h(k)]$. Keys will be stored in distinct table entries (h is perfect) and ordered within T (h is ordered), and without any wasted extra space (h is minimal). An interesting subtlety of these types of hash functions is that the value $h(k)$ can be used as a *lexicographic (integer) name* for the dictionary key k, so we can substitute lexicographic comparisons between pairs of keys with less-than comparisons between hash values, thus exploiting the efficiency of integer comparisons with respect to the possible inefficient comparisons between (possibly long) keys.

Before digging into the technicalities of the construction of h, let us add to these considerations the following subtle one. If the dictionary keys are encoded as variable-length bit strings, then we could assign the rank to each of them by deploying a trie data structure (see Theorem 9.7), but this would incur two main limitations: (i) rank assignment would need a trie search that incurs I/Os in the worst case, rather than the $O(1)$ I/Os required by the hash-based solution; (ii) space occupancy would be linear in the total dictionary length, rather than linear in the dictionary's cardinality. This is because the proposed minimal ordered perfect hash functions do not need the storage of the dictionary S but just $\Theta(n)$ integers. However, the reader has to remember that these hash functions are not able to provide the lexicographic rank of keys *not* belonging to the dictionary S, and thus they are confined to solve just the so-called *lookup* queries. Conversely, if *lexicographic queries* within the dictionary S also have to be supported for the keys *not* in S, then tries are mandatory and they incur larger time and space costs (see Chapter 7).

It is interesting to note that the design of h is based upon three auxiliary functions, denoted h_1, h_2, and g: the first two are universal hash functions over a proper integer codomain, which is larger than n, whereas the third function g is defined from the first two by solving a set of n modulo equations in two variables each, which in turn boils down to solving an interesting *labeling problem* over an undirected and acyclic random graph. Again, random graphs are used to solve concrete problems apparently far removed from a graph formulation: previously we introduced random graphs for designing and analyzing cuckoo hashing, and now we use them for designing and analyzing minimal ordered perfect hash functions.

Let us now dig into the formal definition of the three auxiliary functions h_1, h_2, and g:

- We define h_1 and h_2 as two universal hash functions mapping keys from the universe U to integers in the set $\{0, 1, \ldots, m' - 1\}$, where m' is set to be larger than the dictionary size $n = |S|$. It is worth observing that h_1 and h_2 are not minimal (in fact, $m' > n$) and, in addition, they are not necessarily perfect because they might induce collisions among S's keys. After h_1 and h_2 have been selected from a universal class of hash functions, the algorithm builds a proper undirected graph G, consisting of n edges and m' nodes,[6] and checks whether it is cyclic, in which case it redraws h_1 and h_2; otherwise (i.e. G is acyclic) it proceeds to construct the function g as sketched in the following bullet. The choice of m' impacts on the expected number of redraws, and thus on the efficiency of the construction process: typically, we set $m' = cn$, for a constant $c \geq 3$.[7]

- We define g as a function that maps integers from the range $\{0, \ldots, m' - 1\}$ to integers in the range $\{0, \ldots, n-1\}$. This mapping cannot be perfect, given that $m' > n$, and so some output values of g could be repeated. Nevertheless, the function g is designed in a way that it can be properly combined with h_1 and h_2 to define h in the way we want. The construction of g is obtained via an elegant algorithm that assigns proper integer labels to the nodes of the graph G, which are m' and in correspondence with g's domain values. Such an assignment always exists, if G is acyclic, and can be computed in time linear in G's size by traversing its paths (see later in this section).
- We compose h_1, h_2, and g to define $h(k)$ as follows: $[g(h_1(k)) + g(h_2(k))] \bmod n$, for every $k \in S$. Clearly, h is minimal because it returns values in the range $\{0, \ldots, n - 1\}$; we will prove that it is perfect and ordered by construction.

As far as time and space complexities for the evaluation of h are concerned, we observe the following. The function g is encoded with an integer array of m' entries, whereas universal hash functions h_1 and h_2 take constant space (see Section 8.3). Given that $m' = \Theta(n)$, the total required space is $\Theta(n)$, hence linear in the dictionary's cardinality (and not in the dictionary length). Evaluating $h(t)$ takes constant time: we need to compute the hash functions h_1 and h_2, make two accesses to the array g, and finally execute two sums and one modulo operation. Figure 8.7.a shows an example of a dictionary S with nine strings, and m' set to the prime 13.

We are left with detailing the algorithm that computes the function g so that $h(k)$ is correctly defined according to the formula we have given. The formula actually provides n equality constraints over the n dictionary keys $k \in S$. For each such constraint, $h(k), h_1(k)$, and $h_2(k)$ are known (once the two universal hash functions have been drawn), and so the unknown variables are the two occurrences of $g()$. Referring to the example in Figure 8.7,

- the first key, "abacus," sets the equation $0 = [g(1) + g(6)] \bmod 9$;
- the second key, "cat," sets the equation $1 = [g(7) + g(2)] \bmod 9$;
- and so on... until the last key, "zoo," which sets the equation $8 = [g(5) + g(3)] \bmod 9$.

---

[6] As occurs for the cuckoo graph, in this case too the role of the letters n and m' in denoting the number of edges and nodes, respectively, is swapped.

[7] Choosing $c \geq 3$ gives an acyclic G in $\left\lceil \sqrt{\frac{m'}{m'-2n}} \right\rceil$ trials. This is about two trials if we set $c = 3$ (see [11]).

(a)	Key k	$h(k)$	$h_1(k)$	$h_2(k)$	(b)	x	$g(x)$
	abacus	0	1	6		0	0
	cat	1	7	2		1	5
	dog	2	5	7		2	0
	flop	3	4	6		3	7
	home	4	1	10		4	8
	house	5	0	1		5	1
	son	6	8	11		6	4
	trip	7	11	9		7	1
	zoo	8	5	3		8	0
						9	1
						10	8
						11	6
						12	0

Figure 8.7 An example of a perfect, minimal, and ordered hash function for a dictionary S of $n = 9$ keys (in the form of variable-length strings) which are listed in alphabetic order. Column $h(k)$ reports the lexicographic rank of each key in S. Hash function h is built upon three functions: (a) two random hash functions $h_1(k)$ and $h_2(k)$, for $k \in S$, and having codomain $\{0, 1, \ldots, m' - 1\}$, with $m' = 13 > 9 = n$; and (b) a properly derived function $g(x)$, for $x \in \{0, 1, \ldots, m' - 1\}$, implemented as an array and whose design is explained in the text.

We note from Figure 8.7 that these equations may involve multiple occurrences of the same "variables": for example, $g(1)$ occurs in the equations of "abacus," "home," and "house." So it is not obvious at all that this set of equations admits of a solution. But, surprisingly enough, the computation of g is quite simple and consists of building an undirected graph $G = (V, E)$ with m' nodes labeled $\{0, 1, \ldots, m' - 1\}$ (the same range as the codomain of h_1 and h_2, and the domain of g) and n edges (as many as the keys in the dictionary S). We have one (undirected) edge per key, thus one (undirected) edge per equation: namely, the edge $(h_1(k), h_2(k))$ for every key $k \in S$. We also label every such edge with the *desired* value $h(k)$. Looking at Figure 8.8, and referring to the equations we have given, we note that:

- the first key, "abacus," sets the equation $0 = [g(1) + g(6)] \bmod 9$, which creates the undirected edge $(1, 6)$ and labels it 0;
- the second key, "cat," sets the equation $1 = [g(7) + g(2)] \bmod 9$, which creates the undirected edge $(2, 7)$ and labels it 1;
- and so on... until the last equation for the key "zoo," equal to $8 = [g(5) + g(3)] \bmod 9$, which creates the undirected edge $(3, 5)$ and labels it 8.

It is evident that the topology of G depends only on h_1 and h_2, and thus it is a *random topology* because of the randomness of these two hash functions. The question now is how we solve that set of equations. Here comes the elegant, yet simple idea that hinges upon the property that G is acyclic (as the graph in Figure 8.8); if this is not the case, as we have stated, h_1 and h_2 are redrawn until the corresponding graph does not have any cycles.

The algorithmic idea is to start from any node, say node 0 in Figure 8.8, and assign an arbitrary value, say 0. This corresponds to setting $g(0) = 0$. Then we take an edge

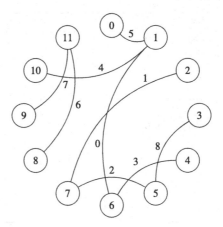

Figure 8.8 Graph corresponding to the string dictionary of Figure 8.7. We do not show node 12 because this value does not occur in the codomain of hash functions h_1 and h_2.

incident on that node, say $(0, 1)$, labeled 5. This edge corresponds to the sixth equation associated with the key "house": $5 = [g(0) + g(1)] \mod 9$. Since $g(0) = 0$, we also can easily derive $g(1) = 5$, and the equation is satisfied. We then proceed in this way, taking another edge incident on a node already labeled with some value. For example, we take the edge $(1, 10)$, labeled 4, which corresponds to the fifth equation associated to the key "home": $4 = [g(1) + g(10)] \mod 9$. Since $g(1) = 5$ from earlier, and $g(10)$ is not set, we set it as $g(10) = 8$, and the equation is satisfied. We continue this way by selecting an edge (u, v) labeled with rank $R(u, v)$ and in which v is labeled with value $g(v)$, but $g(u)$ is not set, and derive $g(u) \geq 0$ so that $g(u) = [R(u, v) - g(v)] \mod 9$. This assignment is always possible provided that $g(u)$ has not been assigned before, which is always the case if the graph is acyclic. If there is an edge incident in two unlabeled nodes, then we assign an arbitrary value to one of them (say value 0 for simplicity), and we continue as before.

Algorithms 8.4 and 8.5 provide the pseudocode of what we have paraphrased here. The first algorithm is the one that triggers the labelling of the graph nodes reachable from a node v that was initially unlabeled and set to the value 0. In this graph visit, if the algorithm meets an already visited node, it has detected a cycle and thus it stops the construction of g. Otherwise, it assigns the correct value to u determined by resolving

---

Algorithm 8.4 Procedure LabelGraph(G)

1: **for** $v \in V$ **do**
2:     $g[v] = \texttt{undef}$
3: **end for**
4: **for** $v \in V$ **do**
5:     **if** $g[v] = \texttt{undef}$ **then**
6:         Label($v, 0$)
7:     **end if**
8: **end for**

---

the corresponding equation in terms of $g(u)$, as we have specified. Array g is correct by construction, and the time complexity of this process is just the one visit of G. We have therefore proved the following.

Algorithm 8.5 Procedure `Label`(v, c)

1: **if** $g[v] \neq$ undef **and** $g[v] \neq c$ **then**
2:      **return** the graph is cyclic; STOP
3: **end if**
4: $g[v] = c$
5: **for** $u \in$ Adj$[v]$ **do**
6:      `Label`$(u, R(u, v) - g(v) \bmod n)$
7: **end for**

Theorem 8.8 *A minimal ordered perfect hash function for a dictionary of n keys can be constructed in $O(n)$ expected time and space. The hash function can be evaluated in $O(1)$ time and uses $O(n)$ space in the worst case.*

The reader can verify that, by applying Algorithm 8.4 to the graph of Figure 8.8, one gets the assignment for the array g specified in Figure 8.7.b.

8.7   Bloom Filters

There are situations in which the universe of keys is very large in cardinality and length, so that hashing solutions could be limited not just by the storage of the table and its pointers, which take $(n + m) \log n$ bits (see Corollary 8.1), but by the storage of the keys, which take $n \log_2 u$ bits. An example is the dictionary of URLs managed by crawlers in search engines: URLs can be hundreds of characters long, so the size of the indexable dictionary in internal memory becomes limited fairly soon, if we attempt to store entire URLs [4]. And, in fact, crawlers do not use either cuckoo hashing or hashing with chaining but, rather, they employ a simple and randomized, yet efficient, data structure named the *Bloom filter* [2].

The crucial property of Bloom filters is that keys are *not explicitly stored*; only a small "fingerprint" of them is stored, and this means that the space needed for the data structure depends on the number of keys rather than their total length (pro), at the drawback of incurring *false positive* answers returned for the membership queries (cons). This is not the case for queries involving keys belonging to the dictionary, for which the Bloom filter is always able to verify the membership correctly: there are no false-negatives in this case. That is the reason why Bloom filters are said to incur *one-side errors*. As for *false positive* errors, they can be controlled and, indeed, their probability *decreases exponentially* with the size of the fingerprints associated to

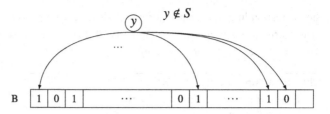

Figure 8.9 Searching key y in a Bloom filter. The four arrows point to the four checked entries $B[h_i(y)]$, since here $r = 4$ and thus $i = 1, 2, 3, 4$. Since one checked entry is 0, key $y \notin S$.

the dictionary keys. Practically speaking, tens of bits (hence, a few bytes) per finger-print are enough to guarantee tiny error probabilities[8] and succinct space occupancy, thus making this solution very appealing in a big-data context. It is useful at this point to recall the Bloom filter mantra: "Wherever a list or set is used, and space is a consideration, a Bloom filter should be considered. When using a Bloom filter, consider the potential effects of false positives."

Let $S = \{x_1, x_2, \ldots, x_n\}$ be a set of n keys and B a bit vector of length m. Initially, all bits in B are set to 0. Suppose we have r universal hash functions $h_i \colon U \longrightarrow \{0, \ldots, m-1\}$, for $i = 1, \ldots, r$. As we have anticipated, every dictionary key k is not represented explicitly in B but, rather, it is fingerprinted by setting r bits of B to 1 as follows: $B[h_i(k)] = 1, \forall\, 1 \leq i \leq r$. Therefore, inserting a key in a Bloom filter requires $O(r)$ time, and sets at most r bits (possibly some hashes may collide; this is called a *standard* Bloom filter). For searching, we state that a key y belongs to the dictionary S if, and only if, all bits of its fingerprint are set to one: that is, $B[h_i(y)] = 1$, $\forall\, 1 \leq i \leq r$. Searching costs $O(r)$ time, as does inserting. Deletions are not supported. In the example shown in Figure 8.9, we can assert that $y \notin S$, since three bits are set to 1 but the rightmost checked bit is zero (i.e. the four checked bits $B[h_i(y)]$ are the ones pointed to by the four arrows).

Clearly, if $y \in S$ then the Bloom filter correctly detects this; but it might be the case that $y \notin S$, and all r bits checked are nonetheless set to 1 because of the setting due to other hashes and keys (possibly not just one). This is the false-positive result we have mentioned, because it induces the Bloom filter to return a positive but erroneous answer to a membership query. It is therefore natural to ask for the probability of a false-positive error, which can be proved to be bounded above by a surprisingly simple formula.

The probability that the insertion of a key $k \in S$ has left null an entry $B[j]$ equals the probability that the r hash functions $h_i(k)$ returned an entry different to j, which is $\left(\frac{m-1}{m}\right)^r$. This value can be approximated with $e^{-\frac{r}{m}}$ for sufficiently large m. After the insertion of all n dictionary keys, the probability that $B[j]$ is still null can then be estimated as $p_0 \approx \left(e^{-\frac{r}{m}}\right)^n = e^{-\frac{rn}{m}}$ by assuming independence among those

---

[8] One could object that errors might occur anyway. But programmers counteract this by claiming that these errors can be made smaller than those incurred by hardware/network failures in data centers or PCs and so they can be disregarded.

hash functions.[9] Hence the probability of a false-positive error (or, equivalently, the *false-positive rate*) is the probability that all r bits checked for a key not in the current dictionary are set to 1, that is: $p_{err} = (1 - p_0)^r \approx \left(1 - e^{-\frac{rn}{m}}\right)^r$.

Not surprisingly, the error probability depends on the three parameters that define the Bloom filter's data structure: the number r of hash functions, the number n of dictionary keys, and the number m of bits in the binary array B. As we anticipated, the total size of dictionary S, which also accounts for the keys' length, does not occur in that formula. It is interesting to note that the fraction $f = m/n \geq 1$ can be read as the average number of bits per dictionary key allocated in B, hence what we termed its *fingerprint* size f. The larger f is, the smaller the error probability p_{err} is, but the larger the space allocated for B. We can optimize p_{err} for a given fingerprint size f by computing its first-order derivative and equalling it to zero: this gets $r_{opt} = (m/n) \ln 2 = f \ln 2$. For this value of r the probability a bit in B gets a null value is $p_0 = 1/2$; which actually means that the array is half filled with 1s and half with 0s. And, indeed, this result could not be different: a larger r induces more 1s in B and thus a larger p_{err}, a lower r induces more 0s in B and thus a larger wasting of (null) space: the optimal choice r_{opt} falls in the middle. For that optimal value of r, we have $p_{err} = (1/2)^{r_{opt}} = (0.693)^{m/n}$, which decreases exponentially by increasing the fingerprint size $f = m/n$.

Nicely enough, we need small values for f in order to achieve tiny false-positive rates: actually, this is $p_{err} = 8 \times 10^{-6}$ for a fingerprint of 32 bits (i.e. $m = 32\,n$), and $p_{err} = 6.4 \times 10^{-11}$ for a fingerprint of 64 bits (i.e. $m = 64\,n$). Figure 8.10 reports the false-positive rate as a function of the number r of hashes for a Bloom filter designed to use $m = 32n$ bits of space, and hence a fingerprint of $f = 32$ bits per key. In this figure we note that $r = 23$ hash functions minimizes the false-positive rate to about 10^{-7}; we also note that for $r \geq 16$, the error rate does not change too much, but these (suboptimal) choices of $16 < r < 23$ speed up the membership queries in practice.

The literature offers many variants of the Bloom filter: two notable examples are the *compressed* Bloom filter and the *spectral* Bloom filter. The former addresses the issue of further squeezing its space occupancy because, in many Web applications, the Bloom filter is a data structure that must be transferred between proxies, thus saving bandwidth and transfer time [9]. The latter addresses the issue of managing multisets, thus allowing the storage and counting of multiplicities of elements, provided that they are below a given threshold (a *spectrum* indeed).

Suppose that we wish to optimize the false-positive rate of the Bloom filter under the constraint that the number of bits to be sent after compression is $z \leq m$. As a compression tool we can use arithmetic coding (see Chapter 12), which well approximates the entropy of the string to be compressed. Surprisingly enough, it turns out that using

---

[9] A more precise analysis is possible, but is very involved and doesn't change the asymptotic result, so we prefer to stick to these simpler (although rougher) calculations [3, 8]. In addition, we mention here that there is another version of the Bloom filter, called the *partitioned* (or *classic*) *Bloom filter* [2], which forces all r bits set to 1 by a single key to be distinct, by, for example, considering r hash tables of size m/r each. The asymptotic behavior of these two types of Bloom filters is the same, although the classic one tends to have a larger false-positive rate because of the presence of more 1s.

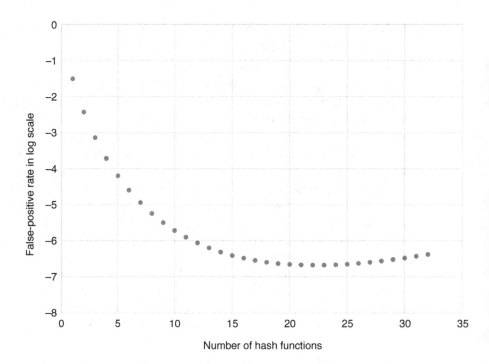

Figure 8.10 Plotting p_{err} (in logarithmic scale) as a function of the number r of hashes for the case $m = 32\,n$. The minimum is achieved for $r = 23$.

a larger, but sparser, Bloom filter can yield the same false-positive rate with a smaller number of transmitted bits; or, in other words, one can transmit the same number of bits with a smaller false-positive rate. As an example, the optimal number of hash functions in a standard Bloom filter with $m = 16n$ is $r_{opt} = 11$, with a false-positive rate equal to 0.000459; by making a sparser Bloom filter with $m = 48n$ and just $r = 3$ hash functions, one can compress the result down to less than $f = 16$ bits per item and also decrease the false-positive rate by roughly a factor of two. Hence a win-win-win situation in terms of false-positive rate, space occupancy, and query speed. However, it goes without saying that the compressed Bloom filter may increase the memory usage at running time (because of decompression), and comes at the computational cost of the additional compression/decompression stages. Nevertheless, some sophisticated compressed indexing approaches are possible that allow direct access to the compressed data without incurring their full decompression: an example is provided by the FM-index data structure, discussed in Chapter 14, which could be built over the binary array B.

As far as the spectral Bloom filter is concerned, recall that it has been introduced to support queries on the multiplicities of dictionary keys, by incurring a small error probability about their estimates, and to support insertions and also deletions among them. In more detail, let $f(k)$ be the multiplicity of the key $k \in S$; this integer can be the number of occurrences of k in a stream or just a value associated to k. A spectral

Bloom filter substitutes the bit vector B with an array C of m counters (thus taking $\Theta(m \log u)$ bits of space, where u is the maximum multiplicity a key in S may occur). The insertion of a key k in the dictionary S consists of adding the value $f(k)$ to all counters identified by the r hash functions $h_i(k)$. Deletion is symmetric. Querying a key k for its multiplicity consists of computing the *minimum* of the values stored at the counters $C[h_i(k)]$, for $i = 1, 2, \ldots r$. The reason for the minimum computation resides in the fact that, due to possible conflicts among the hashes of different keys, each counter $C[i]$ provides an overestimate for the multiplicities of the keys mapped to it: hence $f(k) \le C[h_i(k)]$, for $i = 1, 2, \ldots r$. This observation also allows us to easily prove that the probability that the minimum is different from $f(k)$, and thus its estimate is wrong, equals the probability that there is a collision over all counters $C[h_i(k)]$, and this in turn equals the error rate of a standard Bloom filter built upon the same set of parameters m, n, r. The literature offers variants of the spectral Bloom filter that allow reduction of its space occupancy or its error rate. Probably the most famous one is the adoption of a second-level Bloom filter in which are stored the keys k whose minimum occurs once among the counters $C[h_i(k)]$, for $i = 1, 2, \ldots r$. This *repeated-minimum property* enforces the goodness of the estimates, otherwise it forces the use of another smaller spectral Bloom filter that refines the potentially wrong answers related to single-minimum estimates.

8.7.1 A Lower Bound on Space Occupancy

The question is how small can the bit array B be in order to guarantee a given error rate ϵ for a dictionary of n keys drawn from a universe U of size u. We will answer this difficult question by proving that any data structure offering these features must occupy at least $n \log_2(1/\epsilon)$ bits. This result will allow us to conclude that Bloom filters are asymptotically optimal within a factor of $\log_2 e \approx 1.44$ of this space lower bound.

The proof proceeds as follows. Let us denote by $F(m, \epsilon, X)$ any data structure, requiring m bits of space and solving the membership query on a dictionary $X \subseteq U$ with false-positive rate ϵ. The Bloom filter of the previous section is therefore one of these data structures, with $B = F(m, \epsilon, S)$ for the indexed dictionary S. Clearly, the data structure must work for every possible subset $X \subset U$; they are $\binom{u}{n}$. We say that a data structure $F(m, \epsilon, X)$ accepts a key k if X includes k, otherwise we say that it rejects k.

Let us now consider a specific dictionary S of n elements. Any data structure that is used to represent S must accept each one of its n keys, since no false negatives are admitted, and may also accept at most $(u - n)\epsilon$ other keys of U, because its false-positive rate is ϵ. Therefore, each such data structure accepts at most $n + \epsilon(u - n)$ keys, and can thus be used to represent any of the $w = \binom{n + \epsilon(u-n)}{n}$ subsets of size n of these elements, but it cannot be used to represent any other set.

Since there are 2^m such data structures of m bits, we can conclude that they represent at most $2^m \times w$ subsets of U consisting of n keys and incurring an error rate at most ϵ. Given that we have $\binom{u}{n}$ possible dictionaries drawn from U and consisting of n keys, the following inequality must hold in order to guarantee that an m-bit data structure, such the ones we are aiming for, does exist:

$$2^m \times \binom{n + \epsilon(u - n)}{n} \geq \binom{u}{n},$$

and solving with respect to m we get

$$m \geq \log_2 \left(\binom{u}{n} / \binom{n + \epsilon(u - n)}{n} \right) \geq \log_2 \left(\binom{u}{n} / \binom{\epsilon u}{n} \right) \approx \log_2(1/\epsilon)^n = n \log_2(1/\epsilon),$$

where we used the approximation $\binom{a}{b} \approx \frac{a^b}{b!}$ that holds for $a \gg b$, as it occurs in practice for the parameters u (universe size) and n (dictionary size).

Let us now consider a Bloom filter with the same configuration: namely, error rate ϵ, dictionary size n, and space occupancy of m bits. We know that, in its optimal configuration, it sets $r_{opt} = (m/n) \ln 2$ which translates to an error rate equal to $\epsilon = (1/2)^{(m/n) \ln 2}$. Solving with respect to m, we get

$$m = n \frac{\log_2(1/\epsilon)}{\ln 2} \approx 1.44 \, n \, \log_2(1/\epsilon).$$

This means that Bloom filters are asymptotically optimal in space, and the gap with respect to the optimal space bound is the constant factor 1.44.

8.7.2 A Simple Application

Bloom filters can be used to approximate the intersection of two sets, say A and B, stored in two distinct machines M_A and M_B, by exchanging a small number of bits. Typical applications of this are data replication checking and distributed search engines. This can be efficiently achieved by executing the following steps:

1. Machine M_A builds the Bloom filter $BF(A)$ of $m_A = \Theta(|A|)$ bits, and $r_{opt} = (m_A/|A|) \ln 2$ hash functions;
2. Machine M_A sends $BF(A)$ to machine M_B;
3. Machine M_B constructs Q as the subset of B's elements for which $BF(A)$ answers "yes."

Clearly, $A \cap B \subseteq Q$, so Q contains $|A \cap B|$ keys plus the number of elements belonging to B, but not to A, that, unfortunately, the Bloom filter $BF(A)$ has erroneously identified as being in A too. Therefore, we can conclude that $|Q| = |A \cap B| + |B|\epsilon$ where $\epsilon = 0.6185^{m_A/|A|}$ is the error rate for that design of $BF(A)$. This means that these three steps define a single-round protocol, which allows machine M_B to compute an *approximation* of $A \cap B$ with error rate ϵ. The larger m_A is, the smaller ϵ is, but the larger would be the number of exchanged bits.

By adding the next two steps to this protocol, we get a two-round protocol that allows machine M_A to compute the correct intersection $A \cap B$:

4. Machine M_B sends back Q to M_A;
5. Machine M_A computes $Q \cap A$.

Step 2 exchanges m_A bits and Step 4 exchanges $|Q| \log |U|$ bits, so the total number of bits exchanged by the two-round protocol is $m_A + (|A \cap B| + |B| \times 0.693^{m_A/|A|}) \log |U|$. Conversely, the number of bits exchanged by the obvious protocol that sends the whole of set A to M_B is $|A| \log |U|$. Therefore, the two-round protocol is better than the oblivious one whenever $m_A = c|A|$ for a constant c that is much smaller than $\log |U|$ and, anyway, not too small, as we have observed when commenting on the relation between the size m of the Bloom filter and its error rate ϵ.

References

[1] Martin Aumüller, Martin Dietzfelbinger, and Philipp Woelfel. Explicit and efficient hash families suffice for cuckoo hashing with a stash. In *Proceedings of the 20th European Symposium on Algorithms (ESA)*, Lecture Notes in Computer Science 7501, Springer, 108–20, 2012.

[2] Barton H. Bloom. Space/time trade-offs in hash coding with allowable errors. *Communications of the ACM*, 13(7): 422–6, 1970.

[3] Prosenjit Bose, Hua Guo, Evangelos Kranakis *et al*. On the false-positive rate of Bloom filters. *Information Processing Letters*, 108(4): 210–13, 2008.

[4] Andrei Z. Broder and Michael Mitzenmacher. Survey: Network applications of Bloom filters: A survey. *Internet Mathematics*, 1(4): 485–509, 2003.

[5] Yossi Azar, Andrei Z. Broder, Anna R. Karlin, and Eli Upfal. Balanced allocations. *SIAM Journal on Computing*, 29(1): 180–200, 1999.

[6] Tomas H. Cormen, Charles E. Leiserson, Ron L. Rivest, and Clifford Stein. *Introduction to Algorithms*. The MIT Press, third edition, 2009.

[7] Martin Dietzfelbinger, Torben Hagerup, Jyrki Katajainen, and Martii Penttonen. A reliable randomized algorithm for the closest-pair problem. *Journal of Algorithms*, 25(1): 19–51, 1997.

[8] Fabio Grandi. On the analysis of Bloom filters. *Information Processing Letters*, 129: 35–9, 2018.

[9] Michael Mitzenmacher. Compressed Bloom filters. *IEEE/ACM Transactions on Networks*, 10(5): 604–12, 2002.

[10] Rasmus Pagh and Flemming F. Rodler. Cuckoo hashing. *Proceedings of the 9th European Symposium on Algorithms (ESA)*. Lecture Notes in Computer Science, 2161, 121–33, 2001.

[11] Ian H. Witten, Alistair Moffat, and Timothy C. Bell. *Managing Gigabytes: Compressing and Indexing Documents and Images*, second edition. Morgan Kaufmann, 1999.

[12] Philipp Woelfel. Efficient strongly universal and optimally universal hashing. *Proceedings of the 24th International Symposium on the Mathematical Foundations of Computer Science*, Lecture Notes in Computer Science, 1672, 262–72, 1999.

9   Searching Strings by Prefix

Most discoveries even today are a
combination of serendipity and of
searching.
Attributed to Siddhartha Mukherjee

The problem of searching strings by prefix is experiencing a renewed interest in the algorithmic community because of new applications stemming from Web search engines. Think of the *auto-completion* feature currently offered by major search engines like Google and Bing: it is a prefix search executed on the fly over millions of strings corresponding to past queries by Web users, using the query pattern as the string to search. This problem is made challenging by the size of the dictionary and by the time constraints imposed by the patience of the users.[1] In this chapter we will describe many different solutions to this problem of increasing sophistication and efficiency in time, space, and I/O complexities.

> **The prefix-search problem.** Given a dictionary $\mathcal{D}$ consisting of n strings of total length N, drawn from an alphabet of size σ, the problem consists of preprocessing $\mathcal{D}$ in order to retrieve (or just count) the strings of $\mathcal{D}$ that have P as a prefix.

We mention two other typical string queries: the *exact* search and the *substring* search within the dictionary strings of $\mathcal{D}$. The former is best addressed via hashing because of its simplicity and practical speed; Chapter 8 has already detailed several hashing solutions. The latter problem is more sophisticated and finds application in computational genomics and Asian search engines, just to cite a couple. It consists in finding all positions where the query pattern P occurs as a substring of the dictionary strings. Surprisingly enough, there is a simple *algorithmic reduction* from substring search to prefix search over the set of *all suffixes* of the dictionary strings. This reduction will be discussed in Chapter 10, where the suffix array and the suffix tree data

---

[1] We are simplifying the formulation of the problem to its syntactic form, choosing to ignore the issues regarding the *ranking* of the answers based on features, such as the frequency of the returned queries, the geographic location of the issuing users, and other features to be defined by the search engine with the aim of best matching the underlying user needs.

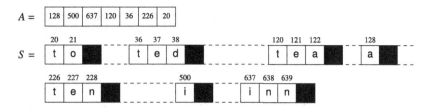

Figure 9.1 The array $S = [to, ted, tea, a, ten, i, inn]$ of (unsorted) strings and the array A of (indirectly sorted) pointers to S's strings.

structures are introduced. As a result, we can conclude that prefix search is the backbone of other important search problems on strings, so the data structures introduced in this chapter offer applications that go far beyond the simple ones discussed below.

9.1 Array of String Pointers

We start with a simple, common solution to the prefix-search problem which consists of an array of pointers to strings stored in arbitrary locations in memory (possibly on disk). Let us call $A[1, n]$ the array of pointers, which are *indirectly* sorted according to the strings pointed to by its entries. We assume that each pointer takes w bytes of memory: typically four bytes (32 bits) or eight bytes (64 bits). Several other representations of pointers are possible, such as variable-length representations, but this discussion is deferred to Chapter 11, where we deal with the efficient encodings of integers.

Figure 9.1 provides a running example in which the dictionary strings are stored in an array S, according to an arbitrary order.

There are two crucial properties that the array A of pointers to (sorted) strings satisfies:

- All dictionary strings prefixed by P occur contiguously when they are lexicographically sorted. So their pointers occupy a subarray, say $A[l, r]$, which is empty if P does not prefix any dictionary string.
- The string P is lexicographically located between $A[l-1]$ and $A[l]$.

Since the prefix search returns either the number of dictionary strings prefixed by P, hence the value $n_{occ} = r - l + 1$, or reports these strings, the key problem to solve is to identify the two positions l and r efficiently. To this aim, we reduce the prefix search problem to the problem of searching for the lexicographic position of a proper pattern string Q among $\mathcal{D}$'s strings, known as a *lexicographic search*. The formation of Q is simple: Q is either the pattern P or the pattern $P\#$, where # is a special symbol that is assumed to be larger than any other alphabet character. It is not difficult to convince yourself that $Q = P$ will precede the string $A[l]$, whereas $Q = P\#$ will follow the string $A[r]$. This actually means that these two lexicographic searches for patterns shorter than $p + 1$ characters are enough to solve the prefix-search problem.

The lexicographic search for Q among $\mathcal{D}$'s strings can be implemented by means of an (indirect) binary search over the (indirectly sorted) array A. It consists of $O(\log n)$ steps, each one requiring a string comparison between Q and the string pointed to by the entry checked in A. The comparison is lexicographic and thus takes $O(p)$ time and $O(p/B)$ I/Os, because it requires in the worst case the scan of all $\Theta(p)$ characters of Q. These poor time and I/O complexities derive from the *indirection*, which elicits no locality in the memory/string accesses of the binary search. The inefficiency is even more evident if we wish to retrieve all n_{occ} strings prefixed by P, and not just count them. After the subarray $A[l, r]$ has been identified, each string reporting incurs at least one I/O, because the strings that are pointed to by $A[l, r]$ may not be contiguous in S.

Theorem 9.1 *The complexity of a prefix search over the array of string pointers is $O(p \log n)$ time and $O(\frac{p}{B} \log n)$ I/Os, and the total space is $N + (1 + w)n$ bytes. Retrieving the n_{occ} strings prefixed by P requires $\Omega(n_{occ})$ I/Os.*

Proof Time and I/O complexities derive from the previous observations. For the space occupancy, A needs n pointers, each taking a memory word w, and all dictionary strings occupy N bytes plus a one-byte delimiter for each of them (commonly \0 in C). ∎

The bound $\Omega(n_{occ})$ may be a major bottleneck if the number of returned strings is large, as it typically occurs in queries that use the prefix search as a preliminary step to select a *candidate set of answers* that have then to be refined via a proper post-filtering process. An example is the solution to the problem of *searching with wild cards*, which involves the presence in P of possibly many special symbols *. The semantics of the wild card symbol is that it matches any substring. In this case if $P = \alpha * \beta * \cdots$, where $\alpha, \beta, \ldots$ are non-empty strings, then we can implement the wild card search by first performing a prefix search for α in $\mathcal{D}$ and then checking by brute-force whether P matches the returned strings given the presence of the wild cards. Of course, this approach can be very expensive, especially when α is not a selective prefix, and thus many dictionary strings are returned as candidate matches. Nevertheless, this provides evidence of how slow a wildcard query could be in a disk environment if solved with such a simple approach.

9.1.1   Contiguous Allocation of Strings

A simple trick to circumvent some of the previous limitations is to store the dictionary strings sorted lexicographically and contiguously on disk. (Pointer) contiguity in A is then reflected in (string) contiguity in S. This has two main advantages:

- **Speed:** when the binary search is confined to a few strings, they will be stored closely both in A and in S, so have probably been buffered by the operating system in internal memory;
- **Space:** compression can be applied to contiguous strings in S, because they typically share some prefix.

Given that S is stored on disk, we can deploy the first observation by blocking strings into groups of B characters each and then storing in A a pointer to the first string of each group. The sampled strings are denoted by $\mathcal{D}_B \subseteq \mathcal{D}$, and their number n_B is upper bounded by $\frac{N}{B}$ because we select at most one string per block. Since A has been squeezed to index at most $n_B \leq n$ strings, the search over A must be changed in order to reflect the *two-level structure* given by the array A and the blocked strings. The idea is thus to decompose the lexicographic search for Q in a two-stages process: in the first stage, we search for the lexicographic position of Q within the sampled strings of $\mathcal{D}_B$; in the second stage, this position is deployed to identify the block of strings where the lexicographic position of Q lies, so that the strings of this block can be eventually scanned and compared with Q for prefix match. We recall that, in order to implement the prefix search, we have to repeat this process for the two strings P and $P\#$, so we have proved the following:

Theorem 9.2 *Prefix search over $\mathcal{D}$ takes $O\left(\frac{p}{B} \log \frac{N}{B}\right)$ I/Os. Retrieving the strings prefixed by P requires $\frac{N_{occ}}{B}$ I/Os, where N_{occ} is their length. The total space is $N + n + n_B w$.*

Proof Once the block of strings $A[l, r]$ prefixed by P has been identified, we can report all of them in $O(\frac{N_{occ}}{B})$ I/Os by scanning the contiguous portion of S that contains those strings. The space occupancy comes from the observation that pointers are stored only for the n_B sampled strings, where $n_B \leq N/B$. ∎

Typically, strings are shorter than B, so $\frac{N}{B} \leq n$, and hence this solution is faster than the previous one. In addition, it can be effectively combined with the compression technique called *front coding* to further lower the space and I/O complexities, as discussed in the following section.

9.1.2 Front Coding

Given a sequence of sorted strings, it is common that adjacent strings share a common prefix. If ℓ is the number of shared characters, then we can substitute them with a proper variable-length binary encoding of ℓ which saves some bits with respect to the classic fixed-size encoding based on four- or eight-bytes. Chapter 11 will detail some of those encoders; here we introduce a simple one to satisfy the curiosity of the reader. The encoder pads the binary representation of ℓ with 0s until an integer number of bytes is used, and then sets the first two bits of the padding (if any, otherwise one more byte is added) to encode the number of used bytes.[2] This encoding is prefix-free, thus it guarantees unique decoding properties; moreover, its byte alignment ensures fast decoding speed in modern processors; it also replaces the initial $\Theta(\ell \log_2 \sigma)$ bits, representing the ℓ characters of the shared prefix, with $O(\log \ell)$ bits of the integer coding, so is advantageous in terms of space. Obviously, the final impact of this solution depends on the amount of shared characters which, in the case of a dictionary of URLs, can be up to 70 percent.

Front coding is a *delta-compression* algorithm, which can be easily defined in an incremental way: given a sequence of strings $(s_1, \ldots, s_n)$, it encodes the string s_i using

---

[2] We are safely assuming that ℓ can be binary encoded in 30 bits, namely $\ell < 2^{30}$.

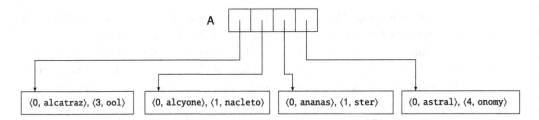

Figure 9.2 Two-level indexing of the set of strings $\mathcal{D} = \{$alcatraz, alcool, alcyone, anacleto, ananas, aster, astral, astronomy$\}$. Strings are partitioned into blocks of two strings each; each block is stored in one disk page and compressed with FC_B. The first string of each block is available uncompressed (in fact, for them we have $\ell = 0$).

the pair $(\ell_i, \hat{s}_i)$, where ℓ_i is the length of the shared prefix between s_i and its predecessor s_{i-1} (0 if $i = 1$), and $\hat{s}_i = s_i[\ell_i + 1, |s_i|]$ is the "remaining suffix" of the string s_i. As an example, consider the dictionary $\mathcal{D} = \{$ alcatraz, alcool, alcyone, anacleto, ananas, aster, astral, astronomy $\}$; its front-coded representation is $(0, \text{alcatraz}), (3, \text{ool}), (3, \text{yone}), (1, \text{nacleto}), (3, \text{nas}), (1, \text{ster}), (3, \text{ral}), (4, \text{onomy})$.

Decoding a string a pair $(\ell, \hat{s})$ is symmetric; we have to copy ℓ characters from the preceding string and then append the remaining suffix $\hat{s}$. This takes $O(|s|)$ time and $O(1 + |s|/B)$ I/Os, provided that the preceding string is available. In general, the reconstruction of a string s_i may require reverse scanning the input sequence up to the first string s_1, which is available in its entirety. So we may possibly need to scan $(\ell_{i-1}, \hat{s}_{i-1}), \ldots, (\ell_1, \hat{s}_1)$ and reconstruct $s_1, \ldots, s_{i-1}$ in order to decode $(\ell_i, \hat{s}_i)$. Therefore, the time cost to decode s_i might be much higher than the optimal $\Theta(|s_i|)$ cost.[3]

To overcome this drawback, it is typical to apply front coding to blocks of strings, thus resorting to the two-level scheme we introduced in Section 9.1.1. The idea is to restart the front-coding at the beginning of every block, so the first string of each block is stored *uncompressed*. This has two immediate advantages for the prefix-search problem: (i) these uncompressed strings are the ones participating in the binary-search process and thus they do not need to be decompressed when compared with Q; (ii) each block is compressed individually and thus the scan of its strings for lexicographically searching Q can be combined with the decompression of these strings without incurring any slowdown. We call this storage scheme *front coding with bucketing*, and denote it by FC_B. Figure 9.2 provides a running example in which the strings "alcatraz", "alcyone", "ananas", and "astral" are stored explicitly because they are the first ones of each block.

As a positive side effect, this approach reduces the number of sampled strings because it can potentially increase the number of strings stored in one disk page: we start from s_1 and we front-compress the strings of $\mathcal{D}$ in order; whenever the compression of a string s_i overflows the current block, a new block is started and the last

---

[3] A smarter solution would be to reconstruct only the first ℓ characters of the previous strings $s_1, s_2, \ldots, s_{i-1}$, because these are the ones involved in s_i's reconstruction.

string is stored there in *uncompressed* form. The number of sampled strings reduces from about $\frac{N}{B}$ to about $\frac{FC_B(\mathcal{D})}{B}$ strings, where $FC_B(\mathcal{D})$ is the space required by FC_B to store all the dictionary strings in blocks of size B. This obviously impacts positively on the number of I/Os needed for a prefix search, given that we execute a binary search over the sampled strings. However, space occupancy increases with respect to $FC(\mathcal{D})$, because $FC_B(\mathcal{D})$ forces the first string of each block to be stored uncompressed; nonetheless, we expect that this increase is negligible because $B \gg 1$.

Theorem 9.3 *Prefix search over $\mathcal{D}$ takes $O\left(\frac{P}{B}\log\frac{FC_B(\mathcal{D})}{B}\right)$ I/Os. Retrieving the strings prefixed by P requires $O\left(\frac{FC_B(\mathcal{D}_{occ})}{B}\right)$ I/Os, where $\mathcal{D}_{occ} \subseteq \mathcal{D}$ is the set of strings in the answer set.*

So, in general, compressing the strings is a good idea because it lowers the space required for storing the strings, and it lowers the number of I/Os. However, we must observe that FC-compression might increase the time complexity of the scan of a block from $\Theta(B)$ to $\Theta(B^2)$ because of the decompression of that block. In fact, take the sequence of strings $(a, aa, aaa, \ldots)$, which is front-coded as $(0,a),(1,a),(2,a),(3,a),\ldots$. In one disk page we can store $\Theta(B)$ such pairs, which represent $\Theta(B)$ strings whose total length is $\sum_{i=0}^{B}\Theta(i) = \Theta(B^2)$.

Despite these pathological cases, the space reduction in practice turns out to be of a constant factor, so the time increase incurred by a block scan is negligible. Therefore, this approach introduces a time/space trade-off driven by the block size B. The longer B is, the better the compression ratio is, the faster the binary search is, but the slower a block scan is. The choice of B also impacts on the occupancy of array A and the possible copy in internal memory of the uncompressed strings it points to, which would reduce the number of I/Os of the binary search.

In order to overcome this trade-off we decouple search and compression issues as follows. We notice that the proposed data structure consists of *two* levels: the "upper" level contains references to the *sampled strings* $\mathcal{D}_B$, and the "lower" level contains the strings themselves stored in a block-wise fashion. The choice of the algorithms and data structures used in the two levels are "orthogonal" to each other, and thus they can be decided independently. It goes without saying that this two-level scheme for searching and storing a dictionary of strings is suitable to be used in a hierarchy of two memory levels, such as also the cache and the internal memory. This is typical in Web search, where $\mathcal{D}$ is the dictionary of terms to be searched by users and disk accesses have to be avoided in order to support each keyword search in few milliseconds.

In the following sections we propose four improvements to the two-level solution: the first is concerned with the compressed storage of the dictionary strings in a way that string decompression is I/O-optimal; the other three solutions refer to the efficient indexing of the sampled strings. These proposals are interesting in themselves, and the reader should not confine their use to the one described in this chpater.

9.2   Locality-Preserving Front Coding$^\infty$

This is an elegant variant of front coding which provides a controlled trade-off between space occupancy and time to decode one string [2]. The key idea is simple, and thus easily implementable, but proving its guaranteed bounds is challenging. We can state the underlying algorithmic idea as follows: *a string is front-coded only if its decoding time is proportional to its length, otherwise it is written uncompressed.* The outcome in time complexity is clear: we compress only if decoding is optimal. But what appears surprising is that, even if we concentrated on the time-optimality of decoding, its "constant of proportionality" also controls the space occupancy of the compressed strings. It seems likes magic – indeed it is!

Formally, suppose that we have front-coded the first $i - 1$ strings $(s_1, \ldots, s_{i-1})$ into the compressed sequence $\mathcal{F} = (0, \hat{s}_1), (\ell_2, \hat{s}_2), \ldots, (\ell_{i-1}, \hat{s}_{i-1})$. We want to compress s_i so we reverse scan at most $c|s_i|$ characters of $\mathcal{F}$ to check whether these characters are enough to reconstruct s_i. This actually means that an uncompressed string is included in those characters, because we have available the first character for s_i. If so, we front-compress s_i into $(\ell_i, \hat{s}_i)$; otherwise s_i is copied uncompressed in $\mathcal{F}$, outputting the pair $(0, s_i)$. Figure 9.3 shows these two cases pictorially.

Figure 9.3 The two cases occurring in locality-preserving front coding (LPFC) when compressing the dictionary string s. Gray rectangles are copied and thus represent the uncompressed strings (in particular, s' is the copied string preceding s); white rectangles represent the front-coded strings.

The key difficulty is to show that the strings that are left uncompressed (i.e. copied), and were instead compressed by the classic front coding scheme, have a length that can be controlled by means of the parameter c, as the following theorem shows (by using the parameter $\epsilon = c/(c - 2)$):

Theorem 9.4 *Locality-preserving front coding (LPFC) takes at most $(1 + \epsilon)FC(\mathcal{D})$ space, and supports the decoding of any dictionary string s in $O\left(\frac{|s|}{\epsilon B}\right)$ optimal I/Os.*

Proof   We call any uncompressed string s a *copied* string, and denote the $c|s|$ characters explored during the backward check as the *left extent* of s. If s is a copied string, there can be no copied string preceding s and beginning in its left extent, otherwise it would have been front-coded. Moreover, the copied string that precedes s may *end* within s's left extent (see the left-hand side of Figure 9.3). For the sake of presentation, the characters belonging to the output suffix $\hat{s}$ of a front-coded string s are referred to as *FC-characters*.

Clearly, the space occupied by the front-coded strings is upper bounded by $FC(\mathcal{D})$. We wish to show that the space occupied by the copied strings, which were possibly

Figure 9.4 The two cases occurring in LPFC. The white rectangles denote the front-coded strings, and thus their FC-characters, while the gray rectangles denote two consecutive copied and thus uncompressed strings, distinguishing the case of crowded (left) and uncrowded (right) copies.

compressed by the classic front coding but are left uncompressed here, sums up to $\epsilon\,FC(\mathcal{D})$, where ϵ is a parameter depending on and equal to $c/(c-2)$ as shown at the end of the proof.

We consider two cases for the copied strings depending on the amount of FC-characters that lie between two consecutive occurrences of them. The first case is called *uncrowded* and occurs when that number of FC-characters is at least $\frac{c|s|}{2}$ (shown in the right part of Figure 9.4); the second case is called *crowded*, and occurs when that number of FC-characters is at most $\frac{c|s|}{2}$ (shown in the left part of Figure 9.4). From Figure 9.4 it is simple to conclude that if the copied string s is crowded then $|s'| \geq c|s|/2$, because s' starts before the left extent of s (otherwise s would not be copied) but ends within the last $c|s|/2$ characters of that extent (otherwise s would be uncrowded). Conversely, again referring to Figure 9.4, we can conclude that if s is uncrowded then it is preceded by at least $c|s|/2$ characters of front-coded strings (FC-characters).

We are now ready to bound the total length of the copied (uncompressed) strings. We partition them into "chains" composed of one uncrowded copied string followed by the maximal sequence of crowded copied strings. By definition, the first string in $\mathcal{D}$ is assumed to be uncrowded, as it is always copied. We prove that the total number of characters in each chain is proportional to the length of its first copied string, which is uncrowded by definition. Precisely, consider the chain $w_1 w_2 \cdots w_x$ of consecutive copied strings, where we have that w_1 is uncrowded and the following w_is are crowded. For any crowded w_i, with $i > 1$, we know that it holds the inequality on crowded strings just proved, namely $|w_{i-1}| \geq c|w_i|/2$ or, equivalently, $|w_i| \leq 2|w_{i-1}|/c = \cdots = (2/c)^{i-1}|w_1|$ for all $i = 2, 3, \ldots, x$. Taking $c > 2$, we derive that the crowded copied strings shrink by a constant factor. Therefore we can upper bound the total number of characters forming a chain by

$$\sum_{i=1}^{x} |w_i| = |w_1| + \sum_{i=2}^{x} |w_i| \leq |w_1| + \sum_{i=2}^{x} (2/c)^{i-1}|w_1|$$

$$= |w_1| \sum_{i=1}^{x} (2/c)^{i} < |w_1| \sum_{i \geq 0} (2/c)^{i} < \frac{c\,|w_1|}{c-2}.$$

By the definition of an uncrowded string, w_1 is preceded by at least $c|w_1|/2$ FC-characters. The total number of these FC-characters is bounded by $FC(\mathcal{D})$, so we can upper bound the total length of the uncrowded strings by $(2/c)FC(\mathcal{D})$. By plugging this into the previous bound on the total length of the chains, we get $\frac{c}{c-2} \times \frac{2FC(\mathcal{D})}{c} = \frac{2}{c-2}FC(\mathcal{D})$. The theorem follows by setting $\epsilon = \frac{2}{c-2}$. ∎

So locality-preserving front coding (LPFC) is a compressed storage scheme for strings that can substitute their plain storage without introducing any asymptotic slowdown in the accesses to the compressed strings and still guaranteeing the space occupancy of the classic front coding up to a constant factor. In this sense it can be considered as a sort of *space booster* for any string-indexing technique.

The two-level indexing data structure described in the previous section can immediately benefit LPFC by making A point to the copied strings of LPFC (which are uncompressed). The buckets delimited by these strings then have *variable length*, but any such string can be decompressed in optimal time and I/Os. So the bounds are the ones stated in Theorem 9.3, but without the pathological cases commented on next to it (cf. previous observation about the $\Theta(B^2)$ size of a bucket in classic FC_B). The scanning of the strings prefixed by P and identified by the binary-search step then takes I/Os and time still proportional to their total length, and hence it is optimal.

The remaining question is, therefore, how to speed up the search over the array A. We foresee two main limitations: (i) the binary-search step has time complexity depending on N or n; (ii) if the strings pointed to by the array A do not fit within the internal memory space allocated by the programmer, or available in cache, then the binary-search step incurs many I/Os and cache misses, and this might be expensive. In Sections 9.3–9.5 we propose three approaches that take full advantage of the distribution of dictionary strings or of some more sophisticated indexing of them.

9.3   Interpolation Search

Let us consider the case of a dictionary of strings that have bounded length, say shorter than b characters drawn from an alphabet of size σ. We can interpret these strings as integers in a universe of size σ^b. In some applications, keys may be short binary strings fitting in the memory-word size so that $b = 4$ or 8 bytes and $\sigma = 256$.

Searching for the lexicographic position of a string P in $\mathcal{D}$ boils down to searching for the integer coding of P among the ordered set of integers encoding the dictionary strings. In this string-to-int transformation some care must be taken; in fact we need to assume that all strings have the same length and, when shorter, they are logically padded with a character assumed to be smaller than any other alphabet character. The search for P and $P\#$ can then be turned into a search for two proper integers, and if the integers generated from the dictionary strings follow some suitable distributions, then there are searching schemes that are faster than binary search. In what follows we describe a variant of the classic *interpolation search* that offers some interesting additional properties (details in [4]).

			B_1		B_3		B_6		B_7		B_{10}		B_{11}	B_{12}
1	2	3	8	9	17	19	20	28	30	32	36

Figure 9.5 An example of interpolation search over a set of 12 integers. The bins are separated by long vertical bars; some bins are empty and thus not shown, such as B_2, B_4, B_5, B_8, and B_9.

Let $X[1, m] = x_1 \ldots x_m$ be the array of sorted integers encoding the dictionary strings, so that $m = n$ (if we encode the whole dictionary $\mathcal{D}$) or $m = n_B$ (if we encode the sampled dictionary $\mathcal{D}_B$). We evenly subdivide the range $[x_1, x_m]$ into m bins $B_1, \ldots, B_m$ of size $b = \frac{x_m - x_1 + 1}{m}$. Hence, we have as many bins as dictionary strings, and $B_i = [x_1 + (i - 1)b, x_1 + ib)$. In order to guarantee the constant-time access to these bins, and for the simplicity of exposition, we keep an additional array $S[1, m]$ of pointers to the first and last integers of B_i in X.

Figure 9.5 gives an example in which we have $m = 12$ integers (and bins). The first integer is $x_1 = 1$, the last integer is $x_{12} = 36$, and thus the bin size is $b = (36 - 1 + 1)/12 = 3$. Only non-empty bins are shown, and the integers of X included in them are separated by long vertical bars.

Given a string P to be lexicographically searched among the dictionary strings, we compute its corresponding integer, say y, and perform the following two steps: first, we determine the index j of the candidate bin where y could occur: that is, $j = \lfloor \frac{y - x_1}{b} \rfloor + 1$; then, we binary search the position of y in B_j by accessing the subarray of X delimited by the two pointers stored in $S[j]$. These two steps take $O(1 + \log |B_j|) = O(\log b)$ time. The value of b depends on the magnitude of the integers present in the indexed dictionary but, in any case, it is $|B_j| \leq n$, so one could be induced to conclude that $O(\log b) = O(\log n)$ in the worst case, thus making this approach not asymptotically faster than binary search.

In what follows, we prove two interesting properties of this approach which concern the distribution of X's integers and impact on the evaluation of its time complexity. We start by defining the parameter Δ as the ratio between the maximum and the minimum gaps between two consecutive integers of the input dictionary. Formally,

$$\Delta = \frac{\max_{i=2\ldots m}(x_i - x_{i-1})}{\min_{i=2,\ldots,m}(x_i - x_{i-1})}.$$

It is interesting to note that the algorithm is oblivious to the value of Δ; nevertheless, the following theorem shows that its time complexity can be bounded in terms of this value. Hence, interpolation search cannot be slower than binary search, but it can be faster depending on the distribution of dictionary keys.

Theorem 9.5 *Interpolation search executed over a dictionary of m integers takes* $O(\log \min\{\Delta, m\})$ *time and* $O(m)$ *extra space in the worst case.*

Proof Correctness is immediate. For the time complexity, we prove that the maximum number of integers that can belong to any bin is no more than b/g, where g is defined as the minimum gap between consecutive integers of X. Then we show that $b/g \leq \Delta$ so that the claim will follow.

We start by observing that the maximum of a series of integers is at least as large as their mean. Here we take as integers the gaps $x_i - x_{i-1}$ between the consecutive sorted integers in X, and write

$$\max_{i=2\ldots m}(x_i - x_{i-1}) \geq \frac{\sum_{i=2}^{m} x_i - x_{i-1}}{m-1} \geq \frac{x_m - x_1 + 1}{m} = b, \qquad (9.1)$$

where the last inequality comes from the following arithmetic property: $\frac{a'}{a''} \geq \frac{a'+1}{a''+1}$ whenever $a' \geq a'' > 0$. This property can be easily proved by solving it, and it holds for the final ratio in equation (9.1) since the integers in X are positive and distinct, so that $x_m - x_1 \geq m - 1$.

Starting from the preliminary observation that $|B_i| \leq b/g$, and then plugging in equation (9.1) and the definition of Δ, we can write

$$|B_i| \leq \frac{b}{g} \leq \frac{\max_{i=2\ldots m}(x_i - x_{i-1})}{\min_{i=2,\ldots,m}(x_i - x_{i-1})} = \Delta.$$ ∎

In the peculiar case where X's integers are uniformly distributed, we can derive a very interesting bound on the maximum bin size, which holds with high probability. In fact, this problem can be rephrased as the maximum load of m bins (i.e. the B_is) among which we distribute m balls (i.e. X's integers) uniformly at random. This maximum value is well known and equal to $O(\log m / \log \log m)$, as we actually proved in Theorem 8.3.

Lemma 9.1 *If the m integers of set X are drawn uniformly at random from $[0, U - 1]$, interpolation search takes $O(\log \log m)$ time with high probability.*

But the issue here is that a uniform input distribution is uncommon in practice. Nevertheless, if we relax the query operation to be just a *membership query* (and not a predecessor query on integers), then we can artificially enforce the uniform distribution over any input by selecting a random permutation $\pi : U \longrightarrow U$ and shuffling X according to π before building the proposed data structure. Care must be taken at query time, since we have to search not for y but for its permuted image $\pi(y)$ in $\pi(X)$. The query performance proved in Lemma 9.1 then holds with high probability for a *membership query* executed on *any indexed set X*. For the choice of π we refer the reader to [8].

If interpolation search is applied to our string context, and assuming that the sampled strings of $\mathcal{D}_B$ are uniformly distributed (which could be the case after the sampling, if B is not too small), then the number of I/Os required to prefix search P among them is $O(\frac{P}{B} \log \log \frac{N}{B})$. This is an exponential reduction in the time and I/O performance of prefix searching executed through the binary search, as reported in Theorem 9.2.

9.4   Compacted Trie

We have already talked about tries in Chapter 7; here we dig further into their properties as efficient data structures for string searching. In this context, the trie is used

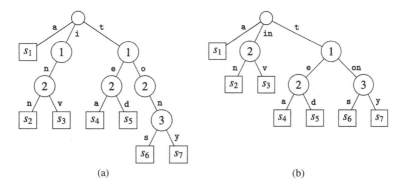

Figure 9.6 An example of uncompacted trie (a) and compacted trie (b) for $n = 7$ strings. The integer shown in each internal node u denotes the length of the string spelled out by the root-to-u path. In uncompacted tries, these integers are useless because they correspond to u's depth. In compacted tries, edge labels are substrings of variable length that can be represented in constant space with triples of integers: for example on could be encoded as $\langle 6, 2, 3 \rangle$, since the sixth string tons includes on from position 2 to position 3.

for indexing the sampled strings $\mathcal{D}_B$ in internal memory. This induces a speed-up in the first stage of the lexicographic search of string Q (either P or $P\#$) in $\mathcal{D}_B$ from $O(\log(N/B))$ time to $O(p)$ time, thus being surprisingly independent of the dictionary size. The reason for this is the power of the RAM model, which allows memory cells of $\Theta(\log N)$ bits to be managed and addressed in constant time. Let us dig more into the use of tries for prefix searching.

A trie is a multi-way tree whose edges are labeled by characters of the indexed strings. An internal node u is associated with a string $s[u]$, which is a *prefix* of a dictionary string. String $s[u]$ is obtained by concatenating the characters found on the downward path that connects the trie's root with the node u. A leaf is associated with a dictionary string. All leaves that descend from a node u are prefixed by $s[u]$. The trie has n leaves and at most N nodes, one per string character.[4] Figure 9.6 provides an illustrative example of a trie built over seven strings. This form of trie is commonly called *uncompacted* because it can have *unary paths*, such as the one leading to string inn.[5]

If we want to check if a string P prefixes some dictionary string, we just have to check if there is a downward path starting from trie's root and spelling out P. All leaves descending from the reached node provide the dictionary strings correctly answering the prefix search. So tries do not need the reduction to the lexicographic search operation introduced for the binary-search approach, whenever the entire dictionary $\mathcal{D}$ is indexed.

But if we want to implement the two-level indexing approach and adopt the uncompacted trie to index the sampled dictionary $\mathcal{D}_B$, in order to route the search toward the

---

[4] We say "at most" because some paths (prefixes) can be shared among several strings.

[5] The trie cannot index strings when one is the prefix of the other. In fact the former string would end up in an internal node. To avoid this case, each string is extended with a special character that is not present in the alphabet and is typically denoted by $.

disk pages storing the strings of $\mathcal{D}$ prefixed by P, then we still need to perform a lexicographic search for the properly built string Q within the uncompacted trie built on $\mathcal{D}_B$. In this case, either Q is spelled out completely, and thus the search ends up at some internal node u, or the downward trie traversal stops at a node v before the scanning of Q is completed, say at character $Q[\ell]$. In the former case, the lexicographic position of Q is found by traversing the leftmost spine of the subtrie rooted at u; in the latter case, ℓ provides us with the longest common prefix between Q and $\mathcal{D}_B$'s strings, and the lexicographic position of Q in $\mathcal{D}_B$ is found by locating $Q[\ell]$ among the edge labels outgoing from v, and thus among the subtries descending from these outgoing edges.

As an example, consider the pattern $Q = \texttt{to}$ and its lexicographic search in the uncompacted trie of Figure 9.6(a). Q prefixes the strings s_6 and s_7 and, in fact, it is fully spelled out in a downward trie traversal which leads to the unary node being the rightmost one in the picture with label 2. Let us now call this node v and assume that the pattern to be lexicographically searched is $Q = \texttt{tod}$. So the downward traversal still reaches v, and then checks whether it has an outgoing edge labeled $\texttt{d}$, which is not the case. So the lexicographic position of Q is found to the left of the descending subtrie, because $\texttt{d}$ is smaller than the character $\texttt{n}$ labeling the single edge outgoing from v.

A big issue is how to efficiently find the "edge to follow" during the downward traversal of the trie, because this impacts on the overall efficiency of the pattern search. The efficiency of this step hinges on a proper storage of the edges (and their labeling characters) outgoing from a node. The simplest data structure that does the job is the *linked list*. Its space requirement is optimal, namely proportional to the number of outgoing edges, but it incurs a $\Theta(\sigma)$ cost in the worst case per traversed node. The result is a prefix search taking $O(p\,\sigma)$ worst-case time, which is too much for large alphabets. If we store the branching characters (and their edges) into a sorted array, then we could binary search it taking $O(\log \sigma)$ time per node. A faster approach consists of using a full-sized array of σ entries, where the non-empty ones store the pointers to the children associated with the existing branching characters. In this case the time to branch out of a node is $O(1)$, and thus $O(p)$ time is the cost for searching the pattern Q; but the space occupancy of the trie grows up to $O(N\sigma)$, which may be unacceptably high for large alphabets. The best approach consists of resorting to a *perfect hash table*, which stores just the existing branching characters and their associated pointers. This guarantees $O(1)$ branching time in the worst case and optimal space occupancy, thus combining the best of the two previous solutions. For details about perfect hashes we refer the reader to Chapter 8.

Theorem 9.6 *The uncompacted trie solves the prefix-search problem in $O(p + n_{occ})$ time and $O(p + n_{occ}/B)$ I/Os, where n_{occ} is the number of strings prefixed by P. The retrieval of those strings takes $O(N_{occ})$ time and, in particular, takes $O(N_{occ}/B)$ I/Os if leaves and strings are stored contiguously and alphabetically sorted on disk. The uncompacted trie consists of $O(N)$ nodes and exactly n leaves, and thus takes $O(N)$ space. Finally, the uncompacted trie also supports the lexicographic search for the pattern P among the indexed strings in $O(p + \log \sigma)$ worst-case time and I/Os.*

Proof Let u be the node such that $s[u] = P$. All strings descending from u are pre-fixed by P, and they can be visualized by visiting the subtree rooted in u. The I/O complexity of the traversal leading to u is $O(p)$ because of the constant-time jumps among trie nodes via perfect hash tables. The retrieval of the n_{occ} leaves descending from the node spelling P takes optimal $O(n_{occ}/B)$ I/Os because we have assumed that trie leaves are stored contiguously on disk, and every node keeps a pointer to its leftmost and rightmost descending leaves. On the other hand, the display of the strings associated with these leaves takes additional $O(N_{occ}/B)$ I/Os, provided that the indexed strings are ordered and stored contiguously on disk. Searching for the lexicographic position of P's mismatch character, i.e. $Q[\ell]$, among the edge labels outgoing from the reached node, takes $O(\log \sigma)$ time by using an array implementation of the branching characters (see Chapter 15 for compressed and faster solutions). ∎

A trie can be wasteful in space if there are long strings with a short common prefix: this would induce a significant number of unary nodes. We can save space by *contracting* the unary paths into one single edge. Edge labels then become (possibly long) substrings rather than single characters, and the resulting trie is termed *compacted*. Figure 9.6(b) shows an example of compacted trie. It is evident that each edge label is a substring of a dictionary string, say $s[i,j]$, so it can be represented via a triple $\langle s, i, j \rangle$. Given that each node is at least binary, the number of internal nodes and edges is $O(n)$ (cf. $O(N)$ in uncompacted tries). So the total space occupied by a compacted trie is also $O(n)$.

Theorem 9.7 *The compacted trie solves the prefix-search problem in $O(p + n_{occ})$ time and $O(p + n_{occ}/B)$ I/Os, where n_{occ} is the number of strings prefixed by P and strings are stored contiguously and alphabetically sorted on disk. The retrieval of those strings takes $O(N_{occ})$ time and, in particular, it takes $O(N_{occ}/B)$ I/Os. The compacted trie consists of $O(n)$ nodes and leaves, so its storage takes $O(n)$ space. It goes without saying that the trie also needs the storage of the dictionary strings to resolve its edge labels, hence additional N space. Finally, the compacted trie also supports the lexicographic search for the pattern P among the indexed strings in $O(p + \log \sigma)$ worst-case time and I/Os.*

Proof Prefix searching is implemented similarly to that for uncompacted tries. The difference is that it alternates character-branches out of internal nodes, and substring matches with edge labels. If the branching characters and the associated edge pointers outgoing from internal nodes are again implemented with perfect hash tables, the stated time and I/O bounds easily follow.

For searching the lexicographic position of the pattern string Q among the indexed strings we can proceed similarly to the approach for uncompacted tries. It is enough to traverse a downward path spelling Q as much as possible until a mismatch character is encountered or the full Q is matched. The difference with uncompacted tries is that the traversal can stop at the middle of an edge, but the conclusions drawn for uncompacted tries still hold here (see Chapter 15 for compressed and faster solutions). ∎

So the compacted trie is an interesting substitute for the array A in the two-level indexing structure of Section 9.1.1, and could be used to support the search for the

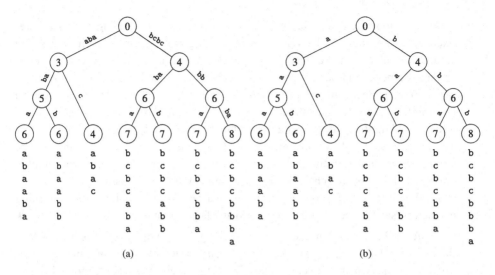

Figure 9.7 An example of compacted trie (a) and the corresponding Patricia trie (b).

candidate bucket where the string P occurs, taking $O(p + \log \sigma)$ time in the worst case. Since each traversed edge can induce one I/O for the retrieval of its labeling substring to be compared with the corresponding one in P, this approach is efficient if the trie and its indexed strings can be fit in internal memory. Otherwise (since σ is typically not much large), it presents two main drawbacks: the linear dependence of the I/Os on the pattern length, and the dependence of its space occupancy on the disk page size (influencing the sampling of $\mathcal{D}$ to get $\mathcal{D}_B$) and on the length of the sampled strings.

The *Patricia trie*, introduced in the next section, solves the former problem, and its combination with the locality-preserving front coding solves both of them.

9.5   Patricia Trie

A Patricia trie built on a string dictionary $\mathcal{D}$ of n strings of total length N is a compacted trie in which edge labels consist just of their initial *single character*, and internal nodes are labeled with integers denoting the *length* of the associated strings. Figure 9.7 illustrates how to convert a compacted trie (left) into a Patricia trie (right).

Even if the Patricia trie strips out some information from the compacted trie, it is still able to support the search for the lexicographic position of a pattern P among a (sorted) sequence of strings, with the significant advantage that this search needs to access only one single string, and hence execute typically one I/O instead of the p I/Os potentially incurred by the edge-resolution step in compacted tries. This algorithm is called *blind search* in the literature [5]. It is a little more complicated than prefix searching in classic tries, because of the presence of only one character per edge label. Technically speaking, blind search consists of three stages:

- **Stage 1 – downward traversal:** Trace a downward path in the Patricia trie to locate a leaf l which points to an "interesting" string of the indexed dictionary. This string does not necessarily identify P's lexicographic position in the dictionary (which is our goal), but it provides *enough information* to find that position in the subsequent stages. The retrieval of the interesting leaf l is done by traversing the Patricia trie from the root and comparing the characters of P with the single characters that label the traversed edges until either a leaf is reached or no further branching is possible. In this latter case, we choose l to be any descendant leaf from the last traversed node.

- **Stage 2 – LCP computation:** Compare P against the string pointed to by leaf l, in order to determine their longest common prefix (LCP). Let ℓ be the length of this shared prefix; it is then possible to prove that (see [5] for details) the leaf l stores one of the strings indexed by the Patricia trie that shares the longest common prefix with P, and denote by $P[\ell + 1]$ and $s[\ell + 1]$ their two mismatched characters.
- **Stage 3 – upward traversal:** Traverse the Patricia trie upward from l to determine the edge $e = (u, v)$ where the mismatch character $s[\ell + 1]$ lies: this is easy because each node on the upward path stores an integer that denotes the length of the corresponding prefix of s, so we have $|s[u]| < \ell + 1 \leq |s[v]|$. If $s[\ell + 1]$ is a branching character (i.e. $\ell = |s[u]|$), then we determine the lexicographic position of $P[\ell + 1]$ among the branching characters of node u. Say this is the i-th child of u; the lexicographic position of P is therefore to the immediate left of the subtree descending from this i-th child. Otherwise (i.e. $\ell > |s[u]|$), the character $s[\ell + 1]$ lies within e and after its first character, so the lexicographic position of P is to the immediate right of the subtree descending from e, if $P[\ell + 1] > s[\ell + 1]$; otherwise it is to the immediate left of that subtree.

A running example is illustrated in Figure 9.8. Stage 1 percolates the Patricia trie downward, matching the rightmost path (depicted in bold), and thus reaching the rightmost leaf $s_7 = $ bcbcbbba. This is because the characters labeling the path edges match the pattern characters at positions $1, 5, 7$. Note that these numbers are "+1" with respect to the numbers labeling the nodes in the traversed path, given that they denote the positions of the branching characters. Stage 2 computes the longest common prefix between $P = $ bcbabcba and s_8, thus finding that it is equal to 3 with mismatches $s_7[4] = c$ and $P[4] = a$. Stage 3 traverses the Patricia trie upward from s_7's leaf, and stops at the edge indicated in Figure 9.8(b), thus finding that P lies to the left of this edge, and thus to the left of its descending subtree. This is indeed the correct lexicographic position of the searched pattern among the indexed dictionary strings.

In the case that the searched pattern is $P = $ ababbb, then Stage 1 stops at the leftmost child of the root because all of its branching characters are different to $P[4] = b$. Then, it selects any leaf descending from that node as leaf l; say it selects the leaf pointing to s_1. It computes the longest common prefix between s_1 and P, thus returning the value 3. Finally, Stage 3 stops its upward traversal from s_1 again at the leftmost child of the root, and finds the position of $P[4] = b$ as occurring between the two branching edges of that node, so the lexicographic position of P lies between the subtrees descending from these two branching edges, that is, between strings s_2 and s_3.

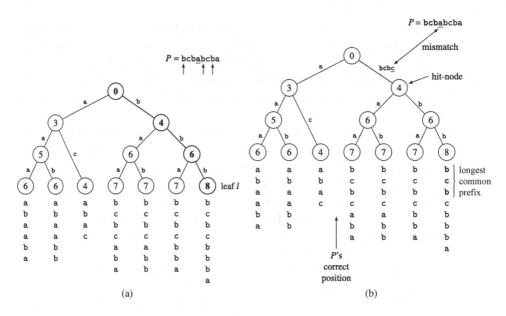

Figure 9.8 An example of the first (a) and second and third (b) stages of the blind search for P in a dictionary of seven strings.

In order to understand why the algorithm is correct, let us take the path spelling out the prefix $P[1, \ell]$ corresponding to the longest common prefix between P and the dictionary strings. We have two cases: either we reached an internal node u such that $|s[u]| = \ell$ or we are in the middle of an edge (u, v), namely $|s[u]| < \ell < |s[v]|$. In the former case, all strings descending from u share ℓ characters with the pattern, and no dictionary string shares more characters (by definition of LCP). The correct lexicographic position therefore falls among them or is adjacent to these strings, and thus it can be found by looking only at the branching characters of the edges outgoing from node u. This is correctly done also by the blind search that stops at u (Stage 1), computes ℓ (Stage 2), and finally determines the correct position of P by comparing u's branching characters against $P[\ell + 1]$ (Stage 3).

In the second case, the blind search reaches node v by skipping the mismatch character that lies within the edge label of (u, v) and, possibly, the traversal goes further down in the Patricia trie because of the possible match between the branching characters of subsequently traversed edges and matched characters of P. Eventually a leaf l descending from v is reached or selected (Stage 1), and the value ℓ is computed correctly given that all leaves descending from v share $|s[v]| > \ell$ characters and thus share ℓ characters with P (Stage 2). So the upward traversal executed in Stage 3 from leaf l reaches correctly the edge (u, v), where $|s[u]| < \ell < |s[v]|$. There, we deploy the mismatch characters $s_l[\ell + 1]$ and $P[\ell + 1]$ to choose the correct lexicographic position of P which is either to the left (i.e. $P[\ell + 1] < s_l[\ell + 1]$) or to the right (i.e. $s_l[\ell + 1] < P[\ell + 1]$) of the leaves descending from v.

We have therefore provided a mathematical ground to the correctness of the blind search which, actually, offers excellent performance in space, time, and I/Os:

Theorem 9.8 *Let us assume that the Patricia trie indexing a dictionary of n strings can be stored in the internal memory of a computer, whereas the dictionary is so large that it has to be stored on disk. The Patricia trie takes $\Theta(n)$ space, hence constant space per indexed string (independent, therefore, of their total length).*

The blind search for the lexicographic position of a pattern string $P[1, p]$ among the dictionary strings takes $O(p + \log \sigma)$ time and no I/Os to traverse the trie's structure (Stage 1 and 3), and $O(p)$ time and $O(p/B)$ I/Os to fetch and compare the single string identified by the blind search (Stage 2).

By searching for P and P#, the blind search determines the range of indexed strings prefixed by P, if any, within the same time and I/O bounds.

This theorem actually states that if $p \leq B$ and $n < M$, which are indeed reasonable conditions in practice, the prefix search for P in a dictionary $\mathcal{D}$ takes just one I/O. If dictionary compression is mandatory, then the performance achieved by the combination of Patricia trie with the LPFC scheme, as stated in the following theorem, is very interesting.

Theorem 9.9 *The two-level indexing data structure composed of the Patricia trie as index in internal memory ("upper level") and the LPFC as compressed storage of the dictionary strings on disk ("lower level") requires $O(n)$ space in memory and $O((1+\epsilon) FC(\mathcal{D}))$ space on disk, where ϵ is the parameter set by LPFC and controlling its I/O–space trade-off.*

A prefix search for a pattern $P[1, p]$ takes $O(\frac{p}{B} + \frac{|s|}{B\epsilon})$ I/Os, where s is the "interesting string" determined in Stage 1 of the blind search. The retrieval of the prefixed strings takes $O(\frac{(1+\epsilon) FC(\mathcal{D}_{occ})}{B})$ I/Os, where $\mathcal{D}_{occ} \subseteq \mathcal{D}$ is the set of returned strings.

Proof The I/O performance comes from the observation that the computation of the value ℓ in Stage 2 of the blind search needs to decode the selected string s from its LPFC representation (Theorem 9.4), and this takes $O(|s|/\epsilon B)$ I/Os. ∎

In the case that $n = \Omega(M)$, we cannot index in the internal-memory Patricia trie the whole dictionary, so we have to resort to a bucketing strategy over its strings and thus index in the Patricia trie only the first string of every disk page. If $N/B = O(M)$, the Patricia trie can index in internal memory all sampled strings, and thus it can support the prefix search for P within the bounds stated in Theorem 9.9, by adding just one I/O due to the scanning of the bucket (i.e. disk page) containing the lexicographic position of P. The previous condition can be rewritten as $N = O(MB)$, which is pretty reasonable in practice, given the current values of $M \approx 32$ GB and $B \approx 32$ KB, which make $M \times B$ of the order of hundreds of terabytes.

9.6   Managing Huge Dictionaries$^\infty$

The final question we address in this chpater is: What if $N = \Omega(MB)$? In this case the Patricia trie is too big to be fit in the internal memory of our computer. We could consider storing the trie on disk without taking much care of the layout of its nodes among the disk pages. But unfortunately, a pattern search could take $\Theta(p)$ I/Os in the two root-to-leaf traversals performed by Stages 1 and 3 of the blind search. Alternatively, we could envision a "packing" of the Patricia trie in disk pages that minimizes the I/Os needed for these root-to-leaf traversals. The idea, in this case, would be to incrementally grow a root page and repeatedly add some node not already packed into that page, where the choice of that node might be driven by various criteria that depend on some access probability or on its depth. When the root page contains B nodes, it is written onto disk and the algorithm recursively lays out the rest of the tree. Surprisingly enough, the obtained packing is far from optimality by a factor of $\Omega(\frac{\log B}{\log \log B})$, but it is surely within a factor of $O(\log B)$ from the optimal [1].

In what follows we describe two distinct optimal approaches to solve the prefix-search problem over dictionaries of *huge size*: the first solution is based on a data structure, called the *String B-tree* [5], which boils down to a B-tree in which the routing table of each node is a Patricia tree; the second solution consists of applying proper *disk layouts of trees* on to the Patricia trie's structure. Both these approaches are briefly described in the following subsections.

9.6.1   String B-Tree

The key idea consists of dividing the big Patricia trie into a set of smaller Patricia tries, each fitting into one disk page, and then linking them all together by means of a B-tree structure. In this section we outline a constructive definition of the String B-tree; for details on this structure and the supported operations we refer the interested reader to the seminal paper [5].

The strings in the dictionary $\mathcal{D}$ are stored on disk contiguously and ordered alphabetically. We denote by $\mathcal{D}^0 = \mathcal{D}$ the pointers to the dictionary strings stored at the leaf level of the String B-tree. These pointers are partitioned into a set of smaller, equally sized chunks $\mathcal{D}_1^0, \ldots, \mathcal{D}_m^0$, each including $\Theta(B)$ strings independently of their length, and thus $m = n/B$. We can then index each chunk $\mathcal{D}_i^0$ with a Patricia trie that fits into one disk page and embed it into a leaf of the B-tree. In order to search for P among this set of leaf nodes, we take from each partition $\mathcal{D}_i^0$ its *first* and *last* (lexicographically speaking) strings s_i^f and s_i^l, defining the set $\mathcal{D}^1 = \left\{ s_1^f, s_1^l, \ldots, s_m^f, s_m^l \right\}$.

Recall that the prefix search for P boils down to the lexicographic search of a pattern Q, properly defined from P: $Q = P$ or $Q = P\#$. If we search Q within $\mathcal{D}^1$, we can discover one of the following three cases:

1. Q falls before the first or after the last string of $\mathcal{D}^1$, because $Q < s_1^f$ or $Q > s_m^l$.
2. Q falls between two chunks, say $\mathcal{D}_i^0$ and $\mathcal{D}_{i+1}^0$, because $s_i^l < Q < s_{i+1}^f$. So we have found Q's lexicographic position in the whole $\mathcal{D}$ between these two adjacent chunks.
3. Q falls among the strings of some chunk $\mathcal{D}_i^0$, because $s_i^f \le Q \le s_i^l$. So the search is continued in the Patricia trie that indexes $\mathcal{D}_i^0$.

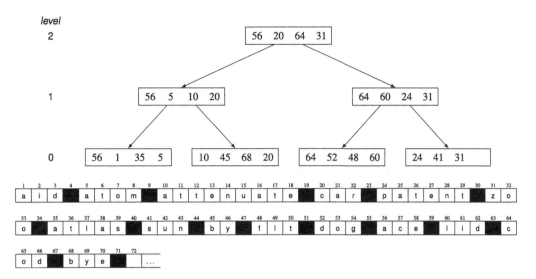

Figure 9.9 An example of String B-tree built on a dictionary of 15 strings stored on disk (in an unsorted order). The strings are stored in the B-tree leaves in alphabetical order by means of their logical pointers. Notice that sorting strings on disk would improve their I/O scanning, and indeed our theorems assume an ordered $\mathcal{D}$ on disk. However, the picture does not force the string sorting in order to show the flexibility of the data structure in supporting the update operations due to string insertions and deletions.

In order to establish which of the three cases occurs, we need to search efficiently in $\mathcal{D}^1$ for the lexicographic position of Q. Now, if $\mathcal{D}^1$ is small and can be fit in memory, we can build on it a Patricia trie and we are done (see Theorem 9.8). Otherwise, we repeat the partitioning process on $\mathcal{D}^1$ to build a smaller set $\mathcal{D}^2$, in which we sample, as before, two strings every B, so $|\mathcal{D}^2| = \frac{2\,|\mathcal{D}^1|}{B}$. We continue this partitioning process for k steps, until $|\mathcal{D}^k| = O(B)$, and thus we can fit the Patricia trie built on $\mathcal{D}^k$ within one disk page.[6]

Note that each disk page gets an even number of strings when partitioning $\mathcal{D}^0, \ldots, \mathcal{D}^k$, and to each pair $\langle s_i^f, s_i^l \rangle$ we associate a pointer to the block of strings that they delimit in the lower level of this partitioning process. The final result of this partitioning process is then a B-tree over string pointers. The *arity* of the tree is $\Theta(B)$, because we index $\Theta(B)$ strings in each single node. The nodes of the String B-tree are then stored on disk. Therefore the String B-tree has height $k = \Theta(\log_B n)$. Figure 9.9 provides an illustrative example for a String B-tree built over 15 strings and height 2.

A (prefix) search for string Q in a String B-tree is simply a traversal of the B-tree, which executes at each node a lexicographic search of Q in the Patricia trie of that node. This search discovers one of the three cases we have mentioned, in particular:

---

[6] Actually, we could stop as soon as $|\mathcal{D}^k| = O(M)$, but we prefer the former to get a standard B-tree structure.

- Case 1 can only happen on the root node; it has found the lexicographic position of Q at the beginning or at the end of dictionary $\mathcal{D}$, so the search in the String B-tree stops;
- Case 2 has found the lexicographic position of Q in the dictionary $\mathcal{D}$ between the strings s_i^f and $s_{(i+1)}^f$, which are adjacent in the dictionary $\mathcal{D}$, so the search in the String B-tree stops;
- Case 3 implies that we have to follow the node pointer associated with the identified chunk delimited in the lower level by the pair of strings $\langle s_i^f, s_i^l \rangle$.

The I/O complexity of the data structure just defined is pretty good: since the arity of the B-tree is $\Theta(B)$, we have $\Theta(\log_B n)$ levels, so a search traverses $\Theta(\log_B n)$ nodes. Since on each node we need to load the node's page into memory and perform a blind search of Q over its Patricia trie (in internal memory), we pay $O(1 + \frac{p}{B})$ I/Os, and thus $O(\frac{p}{B} \log_B n)$ I/Os for the overall prefix search of Q in the dictionary $\mathcal{D}$.

Theorem 9.10 *The prefix search for a pattern $P[1, p]$ in a String B-tree built over a dictionary $\mathcal{D}$ of n strings takes $O\left(\frac{p}{B} \log_B n + \frac{N_{occ}}{B}\right)$ I/Os, where N_{occ} is the total length of the dictionary strings that are prefixed by P. The String B-tree occupies $O(\frac{n}{B})$ disk pages, and strings are stored sorted, uncompressed and contiguously on disk.*

This result is good but not yet *optimal*. The issue that we have to resolve to reach optimality is *pattern rescanning*: each time we do a blind search, we compare Q and one of the strings stored in the currently visited B-tree node starting from their first character. However, as we go down in the String B-tree we can capitalize on the characters of Q that we have already compared in the upper levels of the B-tree, and thus avoid the rescanning of these characters during the subsequent LCP-computations. So if c characters have been already matched in Q during some previous LCP-computations, the next LCP-computation can compare Q with a dictionary string starting from their $(c + 1)$-th character. The pro of this approach is that I/Os are optimal; the con is that strings have to be stored uncompressed in order to support the efficient access to that $(c + 1)$-th character. Working out all the details [5], one can show that:

Theorem 9.11 *The prefix search for a pattern $P[1, p]$ in a String B-tree built over a dictionary $\mathcal{D}$ of n strings takes $O(\frac{p}{B} + \log_B n + \frac{N_{occ}}{B})$ I/Os, where N_{occ} is the total length of the dictionary strings that are prefixed by P. The String B-tree occupies $O(\frac{n}{B})$ disk pages, and strings are stored sorted, uncompressed and contiguously on disk.*

If we want to store the strings compressed on disk, we can either adopt the suboptimal approach of Theorem 9.10 and plug the LPFC scheme over the dictionary $\mathcal{D}$; or, we can keep the I/O-optimality but need to adopt a more sophisticated solution, such as the ones stated in [2, 6]. We refer the interested reader to these papers for details.

9.6.2   Packing Trees on Disk

The advantage of finding a good layout for unbalanced trees among disk pages (of size B) may be unexpectedly large, and therefore must not be underestimated when designing solutions that have to manage large trees on disk. In fact, while balanced trees save a factor $O(\log B)$ when mapped to disk (pack B-node balanced subtrees per page), the mapping of unbalanced trees grows with nonuniformity and approaches, in the extreme case of a linearly shaped tree (i.e. a tree shaped much like a path), a saving factor of $\Theta(B)$ over a naïve memory layout.

This problem is also known in the literature as the *tree packing* problem. Its goal is to find an allocation of tree nodes among the disk pages in such a way that the number of I/Os executed for a root-to-leaf traversal is minimized. Minimization may involve either the total number of loaded pages in internal memory (i.e. I/Os), or the number of distinct visited pages (i.e. working-set size, which may be smaller if some pages are revisited). In this way we model two extreme situations: the case of a one-page internal memory (i.e. a small buffer), or the case of an unbounded internal memory (i.e. an unbounded buffer). Surprisingly, the optimal solution to the tree-packing problem is *independent* of the available buffer size because no disk page is visited twice when I/Os are minimized or the working set is minimum. Moreover, the optimal solution shows a nice *decomposability property*: the optimal tree packing forms in turn a tree of disk pages. These two facts allow us to restrict our attention to the I/O-minimization problem, and thus design recursive solutions for the optimal tree decomposition among B-sized disk pages.

In the rest of this section we present two solutions of increasing sophistication which address two different scenarios: one in which the goal is to *minimize the maximum number* of I/Os executed during a downward root-to-leaf traversal, and the other in which the goal is to *minimize the average number* of I/Os by assuming an access distribution to the tree leaves, and thus to the possible tree traversals. Both solutions assume that B is known; the literature actually offers cache-oblivious solutions to the tree-packing problem, but they are too sophisticated to be discussed in these pages (see [1, 7] for details).

Min-max algorithm. This solution [3] operates greedily and bottom up over the tree to be packed with the goal of minimizing the maximum number of I/Os executed during a downward traversal which starts from the root of the tree. The tree is assumed to be binary; this is not a restriction for Patricia tries because it is enough to encode the alphabet characters with binary strings. The algorithm assigns every leaf to its own disk page and the height of this page is set to 1. Working upward, Algorithm 9.1 is applied to each processed node until the root of the tree is reached.

The final packing may induce a poor page-fill ratio, nonetheless several changes can alleviate this problem in real situations, for example:

1. When a page is closed off, scan its child pages from the smallest to the largest and check whether they can be merged with their parent.

Algorithm 9.1 Min-max algorithm over binary trees (general step)

Let u be the currently visited node;
if both children of u have the same page height d **then**
    if the total number of nodes in both child pages is $< B$ **then**
        Merge the two disk pages and add u;
        Set the height of this new page to d (i.e. as it was for its children);
    else
        Close off the pages of u's children;
        Create a new page for u and set its height to $d + 1$;
    end if
else
    Close off the page of u's child with the smaller height;
    If possible, merge the page of the other child with u and leave its height unchanged;
    Otherwise, create a new page for u with height $d + 1$ and close off both child pages;
end if

---

2. Design logical disk pages and pack many of them into one physical disk page; possibly ignore physical page boundaries when placing logical pages to disk.

It can be shown that Algorithm 9.1 provides a disk packing of a binary tree of n nodes and height H such that every root-to-leaf path traverses $O\left(\frac{H}{\sqrt{B}} + \log_B n\right)$ pages.

Distribution-aware tree packing. We assume that an access distribution to the Patricia trie leaves is known. Since this distribution is often skewed toward some leaves, which are then accessed more frequently than others, the min-max algorithm may be significantly inefficient. The following algorithm is based on a dynamic programming scheme that minimizes the *expected* number of I/Os incurred by any root-to-leaf traversal in the Patricia trie [7].

We denote by τ this optimal tree packing (from tree nodes to disk pages), so $\tau(u)$ denotes the disk page to which node u is mapped. Let $w(f)$ be the probability of accessing a leaf f; we derive a distribution over all other nodes of the tree by just summing up the access probabilities to their descending leaves. We can assume that the tree root r is always mapped to a fixed page $\tau(r) = R$. Consider now the set V of tree nodes that descend from R's nodes but are not themselves in R. We observe that the optimal packing τ induces a tree of disk pages and, consequently, if τ is optimal for the current tree T, then τ is optimal for all subtrees T_v rooted in $v \in V$.

This result allows us to state a recursive computation for τ that first determines which nodes reside in R, and then continues recursively with all subtrees T_v for which $v \in V$. Dynamic programming provides an efficient implementation of this idea, based on the following definition: An *i-confined* packing of a tree T is a packing in which the page R contains exactly i nodes, with $i \le B$. Now, in the optimal packing τ, the

---

Algorithm 9.2 Distribution-aware packing of trees on disk

Initialize $A[v, i] = w(v)$, for all leaves v and integers $i \leq B$;

while there exists an unmarked node v **do**

    mark v;

    update $A[v, 1] = w(v) + A[\texttt{left}(v), B] + A[\texttt{right}(v), B]$;

    for $i = 2$ to B **do**

        update $A[v, i]$ according to the dynamic programming rule specified in the text.

    end for

end while

---

root page R will contain the root r of T, i^* nodes from the left subtree $T_{\texttt{left}(r)}$ and $(B - i^* - 1)$ nodes from the right subtree $T_{\texttt{right}(r)}$, for some $i^* < B$. The consequence is that τ is both an optimal i^*-confined packing for $T_{\texttt{left}(r)}$ and an optimal $(B - i^* - 1)$-confined packing for $T_{\texttt{right}(r)}$.

This property is at the basis of the dynamic programming rule which computes, for a generic node v and integer $i \leq B$, the cost $A[v, i]$ of an optimal i-confined packing of the subtree T_v. The authors of paper [7] showed that $A[v, i]$ can be computed as the access probability $w(v)$ to node v, which accounts for the expected I/Os incurred by visiting v's page (i.e. $1 \times w(v)$), plus the minimum among the following three quantities:

- $A[\texttt{left}(v), i - 1] + w(\texttt{right}(v)) + A[\texttt{right}(v), B]$, which accounts for the (unbalanced) case in which the i-confined packing for v is obtained by storing $i - 1$ nodes from $T_{\texttt{left}(v)}$ into v's page, and $\texttt{right}(v)$ in another page;
- $A[\texttt{right}(v), i - 1] + w(\texttt{left}(v)) + A[\texttt{left}(v), B]$, which is symmetric to the previous rule but here specialized on the right child of v;
- $\min_{1 \leq j < i - 1}\{A[\texttt{left}(v), j] + A[\texttt{right}(v), i - j - 1]\}$, which accounts for the case in which j nodes from $T_{\texttt{left}(v)}$ and $i - j - 1$ nodes from $T_{\texttt{right}(v)}$ are stored in v's page to form the optimal i-confined packing of T_v. (The special case $i = 1$ is given by $A[v, 1] = w(v) + A[\texttt{left}(v), B] + A[\texttt{right}(v), B]$.)

It can be shown that Algorithm 9.2 computes the optimal tree packing in $O(n B^2)$ time and $O(n B)$ space, where optimality here is with respect to the *expected* number of I/Os incurred by any root-to-leaf traversal of the packed binary tree. The packing maps the binary tree into at most $2\lfloor \frac{n}{B} \rfloor$ disk pages.

References

[1] Stefan Alstrup, Michael A. Bender, Erik D. Demaine et al. Efficient tree layout in a multilevel memory hierarchy, 2003. Personal communication: corrected version of a paper that appeared in *Proceedings of the 10th European Symposium on Algorithms (ESA)*, 2002.

[2] Michael A. Bender, Martin Farach-Colton, and Bradley C. Kuszmaul. Cache-oblivious string B-trees. In *Proceedings of the 25th ACM Symposium on Principles of Database Systems*, 223–42, 2006.

[3] David R. Clark and J. Ian Munro. Efficient suffix trees on secondary storage. *Proceedings of the 7th ACM-SIAM Symposium on Discrete Algorithms (SODA)*, pp. 383–391, 1996.

[4] Erik D. Demaine, Thouis Jones, and Mihai Pătraşcu. Interpolation search for non-independent data. In *Proceedings of the 15th ACM–SIAM Symposium on Discrete Algorithms*, 529–30, 2004.

[5] Paolo Ferragina and Roberto Grossi. The String B-tree: A new data structure for string search in external memory and its applications. *Journal of the ACM*, 46(2): 236–80, 1999.

[6] Paolo Ferragina and Rossano Venturini. Compressed cache-oblivious String B-tree. *ACM Transactions on Algorithms*, 12(4): 52:1–52:17, 2016.

[7] Joseph Gil and Alon Itai. How to pack trees. *Journal of Algorithms*, 32(2): 108–32, 1999.

[8] Michael Luby and Charles Rackoff. How to construct pseudorandom permutations from pseudorandom functions. *SIAM Journal on Computing*, 17: 373–86, 1988.

10 Searching Strings by Substring

In this chapter we will look at solving the following problem, known as *full-text searching* or *substring searching*.

> **The substring-search problem.** Given a text string $T[1, n]$, drawn from an alphabet of size σ, preprocess it in a way that it is efficient to subsequently retrieve (or just count) all text positions where a query pattern $P[1, p]$ occurs as a substring of text T.

It is evident that this problem can be solved by brute-forcedly comparing P against every substring of T, thus taking $O(np)$ time in the worst case. But it is also evident that this *scan*-based approach is unacceptably slow when applied to massive text collections subject to a large number of queries, which is the scenario involving genomic databases or search engines. This suggests that we need to "preprocess" the text T before the searches start, by building an *indexing* data structure. A setup cost is required for this construction, but this cost is amortized over the subsequent pattern searches, thus resulting conveniently in a quasi-static environment in which T is changed very rarely.

In this chapter we will describe two main approaches to substring search, based on arrays and another based on trees, which mimic what we have done for the prefix-search problem. The two approaches hinge on the use of two fundamental data structures: the *suffix array* (*SA*) and the *suffix tree* (*ST*). We will describe these data structures in much detail because their use goes far beyond the context of full-text search.

10.1 Notation and Terminology

We assume that text T ends with a special character $T[n] = \$$, which is smaller than any other alphabet character. This ensures that no suffix is a prefix of another suffix. We use $suff_i$ to denote the i-th suffix of text T, namely the substring $T[i, n]$. The following observation is crucial:

> If $P = T[i, i + p - 1]$, then the pattern occurs at text position i and thus we can state that P is a prefix of the i-th text suffix, that is, P is a prefix of the string $suff_i$.

SUF(T)	Positions	Sorted SUF(T)	SA	lcp
mississippi$	1	$	12	0
ississippi$	2	i$	11	1
ssissippi$	3	ippi$	8	1
sissippi$	4	issippi$	5	4
issippi$	5	ississippi$	2	0
ssippi$	6	mississippi$	1	0
sippi$	7	pi$	10	1
ippi$	8	ppi$	9	0
ppi$	9	sippi$	7	2
pi$	10	sissippi$	4	1
i$	11	ssippi$	6	3
$	12	ssissippi$	3	-

Figure 10.1 The set of all text suffixes $SUF(T)$, and the two arrays SA and lcp for the string $T =$ "mississippi$".

As an example, if $P =$ "siss" and $T =$ "mississippi$", then P occurs at text position 4 and prefixes the suffix $suff_4 = T[4, 12] =$ "sissippi$" (see Figure 10.1). For simplicity of exposition, and for historical reasons, we will use this text as running example; note that a text may be an arbitrary sequence of characters, hence not necessarily a single word.

Given this observation, we can form with all text suffixes the dictionary $SUF(T)$ and state that *searching for P as a substring of T boils down to searching for P as a prefix of some string in SUF(T)*. In addition, since there is a bijective correspondence among the text suffixes prefixed by P and the pattern occurrences in T, then:

- the suffixes prefixed by P occur contiguously into the lexicographically sorted $SUF(T)$;
- the lexicographic position of P in $SUF(T)$ immediately precedes the block of suffixes prefixed by P.

An attentive reader may have noticed that these are the properties we deployed to efficiently support prefix searches in Chapter 9. And indeed, the solutions known in the literature for efficiently solving the substring-search problem hinge either on array-based data structures (i.e. the suffix array) or on trie-based data structures (i.e. the suffix tree). So the use of these data structures in pattern searching is pretty immediate. What is challenging is the efficient construction of these data structures and their mapping onto disk to achieve efficient I/O performance. These will be the main issues dealt with in the following sections.

10.2   The Suffix Array

The suffix array for a text T is the array of pointers to all text suffixes ordered lexicographically [14]. We use the notation $SA(T)$ to denote the suffix array built over T,

---

Algorithm 10.1 SUBSTRINGSEARCH(P, T, SA)

1: $L = 1, R = n$;
2: **while** $L \neq R$ **do**
3:      $M = \lfloor (L + R)/2 \rfloor$;
4:      **if** strncmp($P, suff_M, p$) > 0 **then**
5:          $L = M + 1$;
6:      **else**
7:          $R = M$;
8:      **end if**
9: **end while**
10: **if** strncmp($P, suff_L, p$) $= 0$ **then**
11:      **return** L;
12: **else**
13:      **return** -1;
14: **end if**

---

or just *SA* if the indexed text is clear from the context. Because of the lexicographic ordering, $SA[i]$ is the *i*-th smallest text suffix, so $suff_{SA[1]} < suff_{SA[2]} < \cdots < suff_{SA[n]}$, where $<$ is the lexicographic order between strings. For space reasons, each suffix is represented by its starting position in T (i.e. an integer), so *SA* consists of n integers in the range $[1, n]$ and occupies $\Theta(n \log n)$ bits.

Another useful concept is the *longest common prefix* between two consecutive suffixes $suff_{SA[i]}$ and $suff_{SA[i+1]}$, which we have already introduced and deployed in the previous Chapter 9. We store its length in the entry lcp[i] of an array of $n - 1$ entries, each containing values smaller than n. Figure 10.1 provides a running example for the arrays lcp and *SA* given the input text T ="mississippi$". There is an optimal and nonobvious linear-time algorithm to build the lcp array, which will be detailed in Section 10.2.3. The interest in the lcp rests in its usefulness in designing efficient/optimal algorithms to solve various search and mining problems over strings, some of which will be studied in Section 10.4.

10.2.1 The Substring-Search Problem

We observed that the substring-search problem can be reduced to a prefix search over the string dictionary $SUF(T)$, so it can be solved by means of a binary search for P over the array of text suffixes ordered lexicographically, namely $SA(T)$. Algorithm 10.1 encodes a classic binary search, here specialized to compare strings rather than numbers. Therefore, it takes $O(\log n)$ string comparisons, each taking $O(p)$ time in the worst case. We have therefore proved the following result.

Lemma 10.1 *Given the text $T[1, n]$ and its suffix array, we can count the occurrences of a pattern $P[1, p]$ in T taking $O(p \log n)$ time and $O(\log n)$ memory accesses in the worst case. Retrieving the positions of these occ occurrences takes an additional*

	Step 1		Step 2		Step 3		Step 4
$\Longrightarrow$	\$		\$		\$		\$
|	i\$		i\$		i\$		i\$
|	ippi\$		ippi\$		ippi\$		ippi\$
|	issippi\$		issippi\$		issippi\$		issippi\$
|	ississippi\$		ississippi\$		ississippi\$		ississippi\$
|$\rightarrow$	mississippi\$		mississippi\$		mississippi\$		mississippi\$
|	pi\$	$\Longrightarrow$	pi\$		pi\$		pi\$
|	ppi\$	|	ppi\$		ppi\$		ppi\$
|	sippi\$	|	sippi\$		sippi\$		sippi\$
|	sissippi\$	|$\rightarrow$	sissippi\$		sissippi\$		sissippi\$
|	ssippi\$	|	ssippi\$	$\Longrightarrow$	ssippi\$	$\Longrightarrow$	ssippi\$
$\Longrightarrow$	ssissippi\$	$\Longrightarrow$	ssissippi\$	$\Longrightarrow$	ssissippi\$		ssissippi\$

Figure 10.2 Binary search steps to identify the lexicographic position of the pattern $P =$ "ssi" among the suffixes of the text string "mississippi\$". The double right arrows denote the pointers L and R, whereas the single right arrow denotes the pointer M.

$O(occ)$ time. The total required space is $\Theta(n(\log n + \log \sigma))$ bits, where the first term accounts for the suffix array and the second term for the text.

Since each pattern-suffix comparison takes $O(p/B)$ I/Os, then this approach takes $O(\frac{p}{B} \log n)$ I/Os to count the occurrences of a pattern $P[1,p]$ in T; retrieving the positions of these *occ* occurrences takes an additional $O(occ/B)$ I/Os.

Figure 10.2 shows a running example for Algorithm 10.1, which highlights an interesting property: the comparison between P and $suff_M$ does not need to start from their initial character. In fact one could exploit the lexicographic sorting of the suffixes and skip the character comparisons that have already been carried out in previous iterations. This can be done with the help of three arrays:

- The array lcp$[1, n-1]$, which stores in lcp$[i]$ the length of the longest common prefix between suffixes $SA[i]$ and $SA[i+1]$. Let us denote by $lcp(suff_{SA[i]}, suff_{SA[i+1]})$ the function that computes this length.
- Two other arrays $Llcp[1, n-1]$ and $Rlcp[1, n-1]$, which are defined for every triple (L, M, R) that may arise in the inner loop of a binary search over the range $[1, n]$. We define $Llcp[M] = lcp(suff_{SA[L]}, suff_{SA[M]})$ and $Rlcp[M] = lcp(suff_{SA[M]}, suff_{SA[R]})$: that is, $Llcp[M]$ accounts for the length of the longest prefix shared by the leftmost suffix $suff_{SA[L]}$ and the middle suffix $suff_{SA[M]}$ of the range currently explored by the binary search; $Rlcp[M]$ accounts for the length of the longest prefix shared by the rightmost suffix $suff_{SA[R]}$ and the middle suffix $suff_{SA[M]}$ of that range.

Note that each triple (L, M, R) is uniquely identified by its midpoint M because the execution of a binary search actually defines a hierarchical partition of the array SA into smaller and smaller subarrays delimited by (L, R) and thus centered on M. Hence we have $\Theta(n)$ triples overall, and these three arrays occupy $\Theta(n)$ space in total.

We can build the arrays $Llcp$ and $Rlcp$ in time $O(n)$ by exploiting two different approaches. The former approach deploys the observation that the length of the longest common prefix between any two suffixes $suff_{SA[i]}$ and $suff_{SA[j]}$, with

$i < j$, can be computed as the minimum of a range of lcp values, namely $\text{lcp}[i,j] := \min_{k=i,\ldots,j-1} lcp(suff_{SA[k]}, suff_{SA[k+1]}) = \min_{k=i,\ldots,j-1} \text{lcp}[k]$. By associativity of the min operator we can split the computation as $\text{lcp}[i,j] = \min\{\text{lcp}[i,k], \text{lcp}[k,j]\}$, where k is any index in the range $[i,j]$, so we can set $\text{lcp}[L,R] = \min\{\text{lcp}[L,M], \text{lcp}[M,R]\}$. This implies that the arrays $Llcp$ and $Rlcp$ can be computed via a bottom-up traversal of the triplets (L, M, R) in $O(n)$ time. The other approach is to compute $\text{lcp}[i,j]$ on the fly via a range-minimum-query data structure built over the array lcp, as explained in Section 10.4.2. Both these approaches take $O(n)$ time and space, and thus they are asymptotically optimal.

We are left with showing how the binary search can be sped up by using the three arrays SA, $Llcp$, and $Rlcp$. Consider a binary search step in the subarray $SA[L, R]$, and let M be the midpoint of this range (hence $M = \lfloor (L + R)/2 \rfloor$). The lexicographic comparison between P and $suff_{SA[M]}$, executed in Step 4 of Algorithm 10.1, aims at choosing the next search range between $SA[L, M]$ and $SA[M, R]$. There, the string comparison started from the first character of P and $suff_{SA[M]}$; here we compare them by skipping some characters, taking advantage of the previous binary search steps.

Surprisingly enough, this is possible and requires us to know, in addition to $Llcp$ and $Rlcp$, the values $l = lcp\left(P, suff_{SA[L]}\right)$ and $r = lcp\left(P, suff_{SA[R]}\right)$, which denote the number of characters the pattern P shares with the strings at the extremes of the range currently explored by the binary search. Initially (i.e. $L = 1$ and $R = n$), these two values can be computed in $O(p)$ time by explicitly comparing character-by-character the involved strings. At a generic step, we assume that l and r are known inductively, and show next how the binary search step can efficiently recompute them before moving either to $SA[L, M]$ or to $SA[M, R]$.[1]

In fact, we know that P lies between $suff_{SA[L]}$ and $suff_{SA[R]}$, so P shares $\text{lcp}[L, R]$ characters with all suffixes in the range $SA[L, R]$, given that any string in this range must share this number of characters (given that they are lexicographically sorted). Therefore we can conclude that l and r are larger than or equal to $\text{lcp}[L, R]$, and the number of characters m that the pattern P shares with $suff_{SA[M]}$ is also larger than or equal to $\text{lcp}[L, R]$. We can thus take advantage of this last inequality to compare P with $suff_{SA[M]}$, starting from their $(\text{lcp}[L, R] + 1)$-th character.

But actually, we can do better, because we know l and r, and these values can be significantly larger than $\text{lcp}[L, R]$, thus more characters of P have already been involved in previous comparisons and so they are known. We distinguish three main cases by assuming that $l \geq r$ (the other case $l < r$ is symmetric), and aim at not rescanning the characters of P that have been already seen (namely the characters in $P[1, l]$). We define our algorithm in such a way that the order between P and $suff_{SA[M]}$ can be inferred either by comparing characters in $P[l + 1, n]$, or by comparing the values l and $Llcp[M]$ (which give us information about $P[1, l]$).

---

[1] To simplify the presentation, we are using the right-hand range $[M, R]$ instead of $[M + 1, R]$, adopted in Algorithm 10.1. Since the middle element $SA[M]$ is shared by both the left and right ranges, we could end up in an infinite loop whenever $R - L = 1$. Nevertheless, we can easily change the while-condition of that algorithm in $R - L = 1$, and then explicitly check the two delimiting strings.

- If $l < Llcp[M]$, then P is greater that $\mathit{suff}_{SA[M]}$ and we can set $l = m$. In fact, by induction, $P > \mathit{suff}_{SA[L]}$ and their mismatched character lies at position $l + 1$. By definition of $Llcp[M]$ and the hypothesis (i.e. $l < Llcp[M]$), $\mathit{suff}_{SA[L]}$ shares more than l characters with $\mathit{suff}_{SA[M]}$. So $\mathit{suff}_{SA[M]}[l + 1] = \mathit{suff}_{SA[L]}[l + 1]$ and thus the mismatch between P and these two suffixes is the same, hence their comparison gives the same answer – that is, $P > \mathit{suff}_{SA[M]}$. The search can thus continue in the subrange $SA[M, R]$, without incurring any character comparison.
- If $l > Llcp[M]$, this case is similar to the previous one. We can conclude that P is smaller than $\mathit{suff}_{SA[M]}$ and it is $m = Llcp[M]$. So the search continues in the subrange $SA[L, M]$, without incurring any character comparison.
- If $l = Llcp[M]$, then P shares l characters with $\mathit{suff}_{SA[L]}$ and $\mathit{suff}_{SA[M]}$, so the comparison between P and $\mathit{suff}_{SA[M]}$ can start from their $(l + 1)$-th character. Eventually we determine m and their lexicographic order by executing some character comparisons, but the *knowledge* about P's characters advances too.

It is clear that every binary search step either advances the comparison of P's characters, or does not compare any character but halves the range $[L, R]$. The first case can occur at most p times, the second case can occur $O(\log n)$ times. We have therefore proved the following.

Lemma 10.2 *Given the three arrays* lcp, *Llcp, and Rlcp in addition to the suffix array SA built over a text $T[1, n]$, we can count the occurrences of a pattern $P[1, p]$ in the text T taking $O(p + \log n)$ time in the worst case. Retrieving the positions of these occ occurrences takes an additional $O(occ)$ time. The total required space is $O(n)$. All these bounds are optimal in the comparison-based model.*

Proof Remember that searching for all strings that have the pattern P as a prefix requires two lexicographic searches: one for P and the other for $P\#$, where $\#$ is a special character larger than any other alphabet character. So $O(p + \log n)$ character comparisons are enough to delimit the range $SA[i, j]$ of suffixes that have P as a prefix. It is then easy to count the pattern occurrences in constant time, as $occ = j - i + 1$, or print all of their positions in $O(occ)$ time. ∎

10.2.2   The LCP Array and Its Construction$^\infty$

Constructing the longest-common-prefix array lcp$[1, n - 1]$ seems simple and efficient: just scan the $n - 1$ contiguous pairs of text suffixes in SA and compare them character by character.[2] This would take $\Theta(\sum_{i=1}^{n-1}(\text{lcp}[i] + 1))$ time, where the $+1$ comes from the comparison of the mismatched character between $SA[i]$ and $SA[i + 1]$. This time bound can be $\Theta(n^2)$ for some pathological inputs, such as $T = a^n$. In this case $SA[i]$ points to $T[n - i + 1, n]$, for $i = 1, \ldots, n$, so lcp$[i] = i$ and thus the time complexity is $\Theta(\sum_{i=1}^{n-1}(\text{lcp}[i] + 1)) = \Theta(\sum_{i=1}^{n-1}(i + 1)) = \Theta(n^2)$, as claimed. In general, the time complexity is $O(n\ell)$ where ℓ is the average LCP among all T's suffixes.

---

[2] Recall that lcp$[i] = lcp\left(\mathit{suff}_{SA[i]}, \mathit{suff}_{SA[i+1]}\right)$ for $i < n$.

Sorted suffixes	SA	SA positions
<u>abc</u>def...	$j-1$	$p-1$
<u>abc</u>hi...	$i-1$	p
.	.	.
.	.	.
.	.	.
<u>bc</u>def...	j	.
.	.	.
.	.	.
.	.	.
<u>bc</u>h...	k	$q-1$
<u>bc</u>hi...	i	q

Figure 10.3 Relation between suffixes and lcp values in Kasai's algorithm. Suffixes are shown only with their starting characters; the rest is indicated with ... for simplicity.

But surprisingly enough, in 2001 Kasai and colleagues proposed an elegant, deceptively simple, and linear-time optimal algorithm to compute the `lcp` array, provided that the suffix array is known [12]. The linearity is obtained by avoiding the rescanning of text characters, based on some properties of the input text that they proved and deployed in the design of the algorithm, which we show and comment on in the rest of this section.

For the sake of presentation we will refer to Figure 10.3, which illustrates clearly the main algorithmic idea. Let us concentrate on two consecutive suffixes in the text T, say $suff_{i-1} = T[i-1, n]$ and $suff_i = T[i, n]$, which occur at positions p and q in the suffix array SA. That is, $SA[p] = suff_{i-1}$ and $SA[q] = suff_i$. Let us now consider the text suffix that lexicographically precedes $SA[p]$, say $SA[p-1] = suff_{j-1}$ for some j, and assume that we know inductively the value of $lcp[p-1]$, storing the length of longest common prefix between $SA[p-1]$ and $SA[p]$. Similarly, let us denote with $SA[q-1] = suff_k = T[k, n]$, for some k, the text suffix that lexicographically precedes $SA[q]$. By definition of `lcp` array, the entry $lcp[q-1]$ must store their longest common prefix.

Kasai's algorithm scans the text suffixes from left to right (see Algorithm 10.2), hence it examines $T[i, n]$ after having processed $T[i-1, n]$. Our goal is to show that $lcp[q-1]$, which refers to $T[i, n]$, can be efficiently derived from $lcp[p-1]$, which refers to $T[i-1, n]$. Here *efficiently* means that the computation of $lcp[q-1]$ does not need the full rescanning of $T[i, n]$ from its first character but can take advantage of the knowledge of $lcp[p-1]$ and thus start where the comparison between $SA[p-1]$ and $SA[p]$ ended. This will ensure that the rescanning of text characters is avoided and, as a result, we will get a linear-time complexity.

Algorithm 10.2 LCP-BUILD(T, SA)

1: $h = 0$;
2: **for** ($i = 1; i \leq n, i{+}{+}$) **do**
3:      $q = SA^{-1}[i]$;
4:      **if** $q > 1$ **then**
5:           $k = SA[q - 1]$;
6:           **if** $h > 0$ **then**
7:                $h = h - 1$;
8:           **end if**
9:           **while** $T[k + h] = T[i + h]$ **do**
10:               $h = h + 1$;
11:          **end while**
12:          $\texttt{lcp}[q - 1] = h$;
13:     **end if**
14: **end for**

We start from the following property that we already mentioned when dealing with prefix search, and that we restate here in the context of suffix arrays.

Fact 10.1 The longest common prefix (LCP) between the consecutive suffixes $SA[y - 1]$ and $SA[y]$ is not shorter than the LCP between $SA[y]$ and any other previous suffix $SA[x]$, where $x = 1, \ldots, y - 1$.

Proof This property derives from the observation that suffixes in SA are ordered lexicographically, so as we go farther from $SA[y]$ we reduce the length of their shared prefix.   ■

Let us now refer to Figure 10.3, and concentrate on a generic step i of Kasai's algorithm which has compared the pair of consecutive suffixes $SA[p - 1] = suff_{j-1}$ and $SA[p] = suff_{i-1}$, and then moves to compare the pair of consecutive suffixes $SA[q - 1] = suff_j$ and $SA[q] = suff_i$. There are two possible cases: either $\texttt{lcp}[p - 1] > 0$, and thus the two adjacent suffixes $SA[p - 1]$ and $SA[p]$ share some characters in their prefix (as in Figure 10.3), or they do not (i.e. $\texttt{lcp}[p - 1] = 0$).

In the former case we can conclude that, since lexicographically $suff_{j-1}$ comes before $suff_{i-1}$, their next suffixes in T will preserve that lexicographic order, so $suff_j$ will come before $suff_i$. Moreover, since $suff_j$ (resp., $suff_i$) is obtained from $suff_{j-1}$ (resp., $suff_{i-1}$) by dropping its first character, it is $lcp(suff_j, suff_i) = lcp(suff_{j-1}, suff_{i-1}) - 1 = \texttt{lcp}[p - 1] - 1$. In Figure 10.3, we have $\texttt{lcp}[p - 1] = 3$ and the shared prefix is abc, so when we consider the next suffixes their LCP is bc of length 2, and their order is preserved (as $suff_j$ occurs before $suff_i$).

Therefore we have proved the following property, here rephrased using the observation that $j = SA[p - 1] + 1$ and $i = SA[p] + 1$:

Fact 10.2 If $lcp(suff_{SA[p-1]}, suff_{SA[p]}) > 0$ then:

$$lcp(suff_{SA[p-1]+1}, suff_{SA[p]+1}) = lcp(suff_{SA[p-1]}, suff_{SA[p]}) - 1.$$

The next key observation is that, although $suff_{j-1}$ and $suff_{i-1}$ occur contiguously in SA, their next suffixes $suff_j$ and $suff_i$ may not, as Figure 10.3 depicts. Hence, by Fact 10.1 and Fact 10.2, we can derive the key property that $lcp[q-1] \geq \max\{lcp[p-1] - 1, 0\}$. This is algorithmically deployed by Kasai's algorithm to compute $lcp[q-1]$ taking full advantage of what we compared for deriving $lcp[p-1]$.

The pseudocode is shown in Algorithm 10.2, where we make use of the inverse suffix array, denoted by SA^{-1}, which returns for every suffix its position in SA. Referring to Figure 10.3, $SA^{-1}[i] = q$ and $SA^{-1}[i-1] = p$. Algorithm 10.2 hinges on the for-loop that scans the text suffixes $suff_i$ from left to right, and for each of them it retrieves their position in SA, namely $q = SA^{-1}[i]$, and finally sets the content of $lcp[q-1]$ (see Step 12). In order to make this initialization consistent, Step 4 checks whether $suff_i$ occupies the first position of the suffix array (i.e. $q = 1$), in which case the LCP with the previous suffix is undefined, and so the algorithm skips the LCP computation and moves to the next i. Otherwise (i.e. $q > 1$), Step 5 computes the suffix lexicographically preceding $suff_i$ as $k = SA[q-1]$, and then the algorithm extends via character-by-character comparison the LCP between $SA[q-1]$ and $SA[q]$ starting from the offset $h = lcp[p-1]$, which is properly reduced by one unit with Step 6, according to Fact 10.2.

As far as the time complexity is concerned, note that h is decreased at most n times (once per iteration of the for-loop), and it cannot move outside T because of Step 9, since T is terminated by a special character, such as \0 in C. This implies that h can be increased at most $2n$ times and this is therefore the upper bound to the number of character comparisons executed by Algorithm 10.2. The total time complexity is therefore $O(n)$. Clearly, this algorithm is not I/O-efficient because it sets the lcp entries in an arbitrary order. Some heuristics are known to reduce the number of I/Os incurred by the above computation, but an optimal $O(n/B)$ I/O bound, if it is actually possible, is yet to come.

Theorem 10.1 *Given a string $T[1, n]$ and its suffix array SA_T, we can derive the corresponding* lcp *array in $O(n)$ time and space. Running this algorithm in the two-level memory model may be inefficient and takes $O(n)$ I/Os.*

10.2.3   Suffix-Array Construction

Given that the suffix array is a sorted sequence of suffixes, the most intuitive way to construct SA is to use an efficient comparison-based sorting algorithm and specialize the comparison function in such a way that it computes the lexicographic order between strings. Algorithm 10.3 implements this idea in C-style using the built-in procedure QSORT as sorter and a properly defined subroutine Suffix_cmp for comparing suffixes:

```
Suffix_cmp(char **p, char **q){  return  strcmp(*p,*q); };
```

Algorithm 10.3 COMPARISON_BASED_CONSTRUCTION(char *T, int n, char **SA)

1: **for** $(i = 0; i < n; i ++)$ **do**
2:     $SA[i] = T + i;$
3: **end for**
4: QSORT(SA, n, sizeof(char *), Suffix_cmp);

Notice that the suffix array is initialized with the pointers to the real starting positions in memory of the suffixes to be sorted, and not the integer offsets from 1 to n as stated in the formal description of SA at the start of Section 10.2. The reason for this is that, here, Suffix_cmp does not need to know T's position in memory (which would have required the use of a global parameter), because its actual parameters, passed during an invocation, provide directly the starting memory positions of the suffixes to be compared. Moreover, the suffix array SA has indexes starting from 0 as is typical of the C language.

A major drawback of this simple approach is that it is not I/O-efficient, for two main reasons: the optimal number $O(n \log n)$ of comparisons now involves variable-length strings which may consist of up to $\Theta(n)$ characters; and locality in SA does not translate into locality in suffix comparisons because of the fact that sorting permutes the string pointers rather than the strings themselves. Both these issues elicit I/Os, and turn this simple algorithm into a slow one.

Theorem 10.2 *In the worst case, the use of a comparison-based sorter to construct the suffix array of a given string $T[1, n]$ requires $O((\frac{n}{B})n \log n)$ I/Os, and $O(n \log n)$ bits of working space.*

In the rest of this section we describe two I/O-efficient approaches to suffix array construction. One is based on a divide-and-conquer algorithm – the DC3 algorithm proposed by Kärkkäinen and Sanders [11] – which is elegant, easy to code, and flexible enough to achieve the optimal I/O bound in various models of computations. The other – the Scan-based algorithm proposed by Gonnet, Baeza-Yates, and Snider [10] – is also simple and, although incurring a larger number of I/Os, is still interesting because it offers the positive feature of processing the input data in passes (streaming-like) which force prefetching, allow compression, and hence make this approach suitable for slow disks.

The Skew Algorithm

In 2003 Kärkkäinen and Sanders [11] showed that the problem of constructing suffix arrays can be *reduced* to the problem of sorting a set of triplets whose components are integers in the range $[1, O(n)]$. Surprisingly, this reduction takes *linear time and space*, thus turning the complexity of suffix-array construction into the complexity of sorting atomic items, a problem we have discussed deeply in previous chapters and for which we know optimal algorithms for hierarchical memories and multiple disks. More than this, since the items to be sorted are integers bounded in value by $O(n)$, the sorting of the triplets takes $O(n)$ time in the RAM model, so we known how to construct a suffix array in RAM taking linear-time complexity. Really impressive!

The precious feature of this algorithm is that it works in every model of computation for which an efficient sorting primitive is available. It hinges on a divide-and-conquer approach that executes a $\frac{2}{3} : \frac{1}{3}$ split, crucial to make the final merge step easy to implement. Previous approaches used the more natural $\frac{1}{2} : \frac{1}{2}$ split (such as [4]), but they were forced to use a more sophisticated merge step which needed the use of the suffix-tree data structure (described in Section 10.3). Because of the *nonbalancedness* of the underlying divide-and-conquer scheme, the algorithm was originally named *skew*, and then it was named *DC3* (which stands for *difference cover modulo 3*).

For the sake of presentation, we use $T[1, n] = t_1 t_2 \ldots t_n$ to denote the input string and we assume that the characters are drawn from an integer alphabet of size $\sigma = O(n)$. If that is not the case, we can sort the characters of T and rename them with integers in $[0, n-1]$, taking overall $O(n \log \sigma)$ time in the worst case. So T is a text of integers, taking $O(\log n)$ bits each; this will be the case for all texts created during the suffix-array construction process. Furthermore, we assume that $t_n = \$$, a special symbol smaller than any other alphabet character, and logically pad T with an infinite number of occurrences of $\$$.

Given this notation, we can sketch the three main steps of the Skew algorithm:

Step 1: Construct the suffix array $SA^{2,0}$ limited to the suffixes starting at positions

$$P_{2,0} = \{i : i \bmod 3 = 2, \text{ or } i \bmod 3 = 0\}.$$

This consists of the following three substeps:

- Build a special string $T^{2,0}$ of length $(2/3)n$ that compactly encodes all suffixes of T starting at positions $P_{2,0}$.
- Build recursively the suffix array SA' of $T^{2,0}$.
- Derive the suffix array $SA^{2,0}$ from SA'.

Step 2: Construct the suffix array SA^1 of the remaining suffixes, starting at positions

$$P_1 = \{i : i \bmod 3 = 1\}.$$

This consists of the following three substeps:

- Assume we have precomputed the array pos[j] which provides the position of the j-th text suffix $T[j, n]$ in $SA^{2,0}$.
- For every $i \in P_1$, represent suffix $T[i, n]$ with a pair $\langle T[i], \text{pos}[i+1] \rangle$, where it is $i + 1 \in P_{2,0}$.
- Use RADIXSORT over the $O(n)$ pairs.

Step 3: Merge the two suffix arrays $SA^{2,0}$ and SA^1 into one, via the following substep:

- Deploy the decomposition $\frac{2}{3} : \frac{1}{3}$, which ensures a constant-time lexicographic comparison between any pair of suffixes (see details later in section).

This algorithm is detailed in the following pages, and illustrated over the input string $T[1, 12] =$ "mississippi\$" whose suffix array is $SA = (12, 11, 8, 5, 2, 1, 10, 9, 7, 4, 6, 3)$. In this example we have $P_{2,0} = \{2, 3, 5, 6, 8, 9, 11, 12\}$ and $P_1 = \{1, 4, 7, 10\}$.

Step 1. The first step is the most involved, and constitutes the backbone of the entire recursive process. It lexicographically sorts the suffixes starting at the text positions $P_{2,0}$. The resulting array is denoted by $SA^{2,0}$ and represents a *sampled* version of the final suffix array SA because it is restricted to the suffixes starting at positions $P_{2,0}$.

To efficiently obtain $SA^{2,0}$, we reduce the problem to the construction of the suffix array for a string $T^{2,0}$ of length about $2n/3$. This text consists of "characters" which are integers whose maximum value is about $2n/3$. Since we are *again* in the presence of a text of integers, of length proportionally smaller than n, we can construct its suffix array by invoking *recursively* the same construction procedure.

The key difficulty is how to define $T^{2,0}$ so that its suffix array may be used to derive easily $SA^{2,0}$, namely the sorted sequence of text suffixes starting at positions in $P_{2,0}$. The elegant solution proposed in [11] consists of considering the two text suffixes $T[2, n]$ and $T[3, n]$, padding them with the special symbol \$ in order to have multiple-of-three length, and then decomposing the resulting strings into triplets of characters, that is, $T[2, \cdot] = [t_2, t_3, t_4][t_5, t_6, t_7][t_8, t_9, t_{10}] \ldots$ and $T[3, \cdot] = [t_3, t_4, t_5][t_6, t_7, t_8][t_9, t_{10}, t_{11}] \ldots$. The dot expresses the fact that we are considering the smallest integer larger than n that allows those strings to have length which is a multiple of three.

With reference to the previous example, we have:

$$T[2, \cdot] = \underset{2}{[\text{i s s}]} \underset{5}{[\text{i s s}]} \underset{8}{[\text{i p p}]} \underset{11}{[\text{i \$ \$}]} \quad T[3, \cdot] = \underset{3}{[\text{s s i}]} \underset{6}{[\text{s s i}]} \underset{9}{[\text{p p i}]} \underset{12}{[\text{\$ \$ \$}]}$$

We then concatenate these two strings and construct the string $R = T[2, \cdot] \, T[3, \cdot]$:

$$R = \underset{2}{[\text{i s s}]} \underset{5}{[\text{i s s}]} \underset{8}{[\text{i p p}]} \underset{11}{[\text{i \$ \$}]} \underset{3}{[\text{s s i}]} \underset{6}{[\text{s s i}]} \underset{9}{[\text{p p i}]} \underset{12}{[\text{\$ \$ \$}]}$$

The key property on which the first step of the Skew algorithm hinges on is:

Property 1: Every suffix $T[i, n]$ starting at a position $i \in P_{2,0}$ can be put in correspondence with a suffix of the string R consisting of an integral sequence of triplets. Specifically, if $i \bmod 3 = 0$ then $T[i, n]$ coincides exactly with a suffix of R; if $i \bmod 3 = 2$, then $T[i, n]$ prefixes a suffix of R which nevertheless terminates with the special symbol \$.

By the previous running example, take $i = 6 \in P_{2,0}$, because $i \bmod 3 = 0$, and note that the suffix $T[6, 12] = \text{ssippi\$}$ occurs at the second triplet of $T[3, \cdot]$, which is the sixth triplet of R. Similarly, take $i = 8 \in P_{2,0}$, because $i \bmod 3 = 2$, and note that the suffix $T[8, 12] = \text{ippi\$}$ occurs at the third triplet of $T[2, \cdot]$, which is the third triplet of R. Note that, even if $T[8, 12]$ is not a full suffix of R, $T[8, 12]$ ends with two \$s, which will constitute a sort of end delimiter.

Formally speaking, the correctness of this property can be inferred easily by observing that any suffix $T[i, n]$ starting at a position $i \in P_{2,0}$ is clearly a suffix either of $T[2, \cdot]$ or of $T[3, \cdot]$, given that $i > 0$, and $i \bmod 3$ is either 0 or 2. Moreover, since $i \in P_{2,0}$, it has the form $i = 3 + 3k$ or $i = 2 + 3k$, for some $k \geq 0$, and thus $T[i, n]$ occurs within R aligned to the beginning of some triplet.

The final operation to get the string $T^{2,0}$ of $(2n/3)$ integer symbols is then to encode those triplets via integers. This encoding must be implemented in a way that the lexicographic comparison between two triplets can be obtained by comparing those integers. In the literature this is called *lexicographic naming*, and can be easily obtained by using RADIXSORT over the triplets in R and associating with each distinct triplet its *rank* in the lexicographic order. Since we have $O(n)$ triplets, each consisting of symbols in a range $[0, n]$, their RADIXSORT takes $O(n)$ time.

In our example, the sorted triplets are labeled with the following ranks:

[\$ \$ \$]	[i \$ \$]	[i p p]	[i s s]	[i s s]	[p p i]	[s s i]	[s s i]	sorted triplets
0	1	2	3	3	4	5	5	sorted ranks

which allow us to construct the string:

$R =$	[i s s]	[i s s]	[i p p]	[i \$ \$]	[s s i]	[s s i]	[p p i]	[\$ \$ \$]	triplets
	3	3	2	1	5	5	4	0	$T^{2,0}$

As a result of the naming of the triplets in R, we get the new text $T^{2,0} = 33215540$ whose length is $2n/3$. The crucial observation here is that we have a text $T^{2,0}$ which is again a text of integers as T, taking $O(\log n)$ bits per integer (as before), but $T^{2,0}$ has a shorter length than T, so we can invoke recursively the suffix-array construction procedure over it.

It is evident from this discussion that, since the ranks are assigned in the same order as the lexicographic order of their triplets, the lexicographic comparison between suffixes of R (aligned to the triplets) equals the lexicographic comparison between suffixes of $T^{2,0}$. Here Property 1 comes into play, because it defines a bijection between suffixes of R aligned to triplet beginnings, hence suffixes of $T^{2,0}$, with text suffixes starting in $P_{2,0}$. This correspondence is then deployed to derive $SA^{2,0}$ from the suffix array of $T^{2,0}$.

In our running example $T^{2,0} = 33215540$, the suffix-array construction algorithm is applied recursively, thus deriving its suffix array $(8, 4, 3, 2, 1, 7, 6, 5)$. We can turn this suffix array into $SA^{2,0}$ by turning the positions in $T^{2,0}$ into positions in T. This can be done via simple arithmetic operations, given the layout of the triplets in $T^{2,0}$, and obtains in our running example the suffix array $SA^{2,0} = (12, 11, 8, 5, 2, 9, 6, 3)$.

Before concluding the description of Step 1, we add two notes. The first is that, if all symbols in $T^{2,0}$ are different, then we do not need to recurse because suffixes can be sorted by looking just at their first characters. The second observation is for programmers: they should be careful when turning the suffix positions in $T^{2,0}$ into the suffix positions in T to get the final $SA^{2,0}$, because they must take into account the layout of the triplets of R.

Step 2. Once the suffix array $SA^{2,0}$ has been built (recursively), it is possible to sort lexicographically the remaining suffixes of T, namely the ones starting at the text positions $i \bmod 3 = 1$, in a simple way. We decompose a suffix $T[i, n]$ as a pair composed by its first character $T[i]$ and its remaining suffix $T[i + 1, n]$. Since $i \in P_1$, the next position $i + 1 \in P_{2,0}$, and thus the suffix $T[i + 1, n]$ occurs in $SA^{2,0}$. We can then encode the suffix $T[i, n]$ with a pair of integers $\langle T[i], \mathrm{pos}[i + 1] \rangle$, where $\mathrm{pos}[i + 1]$ denotes the lexicographic rank in $SA^{2,0}$ of the suffix $T[i + 1, n]$. If $i + 1 = n + 1$ then we set $\mathrm{pos}[n + 1] = 0$, given that the character $\$$ is assumed to be smaller than any other alphabet character.

Given this observation, two text suffixes starting at positions in P_1 can then be compared in constant time by comparing their corresponding pairs. Therefore SA^1 can be computed in $O(n)$ time by using RADIXSORT on the $O(n)$ pairs encoding its suffixes.

In our example, this boils down to using RADIXSORT on the following pairs $\langle T[i], \mathrm{pos}[i + 1] \rangle$, thus obtaining the suffix array $SA^1 = (1, 10, 7, 4)$.

Starting position in P_1	1		4		7		10
Pairs: char + text suffix	$\langle T[1], T[2, \cdot] \rangle$		$\langle T[4], T[5, 12] \rangle$		$\langle T[7], T[8, 12] \rangle$		$\langle T[10], T[11, 12] \rangle$
	$\langle \mathrm{m}, T[2, \cdot] \rangle$		$\langle \mathrm{s}, T[5, 12] \rangle$		$\langle \mathrm{s}, T[8, 12] \rangle$		$\langle \mathrm{p}, T[11, 12] \rangle$
Pairs: char + suffix position in $SA^{2,0}$	$\langle \mathrm{m}, \mathrm{pos}[2] \rangle$		$\langle \mathrm{s}, \mathrm{pos}[5] \rangle$		$\langle \mathrm{s}, \mathrm{pos}[8] \rangle$		$\langle \mathrm{p}, \mathrm{pos}[11] \rangle$
	$\langle \mathrm{m}, 4 \rangle$		$\langle \mathrm{s}, 3 \rangle$		$\langle \mathrm{s}, 2 \rangle$		$\langle \mathrm{p}, 1 \rangle$
Sorted pairs	$\langle \mathrm{m}, 4 \rangle$	$<$	$\langle \mathrm{p}, 1 \rangle$	$<$	$\langle \mathrm{s}, 2 \rangle$	$<$	$\langle \mathrm{s}, 3 \rangle$
SA^1	1		10		7		4

Step 3. The final step merges the two sorted arrays SA^1 and $SA^{2,0}$ in linear $O(n)$ time by resorting to an interesting observation which motivates the split $\frac{2}{3} : \frac{1}{3}$. Let us take two suffixes $T[i, n] \in SA^1$ and $T[j, n] \in SA^{2,0}$, which we wish to lexicographically compare for implementing the merge step. They belong to two different suffix arrays, so we have no *lexicographic relation* known for them, and we cannot compare them character by character because this would incur a very high cost. We deploy a decomposition idea similar to the one exploited in Step 2, which consists in regarding a suffix as composed of *one or two characters* plus the lexicographic rank of its remaining suffix. This decomposition becomes effective if the remaining suffixes of the compared ones lie in the same suffix array, so their rank is enough to get their order in constant time. Elegantly enough, this is possible with the split $\frac{2}{3} : \frac{1}{3}$, but it would not be possible with the split $\frac{1}{2} : \frac{1}{2}$. This observation is implemented as follows:

1. if $j \bmod 3 = 2$ then we compare $T[j, n]$ against $T[i, n]$ by looking at them as the pairs $\langle T[j], T[j+1, n] \rangle$ and $\langle T[i], T[i+1, n] \rangle$. Both suffixes $T[j+1, n]$ and $T[i+1, n]$

occur in $SA^{2,0}$ (given that their starting positions are congruent to 0 or 2 modulo 3, respectively), so we can derive this lexicographic comparison by comparing the pairs $\langle T[i], \text{pos}[i+1] \rangle$ and $\langle T[j], \text{pos}[j+1] \rangle$. This comparison takes $O(1)$ time, provided that the array pos is available.[3]

2. if $j \bmod 3 = 0$ then we compare $T[j, n]$ against $T[i, n]$ by comparing the triples $\langle T[j], T[j+1], T[j+2, n] \rangle$ against $\langle T[i], T[i+1], T[i+2, n] \rangle$. Both suffixes $T[j+2, n]$ and $T[i+2, n]$ occur in $SA^{2,0}$ (given that their starting positions are congruent to 0 or 2 mod 3, respectively), so we can derive this lexicographic comparison by comparing the triples $\langle T[i], T[i+1], \text{pos}[i+2] \rangle$ and $\langle T[j], T[j+1], \text{pos}[j+2] \rangle$. This comparison takes $O(1)$ time, provided that the array pos is available.

In our running example, $T[8, 11] < T[10, 11]$, and in fact $\langle i, 5 \rangle < \langle p, 1 \rangle$. Also, $T[7, 11] < T[6, 11]$, and in fact $\langle s, i, 5 \rangle < \langle s, s, 2 \rangle$. In the following diagram, we depict for SA^1 all possible pairs or triples which may be involved in a comparison, where ($\star$) and ($\star\star$) denote pairs and triples for rules 1 and 2 above, respectively. In fact, since we do not know which suffix of $SA^{2,0}$ will be compared with a suffix of SA^1 during the merging process, for each of the latter suffixes we need to compute both representations ($\star$) and ($\star\star$), hence as a pair and as a triple.[4] At the end of the merge step we obtain the final suffix array: $SA = (12, 11, 8, 5, 2, 1, 10, 9, 7, 4, 6, 3)$.

	SA^1				$SA^{2,0}$							
1	10	7	4	12	11	8	5	2	9	6	3	suffix positions
$\langle \mathtt{m}, 4 \rangle$	$\langle \mathtt{p}, 1 \rangle$	$\langle \mathtt{s}, 2 \rangle$	$\langle \mathtt{s}, 3 \rangle$		$\langle \mathtt{i}, 0 \rangle$	$\langle \mathtt{i}, 5 \rangle$	$\langle \mathtt{i}, 6 \rangle$	$\langle \mathtt{i}, 7 \rangle$				($\star$)
$\langle \mathtt{m}, \mathtt{i}, 7 \rangle$	$\langle \mathtt{p}, \mathtt{i}, 0 \rangle$	$\langle \mathtt{s}, \mathtt{i}, 5 \rangle$	$\langle \mathtt{s}, \mathtt{i}, 6 \rangle$	$\langle \$, \$, -1 \rangle$					$\langle \mathtt{p}, \mathtt{p}, 1 \rangle$	$\langle \mathtt{s}, \mathtt{s}, 2 \rangle$	$\langle \mathtt{s}, \mathtt{s}, 3 \rangle$	($\star\star$)

From our discussion, it is clear that every step can be implemented via sorting or scanning a set of n atomic items, which are possibly triples of integers taking $O(\log n)$ bits each, so $O(1)$ memory words. Therefore the proposed method can be seen as an *algorithmic reduction* of the suffix-array construction problem to the classic problem of sorting n items.

As far as the RAM model is concerned, the time complexity of the Skew algorithm can be modeled by the recurrence relation $T(n) = T(\frac{2n}{3}) + O(n)$, because Steps 2 and 3 cost $O(n)$ and the recursive call is executed over the string $T^{2,0}$ whose length is $(2/3)n$. This recurrence has solution $T(n) = O(n)$, which is clearly optimal. For the two-level memory model, the Skew algorithm can be implemented in $O(\frac{n}{B} \log_{M/B} \frac{n}{M})$ I/Os, that is, the I/O complexity of sorting n atomic items.

Theorem 10.3 *The Skew algorithm builds the suffix array of a string $T[1, n]$ in $O(\text{Sort}(n))$ I/Os, using $O(n/B)$ disk pages. If the alphabet size σ is polynomial in n, the CPU time is $O(n)$.*

---

[3] Of course, the array pos can be derived from $SA^{2,0}$ in linear time, since it is its inverse.
[4] Recall that $\text{pos}[n] = 0$, and for the sake of the lexicographic order, we set $\text{pos}[j] = -1$, for all $j > n$.

The Scan-Based Algorithm$^\infty$

Before the introduction of the Skew algorithm, the best-known disk-based algorithm was the one proposed by Gonnet, Baeza-Yates, and Snider in 1992 [10]. It is also a divide-and-conquer algorithm whose divide step is strongly unbalanced, thus it executes a quadratic number of suffix comparisons which induce a *cubic* time complexity. Nevertheless, the algorithm is fast in practice because it processes the data into passes, thus deploying the high throughput of modern disks.

Let $\ell < 1$ be a positive constant, fixed to build the suffix array of a text piece of $m = \ell M$ characters in internal memory. Then assume that the text $T[1, n]$ is logically divided into blocks of m characters each, numbered rightward: namely $T = T_1 T_2 \cdots T_{n/m}$ where $T_h = T[hm + 1, (h + 1)m]$ for $h = 0, 1, \ldots$. The algorithm computes *incrementally* the suffix array of T in $\Theta(n/M)$ stages, rather than the logarithmic number of stages of the Skew algorithm. At the beginning of stage h, we assume we have on disk *the array SA^h that contains the sorted sequence of the first hm suffixes of T*. Initially $h = 0$ and thus SA^0 is an empty array. In the generic h-th stage, the algorithm loads the next text piece T^{h+1} in internal memory, builds SA' as the sorted sequence of suffixes *starting* in T^{h+1}, and then computes the new array SA^{h+1} by merging the two sorted sequences SA^h and SA'.

There are two main issues when implementing this algorithmic idea:

- how to efficiently construct SA', since its suffixes start in T^{h+1} but may extend outside that block of characters up to the end of T;
- how to efficiently merge the two sorted arrays SA^h and SA', since they involve suffixes whose length may be up to $\Theta(n)$ characters.

For the first issue, the algorithm does not implement any special trick; it just compares pairs of suffixes character by character in $O(n)$ time and $O(n/B)$ I/Os, thus possibly extending the suffix comparisons outside the block loaded in internal memory. This means that over the total execution of the $O(n/M)$ stages, the algorithm constructs SA' in $O\left(\frac{n}{B} \frac{n}{m} m \log m\right) = O\left(\frac{n^2}{B} \log m\right)$ I/Os.

For the second issue, the algorithm adopts a smart approach to merging SA' with SA^h, by resorting to the use of an auxiliary array $C[1, m + 1]$ which counts in $C[j]$ the number of suffixes of SA^h that are lexicographically greater than the $SA'[j - 1]$-th text suffix and smaller than the $SA'[j]$-th text suffix, where we logically set $SA'[0]$ to be the empty string and $SA'[m + 1]$ to be a special string larger than any other. Since SA^h is increasingly long, it cannot be fit in internal memory, and therefore we process it streaming-like by scanning rightward the text T (from its beginning) and then binary searching each suffix in SA'. If the lexicographic position of the searched suffix is j, then the entry $C[j]$ is incremented. The binary search in SA^h may involve the comparison of some suffix characters outside the block T^{h+1}, currently in internal memory, so we have to count the worst case $O(n/B)$ I/Os per binary search step. Over all n/M stages, the computation of array C takes $O\left(\sum_{h=0}^{n/m-1} \frac{n}{B}(hm) \log m\right) = O\left(\frac{n^3}{MB} \log M\right)$ I/Os (recall that $m = \ell M$).

Array C is then exploited in the next substep to quickly merge the two arrays SA' (residing in internal memory) and SA^h (residing on disk): $C[j]$ indicates how many consecutive suffixes of SA^h lexicographically lie after $SA'[j-1]$ and before $SA'[j]$. Hence a disk scan suffices to perform the merging process in $O(n/B)$ I/Os.

Theorem 10.4 *The Scan-based algorithm builds the suffix array of a string $T[1, n]$ in* $O\left(\frac{n^3}{MB}\log M\right)$ *I/Os, using $O(n/B)$ disk pages.*

Since the worst-case number of total I/Os is cubic, a purely theoretical analysis would classify this algorithm as uninteresting. However, in practical situations it is very reasonable to assume that each suffix comparison finds in internal memory all the characters used to compare the two suffixes involved in a binary search step. And indeed, the practical behavior of this algorithm is better described by the formula $O\left(\frac{n^2}{MB}\right)$ I/Os. Additionally, all I/Os in this analysis are sequential and the actual number of random seeks is only $O(n/M)$ (i.e. at most a constant number per stage). Consequently, the algorithm takes full advantage of the large bandwidth of modern disks and of the high speed of current CPUs. As a final note we remark that the suffix arrays SA^h and the text T are scanned sequentially, so some form of compression can be adopted to reduce the I/O volume, and thus further speed up the underlying algorithm.

Before detailing a significant improvement to the previous approach, let us illustrate the working of the Scan-based algorithm on the same running example used in the previous section for the Skew algorithm, and referring to the following text string.

$$
\begin{array}{ccccccccccccc}
 & 1 & 2 & 3 & 4 & 5 & 6 & 7 & 8 & 9 & 10 & 11 & 12 \\
T[1, 12] = & m & i & s & s & i & s & s & i & p & p & i & \$
\end{array}
$$

Suppose that $m = 3$ and that, at the beginning of stage $h = 1$, the algorithm has already processed the text block $T^0 = T[1, 3] = \text{mis}$, and thus computed and stored on disk the array $SA^1 = (2, 1, 3)$ which corresponds to the lexicographic order of the three text suffixes starting in that block: namely, $\text{mississippi\$}$, $\text{issis-sippi\$}$, and $\text{ssissippi\$}$. During Stage 1, the algorithm loads in internal memory the next block $T^1 = T[4, 6] = \text{sis}$, and lexicographically sorts the text suffixes that start in positions $[4, 6]$ and extend to the end of T, as illustrated in Figure 10.4. Note that, in Step 2, the comparison between the text suffixes $T[4, 12] = \text{sis-sippi\$}$ and $T[6, 12] = \text{ssippi\$}$ involves characters that lie outside the text piece $T[4, 6]$, available in internal memory, so their comparison induces some I/Os. The final step, Step 3, computes the new array SA^2 by merging $SA^1 = (2, 1, 3)$, stored on disk, with $SA' = (5, 4, 6)$, available in internal memory. Figure 10.4 illustrates this merge on our running example with the array $C[1, 4] = [0, 2, 0, 1]$: in fact it is $C[2] = 2$, because two suffixes, $T[1, 12] = \text{mississippi\$}$ and $T[2, 12] = \text{ississippi\$}$, are between the $SA'[1]$-th suffix $T[5, 12] = \text{issippi\$}$ and the $SA'[2]$-th suffix $T[4, 12] = \text{sissippi\$}$; and $C[4] = 1$ because suffix $T[3, 12] = \text{ssissippi\$}$ lies after the $SA'[3]$-th suffix $T[6, 12] = \text{ssippi\$}$.

Stage 1:

(1)   Load into internal memory $T^1 = T[4,6] = \text{sis}$.

(2)   Build SA' for the suffixes starting in $[4,6]$:

Text suffixes	sissippi\$	issippi\$	ssippi\$
		⇓	
		lexicographic ordering	
		⇓	
Sorted suffixes	issippi\$	sissippi\$	ssippi\$
SA′	5	4	6

(3)   Merge SA' with SA^1 exploiting array C:

Suffix arrays	$SA' = [5,4,6]$ $SA^1 = [2,1,3]$
Merge via C	$\underbrace{\qquad}_{\Downarrow\ C=[0,2,0,1]}$
	$SA^2 = [5,2,1,4,6,3]$

Figure 10.4 Stage 1 of the Scan-based algorithm.

Figures 10.5 and 10.6 illustrate the next two stages processing the text substrings $T^2 = T[7,9] = \text{sip}$ and $T^3 = T[10,12] = \text{pi\$}$. In particular, the second stage loads in memory $T^2 = T[7,9]$ and builds the suffix array SA' for the suffixes starting at positions $[7,9]$. This suffix array is then merged with array SA^2, residing on disk and containing the suffixes that start in $T[1,6]$ (illustrated in Figure 10.4). The third and last stage, summarized in Figure 10.6, loads in memory $T^3 = T[10,12]$ and builds the suffix array SA' for the suffixes starting at positions $[10,12]$. This suffix array is then merged with array SA^3, residing on disk and containing the suffixes that start in $T[1,9]$ (illustrated in Figure 10.6). The merged array is the suffix array of the entire string $T[1,12]$.

The asymptotic performance of the Scan-based algorithm claimed in Theorem 10.4 can be improved via a simple observation. Assume that, at the beginning of stage h, in addition to array SA^h we have on disk a bit array, called gt_h, such that $\mathsf{gt}_h[i] = 1$ if and only if the suffix $T[(hm+1)+i,n]$ is greater than (hence gt) the suffix $T[(hm+1),n]$ or, in other words, the text suffix starting at the i-th character of T^h is greater than the text suffix starting at its first character. The computation of gt can be performed I/O-efficiently, but this technicality is left to the original paper [7] and not detailed here.

During the h-th stage the algorithm loads into internal memory the substring $t[1,2m] = T^h T^{h+1}$ (so this is double in size with respect to the previous proposal) and the binary array $\mathsf{gt}_{h+1}[1,m-1]$ (so it refers to the second block of text loaded in internal memory). The key observation is that we can build SA' for the suffixes starting in T^h by deploying the two arrays without performing any I/Os, other than the ones needed to load $t[1,2m]$ and $\mathsf{gt}_{h+1}[1,m-1]$. This seems surprising, but it derives from the fact that any two text suffixes starting at positions i and j within T^h, with $i < j$, can be compared lexicographically by looking first at some of their characters in the

Stage 2:

(1)   Load into internal memory $T^2 = T[7, 9] = \texttt{sip}$.

(2)   Build *SA'* for the suffixes starting in [7, 9]:

Text suffixes	sippi$	ippi$	ppi$
		⇓	
		lexicographic ordering	
		⇓	
Sorted suffixes	ippi$	ppi$	sippi$
SA'	8	9	7

(3)   Merge *SA'* with *SA²* exploiting array *C*:

Suffix arrays	$\underbrace{SA' = [8, 9, 7] \quad SA^2 = [5, 2, 1, 4, 6, 3]}$
Merge via *C*	$\Downarrow C=[0,3,0,3]$
	$SA^3 = [8, 5, 2, 1, 9, 7, 4, 6, 3]$

Figure 10.5 Stage 2 of the Scan-based algorithm.

Stage 3:

(1)   Load into internal memory $T^3 = T[10, 12] = \texttt{pi\$}$.

(2)   Build *SA'* for the suffixes starting in [10, 12]:

Text suffixes	pi$	i$	$
		⇓	
		lexicographic ordering	
		⇓	
Sorted suffixes	$	i$	pi$
SA'	12	11	10

(3)   Merge *SA'* with *SA³* exploiting array *C*:

Suffix arrays	$\underbrace{SA' = [12, 11, 10] \quad SA^3 = [8, 5, 2, 1, 9, 7, 4, 6, 3]}$
Merge via *C*	$\Downarrow C=[0,0,4,5]$
	$SA^4 = [12, 11, 8, 5, 2, 1, 10, 9, 7, 4, 6, 3]$

Figure 10.6 Stage 3 of the Scan-based algorithm.

substring t, namely at the substrings $t[i, m]$ and $t[j, j + m - i]$. These two substrings have the same length and are completely in $t[1, 2m]$, hence in internal memory. If these strings differ, their order is determined and we are done; otherwise, the order between these two suffixes is determined by the order of their remaining suffixes starting at the characters $t[m + 1]$ and $t[j + m - i + 1]$. This order is given by the bit stored in

$gt_{h+1}[j-i]$, also available in internal memory. In conclusion, the two arrays t and gt_{h+1} contain all information needed to build SA^{h+1} by working entirely in internal memory, and thus without performing any I/Os.

Theorem 10.5 *The new variant of the Scan-based algorithm builds the suffix array of a string $T[1,n]$ in $O\left(\frac{n^2}{MB}\right)$ I/Os, using $O(n/B)$ disk pages.*

As an example consider stage $h = 1$ which loads in internal memory the substring $t = T^1T^2 = T[4,9] = $ sis sip, and the array $gt_2 = (0,0)$. The content of gt_2 follows from the fact that $gt_2[1] = 0$ because $T^2[1+1, \cdot] = $ ippi\$ $< T^2[1, \cdot] = $ sippi\$, and $gt_2[2] = 0$ because $T^2[1+2, \cdot] = $ pi\$ $< T^2[1, \cdot] = $ sippi\$. Now consider the positions $i = 1$ and $j = 2$ in t, we can compare the text suffixes starting at these positions by first taking the substrings $t[1,3] = T[4,6] = $ sis with $t[3,5] = T[6,9] = $ ssi. The strings are different so we obtain their order without accessing the disk. Now consider the positions $i = 3$ and $j = 4$ in t; they would not be taken into account by the algorithm since the block has size 3, but let us consider them for the sake of explanation. We can compare the text suffixes starting at these positions by first taking the substrings $t[3,3] = $ s with $t[4,4] = $ s. The strings are not different so we use $gt_2[j-i] = gt_2[1] = 0$, and hence the remaining $(j-i)$-th suffix $T[8, .] = $ ippi\$, is lexicographically smaller than the first suffix $T[7, .] = $ sippi\$, and this can be determined again without any I/Os.

10.3   The Suffix Tree

The *suffix tree* is a fundamental data structure used in many algorithms that process variable-length strings [9]. In its essence it is a compacted trie that stores all suffixes of an input string, where each suffix is represented by a (unique) path from the root of the trie to one of its leaves. We have already discussed compacted tries in Chapter 9; now we specialize that description to the context of a dictionary of strings that are suffixes of one single string.

Let us denote the suffix tree built over an input string $T[1,n]$ as ST_T (or just ST when the input is clear from the context) and assume, as done for suffix arrays, that the last character of T is the special symbol \$ which is smaller than any other alphabet character. The suffix tree has the following properties:

1. Each suffix of T is represented by a *unique* path descending from the root of ST to one of its leaves. So there are n leaves, one per text suffix, and each leaf is labeled with the starting position in T of its corresponding suffix.
2. Each internal node of ST has at least two outgoing edges, since it is a compacted trie. So there are less than n internal nodes and less than $2n - 1$ edges. Every internal node u spells out a text substring, denoted by $s[u]$, which prefixes all of the suffixes descending from u in the suffix tree. Typically the value $|s[u]|$ is stored as satellite information of node u, and we use $occ[u]$ to indicate the leaves (and their text positions) descending from u.

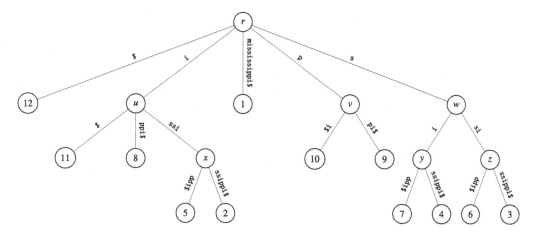

Figure 10.7 The suffix tree of the string $T = \mathtt{mississippi\$}$.

3. The edge labels are nonempty substrings of T. The labels of the edges leaving any internal node start with different characters, called *branching characters*. Edges are assumed to be ordered alphabetically according to their branching characters. So every node has at most σ outgoing edges.[5]

In Figure 10.7 we show the suffix tree built over our exemplar text $T[1, 12] = \mathtt{mississippi\$}$. The presence of the special symbol $T[12] = \$$ ensures that no suffix is a prefix of another suffix of T, and thus every pair of suffixes differs in some character and thus each of them has an associated leaf. So the paths from the root to the leaves of two different suffixes coincide up to their longest common prefix, which ends up in an internal node of ST.

It is evident that we cannot store explicitly the substrings labeling the suffix-tree edges because this could end up in $\Theta(n^2)$ space: Take T as the string consisting of n distinct characters, and observe that the suffix tree consists of one root connected to n leaves with edges representing all suffixes.

We can circumvent this space explosion by encoding the edge labels with pairs of integers which represent the starting position of the labeling substring and its length. With reference to Figure 10.7, the label of the edge leading to leaf 5, namely the substring $T[9, 12] = \mathtt{ppi\$}$, can be encoded with the integer pair $\langle 9, 4\rangle$, where 9 is the offset in T and 4 is the length of the edge label. Other obvious encodings are possible – for example, the pair $\langle 9, 12\rangle$ indicating the starting and ending position of the edge label – but we will not detail them here. Anyway, whatever edge-label encoding is adopted, it uses constant space, and thus the storage of all edge labels takes $O(n)$ space, independently of the indexed string.

Fact 10.3 The suffix tree of a string $T[1, n]$ consists of n leaves, at most $n - 1$ internal nodes, and at most $2n - 2$ edges. Its space occupancy is $\Theta(n)$, provided that a proper constant-sized edge-label encoding is adopted.

[5] The special character $\$$ is included in the alphabet Σ.

As a final point of terminology, the *locus* of a text substring t is the node v whose spelled string is exactly t, hence $s[v] = t$. The *extended locus* of a text substring t' is the locus of its shortest extension that has a defined locus in ST. In other words, the path spelling the string t' in ST ends within an edge label, say the label of the edge (u, v). Then $s[u]$ prefixes t', which in turn prefixes $s[v]$. Of course, if t' has a locus in ST then this coincides with its extended locus. As an example, the node z of the suffix tree in Figure 10.7 is the locus of the substring ssi and the extended locus of the substring ss.

There are few other important properties that the suffix tree satisfies; they pervade most algorithms that hinge on this powerful data structure. We summarize a few of them:

Property 2: Let α be a substring of the text T. There exists an internal node u such that $s[u] = \alpha$ (hence u is the locus of α) if and only if there are at least two occurrences of α in T followed by distinct characters.

As an example, take node x in Figure 10.7: the substring $s[x] = $ issi occurs twice in T at positions 2 and 5, followed by characters i and p, respectively.

Property 3: Let α be a substring of the text T that has an extended locus in the suffix tree. Then every occurrence of α is followed by the same character in T.

As an example, take the substring iss that has node x as extended locus in Figure 10.7. This substring occurs twice in T at positions 2 and 5, always followed by character i.

Property 4: Every internal node u spells out a substring $s[u]$ of T which occurs at the positions $occ[u]$ and is *maximal*, in the sense that it cannot be extended by one character and yet occur at these positions.

Now we introduce the notion of the *lowest common ancestor* (lca) in trees, which is defined for every pair of leaves and denotes the deepest node that is an ancestor of both leaves in input. As an example, in Figure 10.7, u is the lca of leaf 8 and 2. Now we turn lca between leaves into longest common prefix (lcp) between their corresponding suffixes.

Property 5: Let $a(i, j)$ be the lowest common ancestor between the leaves in the suffix tree corresponding to the two suffixes $T[i, n]$ and $T[j, n]$. We have that $s[a(i, j)]$ equals their prefix of length $lcp(T[i, n], T[j, n])$.

As an example, take the suffixes $T[11, 12] = $ i\$ and $T[5, 12] = $ issippi\$. Their longest common prefix is the single character i and, indeed, the lca between their leaves is the node u, which spells out the string $s[u] = $ i.

10.3.1   The Substring-Search Problem

The search for a pattern $P[1, p]$ as a substring of the text $T[1, n]$, with the help of the suffix tree ST, consists of a tree traversal that starts from its root and proceeds downward as pattern characters are matched against characters labeling the tree edges (see Figure 10.8). Note that, since the first character of the edges outgoing from each

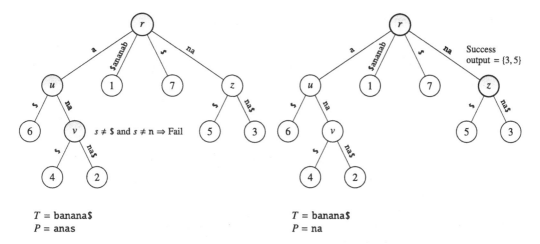

Figure 10.8 Two examples of substring searches over the suffix tree built for the text $T = \text{banana\$}$. The search for the pattern $P = \text{anas}$ fails at node v (left); the search for the pattern $P = \text{na}$ is successful at node z (right).

traversed node is distinct, the matching of P can follow only one downward path. If the traversal determines a mismatched character, the pattern P does not occur in T; otherwise the pattern is fully matched, the extended locus of P is found, say node u, and all leaves of ST descending from u identify all text suffixes that are prefixed by P. The positions $occ[u]$ associated with these descending leaves are the ones indicating the occ occurrences of the pattern P in T. These positions can be retrieved in optimal linear time by visiting the subtree that descends from u; it has $O(occ)$ size because the subtree consists of occ leaves and its internal nodes have (at least) binary fan-out.

In the running example of Figure 10.8, the pattern $P = \text{na}$ occurs twice in T and, in fact, the traversal of ST fully matches P and stops at the node z (the locus of P), from which descend two leaves labeled 3 and 5. These are the positions in T where P occurs, and indeed P prefixes the two suffixes $T[3, 12] = \text{nana\$}$ and $T[5, 12] = \text{na\$}$.

The cost of pattern searching is $O(p\, t_\sigma + occ)$ time in the worst case, where t_σ is the time to branch out of a node during the tree traversal. This cost depends on the alphabet size σ and on the data structure used to store the branching characters of the edges leaving each node. We discussed this issue in Chapter 9, when solving the prefix-search problem via compacted tries. There we observed that it is $t_\sigma = O(1)$ if we use a perfect hash table indexed by the branching characters, whereas it is $t_\sigma = O(\log \sigma)$ if we use a plain array and the branching is implemented by a binary search. In both cases the space occupancy is optimal, that is, linear in the number of branching edges, and thus $O(n)$ overall. We also mentioned that perfect hash tables do not support efficient lexicographic searches.

Fact 10.4 The occ occurrences of a pattern $P[1, p]$ in a text $T[1, n]$ can be found in $O(p + occ)$ time and $O(n)$ space by using a suffix tree built on the input text T, in which the branching characters at each node are indexed via a perfect hash table.

10.3.2   Construction from Suffix Arrays and Vice Versa

It is not difficult to observe that the suffix array SA of the text T, and the corresponding `lcp` array, can be obtained via an in-order visit of its suffix tree ST: each time a leaf is encountered, the suffix index stored in this leaf is written into the suffix array SA; each time an internal node u is encountered, its associated value (i.e. $|s[u]|$) is written into the array `lcp`.

Fact 10.5 Given the suffix tree of a string $T[1, n]$, we can derive in $O(n)$ time and space the corresponding suffix array SA and longest-common-prefix array `lcp`.

Vice versa, we can derive the suffix tree ST from the two arrays SA and `lcp` in $O(n)$ time as follows. The algorithm constructs incrementally ST starting from a tree, say ST_1, that contains the root, denoting the empty string, and the leaf labeled $SA[1]$, denoting the smallest suffix of T. At step $i > 1$, we have inductively constructed the partial suffix tree ST_{i-1} which contains all the $(i-1)$-smallest suffixes of T, according to the lexicographic order, hence the suffixes in $SA[1, i-1]$. During step i, the algorithm inserts in ST_{i-1} the i-th smallest suffix $SA[i]$. This requires the addition of one leaf labeled $SA[i]$ and, as we will prove next, at most one single internal node which becomes the father of the inserted leaf. After n steps, the final tree ST_n will be the suffix tree of the string $T[1, n]$.

The key issue here is to show how to insert the leaf $SA[i]$ into ST_{i-1} in constant amortized time. This will be enough to ensure a total time complexity of $O(n)$ for the overall construction process. The main difficulty consists in the detection of the node u father of the leaf $SA[i]$. This node u may already exist in ST_{i-1}; in this case $SA[i]$ is attached to u; otherwise, u must be created by splitting an edge of ST_{i-1}. Whether u exists or not is discovered by traversing ST_{i-1} upward (and not downward), starting from the leaf $SA[i-1]$, which is the rightmost one in ST_{i-1} because of the lexicographic order, and stopping when a node x is reached such that $\text{lcp}[i-1] \leq |s[x]|$. Recall that $\text{lcp}[i-1]$ is the number of characters that the currently inserted text suffix $suff_{SA[i]}$ shares with the previously inserted text suffix $suff_{SA[i-1]}$. The leaves corresponding to these two suffixes are of course consecutive in the in-order visit of ST. At this point, if $\text{lcp}[i-1] = |s[x]|$, the node x is the father of the leaf labeled $SA[i]$; we connect them and the new ST_i is obtained. Otherwise, if $\text{lcp}[i-1] < |s[x]|$, the edge leading to x has to be split by inserting a node u that has two children: the left child is x and the right child is the leaf $SA[i]$ (because it is lexicographically larger than $SA[i-1]$). This node is associated with the value $\text{lcp}[i-1]$. Readers can run this algorithm over the string $T[1, 12] = \texttt{mississippi\$}$ and convince themselves that the final suffix tree ST_{12} is exactly the one showed in Figure 10.7.

The time complexity of this algorithm derives from an accounting argument that involves the edges traversed by the upward percolation of ST. Since the suffix $suff_{SA[i]}$ is lexicographically greater than the suffix $suff_{SA[i-1]}$, the leaf labeled $SA[i]$ lies to the right of the leaf $SA[i-1]$. So every time we traverse an edge, we either discard it from the next traversals and proceed upward, or we split it and a new leaf is inserted. In particular, all edges from $SA[i-1]$ up to x are never traversed again because they lie to the left of the newly inserted edge $(u, SA[i])$. The total number of these edges is bounded by the total number of edges in ST, which is $O(n)$ from Fact 10.3. The total number of edge-splits equals the number of inserted leaves, which is again $O(n)$.

Theorem 10.6 *Given the suffix array and the longest-common-prefix array of a string $T[1, n]$, we can derive the corresponding suffix tree in $O(n)$ time and space.*

Therefore, we can construct the suffix tree of a string $T[1, n]$ by first running the Skew algorithm to construct the suffix array of T in $O(n)$ time (Theorem 10.3, where we use RADIXSORT in RAM), then the corresponding lcp array in $O(n)$ time (Theorem 10.1), and finally obtain ST via the algorithm described in this section (Theorem 10.6). The overall process takes $O(n)$ optimal time for an integer (or constant-sized) alphabet, and the optimal $O(\texttt{Sort}(n))$ steps in the comparison-based model.

The following subsection presents a classic algorithm for the *direct* construction of suffix trees which takes $O(n \log \sigma)$ time complexity, as stated in Theorem 10.7, but is not very efficient in terms of I/O complexity. Nowadays the space succinctness of suffix arrays and the existence of the Skew algorithm drive programmers to build suffix trees passing through suffix arrays. However, if the *average* LCP among the text suffixes is small, then the direct construction of suffix trees may be still advantageous both in internal memory and on disk. We refer the interested reader to [6] for a deeper analysis of these issues, and to [4] for an I/O-optimal *direct* construction of suffix trees, which is too sophisticated to be discussed in these pages.

10.3.3   McCreight's Algorithm$^\infty$

A naïve algorithm for constructing the suffix tree of an input string $T[1, n]$ could start with an empty trie and then iteratively insert text suffixes, one after the other. It would then maintain the property by which each intermediate trie is a compacted trie of the suffixes inserted so far. In the worst case of a highly repetitive string $T[1, n] = a^{n-1}\$$, the algorithm would cost up to $O(n^2)$ time. The reason for this poor behavior is due to the *rescanning* of some of T's substrings that have already been examined during the insertion of previous suffixes. In 1976 McCreight proposed a now well-known algorithm [15] that circumvents rescanning by the use of some special pointers added to the suffix tree.

These special pointers are called *suffix links* and are defined as follows. The suffix link $SL(z)$ connects the node z to the node z' such that $s[z] = a\,s[z']$, where a is an arbitrary alphabet character. So z' spells out a string that is obtained by dropping the first character from $s[z]$. The existence of node z' in ST is not at all obvious: of course $s[z']$ is a substring of T, given that $s[z]$ is, and thus there exists a path in ST that ends up in the extended locus of $s[z']$; but nothing seems to ensure that $s[z']$ has indeed a locus in ST, and thus that node z' exists. This property is derived by observing that the existence of z implies the existence of at least two suffixes, say $suff_i$ and $suff_j$, that have the node z as their lowest common ancestor in ST, and thus $s[z]$ is their longest common prefix (see Property 5). Then drop the first character of $s[z]$ and obtain $s[z']$, which will surely be, by construction, the longest common prefix of $suff_{i+1}$ and $suff_{j+1}$. So z' will be the lowest common ancestor of the leaves corresponding to these two suffixes.

Looking at Figure 10.7, we can take the node z with $s[z] = \text{ssi}$, and then select the suffixes $suff_3$ and $suff_6$ (which are actually children of z) which have z as their lowest common ancestor. Now consider the two suffixes following these two, namely $suff_4$ and $suff_7$ in the figure. They will share si as their longest common prefix, given that we dropped only their first character, and the suffix tree has indeed a node y (which plays the role of z' in our discussion) such that $s[y] = \text{si}$ and it is their lowest common ancestor. In conclusion, every node z has one suffix link correctly defined; more subtle is the observation that all suffix links form a tree rooted in the root of ST: just observe that $|s[z']| < |s[z]|$ so they cannot induce cycles and eventually end up in the root of the suffix tree (spelling out the empty string).

McCreight's algorithm works in n steps. It starts with the suffix tree ST_1, which consists of a root node, denoting the empty string, and one leaf labeled $suff_1 = T[1, n]$ (namely the entire text). In a generic step $i > 1$, the current suffix tree ST_{i-1} is the compacted trie built over all text suffixes $suff_j$ such that $j = 1, 2, \ldots, i - 1$. Hence suffixes are inserted in ST from the longest one to the shortest, and at any step ST_{i-1} indexes the $(i - 1)$ longest suffixes of T.

To ease the description of the algorithm we need to introduce the notation $head_i$, which denotes the longest prefix of suffix $suff_i$ that occurs in ST_{i-1}. Given that ST_{i-1} is a partial suffix tree, $head_i$ is the longest common prefix between $suff_i$ and any of its previous suffixes in T, namely $suff_j$ with $j = 1, 2, \ldots, i - 1$. We denote by h_i the (extended) locus of the string $head_i$ in the current suffix tree ST_{i-1}, because $suff_i$ has not yet been inserted. After its insertion, $head_i = s[h_i]$ in ST_i, so h_i is the locus of $head_i$, and h_i is set as the parent of the leaf associated with the suffix $suff_i$. As an example, consider the insertion of suffix $suff_5 = \text{byabz\$}$ in the partial suffix tree ST_4 of Figure 10.9. $suff_5$ shares only the character b with the previous four suffixes of T, so $head_5 = \text{b}$ in ST_4, and $head_5$ has extended locus in ST_4 given by the leaf 2. But, after the insertion of $suff_5$, we get the new suffix tree ST_5 in which $h_5 = v$, and this is the locus of $head_5$.

Now we are ready to describe McCreight's algorithm in detail. To produce ST_i, we must locate in ST_{i-1} the (extended) locus h_i of $head_i$. If it is an extended locus, then the edge incident in this node is split by inserting an internal node, which corresponds to h_i, and spells out $head_i$, to which the leaf for $suff_i$ is attached. In the naïve algorithm, $head_i$ and h_i were found tracing a downward path in ST_{i-1} matching $suff_i$ character by character. But we commented that this approach induces a quadratic time complexity in the worst case. Instead McCreight's algorithm determines $head_i$ and h_i by using the information inductively available for string $head_{i-1}$ and its locus h_{i-1}, and the *suffix links* that are already available in ST_{i-1}.

Fact 10.6 In ST_{i-1} the suffix link $SL(u)$ is defined for all nodes $u \neq h_{i-1}$. It may be the case that $SL(h_{i-1})$ is also defined, because that node was already present in ST_{i-1} before inserting $suff_{i-1}$.

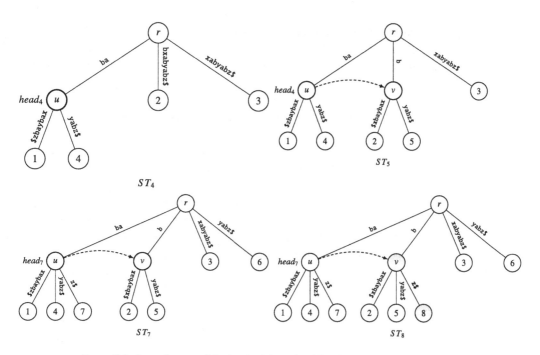

Figure 10.9 Several steps of the McCreight's algorithm for the string $T =$abxabyabz$.

Proof The first statement derives immediately from the way ST_{i-1} is inductively constructed. The question about the possible existence of $SL(h_{i-1})$ comes from the observation that h_{i-1} is the locus of $head_{i-1}$ which prefixes $suff_{i-1}$. Thus the second suffix of $head_{i-1}$ starts at position i and prefixes the suffix $suff_i$. We denote this second suffix with $head_{i-1}^-$, to denote the fact that we have dropped the first character from $head_{i-1}$. By definition, string $head_i$ is the longest prefix shared between $suff_i$ and any one of the previous text suffixes, so that the string $head_{i-1}^-$ prefixes $head_i$, and therefore it is already in ST_{i-1} and could have a locus in this compacted trie. ∎

McCreight's algorithm starts with ST_1, which consists of two nodes: the root and the leaf for $suff_1$. At Step 1 $head_1$ is the empty string, h_1 is the root, and $SL(root)$ points to the root itself. At a generic step $i > 1$, we know $head_{i-1}$ and its locus h_{i-1} (which is the parent of $suff_{i-1}$), and we wish to determine $head_i$ and its locus h_i, in order to insert the leaf for $suff_i$ as a child of h_i. These data are found via the following three substeps:

1. if $SL(h_{i-1})$ is defined, we set $w = SL(h_{i-1})$ and we go to Substep 3;
2. Otherwise we need to perform a *rescanning* whose goal is to find/create the locus w of the string obtained by dropping the first character from $head_{i-1}$, denoted by $head_{i-1}^-$. Given w, we can consequently set the suffix link $SL(h_{i-1}) = w$. The search for w is implemented by taking the parent f of h_{i-1}, jumping via its suffix link $f' = SL(f)$ (which is defined according to Fact 10.6), and then tracing a downward path from f' starting from the $(|s[f']| + 1)$-th character of $suff_i$. Since we know that $head_{i-1}^-$ occurs in T and it prefixes $suff_i$, this downward tracing can be implemented

by comparing only the branching characters of the traversed edges with $head_{i-1}^-$. If the landing node of this traversal is the locus of $head_{i-1}^-$, then this landing node is the searched w; otherwise the landing node is the extended locus of $head_{i-1}^-$, so we split the last traversed edge and insert the node w such that $s[w] = head_{i-1}^-$. In all cases we set $SL(h_{i-1}) = w$.

3. Finally, we locate $head_i$ starting from w and scanning the rest of $suff_i$. If the locus of $head_i$ does exist, then we set it to h_i; otherwise the scanning of $head_i$ stopped within some edge, and so we split it by inserting h_i as the locus of $head_i$. We conclude the process by installing the leaf for $suff_i$ as a child of h_i.

Figure 10.9 shows an example of the advantage gained with suffix links. At Step 8 we have the partial suffix tree ST_7, $head_7 = $ ab, its locus $h_7 = u$, and we need to insert the suffix $suff_8 = $ bz$. Using McCreight's algorithm, we find that $SL(h_7)$ is defined and equal to v, so we reach that node following that suffix link (without rescanning $head_{i-1}^-$). Subsequently, we scan the rest of $suff_8$, namely z$, searching for the locus of $head_8$, but we find that actually $head_8 = head_7^-$, so $h_8 = v$ and we can attach leaf 8 there.

From the point of view of time complexity, the rescanning and scanning steps perform two different types of traversals: the former traverses edges by comparing only the branching characters, since it is rescanning the string $head_{i-1}^-$ which is already known from the previous step $i-1$; the latter traverses edges by comparing their labels in their entirety because it has to determine $head_i$. This last type of traversal always advances in T so the cost of the scanning phase is $O(n)$. The difficulty is to show that the cost of rescanning also is $O(n)$. The proof comes from an observation on the structure of suffix links and suffix trees: if $SL(u) = v$ then all ancestors of u point to a distinct ancestor of v. This comes from Fact 10.6 (all these suffix links do exist), and from the definition of suffix links (which ensures ancestorship). Hence the tree-depth of $v = SL(u)$, say $d[v]$, is larger than $d[u] - 1$ (where -1 is due to the dropping of the first character). Therefore, the execution of rescanning can decrease the current depth at most by 2 (i.e. one for reaching the father of h_{i-1}, one for crossing $SL(h_{i-1})$). Since the depth of ST is most n, and we lose at most two levels per SL-jump, then the number of edges traversed by rescanning is $O(n)$, and each edge traversal takes $O(1)$ time because only the branching character is matched.

The last issue to be considered regards the cost of branching out of a node during the rescanning and scanning steps. Previously we stated that this cost is constant, through using perfect hash tables built over the branching characters of each internal node of ST. In the context of suffix-tree construction, the tree is dynamic and thus we should adopt dynamic perfect hash tables, which is a pretty involved solution. A simpler approach consists of keeping the branching characters and their associated edges within a binary search tree, thus supporting the branching in $O(\log \sigma)$ time. Practically, programmers relax the requirement of worst-case time complexity and use either hash tables with chaining, or cuckoo hashing (described in Chapter 8), or dictionary data structures for integer values (such as the van Emde Boas tree, whose search complexity is $O(\log \log \sigma)$ time) because characters can be looked at as sequences of bits and hence integers.

Theorem 10.7 *McCreight's algorithm builds the suffix tree of a string $T[1, n]$ in $O(n \log \sigma)$ time and $O(n)$ space in the worst case.*

This algorithm is inefficient in an external-memory setting because it may elicit one I/O per edge traversal. Nevertheless, as we have observed, the distribution of the lengths of $head_i$ might be skewed toward small values, so this construction might turn out to be I/O-efficient because the top part of the suffix tree could be cached in the internal memory, and thus will not elicit any I/Os during the scanning and rescanning steps. We refer the reader to [6] for details on this issue.

10.4 Some Interesting Problems

10.4.1 Approximate Pattern Matching

The problem of approximate pattern matching can be formulated as: *finding all substrings of a text $T[1, n]$ that match a pattern $P[1, p]$ with at most k errors.* In this section we restrict our discussion to the simplest type of errors, the ones called *mismatches* or *substitutions*. Here the text substrings that "k-mismatch" the searched pattern P have length p and coincide with the pattern in all but at most k characters. Figure 10.10 provides an example by considering two DNA strings formed over the alphabet of four nucleotide bases $\{A, T, G, C\}$. The reason for using this kind of string is that bio-informatics is the context that spurred interest around the approximate pattern-matching problem. In the figure, pattern P occurs at position 1 in T with two mismatches, indicated by the arrows.

$$
\begin{array}{ccccccccccccc}
C & C & G & T & A & C & G & A & T & C & A & G & T & A \\
C & C & G & A & A & C & T & & & & & & & \\
 & & & \Uparrow & & & \Uparrow & & & & & & &
\end{array}
$$

Figure 10.10 An example of approximate matching between a text string T (top) and a pattern string P (bottom) with $k = 2$ mismatches.

The naïve solution to this problem consists of trying to match P with every possible length-p substring of T, by counting the mismatches and returning the positions where this number is at most k. This would take $O(pn)$ time, independently of k. The inefficiency comes from the fact that each pattern-substring comparison starts from the beginning of P, thus taking $O(p)$ time in the worst case. In what follows we describe a sophisticated solution to the k-mismatch problem which hinges on an elegant data structure that solves an apparently unrelated problem formulated over an array of integers, called a *range minimum query* (RMQ). This data structure is the backbone of many other algorithmic solutions to problems arising in data mining, information retrieval, computational biology, and so on.

Algorithm 10.4 solves the k-mismatches problem in $O(nk)$ time by making the following basic observation. If P occurs in T with $j \leq k$ mismatches, then we can align the pattern P with a substring of T, having the same length p, so that j or $j-1$ substrings coincide and j characters mismatch. Actually, matching substrings and mismatches interleave each other. As an example, consider again Figure 10.10: the pattern occurs

---

Algorithm 10.4 Approximate pattern matching based on LCP computations

---

$matches = \{\}$
for $i = 1$ **to** n **do**
    $m = 0, j = 1;$
    while $m \leq k$ **and** $j \leq p$ **do**
        $\ell = lcp(T[i + j - 1, n], P[j, p]);$
        $j = j + \ell;$
        if $j \leq p$ **then**
            $m = m + 1; j = j + 1;$
        end if
    end while
    if $m \leq k$ **then**
        $matches = matches \cup \{i\};$
    end if
end for
return $matches;$

---

at position 1 in the text T with 2 mismatches, and in fact two substrings of P match their corresponding substrings of T. If neither mismatch had been at the extremes of P, then there would have been three matching substrings.

This observation allows us to conclude that, if we can compare the pattern and a text substring for equality in constant time, then we can execute the naïve approach taking $O(nk)$ time, instead of $O(np)$ time. To be operational, this observation can be rephrased as follows: if $T[i, i+\ell] = P[j, j+\ell]$ is one of these matching substrings, then ℓ is the longest common prefix (LCP) between the pattern and the text suffix starting at the matching positions i and j. Algorithm 10.4 deploys this rephrasing to code a solution that takes $O(nk)$ time provided that LCP computations take $O(1)$ time. In our running example of Figure 10.10, we need to perform two LCP computations and find that $P[1, 7]$ occurs at text position 1 because it equals $T[1, 7]$ with two mismatches:

- The longest common prefix between $T[1, 14] =$ CCGTACGATCAGTA and $P[1, 7] =$ CCGAACT is CCG (i.e. $lcp(T[1, 14], P[1, 7]) = 3$); this means that $T[1, 3] = P[1, 3]$ and the mismatch is at position 4.
- The longest common prefix between $T[5, 14] =$ ACGATCAGTA and $P[5, 7] =$ ACT is AC (i.e. $lcp(T[5, 14], P[5, 7]) = 2$); this means that $T[5, 6] = P[5, 6]$ and the mismatch is at position 7.

Referring to Algorithm 10.4, how do we compute $lcp(T[i + j - 1, n], P[j, p])$ in constant time? We know that suffix trees and suffix arrays have some built-in LCP information, but we similarly recall that these data structures were built on one single string. Here we are talking about suffixes of P and T together. Nevertheless, we can easily circumvent this difficulty by constructing the suffix array, or the suffix tree, over the string $X = T\#P$, where # is a new character not occurring elsewhere. Thus each computation of the form $lcp(T[i + j - 1, n], P[j, p])$ can now be turned into an LCP

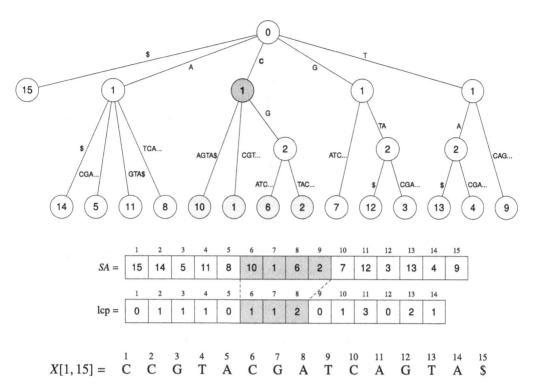

Figure 10.11 An example of suffix tree, suffix array, and `lcp` array for the string X shown in the figure. In the suffix tree we have indicated only a prefix of a few characters for the long edge labels. The number in the internal node u denotes $|s[u]|$, whereas numbers in the leaves denote the starting positions of the corresponding suffixes. The figure highlights that the computation of $lcp(X[2,14], X[10,14]) = 1$ (i.e. the matched character is C) boils down to finding the depth of the `lca` node in ST_X between leaf 2 and leaf 10, as well as solving a range minimum query on the subarray `lcp[6,8]`, since $SA_X[6] = 10$ and $SA_X[9] = 2$.

computation between suffixes of X, precisely $lcp(T[i+j-1, n], P[n+1+j, n+1+p])$, because P starts at position $n+1$ of string X. We are therefore left with showing how these LCP computations can be performed in constant time, whichever is the pair of compared suffixes. This is the topic of the next subsection.

10.4.2 Lowest Common Ancestor, Range Minimum Query, and Cartesian Tree

Let us start with an example, and consider the suffix tree ST_X and the suffix array SA_X built on the string $X = CCGTACGATCAGTA$. This string is not in the form $X = T\#P$ because we wish to stress the fact that the considerations and the algorithmic solutions proposed in this section apply to any string X, not necessarily the ones arising from the k-mismatch problem of the previous subsection.

The key observation builds upon Property 5 of suffix trees, introduced in Section 10.3: there is a strong relation between the problem of computing the longest common prefix between X's suffixes and the problem of computing the *lowest common ancestor* (lca) between leaves of the suffix tree ST_X. Consider the problem of computing $lcp(X[i,x],X[j,x])$, where x is the length of string X. The node $u = \text{lca}(X[i,x],X[j,x])$ in the suffix tree ST_X spells out the LCP between these two suffixes of X, and thus the value $|s[u]|$ stored in node u is exactly the LCP length we are searching for. Equivalently, the same length can be derived by looking at the suffix array SA_X. In particular, take the lexicographic positions i_p and j_p where those two suffixes occur in SA_X, say $SA_X[i_p] = i$ and $SA_X[j_p] = j$ (we are assuming for simplicity that $i_p < j_p$). Because of the lexicographic ordering of X's suffixes, the *minimum value* in the subarray[6] $\text{lcp}[i_p,j_p - 1]$ is equal to $|s[u]|$ since the values contained in that subarray are the values stored in the suffix-tree nodes of the subtree that descends from u (cf. Section 10.3.2). We are actually interested in the smallest value, which corresponds to the shallowest node (namely the root u) of that subtree, hence the minimum computation. As a result, we have two approaches to compute the lcp length in constant time, either through lca computations over ST_X or through RMQ computations over the array lcp (and given SA_X). For the sake of presentation we introduce an elegant solution for the latter, which actually induces in turn an elegant solution for the former, given that they are strongly related. The reader may refer to Figure 10.11 for a running example that will be discussed in the following paragraphs.

In general terms the RMQ problem can be stated as follows:

The range minimum query problem (RMQ). Given an array $A[1,n]$ of elements drawn from an ordered universe, build a data structure RMQ_A that is able to compute efficiently the position of a smallest element in $A[i,j]$, for any given queried range (i,j). We say "a smallest" because that subarray may contain more than one minimum elements.

We underline that this problem asks for the *position* of a minimum element in the queried subarray, rather than its value. This is more general because the value of the minimum can obviously be retrieved from its position in A by accessing this array, which is available.

The simplest, and naïve, solution to achieving constant-time RMQ queries is by means of a table that stores the index of a minimum entry for each possible range (i,j), where $1 \leq i \leq j \leq n$. Such a table requires $\Theta(n^2)$ space and time to be built.

A better solution hinges on the observation that any range (i,j) can be decomposed into two (possibly overlapping) ranges whose size is a power of two, namely $(i, i + 2^L - 1)$ and $(j - 2^L + 1, j)$ where $L = \lfloor \log(j - i) \rfloor$. This allows us to *sparsify* the previous quadratic-size table by storing only ranges whose size is a power of two. Namely, for each position i we store the answers to the queries $\text{RMQ}_A(i, i + 2^\ell - 1)$, for $0 \leq \ell \leq \lfloor \log_2(n - i) \rfloor$. This sparse table occupies $O(n \log n)$ space and still requires constant time to answer RMQ queries: just compute $\text{RMQ}_A(i,j)$ as the position between

---

[6] Recall that the lcp array has size $x - 1$ and stores in lcp[i] the length of the longest common prefix between suffix $SA[i]$ and the next adjacent suffix $SA[i + 1]$, for $i = 1, 2, \ldots, x - 1$.

$\text{RMQ}_A(i, i + 2^L - 1)$ and $\text{RMQ}_A(j - 2^L + 1, j)$ that stores the minimum value, where $L = \lfloor \log(j - i) \rfloor$.

In order to get the optimal $O(n)$ space occupancy, we need to dig into the structure of the RMQ problem and make a twofold reduction which goes back and forth between RMQ computations and `lca` computations [3]: namely, we reduce (i) the RMQ computation over the `lcp` array to an `lca` computation over Cartesian trees (that we define next); we then reduce (ii) the `lca` computation over Cartesian trees to an RMQ computation over a properly defined binary array. This last problem is then solved in $O(n)$ space and constant query time. Clearly, reduction (ii) can be applied to any tree, and thus can be applied to suffix trees in order to solve `lca` queries over them, thus providing a direct solution to the k-mismatch problem.

First reduction step: from RMQ **to** `lca`. We transform the RMQ_A problem "back" into an `lca` computation over a special tree which is known as *Cartesian tree* and is built over the entries of the array $A[1, n]$. The *Cartesian tree* C_A is a binary tree of n nodes, each labeled with one of A's entries (i.e. value and position in A). The labeling is defined recursively as follows: the root of C_A is labeled by the minimum entry in $A[1, n]$ and its position; say this is $\langle A[m], m \rangle$. Then the left subtree of the root is recursively defined as the Cartesian tree of the subarray $A[1, m - 1]$, and the right subtree is recursively defined as the Cartesian tree of the subarray $A[m + 1, n]$. See Figure 10.12 for a simple example over an array of just five positions.

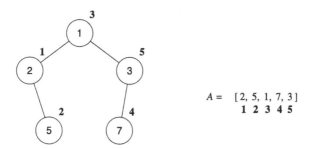

$$A = \quad [2, 5, 1, 7, 3]$$
$$1\ 2\ 3\ 4\ 5$$

Figure 10.12 A Cartesian tree built over the array $A[1, 5] = \{2, 5, 1, 7, 3\}$. Observe that nodes of C_A store as first component of the node label A's value (shown in normal text inside the node) and, as second component of the node label, its position in A (shown in bold outside the node).

Figure 10.13 shows the Cartesian tree built on the `lcp` array depicted in Figure 10.11. Given the construction process, we can state that ranges in the `lcp` array correspond to subtrees of the Cartesian tree. Therefore computing $\text{RMQ}_A(i, j)$ boils down to computing an `lca` query between the nodes of C_A associated with the entries i and j. Differently to what occurred for `lca` queries on ST_X, where the arguments were leaves of that suffix tree, the queried nodes in the Cartesian tree may be internal nodes, and it is possible that one node is the ancestor of the other node, thus, in this case, making the `lca` query trivial. For example, executing $\text{RMQ}_{\text{lcp}}(6, 8)$ is equal to executing `lca(6, 8)` over the Cartesian tree C_{lcp} of Figure 10.13. Queried nodes are highlighted, and the result of this query is the node $\langle \text{lcp}[7], 7 \rangle = \langle 1, 7 \rangle$. Note that we

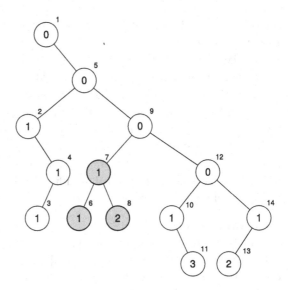

Euler tour = 1 5 2 4 3 4 2 5 9 7 | 6 7 8 | 7 9 12 10 11 10 12 14 13 14 12 9 5 1
     D = 1 2 3 4 5 4 3 2 3 4 | 5 4 5 | 4 3 4 5 6 5 4 5 6 5 4 3 2 1

Figure 10.13 Cartesian tree built on the lcp array of Figure 10.11: inside the nodes we report the LCP's values, outside the nodes we report the corresponding position in the lcp array (in the case of ties, we make an arbitrary choice). As an example, the child of the root is labeled ⟨lcp[5], 5⟩ = ⟨0, 5⟩. On the bottom part of the figure are reported the positions of the nodes encountered during an Euler-tour traversal of the Cartesian tree, and the array D storing the depth of these nodes.

have another minimum value in lcp[6, 8] at lcp[6] = 1, but the algorithm does not "detect" it because it reports the position of "just" one minimum.

Second reduction step: from lca to RMQ. We transform the lca problem over the Cartesian tree C_A "back" into an RMQ problem over a special binary array $\Delta[1, 2e+1]$, where e is the number of edges in the Cartesian tree (of course, $e = O(n)$). It seems strange that this "circular" sequence of reductions now returned us to an RMQ problem. But the current RMQ problem, unlike the original one, is formulated on a binary array that admits an optimal solution in $O(n)$ space.

To build the binary array $\Delta[1, 2e + 1]$, we first build the array $D[1, 2e + 1]$ defined as follows. The *Euler tour* of the Cartesian tree C_A is a sequence of nodes obtained by the pre-order visit of C_A such that each node is written every time the visit passes through it (both at downward and upward edge traversals). Thus an edge is visited twice (which justifies the $2e$ additive term in the size of D), whereas a node is visited (and thus written) as many times as its number of incident edges, with the exception of the root, which is written one more time than its incident edges (hence the +1 in the size of D). We build the array $D[1, 2e + 1]$ by storing in $D[i]$ the depth of the i-th node in the Euler tour traversal of the Cartesian tree $\mathcal{C}_A$. See Figure 10.13 for our running example in which the array A is the lcp array of Figure 10.11.

Given the way the array D is derived from the Euler tour, we can conclude that the query $\text{lca}(i, j)$ in the Cartesian tree $\mathcal{C}_A$ boils down to computing the node of minimum depth in the subarray $D[i', j']$ where i' (resp., j') is the position of the first (resp., last) occurrence of the node i (resp., j) in the Euler tour. In fact, the range (i', j') corresponds to the part of the Euler tour that starts at node i and ends at node j. The node of minimum depth encountered in this subsequence of the Euler tour is properly $\text{lca}(i, j)$.

So we reduced an lca query over the Cartesian tree $\mathcal{C}_A$ into an RMQ query over the array D of node depths. In our running example in Figure 10.13 this reduction transforms the query $\text{lca}(6, 8)$ into a query $\text{RMQ}_D(11, 13)$, which is highlighted by a rectangle. Turning nodes into ranges can be done in constant time simply by storing two integers per node of the Cartesian tree, denoting their first/last occurrence in the Euler tour, thus taking $O(n)$ additional space.

We are again "back" to an RMQ query over an integer array. But the current array D is a special one, because its consecutive entries differ by 1 given that they refer to the depths of consecutive nodes in an Euler tour. And in fact, two consecutive nodes in the Euler tour are connected by an edge and thus one node is the parent of the other, and hence their depths differ by one unit. The net result of this property is that we can solve the RMQ problem over $D[1, 2e + 1]$ in $O(n)$ space and $O(1)$ time by deploying the following two data structures.

First, we split the array D into subarrays D_k of size $d = (1/2) \log e$ each. Next, we find the minimum element in each subarray D_k, and store its position at the entry $M[k]$ of a new array whose size is therefore $(2e + 1)/d = O(e/\log e)$. We finally build on the array M the sparse-table solution previously indicated, which takes $O\left(\left(\frac{e}{\log e}\right) \times \log \frac{e}{\log e}\right) = O(e) = O(n)$ space and solves RMQ queries aligned at the extremes of these subarrays in constant time.

The second data structure is built to efficiently answer RMQ queries in which i and j are in the same block D_k. It is clear that we cannot tabulate all answers to all such possible pairs of indexes, because this would end up in $O(nd) = O(n \log n)$ space occupancy. So the solution we describe here spurs from two simple, but cute, observations whose proof is immediate and left to the reader:

- **Binary entries:** Every block D_k can be transformed into a pair that consists of its first element $D_k[1]$ and a binary array $\Delta_k[i] = D_k[i] - D_k[i-1]$ for $i = 2, \ldots, d$. Entries of Δ_k are either -1 or $+1$ because of the unit difference between adjacent entries of D.
- **Minimum location:** The position of the minimum value in D_k depends only on the content of the binary sequence Δ_k and does not depend on the starting value $D_k[1]$.

Nicely, the possible configurations that every block D_k can assume are infinite, given that infinite is the number of ways we can instantiate the input array A on which we want to issue the RMQ queries; but the possible configurations of the array Δ_k are finite and equal to 2^{d-1}. This suggests to apply the *four Russians trick* to all binary arrays Δ_k, by tabulating all their possible binary configurations and, for each, store the position of the minimum value. Since the blocks Δ_k have length $d - 1 < d = \frac{\log e}{2}$, the total number of their possible binary configurations is at most $2^{d-1} = O(2^{\frac{\log e}{2}}) = O(\sqrt{e}) = O(\sqrt{n})$. Moreover, since both query-indexes i and j can take at most $d = \frac{\log e}{2}$ possible values, being internal in a block D_k, we can have at most $O(\log^2 e) = O(\log^2 n)$ queries of this type. Consequently, we build a lookup table $T[i_o, j_o, \Delta_k]$ that is indexed by the possible query-offsets i_o and j_o within the block D_k and by its binary configuration Δ_k. Table T stores at that entry the position of the minimum value in D_k. We also assume that, for each k, we have stored Δ_k so that the binary representation Δ_k of D_k can be retrieved in constant time. Each of these indexing parameters takes $O(\log e) = O(\log n)$ bits of space, hence one memory word, and thus can be managed in $O(1)$ time and space. In summary, the whole table T consists of $O(\sqrt{n} (\log n)^2) = o(n)$ entries. The time needed to build T is $O(n)$. The power of transforming D_k into Δ_k is evident now; every entry of $T[i_o, j_o, \Delta_k]$ is actually encoding the answer for an infinite number of blocks D_k, namely the ones that can be converted to the same binary configuration Δ_k.

At this point we are ready to design an algorithm that, using the two data structures we have illustrated, answers a query $\texttt{RMQ}_D(i, j)$ in constant time. If i, j are inside the same block D_k then the answer is retrieved in two steps: first we compute the offsets i_o and j_o with respect to the beginning of D_k and determine the binary configuration Δ_k from k; then we use this triple to access the proper entry of T. Otherwise the range (i, j) spans at least two blocks and can thus be decomposed in to three parts: a suffix of some block $D_{i'}$, a consecutive (possibly empty) sequence of blocks $D_{i'+1} \cdots D_{j'-1}$, and finally the prefix of block $D_{j'}$. The minimum for the suffix of $D_{i'}$ and for the prefix of $D_{j'}$ can be retrieved from T, given that these ranges are inside two blocks. The minimum of the range spanned by $D_{i'+1} \cdots D_{j'-1}$ (if non-empty) is stored in M. All this information can be accessed in constant time and the final minimum position can thus be retrieved by comparing these three minimum values, also in constant time.

Theorem 10.8 *Range-minimum queries over an array $A[1, n]$ of elements drawn from an ordered universe can be answered in constant time using a data structure that occupies $O(n)$ space.*

Given the stream of reductions illustrated, we can conclude that Theorem 10.8 also applies to computing $\texttt{lca}$ in generic trees: it is enough to take the input tree in place of the Cartesian tree.

Theorem 10.9 *Lowest-common-ancestor queries over an arbitrary tree of size n can be answered in constant time using a data structure that occupies $O(n)$ space.*

10.4.3   Text Compression

Data compression will be the topic of Chapters 12–15; nonetheless, in this section, we address the problem of compressing a text via the simple algorithm that is at the core of the well-known gzip compressor, named *LZ77* from the initials of its inventors (Abraham Lempel and Jacob Ziv [13]) and from the year of its publication (1977). We will show that there exists an optimal implementation of the LZ77 algorithm taking $O(n)$ time and space, by using suffix trees. (Details on the LZ family of compressors will be given in Chapter 13.)

Given a text string $T[1, n]$, the algorithm LZ77 produces a *parsing* of T into substrings that are defined as follows. Assume that it has already parsed the prefix $T[1, i-1]$ (at the beginning this prefix is empty); then it decomposes the remaining text suffix $T[i, n]$ in to three parts: the longest substring $T[i, i + \ell - 1]$ which starts at i and repeats before in the text T; the next character $T[i + \ell]$; and the remaining suffix $T[i + \ell + 1, n]$. The next substring to add to the parsing of T is $T[i, i + \ell]$, and thus corresponds to the shortest string that is *new* among the ones starting in $T[1, i-1]$. Parsing then continues on the remaining suffix $T[i + \ell + 1, n]$, if any.

Compression is obtained by succinctly encoding the triple of integers $\langle d, \ell, T[i+\ell] \rangle$, where d is the distance (in characters) from i to the previous copy of $T[i, i + \ell - 1]$; ℓ is the length of the copied string; $T[i + \ell]$ is the appended character. By saying "previous copy" of $T[i, i + \ell - 1]$, we mean that this copy starts before position i but it might extend after this position, hence it could be $d < \ell$; furthermore, the "previous copy" can be any previous occurrence of $T[i, i + \ell - 1]$, although space-efficiency issues suggest that we take the closest copy (and thus the smallest d).[7] Finally, we observe that the reason for adding the character $T[i + \ell]$ to the emitted triple is that this character behaves like an *escape* mechanism, when no copy is possible and thus $d = 0$ and $\ell = 0$. Specifically, this occurs when the LZ parsing meets a new character in T, as the running example on the string $T = $ mississippi shows:

1	2	3	4	5	6	7	8	9	10	11
m	i	s	s	i	s	s	i	p	p	i

Output: $\langle 0, 0, m \rangle$

1	2	3	4	5	6	7	8	9	10	11
m	i	s	s	i	s	s	i	p	p	i

Output: $\langle 0, 0, i \rangle$

---

[7] We are not going to discuss the integer-coding issue here, since it will be the topic of Chapter 11; we just mention here that space efficiency is obtained in classic gzip by taking the rightmost copy and by encoding the values d and ℓ via a Huffman coder. However, recent studies [5, 8] have shown that the best previous copy to choose is not necessarily the closest one, which in fact implements Google's open-source compressor, named Brotli [1].

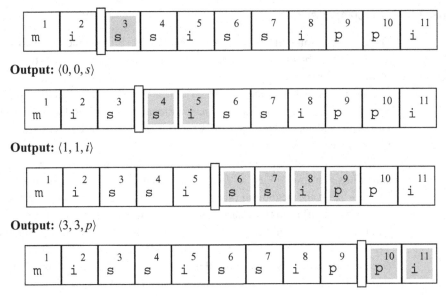

Output: $\langle 0, 0, s \rangle$

Output: $\langle 1, 1, i \rangle$

Output: $\langle 3, 3, p \rangle$

Output: $\langle 1, 1, i \rangle$

We can compute the LZ77 parsing in $O(n)$ time and space via an elegant algorithm that deploys the suffix tree ST built on the text T. The difficulty is to find π_i, the longest substring that occurs at position i and repeats before in the text T, say at distance d from i. We therefore have $\ell = |\pi_i|$, and we can state that π_i is the longest common prefix of the two suffixes $suff_i$ and $suff_{i-d}$. By the properties of suffix trees, the lowest common ancestor of the leaves i and $i - d$ spells out π_i. However, we cannot compute $\mathtt{lca}(i, i - d)$ by issuing a query to the data structure of Theorem 10.9, because we do not know d, which is exactly the information we wish to compute. Similarly, we cannot trace a downward path from the root of ST matching $suff_i$, because all suffixes of T are indexed in the suffix tree and thus we could detect a longer copy that follows position i, instead of preceding it.

To circumvent these problems we preprocess ST via a post-order visit that computes for every internal node u its minimum descending leaf, denoted as $\min(u)$. Clearly, $\min(u)$ is the leftmost position from which we can copy the substring $s[u]$. Given this information we can easily determine π_i: just trace a downward path from the root of ST scanning $suff_i$, and stopping as soon as the reached node v is such that $\min(v) = i$. At this point, we take u as the parent of v and set $\pi_i = s[u]$, and $d = i - \min(u)$. Clearly, the chosen copy of π_i is the farthest one from position i, and not the closest one. However, this does not impact on the number of phrases in which T is parsed by LZ77, but possibly influences the magnitude of these distances and thus their succinct encoding. Devising an LZ77-parser that efficiently determines the closest copy of each π_i is nontrivial and needs much more sophisticated data structures, which we do not describe in this book and thus refer the interested reader to the corresponding literature (such as [8, 2]).

Referring to our running example, take the suffix tree ST in Figure 10.7 and assume that the parsing has processed the prefix $\mathtt{missi}$, emitting the triples: $\langle 0, 0, \mathtt{m} \rangle, \langle 0, 0, \mathtt{i} \rangle, \langle 0, 0, \mathtt{s} \rangle, \langle 1, 1, \mathtt{i} \rangle$. The tracing of the subsequent suffix

$suff_6 = $ ssippi$ down ST stops at node z, because $min(z) = 3 < 6$ and any other additional character from $suff_6$ would have led to leaf 6 (which is not smaller than itself). Consequently, the emitted triple is correctly $\langle 6 - min(z), |s[z]|, T[6+|s[z]|] \rangle = \langle 3, 3, p \rangle$.

The time complexity of this algorithm is linear in the length of T, because the traversal of the suffix tree advances over string T, so this may occur only n times. Branching out of suffix tree nodes can be implemented in $O(1)$ time via perfect hash tables, as observed for the substring-search problem. The construction of the suffix tree costs $O(n)$ time, by using one of the algorithms we described in the previous sections. The computation of the values $min(u)$, over all nodes u, takes $O(n)$ time via a post-order visit of ST.

Theorem 10.10 *The LZ77 parsing of a string $T[1,n]$ can be computed in $O(n)$ time and space. The proposed algorithm copies each substring of the parsing from its farthest previous occurrence.*

10.4.4 Text Mining

In this section we briefly survey two examples of uses of suffix arrays and lcp arrays in the solution of interesting text mining problems.

Let us consider the following problem: *Check whether there exists a substring of $T[1,n]$ that repeats at least twice and has length L.* Solving this in a brute-force way would mean taking every text substring of length L, and counting its number of occurrences in T. These substrings are $\Theta(n)$, searching each of them takes $O(nL)$ time, hence the overall time complexity of this brute-force approach would be $O(n^2L)$. A smarter and faster, actually optimal, solution comes from the use either of the suffix tree or of the array lcp, built on the input text T.

The use of the suffix tree is simple. Let us assume that such a string does exist, and it occurs at positions x and y of T. Now take the two leaves in the suffix tree that correspond to $suff_x$ and $suff_y$ and compute their lowest common ancestor, say $a(x, y)$. Since $T[x, x + L - 1] = T[y, y + L - 1]$, it is $|s[a(x, y)]| \geq L$. We write "greater than or equal to" because it could be the case that a longer substring is shared at positions x and y; in fact L is just fixed by the problem. The conclusion of this argument is that there is an *internal* node u in ST_T whose label is greater than or equal to L, namely $|s(u)| \geq L$. Therefore, a visit of the suffix tree is enough to search for such a node u, thus taking $O(n)$ time.

The use of the suffix array is a little more involved, but follows a similar argument. Recall that suffixes in SA are lexicographically ordered, so the longest prefix shared by a suffix $SA[i]$ is with its adjacent suffixes, namely either with suffix $SA[i - 1]$ or with suffix $SA[i + 1]$. The length of these LCPs is stored in the entries $lcp[i - 1, i]$. Now, if the repeated substring of length L does exist, and it occurs at some text positions, say x and y, then we have $lcp(T[x, n], T[y, n]) \geq L$. These two suffixes are not necessarily contiguous in SA (this may be the case when the substring occurs more than twice); nonetheless, all suffixes occurring among them in *SA* will surely share a prefix of length *L*, because of their lexicographic order. Hence, if suffix $T[x, n]$ occurs at position *i* of the suffix array, namely $SA[i] = x$, then either $\mathtt{lcp}[i - 1] \geq L$ (if $T[y, n] < T[x, n]$) or $\mathtt{lcp}[i] \geq L$ (if $T[y, n] > T[x, n]$). Hence we can solve the problem stated at the start of this section by scanning the array $\mathtt{lcp}$ and searching for an entry whose value is greater than or equal to *L*. This takes $O(n)$ optimal time.

Let us now pose a more sophisticated problem: *Check whether there exists a substring of $T[1, n]$ that repeats at least C times and has length L.* This is the typical query in a text mining scenario, where we are interested not just in a repetitive event but in an event occurring with some *statistical evidence*. We can again solve this problem by trying all possible substrings and counting their occurrences. Again, a faster solution comes from the use either of the suffix tree or of the array $\mathtt{lcp}$. Following the argument provided in the solution to the previous problem, we note that, if a substring of length *L* occurs (at least) *C* times, then there are (at least) *C* text suffixes that share (at least) *L* characters. So there is a node *u* in the suffix tree such that $|s[u]| \geq L$ and the number of descending leaves $|occ[u]|$ is greater than or equal to *C*. Equivalently, there is a subarray of $\mathtt{lcp}$ with length $\geq C - 1$ and whose entries are greater than or equal to *L*. Both approaches provide an answer to the problem in $O(n)$ time.

Let us conclude this section by setting a problem proper for a search-engine scenario: *Given two patterns $P[1, p]$ and $Q[1, q]$, and a positive integer k, check whether there exists an occurrence of P whose distance from an occurrence of Q in an input text $T[1, n]$ is at most k.* This is also called *proximity search* over text *T*, which is given in advance to be preprocessed. The solution passes through the use of any string-search data structure, be it a suffix tree or a suffix array built over *T*, plus some sorting/scanning steps. More precisely, we search for *P* and *Q* in the suffix array, or in the suffix tree, built on *T* and retrieve their *occ* occurrences unsorted. Then we sort them, and scan the ordered list, checking, for every pair of *consecutive* positions of *P* and *Q* occurrences, whether the difference is at most *k*. This takes overall $O(p + q + occ \log occ)$ time, which is clearly advantageous whenever the set of candidate occurrences is small, and thus the queries *P* and *Q* are sufficiently selective.

References

[1]   Jyrki Alakuijala, Andrea Farruggia, Paolo Ferragina *et al.* Brotli: A general-purpose data compressor. *ACM Transactions on Information Systems*, 37(1): article 4, 2019.

[2]   Djamal Belazzougui and Simon J. Puglisi. Range predecessor and Lempel–Ziv parsing. In *Proceedings of the 27th Annual ACM–SIAM Symposium on Discrete Algorithms (SODA)*, 2053–71, 2016.

[3]   Michael A. Bender and Martin Farach-Colton. The LCA problem revisited. In *Proceedings of the 4th Latin American Symposium on Theoretical Informatics (LATIN)*, 88–94, 2000.

[4]   Martin Farach-Colton, Paolo Ferragina, and S. Muthukrishnan. On the sorting-complexity of suffix tree construction. *Journal of the ACM*, 47(6): 987–1011, 2000.

[5] Andrea Farruggia, Paolo Ferragina, Antonio Frangioni, and Rossano Venturini. Bicriteria data compression. *SIAM Journal on Computing*, 48(5): 1603–42, 2019.

[6] Paolo Ferragina. String search in external memory: Algorithms and data structures. In Srinivas Aluru, editor, *Handbook of Computational Molecular Biology*. Chapman & Hall/CRC Computer and Information Science Series, 35-1–35-48, 2005.

[7] Paolo Ferragina, Travis Gagie, and Giovanni Manzini. Lightweight data indexing and compression in external memory. *Algorithmica: Special Issue on Selected Papers of LATIN 2010*, 63(3): 707–30, 2012.

[8] Paolo Ferragina, Igor Nitto, and Rossano Venturini. On the bit-complexity of Lempel–Ziv compression. *SIAM Journal on Computing*, 42(4): 1521–41, 2013.

[9] Dan Gusfield. *Algorithms on Strings, Trees and Sequences: Computer Science and Computational Biology*. Cambridge University Press, 1997.

[10] Gaston H. Gonnet, Ricardo A. Baeza-Yates, and Tim Snider. New indices for text: PAT trees and PAT arrays. In B. Frakes and R. A. Baeza-Yates, editors, *Information Retrieval: Data Structures and Algorithms*, Prentice Hall, 66–82, 1992.

[11] Juha Kärkkäinen and Peter Sanders. Simple linear work suffix array construction. In *Proceedings of the 30th International Colloquium on Automata, Languages and Programming (ICALP)*, Lecture Notes in Computer Science 2791, Springer, 943–55, 2003.

[12] Toru Kasai, Gunho Lee, Hiroki Arimura, Setsuo Arikawa, and Kunsoo Park. Linear-time longest-common-prefix computation in suffix arrays and its applications. In *Proceedings of the 12th Symposium on Combinatorial Pattern Matching (CPM)*, Lecture Notes in Computer Science 2089, Springer, 181–92, 2001.

[13] Jacob Ziv and Abraham Lempel. A universal algorithm for sequential data compression. *IEEE Transactions on Information Theory*, 23(3): 337–43, 1977.

[14] Udi Manber and Gene Myers. Suffix arrays: A new method for on-line string searches. *SIAM Journal on Computing*, 22(5): 935–48, 1993.

[15] Edward M. McCreight. A space-economical suffix tree construction algorithm. *Journal of the ACM*, 23(2): 262–72, 1976.

11   Integer Coding

The trouble with integers is that we have
examined only the very small ones. Maybe
all the exciting stuff happens at really big
numbers, ones we can't even begin to think
about in any very definite way.
Attributed to Ronald Graham

In this chapter we address a basic encoding problem that occurs in many contexts
[4, 9], and whose impact on the total memory footprint and speed performance of the
underlying application is too easily underestimated or neglected.

> **Problem.** Let $S = s_1, \ldots, s_n$ be a sequence of positive integers s_i, possibly
> repeated. The goal is to represent the integers of S as binary sequences that are
> self-delimiting and use just a few bits.

Note that the requirement that s_i are *positive integers* can be relaxed by computing
the minimum value in S among the negative integers, and then summing its absolute
value to all of s_i.

Before digging into the algorithmic solution to this problem, let us comment upon
two exemplar applications. Search engines store for each term t the list of documents
(i.e. Web pages, blog posts, tweets, etc.) in which t occurs; this list is called the *posting
list* of t. Documents are usually represented in posting lists via integer IDs, which are
assigned during Web crawling. Answering a user query, formulated as a sequence of
keywords $t_1 t_2 \ldots t_k$, then consists of finding the docIDs where all t_is occur. This is
implemented by intersecting the posting lists for these k terms. Storing these integers
with a fixed-length binary encoding (i.e., four or eight bytes) may require consider-
able space, and thus time for their retrieval, given that modern search engines index
billions and billions of documents. In order to reduce disk-space occupancy, bandwidth as well as increase the amount of cached lists in internal memory, two kinds of
compression tricks are usually adopted: the first consists of sorting the document IDs
in each posting list, and then encoding each docID as the difference between itself and
its preceding docID in the list, the so-called *gap coding*;[1] the second trick consists

---

[1] Of course, the first docID of a posting list is stored explicitly.

of encoding each gap with a variable-length sequence of bits which is short for small integers [3, 7, 9].

Another example of this problem relates to data compression. We have seen in Chapter 10 that the LZ77 compressor turns input files into sequences of triples in which the first two components are integers. Other well-known compressors (such as MTF, MPEG, RLE, BWT, etc.) produce as intermediate output one or more sets of integers, with smaller values most probable and larger values increasingly less probable. The final coding stage of those compressors must therefore convert these integers into a bit stream, such that the total number of bits is minimized [4, 9].

A final example supporting the generality of the integer compression problem can be obtained by looking at any text T as a sequence of tokens, which may be words or single characters. Each token can be represented with an integer (aka *tokenID*), so that the problem of compressing T can be solved by compressing its sequence of tokenIDs. In order to better deploy integer-coding schemes, one can sort the tokens by decreasing frequency of occurrence in T, and then assign as tokenIDs their *rank* in the ordered sequence. Then the more frequent a token in T is, the smaller its tokenID, and thus the shorter the codeword assigned to it by an integer-coding scheme. It is very well known that words in (linguistic) texts follow a Zipfian distribution [3]: the i-th most frequent word in T has a frequency $c(1/i)^\alpha$, where c is a normalization factor and α is a parameter depending on the input text. Then, any of the following *universal* integer coders (such as the ones in Section 11.1) could be used to encode T's tokenIDs, thus achieving a compression performance close to the *entropy* of the input text.

The main question we address in this chapter is, therefore, how we design a variable-length binary representation for a sequence of (unbounded) integers that takes as a few bits as possible and is prefix-free, that is, the binary encoding of all these integers can be concatenated to produce an output bit stream that preserves decodability, in the sense that the decoder has a means to identify the start and the end of each single integer representation within the bit stream and, thus, get back to its uncompressed representation.

The first and simplest idea to solve this problem is surely the one that takes $m = \max_j s_j$ and then encodes each integer $s_i \in S$ by using $\lceil \log_2(m + 1) \rceil$ bits. This fixed-size encoding is efficient whenever the set S is not very spread out and is concentrated around the value zero. But this is a very unusual situation; in general, $m \gg s_i$, so many bits are wasted in the output bit stream. So why not store each s_i by using its binary encoding with $\lceil \log_2(s_i + 1) \rceil$ bits? The subtle problem with this approach is that this code is not self-delimiting, and in fact we cannot concatenate the binary encoding of all s_i and still be able to distinguish each codeword. As an example, take $S = \{1, 2, 3\}$ and the output bit sequence `11011`, which is produced by using their binary encodings: `1`, `10`, and `11`. It is evident that we could derive many compatible sequences of integers from `11011`, such as $\{6, 1, 1\}$ or $\{1, 2, 1, 1\}$, and several others.

It is therefore clear that this simple encoding problem is challenging and deserves the attention that we dedicate to it in this chapter. We start by introducing one of the simplest and best-known integer codes, the *unary code*. The unary code $U(x)$ for an integer $x \geq 1$ is given by a sequence of $x - 1$ bits set to 0, ended by a (delimiting) bit set to 1. The correctness of the condition that $x \neq 0$ is easily established, although this code can also be made to work on all nonnegative integers just by writing x bits set to 0 rather than $x - 1$. All these trivial technicalities will be neglected in the rest of this chapter, and we will just concentrate on strictly positive s_i. It is clear that $U(x)$ requires x bits, which is *exponentially longer* than the length $\Theta(\log x)$ of its binary code. Nonetheless, this code is efficient for very small integers and soon becomes *space inefficient* as x increases.

This statement can be made more precise by recalling a basic fact deriving from Shannon's coding theorem, which states that *the ideal code length $L(c)$ for a symbol c is equal to $\log_2 \frac{1}{\mathcal{P}[c]}$ bits, where $\mathcal{P}[c]$ is the probability of occurrence of symbol c.* This probability can be known in advance, if we have sufficient information about the source emitting c, or it can be estimated empirically by counting the occurrences of symbol c in S. The reader should be careful in recalling that, in the scenario considered in this chapter, symbols are positive integers, so the ideal code for the integer x consists of $\log_2 \frac{1}{\mathcal{P}[x]}$ bits. So, by solving the equation $|U(x)| = \log_2 \frac{1}{\mathcal{P}[x]}$ with respect to $\mathcal{P}[x]$, we derive the distribution of the integers x for which the unary code is optimal. In this specific case it is $\mathcal{P}[x] = 2^{-x}$. As far as efficiency is concerned, the unary code needs a lot of bit shifts, which are slow operations in modern processors: another reason to favor small integers.

Theorem 11.1 *The unary code of a positive integer x takes x bits, and thus it is optimal for the distribution $\mathcal{P}[x] = 2^{-x}$.*

Using this same argument we can also deduce that the fixed-length binary encoding, which uses $\lceil \log_2(m + 1) \rceil$ bits, is optimal whenever integers in S are *distributed uniformly* within the range $\{1, 2, \ldots, m\}$.

Theorem 11.2 *Given a set S of integers, of maximum value m, the fixed-length binary code represents each of them in $\lceil \log_2(m+1) \rceil$ bits, and thus it is optimal for the uniform distribution $\mathcal{P}[x] = 1/m$.*

In general, integers are not uniformly distributed, and in fact variable-length binary representations must be considered that eventually improve the simple unary code. There are many proposals in the literature, each offering a different *trade-off between space occupancy of the binary code and time efficiency for its decoding*. The following subsections will detail the most useful and most used variable-length binary codes, starting from the simplest ones, which use *fixed encoding models* for the integers in S (such as, e.g., γ and δ codes), and then move on to the more involved interpolative and Elias–Fano codes which use sophisticated (dynamic) models that adapt to the distribution of the integers in S, and thus may induce a much more succinct encoding. Surprisingly enough, we will show that in some cases the interpolative code could end up even shorter than the "optimal" Huffman code (described in Chapter 12). This

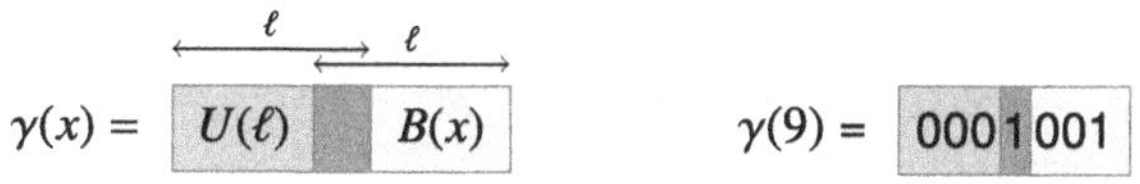

Figure 11.1 (Left) Graphical representation of $\gamma(x)$, for $x > 0$ and $\ell = |B(x)|$. The dark-gray rectangle denotes the binary digit 1 shared between $U(\ell)$ and $B(x)$. (Right) Graphical representation of $\gamma(9)$; note the dark-gray digit 1 shared between the unary code $U(4)$ and the binary code $B(9)$.

apparently contradictory statement comes from the fact that the Huffman code is *optimal* among the family of *static* prefix-free codes, namely the ones that use a fixed code for all occurrences of x in S. Conversely, the interpolative code uses a dynamic model that encodes x according to the distribution of its surrounding integers in S, thus possibly adopting different codes for each of its different occurrences in S. For some integer distributions, this context-aware behavior of the interpolative code may result in a much more compressed representation of the output bit stream.

11.1 Elias Codes: γ and δ

These are two very simple *universal* codes for integers that use a fixed model, which were introduced in the 1960s by Elias [2]. The adjective "universal" here relates to the property that the length of the code is $O(\log x)$ for any integer x. So it is just a *constant factor* longer than the binary code $B(x)$, which has length $\lceil \log(x + 1) \rceil$, with the additional desirable property of being prefix-free.

The γ-code represents an integer x as a binary sequence composed of two parts: a sequence of $|B(x)| - 1$ zeros, followed by the binary representation $B(x)$. The initial sequence of zeros is delimited by the first 1, which also corresponds to the first bit of the binary representation $B(x)$. So $\gamma(x)$ can be decoded easily: count the consecutive number of zeros up to the first 1; say this number is c. Then, fetch the following $c + 1$ bits (including the trailing 1), and interpret the c-long binary sequence as the integer x. Figure 11.1 provides a graphical representation of the γ-code for an arbitrary positive integer x, and an instantiation for $x = 9$.

The γ-code requires $2|B(x)| - 1$ bits, which is equal to $2\lceil \log_2(x+1) \rceil - 1$. In fact, the γ-code of the integer 9 needs $2\lceil \log_2(9 + 1) \rceil - 1 = 7$ bits. From Shannon's condition on ideal codes, we derive that the γ-code is optimal whenever the distribution of the integers in S follows the formula $\mathcal{P}[x] \approx \frac{1}{x^2}$.

Theorem 11.3 *The γ-code of a positive integer x takes $2\lceil \log_2(x + 1) \rceil - 1$ bits, and thus it is optimal for the distribution $\mathcal{P}[x] \approx 1/x^2$. This is within a factor of two from the bit length $|B(x)| = \lceil \log_2(x + 1) \rceil$ of the binary code of x.*

The inefficiency in the γ-code resides in the unary coding of the length $|B(x)|$, which is really costly as x becomes larger and larger. In order to mitigate this problem, Elias introduced the δ-code, which applies the γ-code in place of the unary code. So

Figure 11.2 (Left) Graphical representation of $\delta(x)$, for $x > 0$, $\ell = |B(x)|$ and $\ell' = |B(\ell)|$. The dark-gray rectangle denotes the binary digit 1 shared between $U(\ell')$ and $B(\ell)$.
(Right) Graphical representation of $\delta(14)$, where $\ell = 4$ and $\ell' = 3$. Notice the dark-gray digit 1 shared between the unary code $U(\ell') = U(3)$ and $B(\ell) = B(4)$, given that $|B(x)| = |B(14)| = 4$.

$\delta(x)$ consists of two parts: the first encodes $\gamma(|B(x)|)$, the second encodes x in binary. Note that, since we are using the γ-code for $B(x)$'s length, the first and the second parts do not share any bits; moreover, we observe that γ is applied to $|B(x)|$, which is guaranteed to be a number greater than zero. Decoding $\delta(x)$ is easy: first we decode $\gamma(|B(x)|)$, and then we fetch the next $|B(x)|$ bits which encode the value x in binary. It is interesting to note that the δ-code can also encode the value zero, as $\delta(0) = 1\ 0$, where the first bit corresponds to $\gamma(1) = 1$, which is the length of the (special) binary representation of value 0. Figure 11.2 provides a graphical representation of the δ-code for an arbitrary positive integer x, and an instantiation for $x = 14$.

As for the number of bits taken by $\delta(x)$, we observe that it is $|\gamma(\ell)| + \ell = 2\lceil\log_2(\ell + 1)\rceil - 1 + \ell \approx 2\log\log x + \log x + 1$. This encoding is therefore a factor of $1 + o(1)$ from the length $\ell = |B(x)|$ of the binary code of x, and hence it is universal.

Theorem 11.4 *The δ-code of a positive integer x takes about $1 + \log_2 x + 2\log_2 \log_2 x$ bits, and thus it is optimal for the distribution $\mathcal{P}[x] \approx \frac{1}{x(\log x)^2}$. This is within a factor of $1 + o(1)$ from the bit length $|B(x)| = 2\lceil\log_2(x+1)\rceil$ of the binary code of x.*

In conclusion, γ- and δ-codes are universal and pretty efficient whenever the integers in the set S are concentrated around 1. Moreover, we note that these two codes need a lot of bit shifts to be decoded and thus turn out to be slow for decoding large integers. The codes of the following subsections trade space efficiency with decoding speed and, in fact, they are preferred in practical applications.

11.2   Rice Code

There are situations in which integers are concentrated around some value, different from zero. In this case, the larger this value is, the worse the performance of γ- and δ-codes. Here, Rice coding becomes advantageous both in compression ratio and decoding speed. Its special feature is being a *parametric code*, namely one that depends on a positive integer k, which may be fixed according to the distribution of the integers in the set S. The Rice code $R_k(x)$ of an integer $x > 0$, given the parameter k, consists of two parts: the quotient $q = \lfloor\frac{x-1}{2^k}\rfloor$ and the remainder $r = x - 1 - 2^k q$. We subtract 1 in the quotient and the remainder in order to transform a strictly positive integer sequence into a 0-based one. For sequences where $x \geq 0$ there is no need to perform this subtraction. The quotient is stored in unary using $q + 1$ bits (the +1 is

$$R_k(x) = \boxed{U(q+1) \quad B_k(r)} \qquad R_4(83) = \boxed{000001 \quad 0010}$$

Figure 11.3 (Left) Graphical representation of the Rice code with parameter k. (Right) Graphical representation of $R_4(83)$, where $k = 4, q = \lfloor (83-1)/2^4 \rfloor = 5$, and $r = 83 - 1 - 5 \times 2^4 = 2$.

needed because q may be 0, and we defined the unary code for positive integers); the remainder r is in the range $[0, 2^k)$ and thus it is stored in binary using k bits, denoted with $B_k(r)$. This means that the quotient is encoded in variable length, whereas the remainder is encoded in fixed length. The closer 2^k is to the value of x, the shorter the representation of q is, thus the faster its decoding. For this reason, k is chosen in such a way that 2^k is concentrated around the mean of S's elements. Figure 11.3 provides a graphical representation of the Rice code for an arbitrary positive integer x with parameter k, and an instantiation for $x = 83$ and $k = 4$.

The bit length of $R_k(x)$ is $q + k + 1$. This code is a particular case of the Golomb code [9]; it is optimal when the values to be encoded follow a geometric distribution with parameter p, namely $\mathcal{P}[x] = p(1-p)^{x-1}$. In this case, if $2^k \simeq \frac{ln(2)}{p} \simeq 0.69 \times \mathtt{mean}(S)$, the Rice and all Golomb codes generate an optimal prefix code [9].

Fact 11.1 The Rice code, with parameter k, of a positive integer x takes $\lfloor \frac{x-1}{2^k} \rfloor + 1 + k$ bits, and it is optimal for the geometric distribution $\mathcal{P}[x] = p(1-p)^{x-1}$.

11.3 PForDelta Code

This method for compressing integers supports extremely fast decompression and achieves a small size in the compressed output whenever S's integers follow a Gaussian distribution. Let us assume that most of S's integers fall in an interval $[base, base + 2^b - 2]$. We translate the integers in the new interval $[0, 2^b - 2]$ in order to encode them in b bits; the other integers outside this range are called *exceptions*; they are represented in the compressed list with an *escape symbol* and stored in a separate list using a fixed-size representation of w bits (namely, a whole memory word). The *escape symbol* can be encoded in binary using the b bits representing the configuration $2^b - 1$ which is not part of the range of the encodable integers (see Figure 11.4 for a running example). The good property of this code is that all integers in S are encoded in fixed length, either b bits or $w + b$ bits, so they can be decoded fast and possibly in parallel by packing a few of them in a memory word.

Fact 11.2 The PForDelta code of a positive integer x takes either b bits or $b + w$ bits, depending on whether $x \in [base, base + 2^b - 2]$ or not, respectively.

The design of a PForDelta code for an integer sequence S needs to deal with the choice of b. A rule of thumb is to choose b such that about 90 percent of S's integers fall in

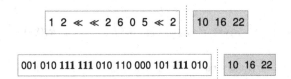

Figure 11.4 An example of PForDelta encoding of the sequence $S = (1, 2, 10, 16, 2, 6, 0, 5, 22, 2)$, with $b = 3$ and $base = 0$. The upper image illustrates that the integers of S falling in the range $[0, 2^b - 2] = [0, 6]$ are encoded explicitly in the white rectangle using b bits, whereas the out-of-range integers are encoded twice: by means of the escape symbol $\ll$ in the white rectangle using b bits, together with a full-size representation in the gray rectangle. The lower image shows the final encoding, in which the escape symbol $\ll$ is represented in three bits using the reserved binary sequence $2^b - 1 = 7 = (111)_2$.

the range $[base, base + 2^b - 2]$, and thus can be encoded in b bits. An alternative solution is to trade between wasting space (choosing a larger b, but reducing the number of exceptions) and saving space (choosing a smaller b, but inducing more exceptions). The authors of [8] have proposed an algorithm based on dynamic programming that computes the largest b for a desired compression ratio, thus ensuring the fastest decompression for a given space-occupancy constraint for the compressed S. The decoding speed of PForDelta is particularly appreciated by the community of software developers: in fact, it can force memory-word alignment over groups of w/b integers, and it can be implemented to avoid branch mispredictions.

11.4   Variable-Byte Code and (*s*, *c*)-Dense Codes

Another class of codes that trade speed and succinctness are (s, c)-*dense codes*. Their simplest instantiation, commonly said to have been introduced by the AltaVista search engine, is the *variable-byte code*, which uses a sequence of bytes to represent an integer, thus achieving a significant decoding speed. This byte-aligned coding is useful for achieving a significant decoding speed. The variable-byte code for x is constructed as follows: its binary representation $B(x)$ is padded to the left with a sequence of 0s in order to guarantee that its length is a multiple of 7; then, this binary sequence is partitioned into groups of seven bits each; finally, a flag bit is appended to each such group to indicate whether it is the last one (bit set to 0) or not (bit set to 1) of x's representation. Figure 11.5 provides a graphical representation of the variable-byte code for an arbitrary positive integer, and its instantiation for $x = 2^{16}$.

The decoding is simple: the byte sequence is scanned until a byte is found whose value is smaller than 128 (hence, its flag bit is 0); then all flag bits are removed and the resulting binary sequence is interpreted as a positive integer. The minimum amount of bits necessary to encode an integer x is 8, and on average four bits are wasted because of the padding. Hence this method is appropriate for large values of x.

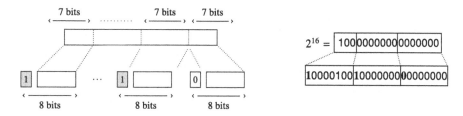

Figure 11.5 (Left) Graphical representation of the variable-byte code for a generic integer. (Right) Graphical representation of the variable-byte code for the integer 2^{16}.

Fact 11.3 The variable-byte code of a positive integer x takes $8 \left\lceil \frac{|B(x)|}{7} \right\rceil$ bits, and thus it is optimal for the distribution $\mathcal{P}[x] \approx \sqrt[7]{1/x^8}$.

The use of flag bits induces a subtle issue that we discuss next, by introducing the design of a more effective family of integer coders: (s, c)-*dense codes*.

The flag bit partitions the $2^8 = 256$ binary configurations of each byte into two sets: the configurations representing integers smaller than 128 (i.e. the flag bit is equal to 0), and the configurations representing integers larger than or equal to 128 (i.e. the flag bit is equal to 1). The former configurations are 128 in number and are called *stoppers* (because they delimit the end of an integer representation); the latter configurations are also 128 in number, and are called *continuers* (because they are in the middle of a byte-aligned integer representation). For the sake of presentation we denote the cardinalities of the two sets by s and c, respectively. In the case of the variable-byte code, $s + c = 2^8 = 256$ and $s = c = 128$. During the decoding phase, whenever we encounter a continuer byte, we go on reading; otherwise we stop and decode the resulting binary sequence, according to the steps we have illustrated.

The drawback of this approach is that for any $x < 128$ we use one byte. Therefore, if the set S consists of very small integers, we are wasting bits. Vice versa, if S consists of integers larger than 128, but smaller than 256, then it could be better to enlarge the set of stoppers in order to still use one byte for them, instead of emitting two bytes. This observation drives us to investigate the design of codes in which we vary the set of stoppers/continuers, still under the constraint that $s + c = 256$. To dig into this, let us first analyze how the choice of s and c changes the number of integers that can be encoded with one or more bytes:

- One byte can encode the first s integers.
- Two bytes can encode the subsequent $s \times c$ integers.
- Three bytes can encode the subsequent $s \times c^2$ integers.
- A sequence of k bytes can encode $s \times c^{k-1}$ integers.

It is simple to derive a closed formula that expresses the number of integers encodable with at most k bytes, and thus with at most $(k - 1)$ continuers and one stopper:

Values	$s = c = 4$		$s = 6, c = 2$	
0		000		000
1		001		001
2		010		010
3		011		011
4	100	000		100
5	100	001		101
6	100	010	110	000
7	100	011	110	001
8	101	000	110	010
9	101	001	110	011
10	101	010	110	100
11	101	011	110	101
12	110	000	111	000
13	110	001	111	001
14	110	010	111	010
15	110	011	111	011
16	111	000	111	100
17	111	001	111	101
18	111	010		
19	111	011		

	$s = c = 4$	$s = 6, c = 2$
s - from	000	000
s - to	011	101
c - from	100	110
c - to	111	111
$0, \ldots, s - 1$	$0, \ldots, 3$	$0, \ldots, 5$
$s, \ldots, c \times s - 1$	$4, \ldots, 19$	$0, \ldots, 17$
$c \times s, \ldots, c^2 \times s$	$20, \ldots, 85$	$18, \ldots, 41$

Figure 11.6 Example of an (s, c)-code using two different pairs of values for s and c.

$$s \times \sum_{i=0}^{k-1} c^i = s \times \frac{c^k - 1}{c - 1}.$$

This formula allows us to immediately derive the number of bytes that are necessary to encode an integer x via an (s, c)-code with $s + c = 256$: it is enough to find the smallest k such that $c^k > x \times ((c - 1)/s) + 1$.

It is evident, at this point, that the previous design is not bounded to byte sequences, and thus to configurations over eight bits. But it can be shaped to fit any number b of bits. In this case, the total number of 2^b configurations can be arbitrarily partitioned in s stoppers and c continuers, provided that $s + c = 2^b$. For simplicity of design, we assume that the first s configurations are stoppers and the remaining c configurations are continuers (as we did for the variable-byte code). The best choice of s and c depends on the *distribution* of the integers to be encoded. For example, assume that we want to design an (s, c)-code over $b = 3$ bits (instead of 8 bits), so we have to choose the number of stoppers and continuers in such a way that $s + c = 2^3 = 8$ (instead of 256). Figure 11.6 shows two different choices for s and c, such that $s + c = 8$: in the first case, the number of stoppers and continuers is equal to 4; in the second case, the number of stoppers is 6 and the number of continuers is 2. Changing s (and thus $c = 8 - s$) changes the number of integers that can be encoded with $3, 6, 9, \ldots$ bits, as Figure 11.6 shows. Note that, while the $(4, 4)$-code can encode only the first four integers with three bits, the $(6, 2)$-code can encode two more integers with three bits. This means that this latter code can lead to a more compressed integer sequence according to the skewness of the distribution of the integers in $\{0, \ldots, 5\}$. Therefore, it can be advantageous to adapt the number of stoppers and continuers to the probability distribution of the integers in S. In particular, if this distribution is concentrated toward 0, then it can be advantageous to choose a small s; on the other hand, the flatter the distribution, the more we could consider choosing larger values of s. The authors of [1] propose an efficient algorithm to calculate that optimal s for a given integer distribution.

11.5   Interpolative Code

This is an integer-coding technique that can be applied to an *increasing* sequence of positive integers. This means that we have to modify the original formulation of our integer-coding problem, over a possibly repeated sequence S of integers, into a new formulation referring to a sequence S' consisting of increasing positive integers. The transformation is easy to define: just set $S'[i] = \sum_{j=1}^{i} S[j]$, so that every integer of S' is obtained as a prefix sum of integers in S.

Let us now concentrate on the increasing sequence $S' = s'_1, \ldots, s'_n$ with $s'_i < s'_{i+1}$. The interpolative code will be very efficient in space compression whenever S' shows *clustered* occurrences of integers, that is, subsequences that are concentrated in small ranges. This is a typical situation that arises in the storage of posting lists of search engines [8].

The design of this integer-coding scheme is *recursive* and proceeds as follows. At each iteration, the algorithm processes the (uncompressed) subsequence $S'_{l,r}$, and knows *inductively* four parameters relating to it:

- the left index l and the right index r delimiting the subsequence to be encoded: that is, $S'_{l,r} = \{s'_l, s'_{l+1}, \ldots, s'_r\}$;
- a lower bound *low* to the lowest value in $S'_{l,r}$, and an upper bound *hi* to the highest value in $S'_{l,r}$, hence $low \le s'_l < \ldots < s'_r \le hi$. The values *low* and *hi* do not necessarily coincide with s'_l and s'_r; they just represent some lower and upper estimates obtained during the recursive calls (both by encoder and decoder).

Initially the subsequence to be encoded is the full sequence $S'[1, n]$, so we have $l = 1, r = n, low = s'_1$, and $hi = s'_n$. These four values are stored in the compressed file so that the decoder can read them at the beginning of the decompression phase.

At each recursive call, the algorithm first encodes the middle element s'_m, where $m = \lfloor \frac{l+r}{2} \rfloor$, given the information available in the 4-tuple $\langle l, r, low, hi \rangle$, and then recursively encodes the two subsequences $s'_l, \ldots, s'_{m-1}$ and $s'_{m+1}, \ldots, s'_r$, by using a properly recomputed 4-tuple for each:

Algorithm 11.1 Interpolative coding of $\langle S', l, r, low, hi \rangle$

1: **if** $r < l$ **then**
2:    **return** the empty string;
3: **end if**
4: **if** $l = r$ **then**
5:    **return** BinaryCode($S'[l], low, hi$);
6: **end if**
7: Compute $m = \lfloor \frac{l+r}{2} \rfloor$;
8: Compute $A_1 =$ BinaryCode($S'[m], low + m - l, hi - r + m$);
9: Compute $A_2 =$ Interpolative coding of $\langle S', l, m - 1, low, S'[m] - 1 \rangle$;
10: Compute $A_3 =$ Interpolative coding of $\langle S', m + 1, r, S'[m] + 1, hi \rangle$;
11: **return** the concatenation of A_1, A_2 and A_3;

- For the subsequence $s'_l, \ldots, s'_{m-1}$, the parameter low is the same as in the previous step, since s'_l has not changed, whereas hi can be set as $s'_m - 1$, since $s'_{m-1} < s'_m$, the integers of S' being distinct and increasing.
- For the subsequence $s'_{m+1}, \ldots, s'_r$, the parameter hi is the same as before, since s'_r has not changed, whereas low can be set as $s'_m + 1$, since $s'_{m+1} > s'_m$.
- The parameters l, r, and n are recomputed accordingly.

In order to succinctly encode s'_m, the algorithm deploys as much information as it can derive from the 4-tuple $\langle l, r, low, hi \rangle$. Specifically, it knows that $s'_m \geq low + m - l$, because to the left of s'_m we have $m - l$ distinct elements of S' and the smallest one is larger than low; and, by a similar argument, it knows that $s'_m \leq hi - (r - m)$. Thus it can infer that s'_m lies in the range $[low + m - l, hi - r + m]$, so it encodes it not explicitly but as the difference between the value s'_m and its known lower bound ($low + m - l$) just by using $\lceil \log_2 B \rceil$ bits, where $B = hi - low - r + l + 1$ is the size of the interval enclosing s'_m. In this way, the interpolative code can use very few bits per s'_m whenever the sequence $S'_{l,r}$ is dense. As a further speciality of this coding scheme, note that, whenever the subsequence to be encoded has the form ($low, low + 1, \ldots, low + n - 1$), the algorithm does not emit any bits, thus achieving a significant compression advantage, indeed.

Algorithm 11.1 provides the details of these steps. In particular, procedure BinaryCode(x, a, b) is used to emit the binary encoding of the integer ($x - a$) in $\lceil \log_2 (b - a + 1) \rceil$ bits, by assuming that $x \in \{a, a + 1, \ldots, b - 1, b\}$. Figure 11.7 shows a running example for the execution of interpolative coding over an increasing sequence of 12 positive integers. Please note the two cases in which the algorithm does not emit any bits (shown as thickly outlined light-gray boxes), because the two ranges of integers, namely $\{1, 2\}$ and $\{19, 20, 21\}$, are fully dense.

We conclude this section by noting that the interpolative coding of an integer s'_i is not fixed but depends on the distribution of the other integers in S'. It is therefore an *adaptive* code which, additionally, turns out to be *not* prefix-free. These two features make it very different from the other codes we have seen in the previous sections,

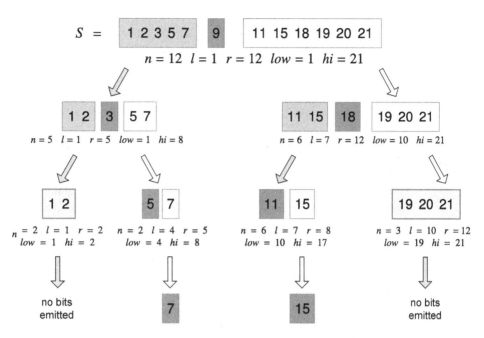

Figure 11.7 The gray and white boxes are, respectively, the left and right subsequences of each recursive iteration of the interpolative coding algorithm. The dark gray boxes highlight the integer s'_m to be encoded. The figure also shows explicitly the number $n = r - l + 1$ of integers to be encoded, for illustrative purposes, as well as the 4-tuple passed to every recursive call. The two thickly outlined light gray boxes show the subsequences for which the interpolative code does not emit any bits. The procedure performs, in practice, a pre-order traversal of a balanced binary tree whose leaves are the integers in S'. The items are encoded in the following order (the actual number encoded is given in parentheses): 9 (3), 3 (0), 5 (1), 7 (1), 18 (6), 11 (1), 15 (4).

and from the Huffman code dealt with in the next chapter, which is optimal among the class of *static* prefix-free codes. As a result, the interpolative code might be much more succinct than Huffman code over dense integer sequences, but this will not surprise us at all because we now know the reason for that.

11.6 Elias–Fano Code

Unlike interpolative coding, the code described in this section provides a space occupancy that does not depend on the distribution of the input data and, more importantly, can be *indexed* (by proper compressed data structures) in order to efficiently access the encoded integers *randomly*. The former feature is a positive one in some settings, and a negative one in other settings. It is positive in the context of storing inverted lists of search engines and adjacency lists of large graphs; it is negative whenever integers are *clustered* and space is a main concern of the underlying application.

$$
\begin{array}{r|c|c}
1 = & 000 & 01 \\
4 = & 001 & 00 \\
7 = & 001 & 11 \\
18 = & 100 & 10 \\
24 = & 110 & 00 \\
26 = & 110 & 10 \\
30 = & 111 & 10 \\
31 = & 111 & 11 \\
\end{array}
$$

$L = 0100111000101011$

bucket $0 \mid 1 \mid 2\mid3\mid 4 \mid5\mid 6 \mid 7$
$H = 10\mid110\mid0\mid0\mid1\mid0\mid0\mid110\mid110$

Figure 11.8 The Elias-Fano code for the integer sequence $S' = 1, 4, 7, 18, 24, 26, 30, 31$.

Some authors have recently proposed a (sort of) dynamic programming approach that turns Elias-Fano coding into a *distribution-sensitive code*, like interpolative code, thus combining the efficiency in randomly accessing the encoded integers of the former with the space succinctness of the latter in compressing clustered integer subsequences [6]. Experiments have shown that interpolative coding is only 2−8 percent smaller than the optimized Elias-Fano code but up to 5.5 times slower, and the variable-byte code is 10−40 percent faster than the optimized Elias-Fano code but at least 2.5 times larger in space. This means that the Elias-Fano code is a competitive choice whenever an integer sequence must be compressed and randomly accessed.

As for the interpolative code, Elias-Fano code works on a *monotonically increasing* sequence $S' = s'_1, \ldots, s'_n$ with $s'_i < s'_{i+1}$. For the sake of explanation, we set the size of the universe $u = s'_n + 1$, and assume that each integer s'_i is represented in binary with $b = \lceil \log_2 u \rceil$ bits. We partition the binary representation of s'_i into two blocks: one denoted by $L(s'_i)$ and consisting of the $\ell = \lceil \log_2(u/n) \rceil$ least significant bits (the rightmost ones), and the other denoted by $H(s'_i)$ and consisting of the $h = b - \ell$ most significant bits (the leftmost ones). Clearly, $b = \ell + h$.

The Elias-Fano code then consists of two binary sequences:

- The sequence L, which is obtained by concatenating the blocks $L(s'_i)$, in the order $i = 1, 2, \ldots, n$, thus resulting in length $n \ell = n \lceil \log_2(u/n) \rceil$ bits.
- The sequence H, which is obtained by iterating over all possible configurations of h bits, namely from $j = 0^h = 0$ to $j = 1^h = 2^h - 1$, and using the *negative unary representation* to encode the number x of elements s'_i for which $H(s'_i) = j$. Specifically, value x is encoded as $1^x 0$ (i.e. 1 is repeated x times), so the binary representation 0 encodes $x = 0$ (i.e. the case that no $H(s'_i) = j$). We call each such negative unary encoding a *bucket*, because it refers to the "bucket" of integers s'_i that have a specific configuration j. The sequence H has n bits set to 1, because every s'_i generates one bit set to 1 in its negative unary representation, and a number of 0s that is equal to the number of buckets, because every 0 delimits their encoding. Now, since the maximum bucket value is $\lfloor u/2^\ell \rfloor$, then the number of 0 can be bounded by $\lfloor u/2^{\lceil \log_2 u/n \rceil} \rfloor \leq u/2^{\log_2(u/n)} = n$. Therefore the binary sequence H has size $2n$ bits, and it has a perfectly balanced number of 0s and 1s.

Figure 11.8 shows a running example of the coding process for a set S' of $n = 8$ integers in a universe of size $u = 32$. Therefore, $b = \lceil \log_2 32 \rceil = 5$ bits are used to represent the integers of S', $\ell = \lceil \log_2(u/n) \rceil = \lceil \log_2(32/8) \rceil = 2$ bits are used to represent their least significant part, and $h = b - \ell = 3$ bits are used to represent their most significant part. The binary sequence L thus has size $\ell n = 2 \times 8 = 16$ bits, and the binary sequence H also consists of 16 bits, because we have $2^3 = 8$ buckets (i.e. configurations of $h = 3$ bits) and $n = 8$ integers to be coded. For illustrative purposes, the figure details which negative unary sequence corresponds to every configuration j of three bits (i.e. $j = 0, 1, \ldots, 7$). In particular, the configuration 001 (i.e. $j = 1$) occurs twice as $H(s_i')$, namely for the integers 4 and 7, so the binary sequence H encodes these two occurrences as 110; instead, the configuration 011 (i.e. $j = 3$) does not occur as $H(s_i')$ and so the binary sequence H encodes that event as 0.

Decoding the Elias-Fano code is easy: just reverse the process we followed to encode S'. Select groups of ℓ bits from L to form the least significant part of the integers of S'. Actually, the i-th group provides the ℓ least significant bits of s_i'. For the h most significant bits of s_i', we iterate over the binary sequence H and, if the i-th bit set to 1 belongs to the j-th negative unary sequence, then we encode j in binary using h bits. We have therefore proved the following:

Theorem 11.5 *The Elias–Fano encoding of a monotonically increasing sequence of n integers in the range $[0, u)$ takes less than $2n + n \lceil \log_2 \frac{u}{n} \rceil$ bits, regardless of their distribution. Compressing and decompressing that integer sequence takes $O(n)$ time. The space bound is almost optimal if the integers are uniformly distributed in $[0, u)$; to be precise, this encoding takes less than two bits per integer in addition to the optimal encoding of $\lceil \log_2(u/n) \rceil$ bits.*

The most interesting property of the Elias-Fano code is that it can be augmented with proper data structures to efficiently support the following two operations:

- Access(i), which, given an index $1 \leq i \leq n$, returns s_i'.
- NextGEQ(x), which, given an integer $0 \leq x < u$, returns the smallest element s_i' that is Greater than or EQual to x.

The key idea underlying the "augmentation" of H is via an auxiliary data structure that efficiently, in time and space, answers a well-known primitive, called $\mathsf{Select}_1(p, H)$, which returns the position in H of the p-th bit set to 1 (or set to 0, in the case of $\mathsf{Select}_0(p, H)$). The implementation of these two operations, and of the succinct data structure for the Select primitive, will be detailed in Chapter 15; we content ourselves here in pointing out that Select can be answered in constant time and $o(|H|) = o(n)$ bits in addition to H (see, e.g., [5]). Given the Select primitive, the two operations Access(i) and NextGEQ(x) can be implemented in $O(1)$ time and $O(\log(u/n))$ time, respectively, as the next Chapter 15 will explain.

A comment is in order at this point which addresses an issue mentioned at the beginning of this section. Since Elias-Fano code represents a monotone sequence of integers regardless of its regularities, clustered sequences get significantly worse compression than what interpolative code is able to achieve. Take, as an illustrative example, the sequence $S' = (1, 2, \ldots, n-1, u-1)$ of n integers. This sequence is highly compressible since the length of the first run and the value of $u-1$ can be encoded in $O(\log u)$ bits each. Conversely Elias-Fano code requires $2 + \lceil \log_2(u/n) \rceil$ bits per element. Some authors have studied how to turn the Elias-Fano code into a *distribution-sensitive* code that takes advantage of the regularities present in the input sequence S' [6]. These authors proposed two approaches. The first is a simple one based on a two-level storage scheme in which the sequence S' is partitioned into n/m chunks of m integers each, where m is a user-defined parameter. The "first level" is then created by using Elias-Fano to encode the last integer of each chunk, hence n/m integers overall; then, the "second level" is created by using a specific Elias-Fano code on each chunk whose integers are gap-encoded with respect to the last integer of the previous chunk (available in the first level). Let u_j be the distance between the first and last integers of the j-th chunk; then the Elias-Fano code will compress its integers in the second level using $(2 + \lceil \log(u_j/m) \rceil)$ bits each, which is advantageous when compared against the cost for Elias-Fano coding the entire sequence S' because (u_j/m) is the average distance within a bucket, whereas (u/n) is the average distance over the entire S'. Nonetheless, we partially lose this advantage due to the space taken by the first indexing level. Overall, this simple integer-coding scheme improves the space occupancy of the classic Elias-Fano code (which operates on the entire S') by up to 30 percent, but it slows down the decompression time by up to 10 percent. Compared to interpolative code, this two-level scheme worsens space occupancy by up to 10 percent, but it achieves three/four times faster decompression. The second approach proposed by the authors of [6] is a more sophisticated approach, hinging on the interpretation of Elias-Fano's encoding of S' as a shortest-path computation over a suitably constructed graph, which comes even closer in space to interpolative code and still achieves very fast decompression.

References

[1] Nieves R. Brisaboa, Antonio Farina, Gonzalo Navarro, and José R. Paramá. Lightweight natural language text compression. *Information Retrieval*, 10: 1–33, 2007.

[2] Peter Fenwick. Universal codes. In Khalid Sayood, editor, *Lossless Compression Handbook*. Academic Press, 55–64, 2002.

[3] Christopher D. Manning, Prabhakar Raghavan, and Hinrich Schütze. *Introduction to Information Retrieval*. Cambridge University Press, 2008.

[4] Alistair Moffat. Compressing integer sequences and sets. In Ming–Yang Kao, editor, *Encyclopedia of Algorithms*. Springer, 178–83, 2009.

[5] Gonzalo Navarro. *Compact Data Structures: A Practical Approach*. Cambridge University Press, New York, 2016.

[6] Giuseppe Ottaviano and Rossano Venturini. Partitioned Elias–Fano indexes. In *Proceedings of the 37th International ACM SIGIR Conference on Research and Development in Information Retrieval*, 273–82, 2014.

[7] Giulio Ermanno Pibiri and Rossano Venturini. Techniques for inverted index compression. *ACM Computing Surveys*, 53(6): 125:1–125:36, 2021.

[8] Hao Yan, Shuai Ding, and Torsten Suel. Inverted index compression and query processing with optimized document ordering. In *Proceedings of the 18th International Conference on World Wide Web (WWW)*, 401–10, 2009.

[9] Ian H. Witten, Alistair Moffat, and Timothy C. Bell. *Managing Gigabytes*. Morgan Kauffman, second edition, 1999.

12 Statistical Coding

Information is the resolution of
uncertainty.
Attributed to Claude Shannon

The topic of this chapter is the *statistical coding* of a sequence S of symbols (aka *texts*) drawn from an alphabet Σ. Symbols may be characters, in which case the problem is named *text compression*, or they can be DNA bases, where the challenge is the one of genomic-database compression, or they can be bits, and in this case we fall in the realm of classic data compression. If symbols are integers, then we have the integer-coding problem addressed in the previous chapter, which can still be solved with a statistical coder just by deriving statistical information on the integers occurring in the sequence S. In this latter case, the code we derive is an *optimal* prefix-free code for the integers of S which, anyway, is slower in both compression and decompression phases when compared against the solutions of the previous chapter.

Conceptually, statistical compression may be viewed as consisting of two phases: a *modeling* phase, followed by a *coding* phase. In the modeling phase, the statistical properties of the input sequence are computed and a *model* is built. In the coding phase, the model is used to derive codewords for the symbols of Σ, and they are then used to compress the input sequence. In the first sections of this chapter we will concentrate only on the coding phase, surveying the best-known statistical compressors: Huffman coding, arithmetic coding, and range coding; whereas in the final Section 12.3, we will introduce a sophisticated modeling technique which will be used to introduce the *prediction by partial matching* (PPM) coder, thus providing a pretty complete picture of what can be done by statistical compressors. As a net result, we will move from a compression performance that can be bounded in terms of 0-th order entropy, namely an entropy function depending on the probability of single symbols (which are therefore considered to occur independently distributed), to the more compact k-th order entropy which depends on the probability of k-sized blocks of symbols and thus models, for example, the case of Markovian sources.

12.1 Huffman Coding

First published in the early 1950s, Huffman coding was regarded as one of the best methods for data compression for several decades, until the arithmetic coding made higher compression rates possible at the end of the 1960s.

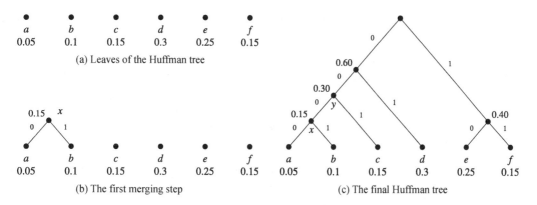

Figure 12.1 Constructing the Huffman tree for the alphabet $\Sigma = \{a, b, c, d, e, f\}$. Probabilities are indicated below every symbol. Tree edges are annotated with the bits 0 (left edge) and 1 (right edge). The final Huffman tree consists of six leaves and five internal nodes.

Huffman coding is based upon a *greedy algorithmic scheme* that constructs a binary tree whose leaves are the symbols σ in Σ, each provided with a probability $\mathcal{P}[\sigma]$ of occurrence in the input sequence to be compressed. These leaves constitute a *candidate set*, which will be kept updated during the construction of the Huffman tree. In a generic step, the Huffman algorithm selects the two nodes with the smallest probabilities from the candidate set, and creates their parent node, whose probability is set equal to the sum of the probabilities of its two children. That parent node is inserted in the candidate set, while its two children are removed from it. Since each step adds one node and removes two nodes from the candidate set, the process stops after $|\Sigma| - 1$ steps, when the candidate set contains only the root of the tree. At the end of this greedy process, the Huffman tree will consist of $t = |\Sigma| + (|\Sigma| - 1) = 2|\Sigma| - 1$ nodes, of which $|\Sigma|$ are leaves and $(|\Sigma| - 1)$ are internal nodes.

Figure 12.1 shows an example of a Huffman tree for the alphabet $\Sigma = \{a, b, c, d, e, f\}$. The first merge (on the left) attaches the symbols a and b as children of the node x, whose probability is set to $0.05 + 0.1 = 0.15$. This node is added to the candidate set, whereas leaves a and b are removed from it. In the second step (see Figure 12.1.b), the two nodes with the smallest probabilities are the leaf c and the (just inserted) node x. Their merging updates the candidate set by deleting x and c, and by adding their parent node y, whose probability is set to be $0.15 + 0.15 = 0.3$. The algorithm continues until there is only one node (the root) left, with probability, of course, equal to 1.

In order to derive the Huffman code for the symbols in Σ, we assign binary labels to the tree edges. The typical labeling consists of assigning 0 to the left edge and 1 to the right edge of each internal node. But this is one of many possible choices. In fact, a Huffman tree can generate $2^{|\Sigma|-1}$ labeled trees, because we have two labeling choices (i.e. 0–1 or 1–0) for the two edges leaving each of the $|\Sigma| - 1$ internal nodes. Given a labeled Huffman tree, the Huffman codeword for a symbol σ is derived by

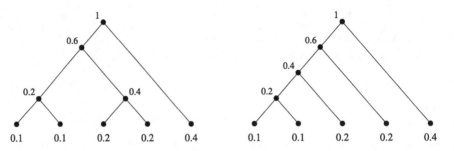

Figure 12.2 An example of two Huffman codes that have the same average codeword length 2.2 bits, but different maximum codeword length, that is, 3 versus 4.

taking the binary labels encountered on the downward path that connects the root to the leaf associated with σ. The length of this codeword equals the depth of the leaf σ in the Huffman tree, and we denote it $L(\sigma)$. The Huffman code is *prefix-free* because every symbol is associated with a distinct leaf, and thus no codeword is the prefix of another codeword.

We observe that the choice of the two nodes with the minimum probability may not be unique, and the actual available choices may induce different codewords all having the same *optimal average* length but, possibly, *different maximum* length. Minimizing this value is useful to reduce the size of the compression/decompression buffer. Figure 12.2 provides an illustrative example of these multiple choices.

A strategy to minimize the maximum codeword length is to choose the two *oldest nodes* among the ones with the same probability in the current candidate set. *Oldest nodes* means that they are either leaves or internal nodes that have been created farther in the past than the other nodes in the candidate set. This strategy can be implemented by using two queues: the first contains the leaves ordered by increasing probability while the second contains the internal nodes in the order they are created by the Huffman algorithm. It is not difficult to observe that the second queue is also sorted by increasing probability. In the presence of more than two minimum-probability nodes, the algorithm looks at the nodes in the first queue, and then looks at the second queue. Figure 12.2 shows on the left the tree resulting from this algorithm and, on the right, the tree obtained by using an approach that makes an arbitrary choice.

The compressed file generated by the Huffman algorithm consists of two parts: the *preamble*, which contains an encoding of the Huffman tree together with the symbol's probabilities, and thus has size $\Theta(|\Sigma|)$, and the *body*, which contains the codewords of the symbols in the input sequence S. The size of the preamble is usually neglected in the evaluation of the length of the compressed file, because it is assumed that $|\Sigma| \ll |S|$. However, it must be noted that there are situations in practice in which the alphabet size is significant and thus the preamble size must be taken into account. In the rest of the section, we will concentrate on the evaluation of the size in bits for the compressed body, and then turn to the efficient encoding of the Huffman tree by proposing the elegant *canonical Huffman,* which offers space succinctness and very fast decoding speed.

Let $L_C = \sum_{\sigma \in \Sigma} L(\sigma) \times \mathcal{P}[\sigma]$ be the average length of the codewords produced by a prefix-free code C, which encodes every alphabet symbol σ in $L(\sigma)$ bits. The following theorem states the *optimality* of Huffman coding:

Theorem 12.1 *If C is a Huffman code, then L_C is the shortest possible average length among all prefix-free codes C', that is, $L_C \leq L_{C'}$.*

To prove this result we first observe that a prefix-free code can be seen as a binary tree (more precisely, we should say binary trie, according to the terminology of Chapter 9), so the optimality of the Huffman code can be rephrased as the *minimality of the average depth* of the corresponding binary tree. This latter property can be proved by deploying the following key lemma, whose proof is left to the reader.

Lemma 12.1 *Let $\mathcal{F}$ be a set of (weighted) binary trees with probabilities associated to their leaves, and minimal average depth among all binary trees with $|\Sigma|$ leaves. There then exists a tree T in $\mathcal{F}$ in which two leaves with minimum probabilities are at the greatest depth, and are children of the same parent node.*

All trees in $\mathcal{F}$ will have two leaves with minimum probabilities at the greatest depth, although they can be attached to different parents. In fact, the deeper the leaf is, the more it weights the average depth of the tree. Hence, it is better to "push" down the leaves of smallest probability to get a minimum average depth. In particular, if a leaf of smallest probability is not at the deepest depth, we can swap it with a leaf at deepest depth and not of smallest probability, and get a tree of smaller average depth. So at least two leaves of smallest probability must be at the deepest depth, but this is not necessarily true for all of them: take the case of four symbols $\{a, b, c, d\}$ with probabilities $[.1, .1, .1, .7]$. The Huffman tree could merge (a, b), and then the resulting node with c, thus making them of different depth. Moreover, as anticipated, the two leaves of smallest probability may not be children of the same parent: take, for example, the case of five symbols $\{a, b, c, d, e\}$ with probabilities $[.1, .1, .11, .11, .58]$, respectively. The Huffman tree would merge (a, b) and then (c, d), and finally make both of them children of the same parent, which is a sibling of the leaf e. Another tree with minimum average depth could be built by merging (a, c) and then (b, d), and finally make both of them children of the same parent, which is again a sibling of the leaf e. But in this latter tree, the two leaves with minimum probabilities will not be children of the same parent node, despite being at the greatest depth. In any case, at least one tree in $\mathcal{F}$ will satisfy both properties as stated in Lemma 12.1.

Before digging into the proof of Theorem 12.1, let us introduce another technical lemma. Assume that the alphabet Σ consists of n symbols, and that symbols x and y have the smallest probability. Let T_C be the binary tree generated by a code C built on this alphabet, and let us denote by R_C the *reduced* tree which is obtained by dropping the leaves for x and y. Thus the parent, say z, of leaves x and y is a leaf of R_C with probability $\mathcal{P}[z] = \mathcal{P}[x] + \mathcal{P}[y]$. So the tree R_C is a binary (weighted) tree with

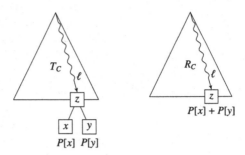

Figure 12.3 Relationship between a binary (weighted) tree T and its corresponding reduced (weighted) tree R, as stated in Lemma 12.2.

$n - 1$ leaves corresponding to the alphabet $\Sigma - \{x, y\} \cup \{z\}$. Figure 12.3 exemplifies the binary trees T_C and R_C, and the following lemma states the relation between their average depths.

Lemma 12.2 *The relation between the average depth of the binary (weighted) tree T with the one of its reduced binary (weighted) tree R is given by the formula $L_T = L_R + (\mathcal{P}[x] + \mathcal{P}[y])$, where x and y are two leaves with the smallest probability.*

Proof It is enough to write down the equalities for L_T and L_R, by summing the lengths of all root-to-leaf paths multiplied by the probability of the landing leaf. So we have $L_T = \left(\sum_{\sigma \neq x,y} \mathcal{P}[\sigma] \times L(\sigma) \right) + (\mathcal{P}[x] + \mathcal{P}[y]) \times (L(z) + 1)$, where z is the parent of x and y, and thus $L(x) = L(y) = L(z) + 1$. Similarly, we can write $L_R = \left(\sum_{\sigma \neq x,y} \mathcal{P}[\sigma] \times L(\sigma) \right) + L(z) \times (\mathcal{P}[x] + \mathcal{P}[y])$. So the thesis follows. ∎

The optimality of the Huffman code (claimed in Theorem 12.1) can now be proved by induction on the number n of alphabet symbols. The base case $n = 2$ is obvious, because any prefix-free code must assign at least one bit to each of Σ's symbols; therefore Huffman is optimal because it assigns the single bit 0 to one symbol and the single bit 1 to the other symbol of Σ.

Let us now assume that $n > 2$ and, by induction, assume that the Huffman code is optimal for an alphabet of $n - 1$ symbols. Take now $|\Sigma| = n$, and let C be an optimal code for Σ and its underlying distribution. Our goal will be to show that $L_C = L_H$, so that Huffman is also optimal for n symbols. Clearly, $L_C \leq L_H$ because C is assumed to be an optimal code for Σ. Now we consider the two reduced trees, say R_C and R_H, which can be derived from T_C and T_H, respectively, by dropping the leaves x and y with the smallest probability and leaving their parent z. By Lemma 12.1 (for the optimal C) and the structure of Huffman's algorithm, this reduction is possible for both trees T_C and T_H. The two reduced trees define a prefix-free code for an alphabet of $n - 1$ symbols; so, given the inductive hypothesis, the code defined by R_H is optimal for the "reduced" alphabet $\Sigma \cup \{z\} - \{x, y\}$. Therefore $L_{R_H} \leq L_{R_C}$ over this "reduced" alphabet. By Lemma 12.2, we can write that the average depth of T_H is $L_H = L_{R_H} + \mathcal{P}[x] + \mathcal{P}[y]$,

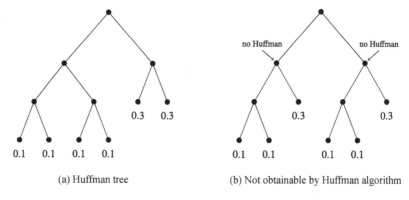

(a) Huffman tree
(b) Not obtainable by Huffman algorithm

Figure 12.4 Example of an optimal code not obtainable by means of the Huffman algorithm.

and that the average depth of T_C is $L_C = L_{RC} + P[x] + P[y]$. So it turns out that $L_H \leq L_C$ which, combined with the previous (opposite) inequality due to the optimality of C, gives $L_H = L_C$. This actually means that Huffman is also an optimal code for an alphabet of n symbols, and thus inductively proves that it is an optimal code for any alphabet size.

This statement does not mean that $C = H$, and indeed, there are optimal prefix-free codes that cannot be obtained via the Huffman algorithm (see Figure 12.4 for an example). Rather, the previous statement indicates that the average codeword lengths of C and H are equal. The next fundamental theorem provides a quantitative upper bound to this average length.

Theorem 12.2 *Let $\mathcal{H}$ be the entropy of the source emitting the symbols of an alphabet Σ, hence $\mathcal{H} = \sum_{\sigma \in \Sigma} P[\sigma] \log_2 \frac{1}{P[\sigma]}$. The average codeword length of the Huffman code satisfies the inequalities $\mathcal{H} \leq L_H < \mathcal{H} + 1$.*

Proof The first inequality comes from Shannon's noiseless coding theorem, whose sophisticated proof can be found in its beautiful original paper [6], or in any other classic text on information theory. To prove the second inequality, we define $\ell_\sigma = \lceil \log_2 (1/P(\sigma)) \rceil$, which is actually the smallest integer upper-bounding Shannon's optimal codeword length given by the entropy term for the symbol σ. By simple arithmetic manipulations, it is easy to derive that $\sum_{\sigma \in \Sigma} 2^{-\ell_\sigma} \leq 1$. So by Kraft's inequality, there exists a binary tree with $|\Sigma|$ leaves whose root-to-leaf paths have lengths ℓ_σ, for every symbol σ. This binary tree provides a code C for Σ's symbols, whose average codeword length is $L_C = \sum_{\sigma \in \Sigma} P(\sigma) \times \ell_\sigma$. Now, by the optimality of Huffman's code (Theorem 12.1), we know that $L_H \leq L_C$, and this proves the thesis because of the definition of the entropy $\mathcal{H}$ and the inequality $\ell_\sigma < 1 + \log_2 (1/P(\sigma))$. ∎

This theorem states that the Huffman code can lose up to one bit per compressed symbol with respect to the entropy $\mathcal{H}$ of the underlying source. This extra bit may make quite a difference or, instead, may be neglected altogether depending on the value of $\mathcal{H}$. Clearly, $\mathcal{H} \geq 0$, because $\mathcal{P}(\sigma) \in [0, 1]$ and thus $\log_2 \frac{1}{\mathcal{P}[\sigma]} \geq 0$. The entropy is equal to zero whenever the source emits just one symbol with probability 1 and all the other symbols with probability 0. Moreover, the entropy is a concave function and its maximum is achieved when all symbols are equiprobable, thus getting the value $\mathcal{H} = \log_2 |\Sigma|$. As a result, $\mathcal{H}$ may get arbitrarily large for a large alphabet of almost equally distributed symbols. In this case (i.e. $\mathcal{H} \gg 1$), the Huffman code is effective and the extra bit is negligible. Otherwise (i.e. $\mathcal{H} \approx 0$), the distribution is *skewed* toward one or a few alphabet symbols, and the (possibly) wasted extra bit makes the Huffman code inefficient because, as for any prefix-free code, Huffman's algorithm cannot use less than one bit per symbol. So the best compression ratio that Huffman can obtain is to encode every symbol with one bit, starting from its full representation of $\log_2 |\Sigma|$ bits. This ideal encoding would achieve a *compression ratio* of $1 / \log_2 |\Sigma|$. If Σ is ASCII, hence $|\Sigma| = 256$, Huffman cannot achieve a compression ratio for any sequence S which is less than $1/8 = 12.57$ percent.

In order to overcome this limitation, Shannon proposed in his famous article of 1948 [6] a simple *blocking scheme* which considers an extended alphabet whose symbols are substrings of k symbols each. The new alphabet has size $|\Sigma|^k$ and thus, if we use Huffman's code on this alphabet, we waste one extra bit per block rather than per symbol. This means that this blocked approach loses a fractional part of a bit per symbol, namely $1/k$, and this is indeed negligible for larger values of k. So how come we do not always select very large values of k? Well, a large k does often improve the compression ratio thanks to the blocking scheme, which captures the interdependency among adjacent symbols. Nevertheless, k cannot be greater than the text length, of course; and, more importantly, a larger k induces a larger Huffman tree, since the number of leaves/symbols in the tree grows as $|\Sigma|^k$, which has to be stored in the preamble of the compressed file. That is why a "smart" compressor should always carefully select the right value for k, which may possibly vary along the text to be compressed. This strategy, albeit viable, is still suboptimal in any case, as we will prove in the following sections.

A final comment regarding the case of very long codewords. If the codeword length exceeds 32 bits the operations can become costly because it is no longer possible to store codewords as a single machine word. Thus it is natural to ask when this pathological case occurs. Given that the optimal code should assign a codeword of length $\lceil \log_2 (1/\mathcal{P}(\sigma)) \rceil$ bits to symbol σ, one could conclude that $\mathcal{P}[\sigma]$ should be around 2^{-33} in order to have $L(\sigma) > 32$, and hence conclude that this bad situation occurs only after about 2^{33} symbols have been processed. Unfortunately, this first approximation is an excessive upper bound. It is enough to consider a Huffman tree skewed to the left, whose leaf i has frequency $F(i) < F(i + 1)$. Moreover, we assume that $\sum_{j=1}^{i} F(j) < F(i + 2)$ in order to induce the Huffman algorithm to join $F(i + 1)$ with the last created internal node rather than with leaf $i + 2$ (or all the other leaves

$i + 3, i + 4, \ldots$). It is not difficult to observe that $F(i)$ may be taken to be the Fibonacci sequence, possibly with different initial conditions, such as $F(1) = F(2) = F(3) = 1$. Here, $F(33) = 3.01 \times 10^6$ and $\sum_{i=1}^{33} F(i) = 1.28 \times 10^7$. The cumulative sum indicates how much text has to be read in order to force a codeword of length 33 bits. Thus, the pathological case can occur after just 10 million symbols, which is considerably less than the preceding estimation! Now, if the pathological case cannot be avoided, then there are methods to reduce the codeword lengths whilst still guaranteeing a good compression performance [8]. One effective approach is the *iterative scaling* of symbol probabilities. It constructs the classic Huffman code over the symbols, whose probabilities are approximated via the number of symbol occurrences in the input text; then, if the longest codeword is larger than the maximum allowed number of bits, say L bits, all the symbol counts are reduced by some constant ratio (e.g. 2 or the golden ratio 1.618) and a new Huffman code is constructed over the newly derived probability distribution for the alphabet symbols. This process is continued until a code of maximum codeword length L or less is generated. In the limit, all symbols will have their counts equal to 1, thus leading to a fixed-length code.

12.1.1 Canonical Huffman Coding

Let us recall the two main limitations incurred by the Huffman code:

- It has to store the structure of the tree, and this can be costly if the alphabet Σ is large, as occurs when coding blocks of symbols, possibly words.
- Decoding is slow because it has to traverse the whole tree for each codeword, and every edge of the path (bit of the codeword) may elicit one cache miss. Thus the total number of cache misses could be equal to the total number of bits constituting the compressed file.

There is an elegant variant of the Huffman code, denoted *canonical Huffman* code, that alleviates these problems by introducing a special restructuring of the Huffman tree that allows extremely fast decoding and a small memory footprint. The idea is to transform the classic Huffman tree into another Huffman tree, equivalent to the previous one in terms of codeword lengths assigned to alphabet symbols, but structured in a way that path lengths do not increase as we move from the leftmost to the rightmost leaf. This "restructuring" is obtained in a surprising way, without manipulating tree pointers but via five steps which involve only arrays and basic arithmetic operations, as detailed here:

1. Compute the codeword length $L(\sigma)$ for each symbol $\sigma \in \Sigma$ according to the classical Huffman's algorithm. Say max is the maximum codeword length (in bits).
2. Construct the array symb[1, max] which stores in the entry symb[ℓ] the list of symbols having Huffman codeword of ℓ bits.
3. Construct the array num[1, max] which stores in the entry num[ℓ] the number of symbols having Huffman codeword of ℓ bits.

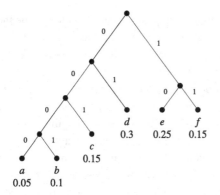

symb	code	ℓ
a	0000	4
b	0001	4
c	001	3
d	01	2
e	10	2
f	11	2

ℓ	symb 0	1	2	num	fc
1				0	2
2	d	e	f	3	1
3	c			1	1
4	a	b		2	0

Figure 12.5 Example of canonical Huffman coding. Note that the Huffman tree is shaped in a way that path lengths do not increase as we move from the leftmost to the rightmost leaf. The table in the top-right corner shows the result of the computation of a classic Huffman algorithm applied to six symbols $\{a, b, c, d, e, f\}$, whose probabilities are specified below the corresponding leaves. The table on the bottom-right corner specifies all arrays computed by the canonical Huffman code, and the binary tree on the left is its graphical representation.

4. Derive from the array num (then discarded), the array fc[1, max], which stores in the entry fc[ℓ] the first codeword of all symbols encoded with ℓ bits. This assignment is tricky; it does not use the Huffman tree structure, but involves arithmetic operations which will be detailed below.
5. Implicitly assign consecutive codewords to the symbols in symb[ℓ], starting from the codeword fc[ℓ] and having length ℓ bits. "Implicitly" here means that they are not stored in memory but they are created on the fly as needed by the encoding/decoding process, as detailed in Algorithm 12.1.

At the end, the canonical Huffman code needs only to store the arrays fc and symb, for a total space complexity that is at most max^2 bits to store fc, and at most $(|\Sigma| + \text{max}) \log_2 (|\Sigma| + 1)$ bits to encode table symb (note that $\text{max} < |\Sigma|$). Consequently, the first key advantage of canonical Huffman is that we do not need to store explicitly the tree structure via pointers, with a saving of $\Theta(|\Sigma| \log_2 |\Sigma|)$ bits. Moreover, in the preamble of the compressed file, we can store just the codeword lengths of the $|\Sigma|$ symbols, for a total of $|\Sigma| \log_2 |\Sigma|$ bits (while the storage of the symbols' frequency would take $|\Sigma| \log_2 n$ bits); this information is enough to rebuild the canonical Huffman code. Figure 12.5 provides a graphical example of a Huffman tree that satisfies the canonical property.

The other important advantage of canonical Huffman resides in its decoding procedure, which does not need to percolate the Huffman tree, but only operates on the two available arrays, thus inducing at most two cache misses per decoded symbol.[1] The pseudocode of the decoding procedure is summarized in the few lines of pseudocode

---

[1] It is reasonable to assume that the number of cache misses is just 1 because the array fc is small and can be fit in cache.

Algorithm 12.1 Decoding one symbol by canonical Huffman

1: $v = \text{next\_bit}()$;

2: $\ell = 1$;

3: **while** $v < \text{fc}[\ell]$ **do**

4: $\quad v = 2v + \text{next\_bit}()$;

5: $\quad \ell{+}{+}$;

6: **end while**

7: **return** $\text{symb}[\ell, v - \text{fc}[\ell]]$;

---

in Algorithm 12.1, where the correctness of the computation of fc-array in Step 4 (proved next) is assumed.

The correctness of the decoding procedure can be inferred from the structure of the canonical Huffman tree. In fact, the while-guard $v < \text{fc}[\ell]$ checks whether the current codeword v, of ℓ bits, is to the left of the first codeword of that level, namely $\text{fc}[\ell]$. If this is the case, because of the left-skewness of the canonical Huffman tree, the codeword v is to the left of *all* symbols encoded with ℓ bits. Therefore, the codeword to be decoded is longer and thus a new bit is fetched by the while-body. On the other hand, if $v \geq \text{fc}[\ell]$, then the current codeword is larger in value than the first codeword represented with ℓ bits, hence v corresponds to a leaf of the canonical Huffman tree at that level ℓ, and this leaf is the one with offset $v - \text{fc}[\ell]$.

In order to better understand these two cases, let us analyze the decoding of the compressed sequence 01, as shown in Figure 12.6. The function next_bit() reads the first incoming bit to be decoded, namely 0. Initially, we have $\ell = 1$, $v = 0$, and $\text{fc}[1] = 2$; so we are in the first case (i.e. $v = 0 < 2 = \text{fc}[1]$), and therefore the algorithm knows that the codeword to be decoded is longer. So ℓ is incremented to the value 2 (next level of the canonical Huffman tree) and v gets the next bit 1, thus $v = 01 = 1$. Now, we are in the second case, for which above because the *while* condition is no longer satisfied: $v = 1 \geq \text{fc}[2] = 1$. Thus the algorithm has detected a codeword of length $\ell = 2$ and, since $v - \text{fc}[2] = 0$, it returns the first symbol of the list pointed to by symb[2], namely $\text{symb}[2, 0] = d$.

A subtle comment is in order at this point: the value $\text{fc}[1] = 2$ seems impossible, because we cannot represent the value 2 with a codeword consisting of one single bit. This is a *special value* which forces the algorithm to always skip to the next level: in fact, fc[1] is larger than any codeword of one bit.

We are finally ready to get down to describing the construction of a canonical Huffman tree, when the underlying symbol distribution does not induce one with such a property. Figure 12.5 shows a Huffman tree that is canonical by construction, thanks to the input symbol distribution. But this is not necessarily the case: take, for example, the Huffman tree shown in Figure 12.7. This is a non canonical tree but, nonetheless, it can be turned into a canonical one by means of the six lines of pseudocode shown in Algorithm 12.2, and for which we detail here the computation of the fc-array, recalling that *max* is the largest codeword length (in the running example, $max = 4$).

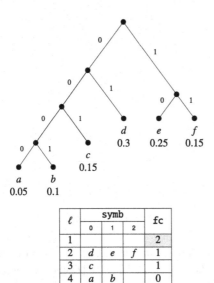

symb	code	ℓ
a	0000	4
b	0001	4
c	001	3
d	01	2
e	10	2
f	11	2

ℓ	symb			fc
	0	1	2	
1				2
2	d	e	f	1
3	c			1
4	a	b		0

ℓ	symb			fc
	0	1	2	
1				2
2	d	e	f	1
3	c			1
4	a	b		0

Figure 12.6 The figure reports on top the Canonical Huffman tree from Figure 12.5, and all codewords for the alphabet symbols. The codeword corresponding to the input bits 01 is highlighted. The first table on the bottom left refers to the entry of the fc-array checked at the first iteration of the while-loop of the decoding process, when fetching the bit 0 from input. The second table on the bottom right refers to the entry of the fc-array checked at the second iteration of the while-loop, when fetching the bit 1 from input. We further comment on this in the text.

Algorithm 12.2 Computing the fc-array of a canonical Huffman code

---

1: fc[*max*] = 0;
2: *i* = *max* − 1;
3: **while** *i* >= 1 **do**
4:      fc[*i*] = (fc[*i* + 1] + num[*i* + 1])/2;
5:      *i* = *i* − 1;
6: **end while**

There are two key remarks to be made before digging into the proof of correctness of Algorithm 12.2. First and foremost, fc[ℓ] is the value of a codeword consisting of ℓ bits, so the reader should keep in mind that, if the binary representation of the value stored in fc[ℓ] is shorter than ℓ bits, then it must be padded with zeros. Second, since the algorithm sets fc[*max*] = 0, the longest codeword is a sequence of max zeros, and so the tree built by the canonical Huffman is totally skewed to the left. Now, let us analyze the formula that computes fc[ℓ], according to this pseudocode, and prove its correctness. By induction, at the level $\ell + 1$, the first codeword is fc[$\ell + 1$] and that level consists of num[$\ell + 1$] leaves. So all codewords from fc[$\ell + 1$] to fc[$\ell + 1$] + num[$\ell + 1$] − 1 can be reserved to all symbols stored in symb[$\ell + 1$]. The first *unused* codeword of $\ell + 1$ bits is therefore given by the value fc[$\ell + 1$] + num[$\ell+1$]. The formula in the pseudocode divides this value by 2, which corresponds

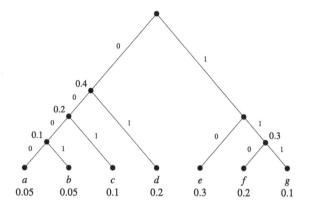

symb	code	ℓ
a	0000	4
b	0001	4
c	001	3
d	01	2
e	10	2
f	110	3
g	111	3

ℓ	symb 0	symb 1	symb 2	num	fc
1				0	2
2	d	e		2	2
3	c	f	g	3	1
4	a	b		2	0

Figure 12.7 From a Huffman tree to the corresponding canonical Huffman tree.

to dropping the most significant bit from the binary encoding of that number. In terms of a binary tree, this is equivalent to taking the parent of the node spelling out the bit string $fc[\ell + 1] + \text{num}[\ell + 1]$, which is at depth ℓ and does not prefix any codeword of length $\ell + 1$. So this bit sequence can be taken as the first codeword $fc[\ell]$. This algorithm computes $fc[1] = 2$ for the example in Figure 12.7, thus obtaining the special case already commented on.

12.2   Arithmetic Coding

The principal strength of arithmetic coding, introduced by Elias in the 1960s, is that it can code symbols arbitrarily close to the 0-th order entropy, by possibly using a fraction of bits per symbol, thus achieving much better compression than Huffman on skewed distributions. So in Shannon's sense it is optimal.

For the sake of clarity, let us consider the following example. Take an input alphabet $\Sigma = \{a, b\}$ with a skewed distribution: $P[a] = \frac{99}{100}$ and $P[b] = \frac{1}{100}$. According to Shannon, the entropy of this source is $\mathcal{H} = \mathcal{P}(a) \log_2 (1/\mathcal{P}(a)) + \mathcal{P}(b) \log_2 (1/\mathcal{P}(b)) \simeq 0.08056$ bits. In contrast, a Huffman coder, like any prefix coder, applied on every symbol of an input text generated by this source must use at least *one bit per symbol*, which is at least 10 times more than the entropy of the source. Consequently, the Huffman code is far in terms of compression ratio from the 0-th order entropy, and clearly, the more skewed the symbol distribution is, the farther Huffman's code is from optimality. As we have already commented, the Huffman code cannot achieve a compression ratio better than $1/\log_2 |\Sigma|$, the best case occurring when we substitute one symbol (encoded plainly with $\log_2 |\Sigma|$ bits) with just one bit. This is $1/8 = 12.5$ percent, in the case where the symbols are the 256 characters of the ASCII code.

To overcome this problem, arithmetic coding relaxes the request to define a prefix-free codeword for each individual symbol by adopting a different strategy in which every bit of the compressed output can represent *more than one* input symbol. This

---

Algorithm 12.3 Converter (x, k)

Require: A real number $x \in [0, 1)$, a positive integer k.
Ensure: The string representing x in k bits.

  1: **repeat**
  2:       $x = 2 \times x$
  3:       **if** $x < 1$ **then**
  4:            $output = output :: 0$
  5:       **else**
  6:            $output = output :: 1$
  7:            $x = x - 1$
  8:       **end if**
  9: **until** k bits are emitted

---

results in a better compression, at the cost of slowing down the algorithm and of losing the capability to access/decode the compressed output from any position. Another interesting feature of arithmetic coding is that it works easily for the case of a *dynamic* model for the probability distribution, namely one in which probabilities $\mathcal{P}(\sigma)$ are updated as the input sequence S is processed. It is enough to set $\mathcal{P}(\sigma) = (\ell_\sigma + 1)/(\ell + |\Sigma|)$, where ℓ is the length of the prefix of S processed so far, and ℓ_σ is the number of occurrences of symbol σ in that prefix. The reader can check that this is a sound probability distribution, initially set to the uniform one, as in fact $\ell = 0$ and $\ell_\sigma = 0$ for all symbols $\sigma \in \Sigma$. These dynamic probabilities can also be kept updated easily enough by the decompression algorithm, so that both compressor and decompressor look at the same input distribution and thus encode/decode the same symbols.

12.2.1   Bit Streams and Dyadic Fractions

A (possibly infinite) bit stream $b_1 b_2 b_3 \ldots b_k$ can be interpreted as a real number in the range $[0, 1)$ by prepending "0." to it:

$$0.b_1 b_2 b_3 \ldots b_k = \sum_{i=1}^{k} b_i \times 2^{-i}.$$

Vice versa, a real number x in the range $[0, 1)$ can be converted into a (possibly infinite) sequence of bits with the algorithm CONVERTER, whose pseudocode is given in Algorithm 12.3. This algorithm consists of a loop where the variable *output* is the output bitstream and where :: expresses concatenation among bits. The loop has to end when a level of accuracy in the representation of x is reached: we can stop when we have emitted a certain number of bits in output, or when we establish that the representation of x is periodic, or the value to encode is zero.

    In order to clarify how CONVERTER works, we apply the pseudocode at the number $x = \frac{1}{3}$ and not fix any upper bound for k:

$$\frac{1}{3} \times 2 = \frac{2}{3} < 1 \rightarrow output = 0$$

$$\frac{2}{3} \times 2 = \frac{4}{3} \geq 1 \rightarrow output = 1$$

In this second iteration x is greater than 1, so CONVERTER emits the bit 1 and updates the value of x by executing Step 7 in the pseudocode: $\frac{4}{3} - 1 = \frac{1}{3}$. Since we have already encountered this value of x, we infer that the output is the periodic representation $\overline{01}$.

Let us consider another example, say execute CONVERTER$(3/32, 5)$:

$$\frac{3}{32} \times 2 = \frac{6}{32} < 1 \rightarrow output = 0$$

$$\frac{6}{32} \times 2 = \frac{12}{32} < 1 \rightarrow output = 0$$

$$\frac{12}{32} \times 2 = \frac{24}{32} < 1 \rightarrow output = 0$$

$$\frac{24}{32} \times 2 = \frac{48}{32} \geq 1 \rightarrow output = 1$$

$$\left(\frac{48}{32} - 1\right) \times 2 = 1 \geq 1 \rightarrow output = 1$$

$$(1 - 1) \times 2 = 0 \rightarrow exit$$

So the final output of CONVERTER is 00011. The same output, in this case, could be obtained by observing that the number to be encoded is represented by a *dyadic fraction*, namely a fraction of the form $\frac{v}{2^k}$, where v and k are positive integers. A dyadic fraction can be encoded exactly and directly, without executing CONVERTER, by emitting the bit sequence $.bin_k(v)$, where $bin_k(v)$ is the binary representation of the integer v as a string of k bits, eventually padded with zeroes. In the previous example, $k = 5$ and $v = 3$, so $bin_5(3) = $ 00011, as computed by CONVERTER.

12.2.2 Compression Algorithm

Compression by arithmetic coding is iterative: each step takes as input a subinterval of $[0, 1)$, representing the prefix of the input sequence compressed so far, the *probabilities* of the alphabet symbols, and their *cumulative probabilities*, and consumes the next input symbol.[2] The input subinterval is further subdivided into smaller subintervals, one for each symbol σ of Σ, whose lengths are proportional to their probabilities $\mathcal{P}(\sigma)$. The step produces as output a new subinterval that is the one associated with the consumed input symbol, and is contained in the previous one. The number of steps is equal to the number of symbols to be encoded, and thus to the length of the input sequence.

In more detail, the algorithm starts by considering the interval $[0, 1)$ and, having consumed the entire input, produces the interval $[l, l + s)$ associated with the last

---

[2] We recall that the cumulative probability of a symbol $\sigma \in \Sigma$ is computed as $\sum_{c < \sigma} \mathcal{P}(c)$, and it is provided by the statistical model constructed during the modeling phase of the compression process. In the case of a dynamic model, the probabilities and the cumulative probabilities change as the input sequence is scanned.

Algorithm 12.4 AC-Coding $(S, \mathcal{P})$

Require: The input sequence $S[1, n]$ and the probabilities $\mathcal{P}(\sigma)$.
Ensure: A subinterval $[l, l + s)$ of $[0, 1)$.

1: Compute the cumulative probabilities $f(\sigma) = \sum_{c<\sigma} \mathcal{P}(c)$, for each alphabet symbol $\sigma \in \Sigma$;
2: $s_0 = 1, l_0 = 0, i = 1$;
3: **while** $i \leq n$ **do**
4:      $s_i = s_{i-1} \times \mathcal{P}[S[i]]$;
5:      $l_i = l_{i-1} + s_{i-1} \times f(S[i])$;
6:      $i = i + 1$;
7: **end while**
8: **return** $\langle x \in [l_n, l_n + s_n), n\rangle$;

---

symbol of the input sequence. The tricky issue here is that the output is not the pair $\langle l, s \rangle$ (hence two real numbers,) but is just one real $x \in [l, l + s)$, chosen to be a dyadic fraction, plus the length of the input sequence.

In the next section we will see how to choose this value in order to minimize the number of output bits; here we will concentrate on the overall compression stage whose pseudocode is provided in Algorithm 12.4: the variables l_i and s_i are, respectively, the left extreme and the length of the interval encoding the i-long prefix of the input sequence. In the case that arithmetic coding uses a semi-static model to estimate the probabilities of the alphabet symbols, the input to Algorithm 12.4 can consist just of the input sequence S, because the probabilities $\mathcal{P}(\sigma)$ are estimated as the frequency of σ in S via a scan taking $O(n)$ time.

As an example, consider the input sequence $S = abac$ and assume the semi-static modeling to estimate the probabilities $\mathcal{P}(a) = \frac{1}{2}, \mathcal{P}(b) = \mathcal{P}(c) = \frac{1}{4}$. The resulting cumulative probabilities are $f(a) = 0, f(b) = \mathcal{P}(a) = \frac{1}{2}$, and $f(c) = \mathcal{P}(a) + \mathcal{P}(b) = \frac{3}{4}$. Following the pseudocode of AC-Coding (S), we have $n = 4$ and thus we repeat the internal while-loop four times. In the first iteration (i.e. $i = 1$), we consider the first symbol $S[1] = a$ of the sequence, and compute the new interval $[l_1, l_1 + s_1)$ given $\mathcal{P}(a)$ and $f(a)$ from the probability model:

$$s_1 = s_0 \times \mathcal{P}(S[1]) = 1 \times \mathcal{P}(a) = \frac{1}{2}$$

$$l_1 = l_0 + s_0 \times f(S[1]) = 0 + 1 \times f(a) = 0.$$

In the second iteration we consider the second symbol, $S[2] = b$ and the (cumulative) probability $\mathcal{P}(b)$ (and $f(b)$), and determine the second interval $[l_2, l_2 + s_2)$:

$$s_2 = s_1 \times \mathcal{P}(S[2]) = \frac{1}{2} \times \mathcal{P}(b) = \frac{1}{8}$$

$$l_2 = l_1 + s_1 \times f(S[2]) = 0 + \frac{1}{2} \times f(b) = \frac{1}{4}.$$

We continue this way for the third and the fourth symbols, namely $S[3] = a$ and $S[4] = c$, thus obtaining the final interval:

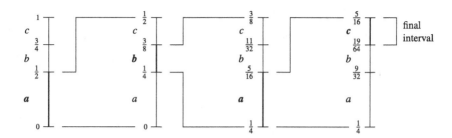

Figure 12.8 A graphical representation of the algorithmic idea behind arithmetic coding.

$$[l_4, l_4 + s_4) = \left[\frac{19}{64}, \frac{19}{64} + \frac{1}{64} \right) = \left[\frac{19}{64}, \frac{20}{64} \right) = \left[\frac{19}{64}, \frac{5}{16} \right).$$

In Figure 12.8 we illustrate the execution of the algorithm in a graphical way. Each step zooms in on the subinterval associated with the current symbol. The final step returns a real number inside the final subinterval, hence this number is *inside all* the previously generated intervals too. This number, together with the length n of the input sequence S, is sufficient to reconstruct it, as we will show in the following subsection. In fact, all input sequences of a fixed length n are associated with distinct subintervals which do not intersect each other, but cover $[0, 1)$; on the other hand, sequences of different lengths might be nested, so n is necessary to reconstruct uniquely S and indeed it is returned as output of AC-Coding.

12.2.3 Decompression Algorithm

The input consists of the stream of bits resulting from the compression stage, the length n of the input sequence to be decompressed, and the symbol probabilities $\mathcal{P}(\sigma)$, for all alphabet symbols $\sigma \in \Sigma$. The output is the original sequence $S[1, n]$, given that arithmetic coding is a *lossless compressor*.

Decoding is correct because the encoder and the decoder use the same statistical model to decompose the current interval (i.e. $\mathcal{P}$ and f), and both start from the interval $[0, 1)$. The difference is that the encoder uses symbols to choose the subintervals, whereas the decoder uses the real number $0.b$ to choose (the same) subinterval to zoom into.

As an example, take the pair $\langle \frac{39}{128}, 4 \rangle$ and assume that the input distribution is $\mathcal{P}(a) = \frac{1}{2}$, $\mathcal{P}(b) = \mathcal{P}(c) = \frac{1}{4}$. The resulting cumulative probabilities are $f(a) = 0$, $f(b) = \mathcal{P}(a) = \frac{1}{2}$, and $f(c) = \mathcal{P}(a) + \mathcal{P}(b) = \frac{3}{4}$. The decoder executes the pseudocode detailed in Algorithm 12.5, starting with the interval $[0, 1)$, and setting $b = 39/128$ and $n = 4$. As the reader will discover at the end of this section, this is the pair returned by Arithmetic coding for the text $S = abac$ of the previous section. So we suggest that readers excute in to parallel the decompression process with the compression one in Figure 12.8, just to convince themselves that coder and decoder are synchronized, as we have observed.

In the first iteration (i.e. $i = 1$), the initial range $[0, 1)$ is subdivided into three subintervals, one per symbol of the alphabet. These intervals follow a predefined

---

Algorithm 12.5 AC-Decoding(b, n, $\mathcal{P}$)

Require: The binary sequence b representing the compressed output, the length n of S, the probabilities $\mathcal{P}(\sigma)$.

Ensure: The original sequence S.

1: Compute the cumulative probabilities $f(\sigma) = \sum_{c < \sigma} \mathcal{P}(c)$, for each alphabet symbol $\sigma \in \Sigma$;

2: $s_0 = 1, l_0 = 0, i = 1$;

3: **while** $i \leq n$ **do**

4:     Subdivide the interval $[l_{i-1}, l_{i-1} + s_{i-1})$ into subintervals of length proportional to the probabilities of the alphabet symbols (taken in a predefined order);

5:     Determine the symbol σ corresponding to the subinterval in which the value $0.b$ lies;

6:     $S = S :: \sigma$;

7:     $s_i = s_{i-1} \times \mathcal{P}(\sigma)$;

8:     $l_i = l_{i-1} + s_{i-1} \times f(\sigma)$;

9:     $i = i + 1$;

10: **end while**

11: **return** S;

---

order; in particular, for this example, the first interval from the bottom is associated with the symbol a, the second with symbol b, and the last one with symbol c (as in Figure 12.8). Algorithm 12.5 computes the size of each subinterval as proportional to the probability of the respective symbol: so we have $[0, \frac{1}{2})$ for a, $[\frac{1}{2}, \frac{3}{4})$ for b, and $[\frac{3}{4}, 1)$ for c. Given the input value $\frac{39}{128}$, the decoding algorithm outputs the symbol a because this value is included in $[0, \frac{1}{2})$. After that, Algorithm 12.5 updates the subinterval as $[0, \frac{1}{2})$. The partitioning in three subintervals and the choice of the one including the value $.b$ (i.e. Steps 4 and 5) are implemented by iterating Steps 7 and 8 for all symbols σ until the correct one is found. That is, $0.b \in [l_1, l_1 + s_1)$ where $s_1 = s_0 \times \mathcal{P}(a) = 1 \times (1/2) = 1/2$ and $l_1 = l_0 + s_0 \times f(a) = 0 + 1 \times 0 = 0$.

In the second iteration (i.e. $i = 1$), the current interval $[0, \frac{1}{2})$ is subdivided into three subintervals whose sizes are proportional to the probabilities of the three alphabet symbols (i.e. again $1/2$ for a, and $1/4$ for b and c). This means that they are $\left[0, \frac{1}{4}\right), \left[\frac{1}{4}, \frac{3}{8}\right), \left[\frac{3}{8}, \frac{1}{2}\right)$. As a result, the second symbol returned in output is b because $\frac{39}{128} \in \left[\frac{1}{4}, \frac{3}{8}\right)$. As a check for the correctness of Algorithm 12.5, Steps 7 and 8 compute $s_2 = s_1 \times \mathcal{P}(b) = (1/2) \times (1/4) = 1/8$ and $l_2 = l_1 + s_1 \times f(b) = 0 + (1/2) \times (1/2) = 1/4$.

Proceeding in this way, the third and the fourth iterations output respectively the symbols a and c, and the initial sequence is thus reconstructed correctly. Algorithm 12.5 stops after four steps, because $n = 4$ was communicated in input to the decoder as the original sequence length.

12.2.4   Efficiency

Intuitively this scheme performs well, because it associates large subintervals to frequent symbols (given that the interval size s_i is proportional to $P(S[i])$), and a large final interval requires fewer bits to specify a number inside it. From Step 4 of Algorithm 12.4 it is easy to derive an explicit formula for the size s_n of the final interval associated to the input sequence S:

$$s_n = s_{n-1} \times P(S[n]) = s_{n-2} \times P(S[n-1]) \times P(S[n]) = \cdots$$

$$= s_0 \times P(S[1]) \times \cdots \times P(S[n]) = 1 \times \prod_{i=1}^{n} P(S[i]). \qquad (12.1)$$

This formula is interesting because it says that s_n depends on the symbols forming S but not on their order within S. So the size of the interval returned by arithmetic coding for S is the same whatever the order. Now, since the size of the interval impacts on the number of bits returned in the compressed output, we derive that the output size is *independent* of the permutation of the symbols in S. This does not contradict the previous statement, which we will go on to prove that arithmetic coding achieves a performance close to the entropy of the sequence S, given that the formula for entropy is also independent of S's symbol ordering.

We are left with the problem of choosing a number within the interval $[l_n, l_n + s_n)$ that has the form of a dyadic fraction $\frac{v}{2^k}$ and can be encoded with a few bits (i.e. a small k). The following lemma is crucial to establish the efficiency and correctness of arithmetic coding.

Lemma 12.3 *Take a real number x represented as the binary sequence $0.b_1 b_2 \cdots$. If we truncate it to its first d bits, we obtain a real number $\mathrm{trunc}_d(x) \in [x - 2^{-d}, x]$.*

Proof The real number x may differ from its truncation in terms of the bits that follow the position d. Those bits have been reset to 0 in $\mathrm{trunc}_d(x)$. Therefore we have:

$$x - \mathrm{trunc}_d(x) = \sum_{i=1}^{\infty} b_{d+i} 2^{-(d+i)} \leq \sum_{i=1}^{\infty} 1 \times 2^{-(d+i)} = 2^{-d} \sum_{i=1}^{\infty} \frac{1}{2^i} = 2^{-d}.$$

On the other hand, $\mathrm{trunc}_d(x) \leq x$ because we may turn bits 1 in the binary representation of x into bits 0 in the binary representation of $\mathrm{trunc}_d(x)$. ∎

Corollary 12.1 *The truncation of $l + \frac{s}{2}$ to its first $\left\lceil \log_2 \frac{2}{s} \right\rceil$ bits falls in the interval $[l, l + s)$.*

Proof It is enough to set $d = \left\lceil \log_2 \frac{2}{s} \right\rceil$ in Lemma 12.3, and observe that $2^{-d} \leq \frac{s}{2}$. ∎

At this point we can substitute the final step, Step 8, in AC-Coding (S) with the invocation of CONVERTER on the real number $l_n + s_n/2$, asking to emit only $\left\lceil \log_2 \frac{2}{s_n} \right\rceil$

bits. Nicely enough, algorithm CONVERTER allows these bits to be incrementally generated.

For the sake of clarity, let us resume the previous example taking the final interval $[l_4, l_4 + s_4) = [\frac{19}{64}, \frac{20}{64})$ found in the compression stage. Hence the value to output is

$$l_4 + \frac{s_4}{2} = \frac{19}{64} + \frac{1}{64} \times \frac{1}{2} = \frac{39}{128}$$

truncated at the first $\lceil \log_2 \frac{2}{s_4} \rceil = \log_2 128 = 7$ bits. The resulting stream of bits associated with this value is obtained by executing the algorithm CONVERTER for seven steps, in this way:

$$\frac{39}{128} \times 2 = \frac{78}{128} < 1 \rightarrow output = 0$$

$$\frac{78}{128} \times 2 = \frac{156}{128} \geq 1 \rightarrow output = 1$$

$$\left(\frac{156}{128} - 1 \right) \times 2 = \frac{56}{128} < 1 \rightarrow output = 0$$

$$\frac{56}{128} \times 2 = \frac{112}{128} < 1 \rightarrow output = 0$$

$$\frac{112}{128} \times 2 = \frac{224}{128} \geq 1 \rightarrow output = 1$$

$$\left(\frac{224}{128} - 1 \right) \times 2 = \frac{192}{128} \geq 1 \rightarrow output = 1$$

$$\left(\frac{192}{128} - 1 \right) \times 2 = 1 \geq 1 \rightarrow output = 1.$$

At the end the encoder returns the pair $\langle 0100111_2, 4 \rangle$. We recall that, to allow the decompression, the decoder must receive not only this pair but also the alphabet $\Sigma = \{a, b, c\}$ and the symbol probabilities $P(a) = \frac{1}{2}, P(b) = P(c) = \frac{1}{4}$.

We are ready now to prove the main theorem of this section, which relates the compression ratio achieved by arithmetic coding with the (empirical) entropy of the input string S. We refer to "empirical" entropy when we estimate the probabilities of the alphabet symbols via their frequency of occurrence in S.

Theorem 12.3 *The number of bits emitted by arithmetic coding for a sequence S of n symbols is at most $2 + n\mathcal{H}$, where $\mathcal{H}$ is the (empirical) entropy of S.*

Proof By Corollary 12.1 and Equation (12.1), we know that the number of output bits is:

$$\left\lceil \log_2 \frac{2}{s_n} \right\rceil < 2 - \log_2 s_n = 2 - \log_2 \left(\prod_{i=1}^{n} P(S[i]) \right) = 2 - \sum_{i=1}^{n} \log_2 P(S[i]).$$

Now we can rewrite the summation by iterating not over the positions i in S but, rather, iterating over the symbols σ and grouping their same occurrences:

$$2 - \sum_{\sigma \in \Sigma} n_\sigma \log_2 \mathcal{P}(\sigma) = 2 - n \left(\sum_{\sigma \in \Sigma} \frac{n_\sigma}{n} \log_2 \mathcal{P}(\sigma) \right),$$

where n_σ is the number of occurrences of symbol σ in S. The final observation is that, if arithmetic coding uses the semi-static model to estimate the probabilities of symbols and thus sets $\mathcal{P}(\sigma) = \frac{n_\sigma}{n}$, then we can rewrite this formula *exactly* as $2 + n\,\mathcal{H}$, where $\mathcal{H}$ is the empirical entropy of S, and the theorem follows. In the case of a static model, the probabilities are fixed in advance and S is emitted according to them. Nevertheless, by the law of large numbers, the ratio n_σ/n converges to $\mathcal{P}(\sigma)$ as n is sufficiently large, and thus the bound stated in the theorem follows asymptotically for the entropy of S's source.   ■

We can draw some conclusions from the result just proved:

- There is a waste of only two bits on an entire input sequence S, hence $\frac{2}{n}$ bits per symbol. This is a vanishing loss as the input sequence becomes increasingly long.
- The size of the output is a function of the set of symbols constituting S with their multiplicities, but not of their order.

In Section 12.1 we saw that Huffman coding requires $n + n\mathcal{H}$ bits for compressing a sequence of n symbols, so arithmetic coding is much better: it turns the additive linear term n into the constant 2. Another advantage is that it calculates the compressed output on the fly and can easily accommodate the use of dynamic modeling. On the other hand, arithmetic coding achieves this efficiency by means of infinite-precision arithmetic operations which are very costly (in time and space) to support. There are several proposals about using *finite*-precision arithmetic, which nonetheless penalizes the compression ratio up to $n\mathcal{H}_0 + \frac{2}{100} n$ (see, e.g., [3, 9]). Even so, arithmetic coding is still more compressed than Huffman coding: $\frac{2}{100}$ versus 1 bit loss. The next subsection describes a practical implementation for arithmetic coding proposed by Witten, Neal, and Clearly [9], sometimes called *range coding*, which is mathematically equivalent to arithmetic coding, but works with subintervals that have *integral extremes*. A more recent proposal working with finite-precision arithmetic and very interesting compression and time performance in practice is *asymmetric numeral systems* (ANS) [2]. Like arithmetic coding, ANS converts a sequence of input symbols into a number that encapsulates a description of the sequence; but, unlike arithmetic coding, ANS generates an *integer* value which *grows* as new symbols are read from the input. So ANS coding adds low-significance bits to that integer, which is proved to diverge from zero according to the reciprocal of the symbol probabilities. So the average number of emitted bits still grows as the (empirical) entropy of the input sequence. (For a clear explanation and comparison of ANS against Huffman and arithmetic codings, we refer the reader to [5].)

Overall, (canonical) Huffman still offers some advantages over arithmetic and ANS codings: it is faster and able to decompress any portion of the compressed file provided that we know its starting codeword. These properties justify the frequent use of (canonical) Huffman coding in the context of Web/text collections, where the efficient decompression of portions of data is essential and symbol distributions are not very skewed. For these applications, an interesting variant of (canonical) Huffman is the one that uses a large alphabet consisting of words or tokens, known as Huffword [8].

12.2.5   Range Coding$^\infty$

In range coding, representing real numbers in finite-precision arithmetic hinges on the following three steps:

1. For every symbol $\sigma \in \Sigma$, we introduce an integer count $c[\sigma]$, denoting the number of occurrences of that symbol in the input sequence, and a cumulative count $C[\sigma]$, which sums the counts of all symbols preceding σ in Σ, hence $C[\sigma] = \sum_{\alpha < \sigma} c[\alpha]$. So we approximate the probability $\mathcal{P}(\sigma)$ and the cumulative probability $f(\sigma)$ as

$$P(\sigma) = \frac{c[\sigma]}{C[|\Sigma| + 1]} \qquad f(\sigma) = \frac{C[\sigma]}{C[|\Sigma| + 1]}.$$

2. The interval $[0, 1)$ is mapped to the integer interval $[0, M)$, where $M = 2^w$ depends on the length w in bits of the memory word.

3. During the i-th iteration of the compression or decompression stages in arithmetic coding, the current subinterval (formerly $[l_i, l_i + s_i)$) will be chosen to have integer endpoints $[L_i, H_i)$ such that

$$L_i = L_{i-1} + \lfloor f(S[i]) \times (H_{i-1} - L_{i-1}) \rfloor$$
$$H_i = L_i + \lfloor P(S[i]) \times (H_{i-1} - L_{i-1}) \rfloor.$$

These approximations induce a compression loss empirically estimated (by the original authors) as 10^{-4} bits per input symbol. In order to clarify how it works, we will first explain the compression and decompression stages, and then we will illustrate an example.

Compression stage. In order to guarantee that every interval $[L_i, H_i)$ has non-empty subintervals, the integer starting point of the next subintervals must be strictly increasing. From their definitions,

$$L_{i+1} = L_i + \lfloor f(S[i+1]) \times (H_i - L_i) \rfloor = L_i + \left\lfloor \frac{C[S[i+1]]}{C[|\Sigma| + 1]} \times (H_i - L_i) \right\rfloor.$$

Since $C[i]$s are strictly increasing, the condition $\frac{H_i - L_i}{C[|\Sigma|+1]} \geq 1$ ensures that the starting points of the subintervals are also increasing. Adding the fact that expansions need to keep numbers smaller than M, it is enough to guarantee that

$$C[|\Sigma| + 1] \leq \frac{M}{4} + 2 \leq H_i - L_i. \tag{12.2}$$

This means that an *adaptive* range coding should reset these counts every $\frac{M}{4} + 2$ input symbols, or rescale them every, for example, $\frac{M}{8} + 1$ input symbols by dividing them by 2.

Rescaling. In order to guarantee (12.2), one can adopt the following *expansion rules*, which are repeatedly checked before each step of the compression process, and until none of them is satisfied:

1. $[L_i, H_i) \subseteq [0, \frac{M}{2}) \rightarrow$ output "0", and the new interval is:

$$[L_{i+1}, H_{i+1}) = [2 L_i, 2 (H_i - 1) + 2).$$

2. $[L_i, H_i) \subseteq [\frac{M}{2}, M) \rightarrow$ output "1", and the new interval is

$$[L_{i+1}, H_{i+1}) = \left[2 \left(L_i - \frac{M}{2} \right), 2 \left(H_i - 1 - \frac{M}{2} \right) + 2 \right).$$

3. If $\frac{M}{4} \leq L_i < \frac{M}{2} < H_i \leq \frac{3M}{4}$, then we cannot output any bit and we have an *underflow condition*, which is managed as follows.

In the case of underflow, we cannot emit any bit until the interval falls in one of the two halves of $[0, M)$ (i.e. cases 1 or 2 above). If we continue and operate on the interval $\left[\frac{M}{4}, \frac{3M}{4} \right)$ as we did with $[0, M)$, by rewriting conditions 1 and 2, the interval size can fall below $\frac{M}{8}$ and thus the same problem arises again. The solution is to use a parameter m that records the number of times that the underflow condition occurred, so that the current interval is within $\left[\frac{M}{2} - \frac{M}{2^{m+1}}, \frac{M}{2} + \frac{M}{2^{m+1}} \right)$; observe that, when the interval eventually does not include $\frac{M}{2}$, we will output 01^m if it is in the first half, or 10^m if it is in the second half. After that, we can expand the interval around its halfway point and count the number of expansions:

- Mathematically, if $\frac{M}{4} \leq L_i < \frac{M}{2} < H_i \leq \frac{3M}{4}$, then we increment the number m of underflows and consider the new interval

$$[L_{i+1}, H_{i+1}) = \left[2 \left(L_i - \frac{M}{4} \right), 2 \left(H_i - 1 - \frac{M}{4} \right) + 2 \right).$$

- When expansion rules 1 or 2 are operated, after the output of the bit, we also output m copies of the complement of that bit, and reset m to 0.

End of the input sequence. At the end of the input sequence, because of interval expansions, the current interval satisfies at least one of the following two inequalities:

$$L_n < \frac{M}{4} < \frac{M}{2} < H_n \quad \text{or} \quad L_n < \frac{M}{2} < \frac{3M}{4} < H_n. \qquad (12.3)$$

In the case that $m > 0$, range coding completes the output bit stream as follows:

- If the first inequality holds, we can emit 01^{m+1} (if $m = 0$, this means encoding $\frac{M}{4}$).
- If the second inequality holds, we can emit 10^{m+1} (if $m = 0$, this means encoding $\frac{3M}{4}$).

Decompression stage. The decoder must mimic the computations operated during the compression stage. It maintains a shift register v of $\lceil \log_2 M \rceil$ bits, which plays the role of x (in the classic arithmetic coding), and it is thus used to find the next subinterval from the partitioning of the current interval. When the interval is expanded, v is modified accordingly, and a new bit from the compressed stream is loaded through the function next_bit (which is assumed to fetch a bit 0 whenever the input stream is exhausted). As in the compression stage, the following expansion rules are repeatedly checked until none is satisfied:

1. $[L_i, H_i) \subseteq [0, \frac{M}{2}) \rightarrow$ consider the new interval

$$[L_{i+1}, H_{i+1}) = [2 L_i, 2 (H_i - 1) + 2),$$
$$v = 2v + \texttt{next\_bit}.$$

2. $[L_i, H_i) \subseteq [\frac{M}{2}, M) \rightarrow$ consider the new interval

$$[L_{i+1}, H_{i+1}) = \left[2\left(L_i - \frac{M}{2}\right), 2\left(H_i - 1 - \frac{M}{2}\right) + 2\right),$$
$$v = 2\left(v - \frac{M}{2}\right) + \texttt{next\_bit}.$$

3. if $\frac{M}{4} \leq L_i < \frac{M}{2} < H_i \leq \frac{3M}{4}$ consider the new interval

$$[L_{i+1}, H_{i+1}) = \left[2\left(L_i - \frac{M}{4}\right), 2\left(H_i - 1 - \frac{M}{4}\right) + 2\right),$$
$$v = 2\left(v - \frac{M}{4}\right) + \texttt{next\_bit}.$$

In order to understand range coding better, let us resume the example of the previous sections with the same input sequence $S = abac$ of length $n = 4$, ordered alphabet $\Sigma = \{a, b, c\}$, probabilities $\mathcal{P}(a) = \frac{1}{2}$, $\mathcal{P}(b) = \mathcal{P}(c) = \frac{1}{4}$, and cumulative probabilities $f(a) = 0, f(b) = \frac{1}{2}$, and $f(c) = \frac{3}{4}$. We rewrite these probabilities by using the approximations that we saw at the start of this section, hence $C[|\Sigma| + 1] = 4$, and we set the initial interval as $[L_0, H_0) = [0, M)$, where M is chosen to satisfy (12.2):

$$C[|\Sigma| + 1] \leq \frac{M}{4} + 2 \iff 4 \leq \frac{M}{4} + 2.$$

We take $M = 16$, so that $\frac{M}{4} = 4$, $\frac{M}{2} = 8$, and $\frac{3M}{4} = 12$ (of course, this value of M is not based on the real machine word length but it is useful for our example). At this point, we have the initial interval

$$[L_0, H_0) = [0, 16),$$

and we are ready to compress the first symbol $S[1] = a$ using the expressions for the endpoints from the start of this section:

$$L_1 = L_0 + \lfloor f(a) \times (H_0 - L_0) \rfloor = 0 + \lfloor 0 \times 16 \rfloor = 0$$
$$H_1 = L_1 + \lfloor \mathcal{P}(a) \times (H_0 - L_0) \rfloor = 0 + \left\lfloor \frac{2}{4} \times 16 \right\rfloor = 8.$$

The new interval $[L_1, H_1) = [0, 8)$ satisfies the first expansion rule $[L_1, H_1) \subseteq [0, \frac{M}{2})$, hence range coding outputs "1" and expands the current interval as:

$$[L_1, H_1) = [2 L_1, 2 (H_1 - 1) + 2) = [0, 16).$$

In the second iteration, we consider the second input symbol $S[2] = b$, and the endpoints of the new interval are:

$$L_2 = L_1 + \lfloor f(b) \times (H_1 - L_1) \rfloor = 8$$
$$H_2 = L_2 + \lfloor P(b) \times (H_1 - L_1) \rfloor = 12.$$

This interval satisfies the second expansion rule $[L_2, H_2) \subseteq [\frac{M}{2}, M)$, hence range coding outputs the bit "1" and expands the current interval as:

$$[L_2, H_2) = \left[2 \left(L_2 - \frac{M}{2} \right), 2 \left(H_2 - 1 - \frac{M}{2} \right) + 2 \right) = [0, 8).$$

This interval satisfies the first expansion rule, thus range coding applies it before reading the next input symbol. So it outputs "0" and obtains the new expanded interval:

$$[L_2, H_2) = [2 L_1, 2 (H_2 - 1) + 2) = [0, 16).$$

The third input symbol $S[3] = a$ is equal to the first one and is encoded within the same interval, so we know that range coding outputs "0" and obtains the new interval $[L_3, H_3) = [0, 16)$. For the final, fourth input symbol $S[4] = c$, range coding computes the new interval as:

$$[L_4, H_4) = [L_3 + \lfloor f(c) \times (H_3 - L_3) \rfloor, L_4 + \lfloor P(c) \times (H_3 - L_3) \rfloor) = [12, 16).$$

This interval lies after $M/2$ so range coding emits "1" and applies the second expansion rule:

$$[L_4, H_4) = \left[2 \left(L_4 - \frac{M}{2} \right), 2 \left(H_4 - 1 - \frac{M}{2} \right) + 2 \right) = [8, 16).$$

This interval must be expanded again according to the second expansion rule, so range coding outputs "1" and obtains the final interval:

$$[L_4, H_4) = \left[2 \left(L_4 - \frac{M}{2} \right), 2 \left(H_4 - 1 - \frac{M}{2} \right) + 2 \right) = [0, 16).$$

The reader can verify that this last interval satisfies (12.3), and that the compressed bit sequence `010011` is actually one bit shorter than the one generated by the classic arithmetic coding. This bit sequence encodes the dyadic fraction $\frac{19}{64}$, which is correctly within the range $[\frac{19}{64}, \frac{5}{16})$ identified by arithmetic coding in Figure 12.8.

As far as the decoding stage is concerned, the first step initializes the shift register v (of length $\lceil \log_2 M \rceil = \lceil \log_2 16 \rceil = 4$) with the first $\lceil \log_2 16 \rceil = 4$ bits of the compressed sequence, hence $v = 0100_2 = 4_{10}$.[3] At this point the initial interval $[L_0, H_0) = [0, 16)$ is subdivided into three different subintervals, one for every symbol in the alphabet, according to their countings: $[0, 8)$, $[8, 12)$, and $[12, 16)$. The

---

[3] The notation x_2 (resp. x_{10}) denotes that x is written in base 2 (resp. 10).

symbol output at the first iteration is then a because $v = 4 \in [0, 8)$. At this point, range coding applies the first expansion rule of the decompression process because $[L_1, H_1) = [0, 8) \subseteq [0, \frac{M}{2})$, obtaining:

$$[L_1, H_1) = [2L_1, 2(H_1 - 1) + 2) = [0, 16)$$
$$v = 2v + \texttt{next\_bit} = \texttt{shift}_{sx}(0100_2) + 1_2 = 1000_2 + 1_2 = 1001_2 = 9_{10}.$$

In the second iteration, the interval $[0, 16)$ is subdivided into the same ranges as before, and the output symbol is now b because $v = 9 \in [8, 12)$. This last interval satisfies the second expansion rule, which produces the new interval:

$$[L_2, H_2) = \left[2\left(L_2 - \frac{M}{2}\right), 2\left(H_2 - 1 - \frac{M}{2}\right) + 2\right) = [0, 8)$$
$$v = 2\left(v - \frac{M}{2}\right) + \texttt{next\_bit} = \texttt{shift}_{sx}(1001_2 - 1000_2) + 1_2 = 0011_2 = 3_{10}.$$

Since the current interval $[0, 8)$ satisfies the first expansion rule, we apply it (the function $\texttt{next\_bit}$ returns "0" if there are not more bits in the compressed sequence):

$$[L_2, H_2) = [2L_2, 2(H_2 - 1) + 2) = [0, 16)$$
$$v = 2v + \texttt{next\_bit} = \texttt{shift}_{sx}(0011_2) + 0_2 = 0110_2 = 6_{10}.$$

This interval is subdivided as in the first iteration, and range coding outputs a because $v = 6 \in [0, 8)$. By following the same calculations as in the first iteration, the new interval is $[L_3, H_3) = [0, 16)$ and

$$v = 2v + \texttt{next\_bit} = \texttt{shift}_{sx}(0110_2) + 0_2 = 1100_2 = 12_{10}.$$

The last output symbol is c because $v = 12 \in [12, 16)$, and thus the entire input sequence is exactly reconstructed. The algorithm can stop because it has generated four symbols, and 4 was provided as input to the decoder to specify the length of S.

12.3   Prediction by Partial Matching$^\infty$

In order to improve compression, we need better models for the symbol probabilities. A typical approach consists of estimating them by considering not just individual symbols, and thus assuming that they occur independently of each other, but evaluating the *conditional probability* of their occurrence in S given a few previous symbols: the so-called *context*. In this section we will look at a particular *adaptive* technique to build a context model that can be combined very successfully with arithmetic coding, because it generates skewed probabilities and thus high compression. This method is called *prediction by partial matching* (PPM); it allows us to move from 0-th order entropy coders to k-th order entropy coders. The recent advent of *deep neural networks* as sophisticated probability distribution models has opened the way to new modeling approaches which could be used in combination with the previous statistical coders in order to achieve even better compression performance, whose time and space efficiency has yet to be investigated with care.

The implementation of PPM suffers two main problems: (i) it needs proper data structures to maintain updated in a time- and space-efficient manner all conditional probabilities, as the input sequence is scanned; (ii) at the beginning, the estimates of the context-based probabilities are poor, so proper adjustments have to be made in order to quickly establish good statistics for all input symbols. In the rest of this section, we concentrate on the second issue, and refer the reader to the literature for the first one (see, e.g., [4, 8]), also pointing out some recent results concerning the compressed encoding of the tree-based data structures that could be adopted for (i), this being another key efficiency problem when the alphabet and the context lengths grow (see also Chapter 15).

PPM uses a suite of finite contexts of length $\ell \leq K$ (aka ℓ-order contexts) in order to predict the next symbol. The maximum context length K influences the time and space efficiency of the data structures used to index those contexts and, as such, it has to be chosen with care, as we highlighted in point (i). At step i, PPM has to execute two phases: one consists of encoding the current symbol $\sigma = S[i]$ according to the probability estimates that the suite of contexts provides for it; the other consists of updating the counts for σ and all of its previous contexts $\alpha = S[i - \ell, i - 1]$ of length up to K, so that it keeps track of how many times the string $\alpha \sigma$ occurs in the prefix of S processed so far.

The choice of the *best* context to use for the encoding of $S[i]$ is tricky, and done in PPM starting from the longest possible context of length K that precedes $S[i]$, namely $S[i - K, i - 1]$. If PPM establishes that it has not much *statistical information* for predicting "$S[i]$ after $S[i - K, i - 1]$," then it switches to shorter and shorter ℓ-order contexts until it finds the one, say $S[i - \ell, i - 1]$ with $\ell < K$, that is able to predict $S[i]$ with enough statistical significance. This check deploys the statistics (i.e. counts) that PPM keeps for all symbols occurring after all contexts of length up to K in the prefix of the sequence S processed so far. Therefore, it can estimate the probability that $S[i]$ follows $S[i - \ell, i - 1]$ by accessing the corresponding count, and using it if larger than 0. Note that the 0-order context corresponds to probabilities estimated just by the frequency counts of the individual symbols, exactly as in the classic arithmetic coding. Otherwise (i.e. the count for $S[i]$ following $S[i - \ell, i - 1]$ is null), PPM scales to a shorter ℓ-order context. At the start, some contexts may be missing; in particular, when $i \leq K$, the encoder and the decoder can use at most the context of length $(i - 1) < K$. In order to avoid the pathological cases in which no statistics is available for "$S[i]$ after $S[i - \ell, i - 1]$," for all $0 \leq \ell \leq K$, PPM additionally maintains a *special* (-1)-*order context*, which corresponds to a model in which all symbols have the same probability. This context ensures that, in the context-scaling process, there will always be one in which symbol $S[i]$ has non-null probability.

The key compression issue is then how to encode the length ℓ of the model adopted to compress $S[i]$, so that the decoder can also use that context in the decompression phase. We could use an integer coder (see Chapter 11), of course, but this would take an integral number of bits per symbol, thus undoing all our previous efforts for a good modeling. The smart idea adopted by PPM is to turn this problem into a symbol-encoding problem, by introducing an *escape* symbol (esc) which is emitted every time a context switch, to the next shorter context, has to be performed. This *escaping process* continues till a model where the symbol is not novel (and thus its count is more than 0), is reached. This is eventually the special (-1)-order context. Using such strategy, the probability associated to a symbol is always the one that has been calculated in the longest context where the symbol has previously occurred; so it should be more precise than just the probabilities based on individual counts for the symbols in Σ, as adopted for arithmetic and Huffman codings.

To better understand how PPM works, we consider the following example. Let the input sequence S be the string *abracadabra*, and let $K = 2$ be the longest context used in the computation of the *conditional probabilities* for all alphabet symbols. As previously said, the only model available when the algorithm starts is the (-1)-order model. So when the first symbol a is read, no escape symbols have to be emitted, and the (-1)-order context is used to assign to $S[1] = a$ the uniform probability $\frac{1}{|\Sigma|}$ (typically, symbols are byte encoded and thus $|\Sigma| = 256$). At the same time, PPM updates the frequency counts in the 0-order model, by assigning a probability $\mathcal{P}(a) = \frac{1}{2}$ and $\mathcal{P}(esc) = \frac{1}{2}$. In this running example we assume that the escape symbol is given a count equal to the total number of different characters in the model. Other strategies to define its probability will be discussed in detail in the following subsection.

PPM then reads $S[2] = b$ and tries the 0-order model, which is currently the longest one available, as has been explained. An escape symbol is transmitted since b has never been read before. The (-1)-order model is so used to compress b, and then both the 1-order and the 0-order models are updated. In the 0-order model we have $\mathcal{P}(a) = \frac{1}{4}$, $\mathcal{P}(b) = \frac{1}{4}$, $\mathcal{P}(esc) = \frac{2}{4} = \frac{1}{2}$ (two distinct symbols have been read). In the 1-order model the probabilities are $\mathcal{P}(b|a) = \frac{1}{2}$ and $\mathcal{P}(esc|a) = \frac{1}{2}$ (only one distinct symbol is read).

Now let us skip the coding of the first five symbols and suppose that PPM has to encode $S[6] = d$. Since it is the first occurrence of d in S, three escape symbols will be emitted for switching from the 2-order to the (-1)-order model. Figure 12.9 shows the statistics computed by PPM after it has processed the entire sequence S. PPM offers probability estimates that can then be used by an arithmetic coder or any other statistical coder to compress a sequence of symbols in $\Sigma \cup \{esc\}$. This is the reason why PPM is often regarded as a context-modeling technique rather than a compressor.

12.3.1   On the Estimation of Symbol Probabilities

It is possible to use the knowledge about symbol frequencies in the ℓ-order models to improve the compression rate when scaling through increasingly shorter contexts. Suppose that the whole input sequence S of the previous example has been processed and that the following symbol to be encoded is c and $K = 2$. The current 2-order context is ra, so the entry for $ra \rightarrow c$ in Figure 12.9 is considered, and thus c is encoded with a probability of $\frac{1}{2}$, thus using 1 bit.

Order $k = 2$

Predictions		c	$\mathcal{P}$
ab	→ r	2	$\frac{2}{3}$
	→ esc	1	$\frac{1}{3}$
ac	→ a	1	$\frac{1}{2}$
	→ esc	1	$\frac{1}{2}$
ad	→ a	1	$\frac{1}{2}$
	→ esc	1	$\frac{1}{2}$
br	→ a	2	$\frac{2}{3}$
	→ esc	1	$\frac{1}{3}$
ca	→ d	1	$\frac{1}{2}$
	→ esc	1	$\frac{1}{2}$
da	→ b	1	$\frac{1}{2}$
	→ esc	1	$\frac{1}{2}$
ra	→ c	1	$\frac{1}{2}$
	→ esc	1	$\frac{1}{2}$

Order $k = 1$

Predictions		c	$\mathcal{P}$
a	→ b	2	$\frac{2}{7}$
	→ c	1	$\frac{1}{7}$
	→ d	1	$\frac{1}{7}$
	→ esc	3	$\frac{2}{7}$
b	→ r	2	$\frac{2}{3}$
	→ esc	1	$\frac{1}{3}$
c	→ a	1	$\frac{1}{2}$
	→ esc	1	$\frac{1}{2}$
d	→ a	1	$\frac{1}{2}$
	→ esc	1	$\frac{1}{2}$
r	→ a	2	$\frac{2}{3}$
	→ esc	1	$\frac{1}{3}$

Order $k = 0$

Predictions	c	$\mathcal{P}$
→ a	5	$\frac{5}{16}$
→ b	2	$\frac{2}{16}$
→ c	1	$\frac{1}{16}$
→ d	1	$\frac{1}{16}$
→ r	2	$\frac{2}{16}$
→ esc	5	$\frac{5}{16}$

Order $k = -1$

Predictions	c	$\mathcal{P}$
→ $\forall \sigma[i]$	1	$\frac{1}{|\Sigma|}$

Figure 12.9 Method C of PPM model after processing the whole string $S = abracadabra$.

Suppose now that, instead of c, the character d follows $S = abracadabra$. In this case, no entry $ra \rightarrow d$ does exist in Figure 12.9. PPM emits an esc symbol (encoded with probability $\frac{1}{2}$) and it switches to the 1-order context a. The entry $a \rightarrow d$ does exist in Figure 12.9, and thus d can be encoded with probability $\frac{1}{7}$. An interesting observation, called the *exclusion principle*, allows us to improve the estimate for the probability $\mathcal{P}(d|a)$. Since the 2-order model was discarded, the encoder (and the decoder) can infer that the current symbol cannot be any of the ones tabulated after context ra in Figure 12.9. Consequently, the shorter 1-order model knows that the current symbol cannot be c (because of the entry $ra \rightarrow c$), and thus it can "exclude" the entry $a \rightarrow c$ and reduce the frequency count of the context a by one unit (i.e. the frequency of ac). As a result, symbol d can be encoded with probability $\frac{1}{6}$.

Suppose now that after *abracadabra*, the novel symbol e occurs. In this case, a sequence of esc symbols is emitted to make the decoder switch to the (-1)-order context. Without *exclusion*, the novel symbol would be encoded with a probability of $\frac{1}{|\Sigma|}$. Instead, PPM can exclude from the (-1)-order context all symbols that occurred after the previously longer contexts, such as *ra*, *a*, and the empty context. These are indeed all symbols seen so far, namely $\{a, b, c, d, r\}$, so the probability assigned to the novel symbol is $\frac{1}{|\Sigma|-5}$. Performing this technique takes a little extra time but gives a reasonable payback in terms of extra compression, because all nonexcluded symbols have their probability increased.

A final comment concerns the maximum length K of the contexts maintained by PPM and the encoding of the `esc` symbol. It may seem that PPM's performance should improve when K increases, but this is not necessarily the case, because the input sequence is finite, and with longer contexts there is a greater probability of emitting as many escape symbols as is needed to reach the context length for which non-null predictions are available. Therefore, K cannot be very large (typically it is chosen as $K \leq 5$), and much care must be adopted when estimating the probability of `esc`, because this impacts on the overall compressed space achieved by PPM. We conclude this chapter by commenting on some famous methods to estimate this probability (see, e.g., [1, 4, 7]), using the following notation: α denotes a context; σ is a symbol; $c(\sigma)$ is the number of times that σ has occurred after context α; n_α is the number of times the current context α has occurred; q the total number of distinct symbols read in the context α.

Method A. This method estimates the probability that symbol σ occurs (hence $c(\sigma) > 0$) in a context α by $P(\sigma \mid \alpha) = \frac{c(\sigma)}{1+n_\alpha}$. It then estimates the probability that a novel symbol occurs in a context α as:

$$P(\text{esc} \mid \alpha) = 1 - \sum_{\sigma \in \Sigma, c(\sigma) > 0} P(\sigma \mid \alpha) = 1 - \sum_{\sigma \in \Sigma, c(\sigma) > 0} \frac{c(\sigma)}{1 + n_\alpha}$$

$$= 1 - \frac{n_\alpha}{1 + n_\alpha} = \frac{1}{1 + n_\alpha},$$

where we deployed the equality $\sum_{\sigma \in \Sigma} c(\sigma) = n_\alpha$, by definition of these parameters.

Method B. The second method classifies a symbol as novel unless it has already occurred twice. The motivation for this is that a symbol that has occurred only once can be an anomaly. The probability of a symbol occurring in a context is thus estimated by $P(\sigma \mid \alpha) = \frac{c(\sigma)-1}{n_\alpha}$, and q is set as the number of distinct symbols seen so far in the input sequence. This method then estimates the probability that a novel symbol occurs in a context α as:

$$P(\text{esc} \mid \alpha) = 1 - \sum_{\sigma \in \Sigma, c(\sigma) > 0} \frac{c(\sigma) - 1}{n_\alpha}$$

$$= 1 - \frac{1}{n_\alpha} \left(\sum_{\sigma \in \Sigma, c(\sigma) > 0} c(\sigma) - \sum_{\sigma \in \Sigma, c(\sigma) > 0} 1 \right)$$

$$= 1 - \frac{1}{n_\alpha} (n_\alpha - q) = \frac{q}{n_\alpha}.$$

Method C. This is a hybrid between the previous two methods A and B. When a novel symbol occurs, a count of 1 is added both to the escape count and to the new symbol count, so the total count increases by 2. Thus this method estimates the probability of a symbol σ in a context α as $\mathcal{P}(\sigma \mid \alpha) = c(\sigma) / (n_\alpha + q)$, and evaluates the escape probability as

$$\mathcal{P}(\mathrm{esc} \mid \alpha) = 1 - \sum_{\sigma \in \Sigma, c(\sigma) > 0} \frac{c(\sigma)}{n_\alpha + q} = \frac{q}{n_\alpha + q}.$$

Method D. This is a minor modification of method C, which treats in a more uniform way the occurrence of a novel symbol: instead of adding 1, it adds $\frac{1}{2}$ both to the escape and to the new symbol counts. Hence this method estimates the probability of a symbol σ in a context α as $\mathcal{P}(\sigma \mid \alpha) = (2c(\sigma) - 1)/(2n_\alpha)$, and evaluates the escape probability as $\mathcal{P}(\mathrm{esc} \mid \alpha) = (q / 2n_\alpha)$.

Previous methods do not make any assumptions on the distribution of symbol occurrences in some specific context. For example, under the hypothesis that symbols appear according to a Poisson process, and denoting with t_i the number of distinct symbols occurring exactly i times in a sample of size n_α, we could approximate the probability that the next symbol is novel by $t_1 - t_2 + t_3 - \cdots$. A simplification is to compute only the first term of the series, since in most cases n_α is very large and t_i decreases rapidly as i increases: namely, $\mathcal{P}(\mathrm{esc} \mid \alpha) = t_1 / n_\alpha$. This corresponds to counting only the symbols that have occurred once after context α. There are other approaches to more sophisticated evaluations of $\mathcal{P}(\mathrm{esc} \mid \alpha)$ that mix these latter methods with the previous ones, but for those ones we refer the reader to [1, 4, 7, 8].

References

[1] John G. Clearly and Ian H. Witten. Data compression using adaptive coding and partial string matching. *IEEE Transactions on Communications*, 32: 396–402, 1984.

[2] Jarosław Duda. Asymmetric numeral systems: Entropy coding combining speed of Huffman coding with compression rate of arithmetic coding. *CoRR abs/1311.2540*, 2013.

[3] Paul Howard and Jeffrey S. Vitter. Arithmetic coding for data compression. *Proceedings of the IEEE*, 857–65, 1994.

[4] Alistair Moffat. Implementing the PPM data compression scheme. *IEEE Transactions on Communications*, 38: 1917–21, 1990.

[5] Alistair Moffat and Matthias Petri. Large-alphabet semi-static entropy coding via asymmetric numeral systems. *ACM Transactions on Information Systems*, 38(4): 33.1–33.33, 2020.

[6] Claude E. Shannon. A mathematical theory of communication. Reprinted with corrections from *The Bell System Technical Journal*, 27: 379—423, 623—56, 1948. https://people.math.harvard.edu/ ctm/home/text/others/shannon/entropy/entropy.pdf

[7] Ian H. Witten and Timothy C. Bell. The zero-frequency problem: Estimating the probabilities of novel events in adaptive text compression. *IEEE Transactions on Information Theory*, 37: 1085–94, 1991.

[8] Ian H. Witten, Alistair Moffat, and Timothy C. Bell. *Managing Gigabytes*. Morgan Kauffman, second edition, 1999.

[9] Ian H. Witten, Radford M. Neal, and John G. Clearly. Arithmetic coding for data compression. *Communications of the ACM*, 30(6): 520–40, 1987.

13 Dictionary-Based Compressors

The first step was to try and understand
how to cope with the case where you don't
know what the statistics are and you have to
cleverly learn what it is.
Jacob Ziv

In this chapter we further discuss data-compression techniques, but following a different approach to the statistical one. The algorithms we are going to analyze do not derive statistics about the source generating the input sequence S; rather, they derive a *dictionary of strings* from S, and use it to replace occurrences in S of those strings via proper *tokens* (aka IDs), which are *indexes* for that dictionary. The choice of the dictionary is of course crucial in determining how well the file is compressed. An English dictionary will have a hard time to compress an Italian text, for instance; and it would be totally inappropriate to compress an executable file. Thus, while a *static* dictionary can work very well for compressing some specific file types that are known in advance, it cannot be used for a good *general-purpose compressor*. Moreover, sometimes it is ineffective to transmit the full dictionary along with each compressed file, and it is often unreasonable to assume that the receiver already has a copy of it.

Starting from 1977, Abraham Lempel and Jacob Ziv introduced a family of compressors which addressed these problems successfully by designing two algorithms, named LZ77 and LZ78 after the initials of the inventors and the years of the proposals, which use the input sequence they are compressing as the dictionary, and substitute each occurrence of an already seen string with either the offset of its previous position or an ID assigned incrementally to new dictionary phrases. The dictionary is *dynamically built* in the sense that it is initially empty, and then it grows as the input sequence is processed; at the beginning, low compression is achieved, but after some kilobytes, we can expect to achieve good compression ratios, provided that the input sequence shows some degree of *repetitiveness*. For typical textual files, those methods achieve about one-third of compression ratio. Lempel–Ziv compressors are very popular because of their `gzip` instantiation, and constitute the base of more sophisticated compressors in use today, such as `7zip`, `Brotli`, `LZ4`, `LZMA`, and `ZSTD`. In the following paragraphs, we will describe them in detail, along with some interesting variants.

13.1   LZ77

In their seminal paper of 1977 [7], Lempel and Ziv described their contribution as follows "universal coding scheme which can be applied to any discrete source and whose performance is comparable to certain optimal fixed code book schemes designed for completely specified sources." The key expression here is "comparable to [...] fixed code book schemes designed for completely specified sources," because the authors compare their scheme to previously designed statistical compressors, such as Huffman and arithmetic, for which a statistical characterization of the source was necessary. Conversely, their dictionary-based compressors waive this characterization, which is derived *implicitly* by observing *substring repetitiveness* via a fully syntactic approach.

In the following pages, we will not dig into the observations that provide a mathematical ground to these comments (see [1, 7]); rather, we will concentrate on the algorithmic issues underlying their design. LZ77's compressor is based on a *sliding window* $W[1, w]$, which contains a portion of the input sequence that has been processed so far, typically consisting of the last w symbols, and a *look-ahead buffer B*, which contains the suffix of the text still to be processed. In the following example, the window $W = aabbababb$ is of size 9 (surrounded by a rectangular box), and the rest of the input sequence is $B = baababaabbaa\$$:

$$\longleftarrow \cdots \boxed{aabbababb}\ baababaabbaa\$ \longrightarrow$$

The algorithm works inductively by assuming that everything occurring before B has been processed and compressed by LZ77, and W is initially set to the empty string. The compressor operates in two main stages: *parsing* and *encoding*. Parsing consists of transforming the input sequence S into a sequence of triples of integers (called *phrases*). Encoding turns these triples into a (compressed) bit stream by applying either a statistical compressor (e.g. Huffman or arithmetic) or an integer-coding scheme to each triplet component individually.

So the most interesting algorithmic stage is the parsing stage, which works as follows. LZ77 searches for the longest prefix α of B that occurs as a substring of $W \cdot B$. We write the concatenation $W \cdot B$ rather than the single string W because the previous occurrence we are searching for may start in W and extend up to within B. Say α occurs at distance d from the beginning of B, and it is followed by symbol c in B; then the triple generated by LZ77 is $\langle d, |\alpha|, c \rangle$, where $|\alpha|$ is the length of the *copied* string. If a match is not found, the output triple becomes $\langle 0, 0, B[1] \rangle$. We note that any occurrence of α in $W \cdot B$ must be followed by a symbol different from c, otherwise α would *not* be the longest prefix of B that repeats in $W \cdot B$.

After this triple is emitted, LZ77 advances in B by $|\alpha| + 1$ positions, and slides W accordingly. In the case that $|W| = +\infty$, the window is unbounded and thus LZ77 parsing can copy up to the beginning of the file to be compressed. It is not difficult to convince ourselves that this parsing process *minimizes* the number of emitted phrases.

We refer to LZ77 as a dictionary-based compressor because "the dictionary" is not explicitly stored; rather it is implicitly formed by all substrings of S that start in W and extend rightward, possibly ending in B. Each of those substrings is represented by the pair $\langle d, |\alpha| \rangle$. The dictionary is *dynamic* because at every shift it has to be updated by removing the substrings starting in $W[1, |\alpha| + 1]$, and adding the substrings starting in $B[1, |\alpha| + 1]$.

The role of the sliding window is easy to explain: it delimits the size of the dictionary, which depends on W's and S's length, because it includes $|W|$'s strings of length up to $|S|$. So W impacts significantly on the time cost for the search of α. As a running example, let us consider the following sequence of LZ77-parsing steps, where the bar | separates W and B:

$$\boxed{\;|\text{aabbabab}\qquad} \Longrightarrow \text{no copy is found; it emits } \langle 0, 0, a \rangle$$

$$\boxed{a|\text{abbabab}\qquad} \Longrightarrow \text{it copies ``a'', thus emitting } \langle 1, 1, b \rangle$$

$$\boxed{\text{aab}|\text{babab}\qquad} \Longrightarrow \text{it copies ``b'', thus emitting } \langle 1, 1, a \rangle$$

$$\boxed{\text{aabba}|\text{bab}\qquad} \Longrightarrow \text{an overlapping copy is found; it emits } \langle 2, 3, EOF \rangle$$

It is interesting to note that the last phrase $\langle 2, 3, EOF \rangle$ presents a copy-length which is larger than the copy-distance; this actually indicates the special situation we mentioned in which α starts in W and ends in B. Even if this *overlapping* occurs, the copy-step that must be executed by LZ77 in the decompression stage is not affected, provided that it is executed sequentially according to the following snippet of code:

```
for i = 0 to L-1 do { S[s+i] = S[s-d+i]; }
s = s+L;
```

where the triple to be decoded is $\langle d, L, c \rangle$ and $S[1, s - 1]$ is the prefix of the input sequence which has been already decompressed. Since $d \le |W|$ and the window size is up to a few megabytes, the copy operation does not elicit any cache miss, thus making the decompression process very fast indeed. The longer the window W, the longer the phrases may be, the fewer their number, and thus possibly the shorter the compressed output; but in terms of compression time, the longer the time to search for the longest copied α. Vice versa, the shorter W is, the worse the compression ratio, but the faster the compression time. This trade-off is evident and its magnitude depends on the input sequence. Surprisingly enough, the performance of the decompression stage is the opposite of the one experienced in the compression stage, since the number of phrases impacts on the number of copies to be executed and, thus, on the efficacy of the caching and prefetching in modern computers.

To slightly improve compression we make the following observation, which is due to Storer and Szymanski [5] and dates back to 1982. In the parsing process two situations may occur: either a (longest) match has been found, or it has not. In the former case, it is not reasonable to add the symbol following α (the third component in the triple), given that we advance anyway in the input sequence. In the latter case, it is not reasonable to emit two 0s (first two components of the triple) and thus waste one integer code. The simplest solution to these two inefficiencies is to always output a pair, rather than a triple, with the form $\langle d, |\alpha| \rangle$ or $\langle 0, B[1] \rangle$. This variant of LZ77 is named LZss, and it is often confused with LZ77, so we will use it from this point on.

By referring to the previous running example, LZss would obtain the following parsing:

$$\boxed{|\text{aabbabab}} \implies \langle 0, a \rangle$$
$$\boxed{\text{a}|\text{abbabab}} \implies \langle 1, 1 \rangle$$
$$\boxed{\text{aa}|\text{bbabab}} \implies \langle 0, b \rangle$$
$$\boxed{\text{aab}|\text{babab}} \implies \langle 1, 1 \rangle$$
$$\boxed{\text{aabb}|\text{abab}} \implies \langle 3, 2 \rangle$$
$$\boxed{\text{aabbab}|\text{ab}} \implies \langle 2, 2 \rangle$$

At decompression time, distinguishing which kind of pair is available is simple: just read the first integer and if it is zero then we are in the presence of a one-symbol phrase and the next bits encode that symbol; otherwise, we are in the presence of a copied phrase, whose distance is encoded in the read integer (larger than zero) and its length is encoded in the following bits.

gzip: a classic, nice, and fast implementation of LZ77. The key programming problem when implementing LZ77 is the *fast search* for the longest prefix α of B that starts in W. A brute-force algorithm that checks the occurrence of every prefix of B starting in W, via a linear backward scan, would be very time-consuming and thus unacceptable for compressing long files.

Fortunately, this process can be accelerated by using a suitable data structure. gzip, the most popular and classic implementation of LZ77, uses a hash table to determine α and find its previous occurrence in W. The idea is to store in the hash table all 3-grams occurring in $W \cdot B[1, 2]$, that is, all triplets of contiguous symbols, by using as *key* the 3-gram and as its *satellite* data the position in W where that 3-gram occurs. Since a 3-gram may repeat multiple times, the hash table saves for a given 3-gram all of its multiple occurrences, sorted by increasing position in S. Then when W shifts to the right, because of the emission of the pair $\langle d, \ell \rangle$, the hash table can be updated by deleting the 3-grams starting at $W[1, \ell]$, and inserting the 3-grams starting at $B[1, \ell]$. In total, this takes ℓ deletions from the hash table, and ℓ insertions into it.

The search for α is implemented as follows:

- First, the 3-gram $B[1, 3]$ is searched in the hash table. If it does not occur, then gzip emits the phrase $\langle 0, B[1] \rangle$, and the parsing advances by one single symbol. Otherwise, it determines the list $\mathcal{L}$ of occurrences of $B[1, 3]$ in $W \cdot B[1, 2]$.
- Then, for each position i in $\mathcal{L}$ (which is expressed as absolute position in S), the algorithm compares symbol-by-symbol the suffix $S[i, n]$ against B in order to compute their longest common prefix. At the end, the position $i^* \in \mathcal{L}$ sharing this longest common prefix is determined, hence α has been found.
- Finally, let p be the current position of B in S; the algorithm emits the pair $\langle p - i^*, |\alpha| \rangle$, and advances the window W and B of $|\alpha|$ positions.

gzip implements the encoding of the phrases by using Huffman over two alphabets: the one formed by the lengths of the copies plus the literals, and the other formed by the distances of the copies. This trick saves one extra bit in distinguishing between the two types of pairs. In fact, $\langle 0, c \rangle$ is represented as the Huffman encoding of c, and $\langle d, \ell \rangle$ is represented reversed by anticipating the Huffman encoding of ℓ. Given that literals and copy-lengths are encoded within the same alphabet, the decoder fetches the next codeword and decompresses it, so is able to distinguish whether the next item is a symbol c or a length ℓ. According to the result, it can either restart the decoding of the next pair (c has been decoded), or it can decode d (ℓ has been decoded) by using the other Huffman code.

`gzip` deploys an additional programming trick that further speeds up the compression process. It consists of sorting the list of occurrences of the 3-grams from the most recent to the oldest matches, and possibly stops the search for α when a sufficient number of candidates have been checked. This trades the length of the longest match against the speed of the search. As far as the size of the window W is concerned, `gzip` allows us to specify at the command line the options $-1, \ldots, -9$, which in fact means that W's size may vary from 100 KB to 900 KB, with a consequent improvement of the compression ratio, at the cost of slowing down the compression speed. As we have observed, the longer W is, the faster the decompression, because the smaller the number of encoded phrases, and thus the smaller the number of memory copies and cache misses induced by the Huffman decoding process.

For other implementations of LZ77, the reader can refer to Chapter 10, where we discussed the use of the suffix tree in the case of an unbounded window. Other interesting issues arise when we take into account the size of the compressed output (in bits), rather than just the number of phrases. The compressed size clearly depends on the number of phrases, but also upon the values of their integer components, in a way that cannot be underestimated [2]. Briefly, it is not necessarily the case that a longer α induces a shorter compressed file, because its copy might occur at a very far distance d, thus taking many bits for its encoding. Conversely, it might be better to divide α into two substrings which can be copied closely enough that the total number of bits required for their encoding is less than the ones needed for d.

13.2   LZ78

The sliding window used by LZ77 on the one hand speeds up the search for the longest phrase to encode, but on the other hand limits the search space, and thus the ultimate compression ratio. In order to avoid this problem and still keep a fast compression stage, Lempel and Ziv devised in 1978 another algorithm, which is consequently called LZ78 [8]. The key idea is to build *incrementally* an *explicit dictionary* that contains only a subset of the substrings of the input sequence S, selected according to a simple rule that we detail in the following paragraph. Concurrently, S is decomposed into phrases that are taken from the current dictionary, and encoded by compression schemes similar to the ones adopted for LZ77's phrases.

Phrase detection and dictionary update are deeply intermingled in LZ78. Adopting a similar notation as for LZ77, let B be the sequence yet to be parsed, and let $\mathcal{D}$ be

Input	Output	Dictionary
-	-	0: empty string
a	<0, a>	1: a
ab	<1, b>	2: ab
b	<0, b>	3: b
aba	<2, a>	4: aba
bb	<3, b>	5: bb
ba	<3, a>	6: ba
abab	<4, b>	7: abab
aa	<1, a>	8: aa

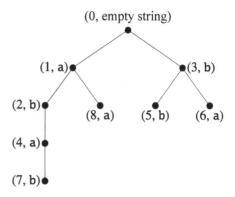

Figure 13.1 LZ78 parsing of the string $S = aabbababbbaababaa$, and the uncompacted trie built by the parsing algorithm upon the corresponding dictionary.

the current dictionary in which every phrase f is identified via the integer $\mathtt{id}(f)$. The parsing of B consists again of determining its longest prefix α that is also a phrase of $\mathcal{D}$, and substituting it with the pair $\langle \mathtt{id}(\alpha), c \rangle$, where c is the symbol following α in B, hence $c = B[|\alpha| + 1]$. Next, $\mathcal{D}$ is updated by adding the new phrase αc. Therefore, the dictionary is *prefix-complete* because it will contain all prefixes of all phrases in $\mathcal{D}$. Moreover, its size grows with the length of the input sequence. As occurred for LZ77, the stream of pairs generated by the LZ78 parsing can be encoded via a statistical compressor (such as Huffman or arithmetic) or via any variable-length integer coder. This will produce the compressed bit stream which is the eventual output of LZ78.

The decompressor works in a very similar way: it reads a pair $\langle \mathtt{id}, x \rangle$ from the compressed stream, determines the phrase α corresponding to the integer $\mathtt{id}$ in the current dictionary $\mathcal{D}$, emits the substring αc, and updates the current dictionary by adding that substring as a new phrase.

As an illustrative example, let us consider the sequence S depicted in Figure 13.1. The table on the left shows the sequence of phrases α detected in S by the LZ78 parsing, specified in the column Input, and substituted by pairs $\langle \mathtt{id}(\alpha), c \rangle$, specified in the column Output. The last column of the table shows the corresponding phrases αc incrementally added to the dictionary $\mathcal{D}$, and the $\mathtt{id}$s assigned to them. On the right of Figure 13.1 is shown the data structure adopted by LZ78 to implement, efficiently in time and space, the dictionary $\mathcal{D}$. This data structure is the *trie* (see Chapter 9), given that it supports fast insertion and prefix searches of strings. The prefix-complete property satisfied by $\mathcal{D}$ ensures that the trie is *uncompacted*, that is, every edge is labeled with a single symbol. In the figure, the trie shows close to each node u the pair $(\mathtt{id}(f), c)$ such that character c is the label of the trie edge incident into node u, and f is the phrase spelled out by the downward path starting from the trie root and leading to u. As an example, the node labeled with the pair $(8, a)$ corresponds to the dictionary string aa with $\mathtt{id} = 8$. It is not surprising to note that $\mathtt{id}$s are increasing as we traverse the trie downward, because longer phrases lengthen shorter phrases by appending just one symbol at a time. The encoding algorithm fits nicely on the trie structure. In fact, searching for the longest prefix of B, which is a dictionary phrase, can be implemented by traversing the trie according to B's symbols and matching edge labels until a trie leaf v is reached. The string spelled out by v is the detected phrase α. Then, the new phrase αc is easily inserted into the trie (and thus in $\mathcal{D}$) by just appending a new leaf to v, and labeling it with the symbol $c = B[|\alpha| + 1]$ and the id equal to the size of the dictionary before its insertion. As a final note, the size of the trie equals the *number* of dictionary strings and not their total length, because of the prefix-completeness property of LZ78's dictionaries.

The final question is how LZ78 manages large files and, thus, large dictionaries which host increasingly long phrases. There are a few possibilities to cope with this problem; we sketch here the most common ones. As soon as a maximum dictionary size is reached, (i) the dictionary is frozen by disallowing the entry of new strings (this approach may be advantageous in the case of an input sequence S that has the same recurring pattern of substrings); or (ii) the dictionary is discarded, and a new empty one is started (this approach may be advantageous whenever the input sequence S is structured in blocks, each with its own recurring pattern of substrings); or, finally, (iii) the dictionary is updated by inserting the new phrase and deleting one of the least recently used (this solution recalls a sort of LRU model in the way the dictionary is managed.)

13.3　LZW

A very popular variant of LZ78 is LZW, developed by Welch in 1984 [6], which is the reason for the addition of the letter W at the end of the algorithm's name. Its main objective is to avoid the need for the second component of the pair $\langle \text{id}(\alpha), c \rangle$, and thus for the byte representing the additional symbol. To accomplish this goal, before the start of the algorithm, all possible one-symbol strings are written to the dictionary. This means that the phrase-ids from 0 to 255 have been allocated to these one-byte symbols. Next, the parsing of S starts by searching, as usual, for the longest prefix α that matches a phrase in $\mathcal{D}$. Since the next prefix αc of B does not occur in $\mathcal{D}$, αc is then added to the dictionary, taking the next available id, and the next phrase to detect starts from c rather than from the following symbol, as is done in LZ78 and LZ77. So parsing and dictionary updating are *misaligned*, which makes decoding a bit tricky.

In fact, assume that decoding has to process two consecutive ids i' and i'', and call their corresponding dictionary phrases α' and α''. The decoder, in order to realign the dictionary, has to create the new phrase f from the reading of i' and i'', setting $f = \alpha' \alpha''[1]$, where $\alpha''[1]$ is the first character of the phrase α''. This seems easy to do but, indeed, it is not because α'' might not yet be available in $\mathcal{D}$.

For better understanding this concept, let us consider the time at which the compressor emitted i' for α' and inserted $f = \alpha' \alpha''[1]$ in $\mathcal{D}$. Clearly, the compressor knows α'' (because it knows S), and so it can construct f and insert it in the dictionary. But if the next phrase is exactly the one just inserted, namely $\alpha'' = f$, then the decompressor is in trouble, because it needs to construct f as $\alpha' \alpha''[1] = \alpha' f[1]$, and thus it needs

Input	Output	Dictionary
a	-	0-255:'\0'-'\255'
a	97 (a)	256: aa
b	97 (a)	257: ab
b	98 (b)	258: bb
ab	98 (b)	259: ba
aba	257 (ab)	260: aba
eof	260 (aba)	261: aba EOF

Input	Dictionary		Output
-	0-255:'\0'-'\255'		
97	256:	a?	a
97	256:	aa	a
	257:	a?	
98	257:	ab	b
	258:	b?	
98	258:	bb	b
	259:	b?	
257	259:	ba	ab
	260:	ab?	
260	261:	aba	aba

Figure 13.2 We assume that the LZW dictionary starts with all single ASCII symbols into it, having ids from 0 to 255. (Left) LZW encoding of $S = aabbabab$; 97 and 98 are the ASCII codes for a and b. (Right) LZW decoding of the id-stream: $97, 97, 98, 98, 257, 260$.

the first symbol of the phrase under construction. However, this recursive definition of f can be solved by noting that $|\alpha'| \geq 1$, so $f[1] = \alpha'[1]$. Hence the LZW decoder can construct f as $\alpha'\alpha'[1]$, thus using only phrases available in the current dictionary. Then f is inserted in $\mathcal{D}$, and thus LZW realigns the dictionaries available at the compression and decompression stages after the reading of i'.

Figure 13.2 shows a running example for the encoding (left) and the decoding (right) stages of LZW, applied to the string $S = aabbabab$. The dictionary starts with all the possible 256 symbols in the ASCII code, so the new phrases take ids from 256 on. The question mark (i.e. ?), specified closely to each phrase in the column Dictionary of the right-hand table, indicates the misalignment of the decoding stage, which needs to defer the construction of the current dictionary phrase until the next one is available. And, in fact, the right-hand table reports pairs of lines per each constructed phrase. All of these constructions are possible, because they involve available dictionary phrases, except for the last one with $id = 260$. In fact, that id triggers the special case we have discussed, because after reading the $id = 257$, its corresponding phrase $\alpha' = ab$ is available in $\mathcal{D}$, but the phrase α'' with $id = 260$ is not yet in the dictionary. Nevertheless, by using this observation, we can conclude that $f = \alpha'\alpha'[1] = ab\,a$, and can insert it into the dictionary, and thus realign the dictionaries available at the LZW's encoder and decoder.

Similarly to the LZ77 algorithm, LZW has many commonly used implementations, among which is the popular GIF image format.[1] It assumes that the original (uncompressed) image uses eight bits per pixel, so the alphabet has size 256, and the input sequence S comes as a stream of bytes, obtained by reading the pixels of the image row by row.[2] Since eight bits are very few to represent all possible colours of an image,

---

[1] See "GIF" at https://en.wikipedia.org/wiki/GIF.

[2] Actually, the GIF format can also present the rows in an *interleaved* format, the details of which are out of the scope of this brief discussion; the compression algorithm is, however, the same.

each value is actually an index in a *palette*, whose entries are 24-bit descriptions of the actual colour (the typical RGB format). In any case, this restricts the maximum number of different colours present in an image to 256. Some researchers [3] also explored the possibility of introducing a *lossy* variant of GIF compression, without changing the way the output is represented [5]. The basic idea is quite simple: instead of looking for the longest *exact* match in the dictionary while parsing, it performs some kind of *approximate* matching, thus finding potentially longer phrases, which reduces the output size, but at the cost of representing a slightly different image. Approximate matching of two strings of colours is done with a measure of difference based on their actual RGB values, which must be guaranteed to not exceed a threshold in order to not distort the original image too much.

13.4   On the Optimality of Compressors$^\infty$

The literature shows many results regarding the optimality of LZ-inspired algorithms. Lempel and Ziv themselves demonstrated that LZ77 is optimal for a certain family of sources (see [7]), and that LZ78 asymptotically reaches the best compression ratio among finite-state compressors (see [8]). Optimality here means that, assuming the string to compress is infinite and is produced by a *stationary ergodic source with a finite alphabet*, then the compression ratio asymptotically approaches to the entropy of the underlying source. More recent results made it possible to have a quantitative estimate of an algorithm's *redundancy*, which is a measure of the distance between the source's entropy and the compression ratio, and can thereby be seen as a measure of "how fast" the algorithm reaches the source's entropy.

All these measures are very interesting, but unrealistic because it is quite unusual, if not impossible, to know the entropy of the source that generated the string we are going to compress. In order to circumvent this problem, a different empirical approach has been taken by introducing the notion of *k-th order empirical entropy* of a string S, denoted by $\mathcal{H}_k(S)$. In Chapter 12 we discussed the case $k = 0$, which depends on the frequencies of the individual symbols occurring in S. Here, we wish with $\mathcal{H}_k(S)$ to empower the entropy definition by considering the frequencies of k-grams in S, thus taking into account subsequences of symbols, hence the *compositional structure* of S.

More precisely, let S be a string over an alphabet $\Sigma = \{\sigma_1, \ldots, \sigma_h\}$, and let us denote by n_ω the number of occurrences of the substring ω in S. We use the notation $\omega \in \Sigma^k$ to specify that the length of ω is k. Given this notation, we can define

$$\mathcal{H}_k(S) = \frac{1}{|S|} \sum_{\omega \in \Sigma^k} \left(\sum_{i=1}^{h} n_{\omega\sigma_i} \log\left(\frac{n_\omega}{n_{\omega\sigma_i}} \right) \right).$$

A compression algorithm is then defined as being *coarsely optimal* if and only if, for all k there exists a function $f_k(n)$ approaching to 0 as $n \to \infty$ such that, for all sequences S of increasing length, it holds that the compression ratio of the evaluated algorithm is at most $\mathcal{H}_k(S) + f_k(|S|)$. Plotnik, Weinberger, and Ziv proved the coarse optimality of LZ78 [4]; Kosaraju and Manzini [1] noted that the notion of coarse optimality does not necessarily imply a good algorithm because, if the entropy of the string S approaches zero, the algorithm can still compress badly because of the additive term $f_k(|S|)$.

Lemma 13.1 *There exist strings for which the compression ratio achieved by LZ78 is at least $g(|S|) \times \mathcal{H}_0(S)$, where $\lim_{n\to\infty} g(n) = \infty$.*

Proof Consider the string $S = 01^{n-1}$, which has entropy $\mathcal{H}_0(S) = \Theta(\frac{\log n}{n})$. It is easy to see that LZ78 parses S with $\Theta(\sqrt{n})$ phrases. Thus we get $g(n) = \frac{\sqrt{n}}{\log n}$. So $\mathcal{H}_0(S)$ decreases for increasingly long S, but LZ78's compression ratio decreases at a slower rate. ∎

This observation is equivalent to the one we made for Huffman, related to the extra bit needed for each encoded symbol. That extra bit was okay for large entropies, but it was considered bad for entropies approaching 0. To circumvent these inefficiencies, Kosaraju and Manzini introduced a stricter version of optimality, called λ-optimality, which applies to any algorithm whose compression ratio can be bounded by $\lambda \mathcal{H}_k(S) + o(\mathcal{H}_k(S))$. As the previous lemma clearly demonstrates, LZ78 is not λ-optimal; however there is a modified version of LZ78, combined with run-length compression (described in the next chapter), which is 3-optimal with respect to $\mathcal{H}_0$, but it has been shown to be not λ-optimal for all $k \geq 1$.

Let us now turn our attention to LZ77, which seems to be more powerful than LZ78, given that its dictionary is richer in substrings. The practical variant of LZ77 that uses a fixed-size compression window is not much good, and is actually worse than LZ78:

Lemma 13.2 *The LZ77 algorithm, with a bounded sliding window, is not coarsely optimal.*

Proof For each size L of the sliding window, we can find a string S for which the compression ratio exceeds its k-th order entropy. Consider the string $(0^k 1^k)^n 1$ of length $2kn + 1$ bits, and choose $k = L - 1$. Due to the sliding window, LZ77 parses S in the following way:

$$\underline{0}\ 0^{k-1}1\ 1^{k-1}0\ 0^{k-1}1 \ldots 1^{k-1}0\ 0^{k-1}1\ 1^k.$$

Every phrase then has a length up to k, splitting the input into $\Theta(n)$ phrases, and thus achieving an output size $\Omega(n)$.

In order to compute $\mathcal{H}_k(S)$ we need to work on all different k-length substrings of S, which are $2k$: $\{0^i 1^{k-i}\}_{i=1\ldots k} \cup \{1^i 0^{k-i}\}_{i=1\ldots k}$. Now, all strings having the form $0^i 1^{k-i}$ are always followed by a 1. Similarly, all strings having the form $1^i 0^{k-i}$ are always followed by a 0. Only the string 1^k is followed $n-1$ times by a 0, and once by a 1. So we can split the sum over the k-grams ω within the definition of $\mathcal{H}_k(S)$ into four parts:

$\omega \in \{0^i 1^{k-i}\}_{i=1\ldots k}$	$\to n_{\omega 0} = 0$	$n_{\omega 1} = n$
$\omega \in \{1^i 0^{k-i}\}_{i=1\ldots k-1}$	$\to n_{\omega 0} = n$	$n_{\omega 1} = 0$
$\omega = 1^k$	$\to n_{\omega 0} = n-1$	$n_{\omega 1} = 1$
else	$\to n_{\omega 0} = 0$	$n_{\omega 1} = 0$.

It is now easy to calculate

$$|S|\,\mathcal{H}_k(S) = \log n + (n-1)\log\frac{n}{n-1} \;=\; \Theta(\log n),$$

and the lemma follows. ∎

If we waive the sliding window, then LZ77 is coarsely optimal and also δ-optimal with respect to $\mathcal{H}_0$. However, it is not λ-optimal for any $k \geq 1$:

Lemma 13.3 *There exist strings for which the compression ratio of LZ77, with no sliding window, is at least $g(|S|) \times \mathcal{H}_1(S)$, with $\lim_{n\to\infty} g(n) = \infty$.*

Proof Consider the string $10^k\,2^{2^k}\,1\,101\,10^2 1\,10^3 1\ldots 10^k 1$ of length $2^k + O(k^2)$, and k-th-order entropy bound $|S|\,\mathcal{H}_k(S) = k\log k + O(k)$. The string is parsed with $k+4$ phrases:

$$\underline{1}\,\underline{0}\,\underline{0^{k-1}2}\,\underline{2^{2^k-1}1}\,\underline{101}\,\underline{10^2 1}\ldots\underline{10^k 1}.$$

The problem is that the last k phrases refer back to the beginning of S, which is 2^k characters away. This generates $\Omega(k)$ long phrases, thus an overall output size of $\Omega(k^2)$ bits. ∎

So LZ77 is better than LZ78, as expected, but not as good as we would like, for $k \geq 1$. The next chapter will introduce the Burrows–Wheeler transform, proposed in 1994, which addresses the inefficiencies of LZ-based methods by devising a novel approach to data compression which achieves λ-optimality, for very small λ and simultaneously for all $k \geq 0$. It is therefore not surprising that the BWT-based compressor `bzip2`, available in most operating system distributions, produces a more succinct output than `gzip` and has got much visibility and interest within the data compression community, and elsewhere.

References

[1] S. Rao Kosaraju and Giovanni Manzini. Compression of low entropy strings with Lempel–Ziv algorithms. *Siam Journal on Computing*, 29(3): 893–911, 1999.

[2] Paolo Ferragina, Igor Nitto, and Rossano Venturini. On the bit-complexity of Lempel–Ziv compression. *SIAM Journal on Computing*, 42(4): 1521–41, 2013.

[3] Steven Pigeon. An optimizing lossy generalization of LZW. *Proceedings of the IEEE Data Compression Conference*, 509, 2001.

[4] Eli Plotnik, Marcelo Weinberger, and Jacob Ziv. Upper bounds on the probability of sequences emitted by finite-state sources and on the redundancy of the Lempel–Ziv algorithm. *IEEE Transactions on Information Theory*, 38: 16–24, 1992.

[5] James A. Storer and Thomas G. Szymanski. Data compression via textual substitution. *Journal of the ACM*, 29(4): 928–51, 1982.

[6] Terry A. Welch. A technique for high-performance data compression. *Computer*, 17(6): 8–19, 1984.

[7] Jacob Ziv and Abraham Lempel. A universal algorithm for sequential data compression. *IEEE Transactions on Information Theory*, 23(3): 337–43, 1977.

[8] Jacob Ziv and Abraham Lempel. Compression of individual sequences via variable-rate coding. *IEEE Transactions on Information Theory*, 24(5): 530–6, 1978.

14 Block-Sorting Compression

Years passed, and it became clear that David
had no thought of publishing the algorithm –
he was too busy thinking of new things.
Mike Burrows

This chapter describes a lossless data compression technique devised by Mike Burrows and David Wheeler at the DEC Systems Research Center.[1] This technique was published in a technical report of the company [4, 9], and since it was rejected by the 1994 IEEE Data Compression Conference (as Mike Burrows stated in its foreword to [10][2]), the two authors decided not to publish their paper anywhere. Fortunately, Mark Nelson drew attention to it in an article in *Dr. Dobb's Journal*, and that was enough to ensure its survival and successful spread through the scientific community.

In fact, a wonderful thing about publishing an idea is that a greater number of minds can be brought to bear on the surrounding problems. This is what happened with the Burrows–Wheeler transform, whose studies exploded around the year 2000, leading a group of researchers to celebrate a ten-year-later resume in a special issue of *Theoretical Computer Science* [10]. In that volume, Mike Burrows again declined to publish the original technical report but wrote a wonderful foreword dedicated to the memory of David Wheeler, who passed away in 2004, and stated at the end "This issue of Theoretical Computer Science is an example of how an idea can be improved and generalized when more people are involved. I feel sure that David Wheeler would be pleased to see that his technique has inspired so much interesting work."

The *Burrows–Wheeler transform* (BWT) offered a revolutionary alternative to dictionary-based and statistical compressors by initiating a new class of data compression approaches (such as `bzip2` [19] or booster [7]), as well as a new powerful class of compressed indexes (such as, the FM-index [8], and many variations of it [16]). In the following we will detail the BWT and the other two simple compressors, Move-to-Front and Run-Length Encoding, whose combination constitutes the design core

---

[1] Mike Burrows: "In the technical report that described the BWT, I gave the year as 1981, but later, with access to the memory of his wife Joyce, we deduced that it must have been 1978." [10].

[2] Mike Burrows: "Years passed, and it became clear that David had no thought of publishing the algorithm – he was too busy thinking of new things. Eventually, I decided to force his hand: I could not make him write a paper, but I could write a paper with him, given the right excuse."

of `bzip`-based compressors, also known as *block-sorting compressors*. We will also briefly mention some theoretical issues about the BWT performance expressed in terms of the k-th order empirical entropy of the data to be compressed, and sketch the main algorithmic issues that underlie the design of the first provably compressed index to date, namely the FM-index.

14.1 The Burrows–Wheeler Transform

The *Burrows–Wheeler transform* is not a compression algorithm per se, as it does not squeeze the input size. It is a *permutation* (and thus, a lossless transformation) of the input symbols, which are laid down in a way that the resulting string is most suitably compressed via simple algorithms, such as *Move-to-Front coding* (MTF) and *Run Length Encoding* (RLE), both to be described in Section 14.2. This permutation forces some "locally homogeneous" properties in the ordering of the symbols that can be fully deployed, efficiently and efficaciously, by the combination MTF + RLE. A last statistical encoding step (e.g. Huffman or arithmetic) is finally executed in order to eventually squeeze the output bit stream. All these steps constitute the backbone of any `bzip`-like compressor, which will be discussed in Section 14.3.

The BWT consists of a pair of inverse transformations: a *forward transform*, which rearranges the symbols in the input string; and a *backward transform*, which somewhat magically reconstructs the original string from its BWT. It goes without saying that the invertibility of BWT is necessary to guarantee the decompression of the input file.

14.1.1 The Forward Transform

Let $S[1, n]$ be an input string on n symbols drawn from an *ordered* alphabet Σ. We append to S a special symbol $ which does not occur in Σ and is assumed to be smaller than any other symbol in the alphabet, according to its total ordering.[3]

The forward transform proceeds as follows:

1. Build the string S.
2. Consider the *conceptual* matrix $\mathcal{M}$ of size $(n + 1) \times (n + 1)$, whose rows contain all the cyclic left-shifts of string S. $\mathcal{M}$ is called the *rotation matrix* of S.[4]
3. Sort the rows of $\mathcal{M}$ reading them *left to right* and according to the ordering defined on the alphabet $\Sigma \cup \{\$\}$. The final matrix is called $\mathcal{M}'$. Since $ is smaller than any other symbol in Σ, the first row of $\mathcal{M}'$ is S.
4. Set $bw(S) = (\widehat{L}, r)$ as the output of the algorithm, where $\widehat{L}$ is the string obtained by reading the last column of $\mathcal{M}'$, sans symbol $, and r is the position of $ there.

---

[3] The step that concatenates the special symbol $ to the initial string was not part of the original version of the algorithm as described by Burrows and Wheeler. It is introduced here with the intent of simplifying the description.

[4] The left shift of a string $a\alpha$ is the string αa, that is, the first symbol is moved to the end of the original string.

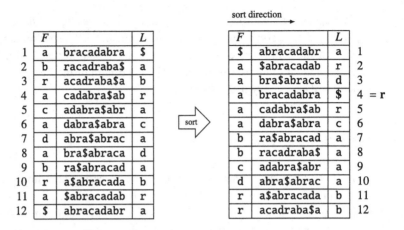

Figure 14.1 Forward Burrows–Wheeler transform of the string $S =$ abracadabra.

We have called $\mathcal{M}$ a conceptual matrix because we have to avoid its explicit construction, which otherwise would make the BWT just an elegant mathematical object: the size of $\mathcal{M}$ is quadratic in $bw(S)$'s length, so the conceptual matrix would have the size of terabytes just for transforming a string of a few megabytes. In Section 14.3 we will show that $\mathcal{M}'$ can be built in time and space linear in the length of the input string S, by resorting to the construction of suffix arrays (introduced in Chapter 10).

An alternate enunciation of the algorithm, less frequent yet still present in the literature [20], constructs matrix $\mathcal{M}'$ by sorting the rows of $\mathcal{M}$ reading them *right to left* (i.e. starting from the last symbol of every row). Then, it takes the string $\widehat{F}$ formed by scanning the first column of $\mathcal{M}'$ top to bottom and, again, skipping symbol $ and storing its position in r'. The output is then $bw(S) = (\widehat{F}, r')$. This enunciation is somewhat equivalent of the one already described because it is possible to formally prove that strings $\widehat{F}$ and $\widehat{L}$ both exhibit the same *local homogeneity* properties, and thus compression. In the rest of the chapter we will refer to the left-to-right sorting of $\mathcal{M}$'s rows and to $(\widehat{L}, r)$ as the BWT of the string S.

In order to better understand the power of the Burrows–Wheeler transform, let us consider the following running example formulated over the string $S =$ abracadabra. The left side of Figure 14.1 shows the rotated matrix $\mathcal{M}$ built over S, whereas the right side of Figure 14.1 shows the sorted matrix $\mathcal{M}'$. Because the first row of $\mathcal{M}$ is the only one to end with $, which is the lowest-ordered symbol in the alphabet, row $abracadabra is the first row of $\mathcal{M}'$. The other three rows of $\mathcal{M}'$ are the ones beginning with a, and then follow the rows starting with b, c, d, and finally r, respectively.

If we read the first column of $\mathcal{M}'$, denoted by F, we obtain the string $aaaaaabbcdr which is the sorted sequence of all symbols in the input string $S$$. We finally obtain $\widehat{L}$ by excluding the single occurrence of $ from the last column L, so $\widehat{L} =$ ardrcaaaabb, and set $r = 4$.

This example is illustrative of the locally homogeneous property we have mentioned: the last six symbols of the last column of $\mathcal{M}$ form a highly repetitive string aaaabb which can be easily and highly compressed via the two simple compressors MTF + RLE (described in Section 14.2). The soundness of this statement will be mathematically sustained in the following pages; here we content ourselves with observing that this repetitiveness does not occur by chance but is induced by the way $\mathcal{M}$'s rows are sorted (left to right) and texts are written by humans (left to right). The nice issue here is that there are many real sources (called Markovian) that generate data sequences, other than texts, that can be converted to be locally homogeneous via the Burrows–Wheeler transform, and thus can be highly compressed by bzip-like compressors.

14.1.2 The Backward Transform

We observe, both by construction and from the example we have provided, that each column of the sorted cyclic-shift matrix $\mathcal{M}'$ (and, indeed, also $\mathcal{M}$) contains a permutation of $S\$$. In particular, its first column $F = \$aaaaabbcdr$ is alphabetically sorted and thus it represents the most-compressible transformation of the input string $S\$$. But unfortunately F cannot be used as BWT because it is not invertible: every text of length 10 and consisting of five occurrences of symbol a, two occurrences of b, and one occurrence each of c, d, r respectively, generates a BWT whose F is the same as the one of the string $S\$$. The Burrows–Wheeler transform represents, in some sense, the best column of $\mathcal{M}'$ to be chosen as a transformation of the input string in terms of its reversibility and compressibility.

In order to prove these properties more formally, let us define a useful function that tells us how to locate in $\mathcal{M}'$ the predecessor of a symbol at a given index in S.

Fact 14.1 For $1 \leq i \leq n + 1$, let $S[k_i, n]$ denote the (possibly empty) suffix of S prefixing row i of $\mathcal{M}'$. Clearly, this suffix is then followed in row i by symbol $\$$, and then by the (possibly empty) prefix $S[1, k_i - 1]$ because of the leftward cyclic shift of the rows in $\mathcal{M}'$.

For example, in Figure 14.1, row 3 of $\mathcal{M}'$ is prefixed by abra, followed by $\$$, and then by abracad.

Property 1: The symbol $L[i]$ precedes the symbol $F[i]$ in the string S except for the row i ending with $\$$ (i.e. $L[i] = \$$), in which case $F[i] = S[1]$.

Proof Because of Fact 14.1, the last symbol of the row i is $L[i] = S[k_i - 1]$ and its first symbol is $F[i] = S[k_i]$. So the statement follows. ∎

Intuitively, this property derives from the very nature of every row in $\mathcal{M}$ and $\mathcal{M}'$ that is a *left* cyclic shift of $S\$$, so if we take two extremes of each row, the symbol on the right extreme (i.e. on L) is immediately followed by the one on the left extreme (i.e. on F) over the string S. The following property is the key one to design the BWT's backward transform.

Property 2: All the occurrences of a same symbol c in L maintain the same relative order as in F. This means that the k-th occurrence in L of symbol c corresponds to the k-th occurrence of the symbol c in F.

Proof Given two strings t and t', we shall use the notation $t \prec t'$ to indicate that string t lexicographically precedes string t'. Fix now a symbol c occurring in the input string S. If c occurs once, then the proof derives immediately because the single occurrence of c in F obviously maps to the single occurrence of c in L. (Both columns are permutations of S.)

To prove the more complex situation where c occurs at least twice in S, let us fix two of these occurrences in F, say F[i] and F[j] with $i < j$, and pick their rows (strings) in the sorted matrix $\mathcal{M}'$, say $r(i)$ and $r(j)$. We can observe a few interesting things:

- Row $r(i)$ precedes lexicographically row $r(j)$, given the ordering of $\mathcal{M}'$'s rows and the fact that $i < j$, by assumption.
- Both rows $r(i)$ and $r(j)$ start with symbol c, by assumption.
- Given that $r(i) = c\alpha$ and $r(j) = c\beta$, we have $\alpha \prec \beta$.

Since we are interested in the respective positions of those two occurrences of c when they are mapped to L, we consider the two rows $r(i')$ and $r(j')$ that are obtained by rotating $r(i)$ and $r(j)$ leftward by one single symbol: $r(i') = \alpha c$ and $r(j') = \beta c$. This rotation then brings the first symbol $F[i]$ (resp. $F[j']$) to the last symbol $L[i']$ (resp. $L[j']$) of the rotated rows. By assumption $\alpha \prec \beta$, so we have $r(i') \prec r(j')$ and so the ordering in L of that pair of occurrences of c is preserved. Given that this order-preserving property holds for every pair of occurrences of c in F and L, it holds true for all of them.   ∎

We now have all the mathematical tools to design an algorithm that reconstructs S from its $bw(S) = (\widehat{L}, r)$ by exploiting the following LF-mapping.

Definition 14.1 $LF[1, n + 1]$ is an array of $n + 1$ integers in the range $[1, n + 1]$ such that $LF[i] = j$ if and only if the symbol $L[i]$ maps to symbol $F[j]$. Thus, if $L[i]$ is the k-th occurrence in L of symbol c, then $F[LF[i]]$ is the k-th occurrence of c in F.

Building LF is pretty straightforward for symbols that occur only once, as is the case for $, c, and d in our running example of $S = $ abracadabra$; see Figure 14.1. But when it comes to symbols a, b, and r, which occur several times in the string S, computing LF efficiently is no longer trivial. Nonetheless, it can be solved in optimal $O(n)$ time thanks to Property 2, as Algorithm 14.1 details. This algorithm uses an auxiliary vector C, of size $|\Sigma| + 1$, because of the addition of $ to S. For the sake of description, we assume that array C is indexed by a *symbol* rather than by an integer.[5]

---

[5] Just implement C as a hash table, or observe that in practice any symbol is encoded via an integer (ASCII code maps to the range $0, \ldots, 255$) which can be used as its index in C.

Algorithm 14.1 Constructing the LF-mapping from column L

 1: **for** $i = 1, \ldots, n + 1$ **do**
 2:      $C[L[i]]$++;
 3: **end for**
 4: $temp = 0$, $sum = 1$;
 5: **for** $i = 1, \ldots, |\Sigma| + 1$ **do**
 6:      $temp = C[i]$;
 7:      $C[i] = sum$;
 8:      sum += $temp$;
 9: **end for**
10: **for** $i = 1, \ldots, n$ **do**
11:      $LF[i] = C[L[i]]$;
12:      $C[L[i]]$++;
13: **end for**

The first for-loop in Algorithm 14.1 computes, for each symbol c, the number n_c of its occurrences in L, and thus it sets $C[c] = n_c$ (we assume that C's entries are null at the beginning and that their indexes are given by symbols' rank). Then, the second for-loop turns these symbol-wise occurrences into a cumulative sum, so that the new value in $C[c]$ denotes the total number of occurrences in L of symbols *smaller than c* increased by 1, namely $C[c] = 1 + \sum_{x<c} n_x$. This is done by adopting two auxiliary variables (i.e. temp and sum), so that the overall working space is still $O(n)$. We note that $C[c]$ after Step 7 gives the first position in F where symbol c occurs. Therefore, before the last for-loop starts, $C[c]$ is the landing position in F of the first c in L (we thus know the LF-mapping for the first occurrence of every alphabet symbol). Finally, the last for-loop scans the column L and, whenever it encounters symbol $L[i] = c$, it sets $LF[i] = C[c]$. This is correct when c is met for the first time; then $C[c]$ is incremented in line 12 so that the next occurrence of c in L will map to the next position in F (given the contiguities in F of all rows starting with that symbol). So the algorithm keeps the invariant that $LF[c] = \sum_{x<c} n_x + k$, after $k - 1$ occurrences of c in L have been processed. It is easy to derive the time complexity of such computation, which is $O(n)$.

Given the LF-mapping and the fundamental properties we have shown, we are able to reconstruct S backwards, starting from the transformed output $bw(S) = (\widehat{L}, r)$ in $O(n)$ time and space. Clearly, it is easy to construct L from $bw(S)$: just insert $ at position r of $\widehat{L}$. The algorithm then picks the last symbol of S, namely $S[n]$, which can be easily identified at $L[1]$, given that the first row of $\mathcal{M}'$ is $S. Then it proceeds by moving one symbol at a time to the left in S, deploying the two properties above: Property 2 allows us to map the current symbol occurring in L (initially $L[1]$) to its corresponding copy in F; then Property 1 allows us to find the symbol which precedes that copy in F by taking the symbol at the end of the same row (i.e. the one in L). This double step, which returns the algorithmic focus to L, allows us to move one symbol leftward in S. Repeating this for $n - 1$ steps, we are able to reconstruct the original

---

Algorithm 14.2 Reconstructing S from $bw(S)$

1: Derive column L from $bw(S)$;

2: Compute $LF[1, n + 1]$ from L;   // by Algorithm 14.1

3: $k = 1$; $i = n$;

4: **while** $i > 0$ **do**

5:     $S[i] = L[k]$;

6:     $k = LF[k]$;

7:     $i--$;

8: **end while**

---

input string S. The pseudocode of the BWT-backward transformation is reported in Algorithm 14.2.

As an example, refer to Figure 14.1, where $L[1] = S[n] = $ a, and execute the while-loop of Algorithm 14.2. Definition 14.1 guarantees that $LF[1]$ points to the first row starting with a; this is row 2. So that copy of a is LF-mapped to $F[2]$ (and in fact $F[2] = $ a), and the preceding symbol in S is thus $L[2] = $ r. These two basic steps are repeated until the whole string S is reconstructed. Continuing the previous running example, $L[2] = $ r is LF-mapped to the symbol in F at position $LF[2] = 11$ (and indeed, $F[11] = $ r). In fact, $L[2]$ and $F[11]$ are the first occurrence of symbol r in both columns L and F, respectively. The algorithm then takes as the preceding symbol of r in S the symbol $L[11] = $ b. And so on...

Theorem 14.1 *The original input string S can be reconstructed from its BWT in $O(n)$ time and space. Algorithm 14.2 may elicits one cache miss per symbol.*

Several recent studies have addressed the problem of reducing the number of cache misses as well as the working space of algorithms inverting the BWT. Some progress has been made in the literature (see, e.g., [18, 13, 14, 12]), but so far the improvements have been limited, for example small constants for the cache misses, which get larger if the data is highly repetitive. There is still much to be discovered here!

14.2   Two Other Simple Transforms

Let us now focus on two simple algorithms that turn out to be very useful in designing the compressor bzip2. These algorithms are called *Move-to-Front* (MTF) and *Run-Length Encoding* (RLE). The former maps symbols into integers, and the latter maps runs of equal symbols into pairs of the form ⟨symbol, integer⟩. For the sake of completeness we observe that RLE is actually a compressor, because the output sequence may be reduced in length in the presence of long runs of equal symbols, while MTF can be turned into a compressor by encoding the output integers via proper variable-length encoders. In general, the compression performance of those algorithms is very poor: BWT is, magically, their killer application!

S: "bananacocco"
Σ : $\{a, b, c, n, o\}$

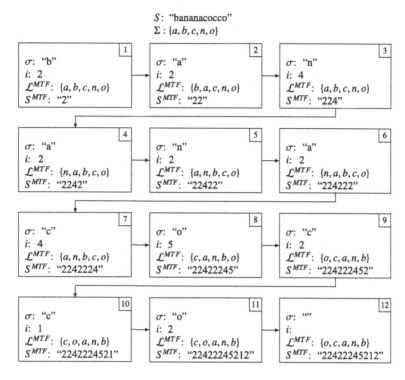

Figure 14.2 An example of MTF transform over the string S = bananacocco, alphabet $\Sigma = \{a, b, c, n, o\}$ and thus index set $\{1, 2, 3, 4, 5\}$ for the list $\mathcal{L}^{MTF}$.

14.2.1 The Move-to-Front Transform

The MTF-transform is discussed in [3], and implements the idea that every symbol of a string S can be replaced with its index in a proper *dynamic* list $\mathcal{L}^{MTF}$ containing all alphabet symbols. The string produced in output, denoted hereafter as S^{MTF}, is initialized to the empty string and contains as symbols integers in the range $[1, |\Sigma|]$. At each step i, MTF processes the symbol $S[i]$ and finds its position p in $\mathcal{L}^{MTF}$ (counting from 1). Then p is appended to the string S^{MTF}, and $\mathcal{L}^{MTF}$ is modified by *moving* the symbol $S[i]$ to the *front* of the list.

It may be greatly advantageous to apply this processing over the column L of $bw(S)$ because, as will soon be clear, it transforms *locally homogeneous substrings* of L into a *globally homogeneous string* L^{MTF}, in which small integers abound. At this point we can apply any integer compressor, described in Chapter 11, or deploy, as bzip does, the structural properties of L^{MTF} to apply, in cascade, RLE and finally a statistical encoder (such as Huffman, arithmetic, or some of their "variants" see Chapter 12).

Figure 14.2 shows a running example for MTF over the string S = bananacocco, which consists of five distinct symbols $\{a, b, c, n, o\}$ and thus index set $\{1, 2, 3, 4, 5\}$ for the list $\mathcal{L}^{MTF}$. It is evident that the most frequent symbols are frequently to the front of the list $\mathcal{L}^{MTF}$, and thus get smaller indices in S^{MTF}; this is the principle exploited

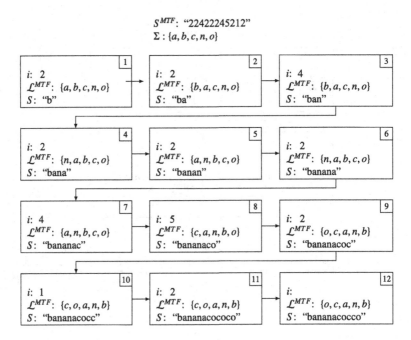

S^{MTF}: "22422245212"
Σ : $\{a, b, c, n, o\}$

Figure 14.3 An example of MTF-inversion over the string $S^{MTF} = 22422245212$, starting with the list $\mathcal{L}^{MTF} = \{a, b, c, n, o\}$.

in [3] to prove some compressibility bounds for the compressor that applies γ-coding over the integers in S^{MTF} (see the following Theorem 14.3).

We notice two local homogeneous substrings in S – namely, "anana" and "cocco" – which show individually some redundancy in a few symbols (such as $\{a, n\}$ and $\{c, o\}$, respectively). The nice thing about the MTF-mapping is that such homogeneous substrings are changed into substrings of S^{MTF}, consisting of small integers. As a result, the strong local-homogeneity properties of the column L in $bw(S)$ will thus make L^{MTF} full of 1s, so the use of the *simple compressor* RLE is worth and effective.

Inverting S^{MTF} is easy, provided that we start with the same initial list $\mathcal{L}^{MTF}$ used for the MTF transformation of S. Therefore, the initial $\mathcal{L}^{MTF}$ should be part of the preamble of the compressed file produced by MTF. A running example is provided in Figure 14.3. The algorithm turns every integer i in S^{MTF} into the symbol that occurs at position i in $\mathcal{L}^{MTF}$, and then moves that symbol to the front of the list. The inversion algorithm thus mimics the transformation algorithm, by keeping both MTF lists synchronized.

Theorem 14.2 *Transforming a string S via MTF takes $O(|S|)$ time and $O(|\Sigma|)$ working space.*

A key concept for evaluating the compression performance of MTF is the one named *locality of reference*, which we have previously refered to as *locally homogeneous substrings*. Locality of references in S means that the distance between consecutive occurrences of the same symbol is small. For example, the string bananacocco shows this feature in the substrings anana and cocco. We are perfectly aware that this concept is roughly specified but, for now, let us stick to this intuitive formulation, which we will soon make mathematically precise.

If the input string S exhibits locality of references, then the MTF-compressor (namely one that MTF transforms S and then compresses the integers in S^{MTF}) performs better than the Huffman compressor. This might appear surprising, because the Huffman compressor is an *optimal prefix-free code* (as proved in Chapter 12); but, actually, it should not be surprising, because the MTF-compressor is not a prefix-free code, given that a symbol may be *dynamically* associated to different codewords. As an example, look at Figure 14.2 and note that the symbol c gets three different numbers in S^{MTF} – i.e. $4, 2, 1$ – and thus three different codewords.

Lemma 14.1 *The compressor based on the combination of the MTF transform and γ-code can be better than the Huffman compressor by the unbounded factor $\Omega(\log n)$, where n is the length of the string to be compressed.*

Proof Take the string $S = 1^n 2^n \cdots n^n$ defined over an integer alphabet of size n and having length n^2. Since every symbol occurs n times, the distribution is uniform and thus Huffman code uses for each symbol $\Theta(\log_2 n)$ bits. The overall compression of S by Huffman code then takes $\Theta(|S| \log n) = \Theta(n^2 \log n)$ bits.

If we apply the MTF transform to S, we get the string $S^{MTF} = 1^n 2 1^{n-1} 3 1^{n-1} 4 \cdots$. Compressing this string via the γ-code, we get an output bit sequence of length $O(n^2 + n \log n)$. This is due to the fact that the $\Theta(n^2)$ integers equal to 1 are encoded as $\gamma(1) = 1$, thus taking one bit, whereas all other integers (they are $n - 1$ and of value at most n) are encoded with $O(\log n)$ bits each. ∎

Conversely, if the input string S does not exhibit any kind of locality of reference (e.g. it is a (quasi-)random string over the alphabet Σ), then the MTF-compressor performs worse than the Huffman compressor, but not actually by much. Theorem 14.3 makes this rough and intuitive analysis precise by combining the MTF transform with the γ-code. It goes without saying that the upper bound in the theorem could be made closer to the (0-th order) empirical entropy $\mathcal{H}_0$ of the string S by substituting the γ-code with the δ-code, or any other better universal compressor for integers (see Chapter 11).

Theorem 14.3 *Let n_c be the number of occurrences of a symbol c in the input string S, whose total length is n. We denote by $\rho_{MTF}(S)$ the average number of bits per symbol output by the compressor that squeezes the string S^{MTF} using the γ-code over its integers. As $\rho_{MTF}(S) \leq 2\mathcal{H}_0 + 1$, we can conclude that this compressor cannot be more than twice worse than the Huffman compressor.*

Proof Let $p_1, \ldots, p_{n_c}$ be the positions in S where symbol c occurs. Clearly, between any two consecutive occurrences of c, say p_{i-1} and p_i, there may exist no more than $p_i - p_{i-1}$ distinct symbols (including c itself). So the index encoded by the MTF-compressor for the occurrence of c at position p_i is at most $p_i - p_{i-1}$. In fact, when processing position p_{i-1}, the symbol c is moved to the front of the list (i.e. in position 1), then it can move (at most) one position back per symbol processed subsequently, until we reach the occurrence of c at position p_i. This means that the integer emitted for the occurrence of c at position p_i is at most $p_i - p_{i-1}$. This integer is then encoded via γ-code using at most $|\gamma(p_i - p_{i-1})| \leq 2(\log_2(p_i - p_{i-1})) + 1$ bits. As far as the first occurrence of c is concerned, we can assume that $p_0 = 0$, and thus encode it with at most $|\gamma(p_1)| \leq 2(\log_2 p_1) + 1$ bits. Overall, the cost in bits for storing the occurrences of c in string S is

$$\leq |\gamma(p_1)| + \sum_{i=2}^{n_c} |\gamma(p_i - p_{i-1})|$$

$$\leq 2\log_2(p_1) + 1 + \sum_{i=2}^{n_c} \left(2\log_2(p_i - p_{i-1}) + 1\right)$$

$$= \sum_{i=1}^{n_c} \left(2\log_2(p_i - p_{i-1}) + 1\right).$$

By applying Jensen's inequality to the summation of the logarithms, we can move the logarithm function outside the summation and average its arguments, resulting in a telescopic sum:

$$\leq n_c \left(2\log_2\left(\frac{1}{n_c}\left(\sum_{i=1}^{n_c}(p_i - p_{i-1})\right)\right) + 1\right)$$

$$\leq n_c \left(2\log_2\left(\frac{n}{n_c}\right) + 1\right),$$

where the last inequality comes from the simple observation that the position p_{n_c} of the last occurrence of symbol c in S cannot be more than its length n. If we now sum over all symbols $c \in \Sigma$ and divide by the string length n, because $\rho_{MTF}(S)$ denotes number of bits per symbol in S, we get

$$\rho_{MTF}(s) \leq 2\left(\sum_{c \in \Sigma} \frac{n_c}{n}\log_2\left(\frac{n}{n_c}\right)\right) + 1 = 2\mathcal{H}_0 + 1.$$

The thesis follows because $\mathcal{H}_0$ lower-bounds the average codeword length of the Huffman code.   ∎

14.2.2   The RLE Transform

This is a very simple string transformation which maps every maximal contiguous substring of ℓ occurrences of symbol c into a pair $\langle \ell, c \rangle$. As an example, suppose we have to compress the following string, which represents a line of pixels of a monochromatic bitmap (where W stands for "white" and B for "black").

$$WWWWWWWWWWWBWWWWWWWWWWWWWBBBBBWWWWWW$$

We can take the first block of W and compress it in the following way:

$$\underbrace{WWWWWWWWWWW}_{\langle 11, W \rangle} BWWWWWWWWWWWWWBBBBBWWWWWW$$

We can proceed in the same way until the end of the line is encountered, thus obtaining the sequence of pairs $\langle 11, W \rangle, \langle 1, B \rangle, \langle 12, W \rangle, \langle 5, B \rangle, \langle 6, W \rangle$. It is easy to see that the encoding is lossless and simple to reverse. A remarkable observation is that if $|\Sigma| = 2$, as in the previous example, the input string would have alternating maximal runs of Ws and Bs, so we could simply emit the run lengths plus the first symbol of the string to compress, and still be able to get back the original string. In the previous example, we could emit: $W, 11, 1, 12, 5, 6$.

Run-length encoding is actually more than a transform, because it can be turned into a simple compressor by combining it with an integer coder (as we did for MTF). Its best-known context of application is fax transmission: a sheet of paper is viewed as a binary (i.e. monochromatic) bitmap, this bitmap is first transformed by XORing two consecutive lines of pixels, then every output line is RLE-transformed, and, finally, the integers are compressed via Huffman or arithmetic (recall that in binary images, the alphabet has size two). Provided that the paper to be faxed is pretty regular, the XORed lines will be full of 0s, and thus their RLE transformation will generate a few runs, whose compression will be significant. Nothing prevents applying this argument to coloured images, but the XORing of contiguous lines will get fewer 0s. More sophisticated approaches are needed in this setting.

Run-length encoding can perform better or worse than the Huffman compressor: this depends on the string we want to squeeze. The following lemma shows that RLE can be much better than Huffman, by adopting the same string we used to prove Lemma 14.1.

Lemma 14.2 *The compressor based on the combination of the RLE transform and the γ-code can be better than the Huffman compressor by an unbounded factor $\Omega(n)$, where n is the length of the string to be compressed.*

Proof Take the string $S = 1^n 2^n \cdots n^n$, and recall from the proof of Lemma 14.1 that the Huffman code takes $\Theta(n^2 \log n)$ bits to compress it. If we apply the RLE transform to S we get the string $S^{RLE} = \langle 1, n \rangle \langle 2, n \rangle \langle 3, n \rangle \cdots \langle n, n \rangle$. The γ-code over the integers of S^{RLE} will use $O(\log n)$ bits per pair, and thus $O(n \log n)$ bits overall. ∎

But there are cases, of course, in which the RLE-compressor can perform much worse than Huffman's one. Just consider a string S in which runs are very short, as in any English text where runs are typically of length 1.

14.3   The `bzip` Compressor

As we anticipated in the previous sections, the compressor `bzip` hinges on the sequential combination of three transforms – BWT, MTF, and RLE – which produce an output that is suitable to be highly squeezed by a classical statistical compressor, such as Huffman, arithmetic, or one of their variants. The most time-consuming step in this sequence is the computation/inversion of the BWT, at compression/decompression time, respectively. This is not just in terms of the number of operations, which is $\Theta(n)$ overall, but because of the pattern of memory accesses, which is very scattered, thus inducing a lot of cache misses. This is an issue that we will now comment on in depth.

The key property that makes `bzip` work well is the local homogeneity of the string produced by the Burrows–Wheeler transform, as we have broadly mentioned. Here, we provide more hints about this issue, and leave to Section 14.4 the task of digging into some more mathematical insights. Let us consider the input string S and one of its substrings w, which is assumed to occur n_w times in S. Say $c_1, \ldots, c_{n_w}$ are the symbols preceding these occurrences of w. Given the way $bw(S)$ is constructed, we can conclude that all rows prefixed by w in $\mathcal{M}'$ (they are of course n_w) are contiguous but possibly shuffled, with respect to their positions in S, in accordance with the symbols that follow w in each of those rows. In any case, the symbols c_i that precede w are contiguous in L (shuffled, accordingly), and thus constitute a substring of L. If the string S is Markovian, in the sense that symbols are emitted based on their previous ones (like in linguistic texts), then the symbols c_i are expected to be a few distinct ones, and this property holds the longer w is. This homogeneity is the core property that makes the subsequent steps in `bzip` very effective in compressing L.

For the sake of clarity, let us consider the following example, which runs `bzip` over the string S defined as the string `mississippi` repeated three times, which will entail a high degree of repetitiveness in S. The first step consists of computing $bw(S)$; for space reasons we do not detail this computation but just show the result, which can be checked by hand: $L =$ `ippp ssss ssmm miip ppii isss sssi iiii i`, where we have grouped symbols in 4-grams to simplify the reading, and $r = 16$ (counting from 1). The next step is to apply the MTF transform to L starting with a list $\mathcal{L}^{MTF} = \{i, m, p, s\}$. The storage of r (using 4–8 bytes) and of $\mathcal{L}^{MTF}$ (plainly) occurs in the preamble of the compressed file. The result of the MTF is the string

$$L^{MTF} = 1311\ 4111\ 1141\ 1414\ 1121\ 1411\ 1112\ 1111\ 1.$$

Note that runs of equal symbols generate runs of 1, except for the first symbol of each run, which is mapped to an integer representing its position in $\mathcal{L}^{MTF}$ at the time of its processing.

The first speciality introduced by `bzip` is that RLE is not applied to runs of all possible symbols; rather it applies a restricted variant, called RLE1, which squeezes only the runs consisting of 1s. So L^{MTF} can be regarded as a smart way to reserve the symbols (integers) 0 and 1 for the binary encoding of the lengths of 1-runs. More precisely, the run `11111`, consisting of five occurrences of 1, is encoded according to the following scheme, known as Wheeler's code: the length of the run is increased by 1, hence $5 + 1 = 6$, then the binary encoding of 6 is computed, hence `110`, and finally the first bit (surely 1) is removed, thus outputting the binary sequence `10`. The first increment guarantees that the (increased) run length is at least 2, and thus it is represented in at least two binary digits, of which the first is surely a 1. So the 1-bit removal leaves at least one bit to be output. Decoding Wheeler's code is easy – just repeat these steps in reverse order.

The key property of Wheeler's code is that the output bit sequence consists of no more digits than symbols in L^{MTF}, so this step can be considered as a preliminary compression, which is increasingly effective as the 1-runs in L^{MTF} increase in length. The binary output for the sequence of our running example is:

$$\text{RLE1} = 0314 \ 1041 \ 4031 \ 4141 \ 0210.$$

It is evident that the decompressor can easily identify the run's encodings, because they consist of maximal sequences of 0s and 1s; recall that these numbers have been reserved explicitly for this purpose.

Finally, RLE1 is compressed by using a statistical compressor that operates on an alphabet which consists of integers in the range $[1, |\Sigma| + 1]$. The reader can look at the home page of `bzip2` [19] for further details,[6] especially regarding the statistical-encoding step, and at the Squash compression benchmark[7] to access a plethora of compressors, datasets, and machines to perform the widest possible comparison.

An immediate conclusion about the practical performance of the compressors we have seen in this book is that LZ-based compressors are the fastest in (de)compression performance, because of their cache-friendly algorithmic structure, and they also achieve very interesting compression ratios; on the other hand, BWT-based compressors are quite slow, which is not a surprise because of the BWT-algorithmic structure, but they reach significant compression rates. Since $bw(S)$ is costly to be computed, its implementations divide the input file into blocks and then apply the transform *block-wise*. This is the reason why BWT-based compressors are called *block-wise compressors*. As for dictionary-based compressors, the size of the block impacts on the trade-off compression ratio versus compression speed; but, unlike dictionary-based compressors, this also impacts unfavorably on the decompression speed, which slows when working on longer blocks. Regardless, the current implementation of `bzip2` allows us to specify the size of the block at compression time with the command-line options `-1, . . ., -9`, which actually indicate a block of size 100 KB, . . ., 900 KB.

We are left with the problem of constructing the Burrows–Wheeler forward transform given that, as we have observed, we cannot construct explicitly the rotation matrix $\mathcal{M}$, and a fortiori its sorted version $\mathcal{M}'$, since this would take $\Theta(n^2)$ working space for an input of length n. This is why most BWT-based compressors exploit some "tricks" in order to avoid the construction of these matrices. One such "trick" involves the

---

[6] There, positions are counted from 0, so that RLE works on 0-runs and all other numbers are increased by 1 in order to still reserve the symbols 0 and 1 to encode the run's lengths.

[7] See https://quixdb.github.io/squash-benchmark/.

suffix	index	sorted suffix	index	$\mathcal{M}'$	L
abracadabra$	1	$	12	$abracadabra	a
bracadabra$	2	a$	11	a$abracadabr	r
racadabra$	3	abra$	8	abra$abracad	d
acadabra$	4	abracadabra$	1	abracadabra$	$
cadabra$	5	acadabra$	4	acadabra$abr	r
adabra$	6	adabra$	6	adabra$abrac	c
dabra$	7	bra$	9	bra$abracada	a
abra$	8	bracadabra$	2	bracadabra$a	a
bra$	9	cadabra$	5	cadabra$abra	a
ra$	10	dabra$	7	dabra$abraca	a
a$	11	ra$	10	ra$abracadab	b
$	12	racadabra$	3	racadabra$ab	b

Figure 14.4 Suffix Array *versus* sorted rotated matrix $\mathcal{M}'$ over the string $S =$ abracadabra$. We show the matrix $\mathcal{M}'$ and we copy in L the last symbol of each of its rows.

usage of suffix arrays, which were described in Chapter 10, where we also detailed several algorithms to build them efficiently. The construction of BWT deploys one of these algorithms,[8] and this motivates the increased interest in the literature about the suffix-array construction problem after the BWT publication (see, e.g., [15, 17, 1]).

To see why suffix arrays and BWT are connected, let us consider the following example Take the string $S =$ abracadabra$ and compute its suffix array $SA =$ [12, 11, 8, 1, 4, 6, 2, 5, 7, 10, 3]. Figure 14.4 summarizes these data structures for the running example at hand. The first four columns show the suffixes of the string S and its suffix array SA. The fifth column shows the corresponding sorted-rotated matrix $\mathcal{M}'$ with its last column L. It is easy to see that sorting suffixes is equivalent to sorting rows of $\mathcal{M}$, given the presence of the sentinel symbol $. The reader can check that the formula below ties SA with L:

$$ L[i] = \begin{cases} S[SA[i] - 1] & \text{if } SA[i] \neq 1 \\ \$ & \text{otherwise} \end{cases} $$

We know that every symbol $L[i]$ precedes symbol $F[i]$ in S (see Property 1). Symbol $F[i]$ is the first symbol of row i in $\mathcal{M}'$, and thus it is the first symbol of the suffix starting at $SA[i]$. Therefore we can conclude that $L[i]$ equals the symbol of S that precedes position $SA[i]$. The special case is the row corresponding to S, hence prefixed by the first suffix, for which $ will be used as preceding symbol. So, given the suffix array of string S, it takes only linear time to derive the string L, by applying this formula. We have therefore proved the following:

Theorem 14.4 *Given an input string S, constructing bw(S) takes the time and I/O complexity of Suffix array construction. By using the DC3 algorithm of Chapter 10,*

---

[8] M. Burrows: "So I enlisted his help in finding ways to execute the algorithm's sorting step efficiently, which involved considering constant factors as much as asymptotic behaviour. We tried many things, only some of which made it into the paper, but we met my goals: we showed that the algorithm could be made fast enough to see practical use on modern machines ..." [10].

the overall cost of building $bw(S)$ is optimal in several models of computation. In particular, it is $O(n)$ in the RAM model, and $O(\text{Sort}(n))$ in the two-level memory model, where $\text{Sort}(n)$ is the I/O cost of sorting n atomic items.

14.4 On Compression Boosting$^\infty$

Let us first recall the notion of k-th order empirical entropy as a measure of uncertainty (or information) associated with string S drawn from an alphabet $\Sigma = \{\sigma_1, \ldots, \sigma_h\}$, and let us denote by n_ω the number of occurrences of the substring ω in S. We use the notation $\omega \in \Sigma^k$ to specify that the length of ω is k. As introduced in Section 13.4, we define

$$\mathcal{H}_k(S) = \frac{1}{|S|} \sum_{\omega \in \Sigma^k} \left(\sum_{i=1}^h n_{\omega \sigma_i} \log \left(\frac{n_\omega}{n_{\omega \sigma_i}} \right) \right).$$

Setting $k = 0$, we get the classical 0-th order empirical entropy, which is computed with respect to the frequencies of the individual symbols in S, therefore without exploiting any k-length context. Clearly, $\mathcal{H}_k(S) \le \mathcal{H}_0(S)$, but it can be much smaller, and for growing $|S|$ and k this value converges to the entropy of the source that emitted S.

We are interested in this formula because it suggests a way to design a compressor that achieves $\mathcal{H}_k(S)$ starting from a compressor that achieves $\mathcal{H}_0(S)$ of its input string, such as arithmetic or Huffman compressors. This kind of algorithm is called a *compression booster*, because it is able to boost a compression performance up to $\mathcal{H}_0$ into a compression performance up to $\mathcal{H}_k$. The algorithmic tool to achieve this is, surprisingly, the Burrows–Wheeler transform [7]. In order to illustrate this innovative and powerful idea, let us consider a generic 0-order statistical compressor $\mathcal{C}_0$ whose performance, in bits per symbol, over a string S is bounded by $\mathcal{H}_0(S) + f(|S|)$ bits. We note that the function $f(|S|) = 2/|S|$ is the one achieved by arithmetic coding, and it is $f(|S|) = 1$ for Huffman coding (see Chapter 12).

In order to turn $\mathcal{C}_0$ into an effective k-th order compressor $\mathcal{C}_k$, we proceed as follows.

- Compute the Burrows–Wheeler transform $bw(S)$ of the input string S.
- Take all possible substrings ω of the string S, and partition the column L so as to form substrings L_ω, each formed by the last symbols of the rows prefixed by ω.
- Compress each L_ω with $\mathcal{C}_0$, and concatenate the output bit sequences by alphabetically increasing ω (or, equivalently, by occurrence of L_ω in L).

It can be seen immediately that L_ω is a substring of L, because rows prefixed by ω in $\mathcal{M}'$ are contiguous. Given the lcp array of string S, the partitioning of L takes linear time (see Chapter 10), and thus it does not impact on the efficiency of the final compressor $\mathcal{C}_k$. As far as the compression performance in bits per symbol is concerned, we easily derive that it can be bounded by

$$\frac{1}{|S|} \sum_{\omega \in \Sigma^k} |L_\omega| \left(\mathcal{H}_0(L_\omega) + f(|L_\omega|)\right) = \mathcal{H}_k(S) + O(|\Sigma|^k),$$

where we have applied the definition of $\mathcal{H}_k(S)$ to the summation of the $\mathcal{H}_0(L_\omega)$, and the fact that $f(|L_\omega|) \leq 1$ for Huffman and arithmetic compressors. It is clear that the more effective the 0-th order compressor, the closer it is to $\mathcal{H}_0$, the smaller is the term $f(|L_\omega|)$, and thus the additive term $O(|\Sigma|^k)$ becomes negligible. In [7] the authors showed that one actually does not need to fix k, since there is a compression booster that identifies in optimal $O(|S|)$ time a partition of L which achieves a compression ratio that is better than the one obtained by C_k, for any possible $k \geq 0$. The algorithm is elegant and not too involved, but it would require some space to be described in sufficient details, so that we refer the interested reader to that paper.

14.5   On Compressed Indexing$^\infty$

We have already highlighted the bijective correspondence between the rows of the rotated matrix $\mathcal{M}$ and the suffixes of the string S, as well as the relationship between the string L and the suffix array built on S (see Figure 14.4). These are at the core of the FM-index's design, which has been the first compressed full-text index to achieve efficient substring search and space occupancy bounded above by the k-th order empirical entropy of the indexed string. We can look at the FM-index as the *compressed version* of the suffix array, or as the *searchable version* of a bzip-compressed file. The nature of these notes does not allow us to dig into the technical details of the FM-index, so in the rest of this section we will just fly over its technicalities and concentrate on the main algorithmic ideas; the interested reader may look at the seminal paper [8] and the survey [16] for further details.

In order to simplify the presentation, we distinguish between three basic operations:

- Count(P) returns the *range of rows* [*first*, *last*] in $\mathcal{M}'$ (and thus suffixes in the suffix array) that are prefixed by the string $P[1,p]$. The value (*last* − *first* + 1) accounts for the number of these pattern occurrences.
- Locate(P) returns the *list* of all positions in the indexed string S where P occurs (they are possibly unsorte).
- Extract(i,j) returns the substring $S[i,j]$ by accessing its compressed representation in the FM-index.

For example, in Figure 14.4 for the pattern $P = $ ab we have *first* = 3 and *last* = 4 for a total of two occurrences. These two rows correspond, as the figure clearly illustrates, to the two suffixes $S[1, 12]$ and $S[8, 12]$ which are prefixed by P.

Let us start from the description of Count(P). The retrieval of the rows *first* and *last* is not implemented via a binary search, as occurred in suffix arrays, but it uses a peculiar search method which deploys the column L, the array C (which stores in $C[c]$ the position of the first occurrence of symbol c in column F, see Step 7 in Algorithm 14.1), and an additional data structure which supports efficiently the very basic counting Rank(c, k), which reports the number of occurrences

---

Algorithm 14.3 Counting the occurrences of pattern P[1,p] in S

1: $i = p, c = P[p]$;
2: $first = C[c], last = C[c + 1] - 1$;
3: **while** ($first \leq last$ **and** $i > 1$) **do**
4:     $c = P[i - 1]$;
5:     $first = C[c] + \text{Rank}(c, first - 1)$;
6:     $last = C[c] + \text{Rank}(c, last) - 1$;
7:     $i = i - 1$;
8: **end while**
9: **return** $(first, last)$.

---

of the symbol c in the string prefix $L[1, k]$. We mention that the array C is small in that its size is proportional to the alphabet cardinality; whereas the string L and the data structure to implement $\text{Rank}(c, k)$ over it can be kept compressed and they are still able to support efficiently the retrieval of $L[i]$ and $\text{Rank}(c, k)$. The literature offers many solutions for this latter problem (see, e.g., some classic results in [8, 11, 2, 16]); here we report some of them (possibly no longer the best ones at the time of writing given the effervescence of this research field):

Theorem 14.5 *Let $S[1, n]$ be a string over alphabet Σ, and let L be its BWT.*

- *If $|\Sigma| = O(\texttt{polylog}(n))$, there exists a data structure that supports* Rank *queries on L in $O(1)$ time using $nH_k(S) + o(n)$ bits of space, for any $k = o(\log_{|\Sigma|} n)$, and retrieves any symbol L in the same time bound.*
- *For general Σ, there exists a data structure that supports* Rank *queries on L in $O(\log \log |\Sigma|)$ time, using $nH_k(S) + o(n \log |\Sigma|)$ bits of space, for any $k = o(\log_{|\Sigma|} n)$, and retrieves any symbol of L in the same time bound.*

This means that Rank can be implemented in constant, or "almost" constant time, and in space that is very much close to the k-th order entropy of the string S we wish to index. The array C takes only $O(|\Sigma|)$ space, which is negligible for real alphabets. This means that this ensemble of data structures is very compact indeed.

We are left to show how this ensemble allows us to implement Count(P). Algorithm 14.3, nowadays called a *backward search*, reports the pseudocode of such an implementation which works in p phases numbered from p to 1. The i-th phase preserves the following invariant: *the parameter "first" points to the first row of the sorted rotated matrix $\mathcal{M}'$ prefixed by the suffix $P[i, p]$, and the parameter "last" points to the last row of $\mathcal{M}'$ prefixed by the same suffix $P[i, p]$*. Initially the invariant is true by construction: $C[c]$ is the first row in $\mathcal{M}'$ starting with c, and $C[c + 1] - 1$ is the last row in $\mathcal{M}'$ starting with c (recall that rows are numbered from 1). As a running example, take $P = ab$ and refer to the matrix $\mathcal{M}'$ of Figure 14.4: at the beginning we have $p = 2$, $P[2] = b$ and $C[b] = 7$ (we count one occurrence of \$ and five occurrences of a in S), and $C[b + 1] = C[c] = 9$ (we count two more occurrences of b in S). Thus $[7, 8]$ is the correct range of rows prefixed by the single symbol $P[2] = b$ before the backward search starts.

At each subsequent phase, Algorithm 14.3 has inductively found the range of rows [*first, last*] prefixed by $P[i, p]$. Then it determines the new range of rows [*first, last*] prefixed by the pattern suffix $P[i - 1, p] = P[i - 1] \cdot P[i, p]$, which is one symbol longer than the previously processed pattern suffix, namely $P[i, p]$. This inductive step works as follows. First it determines the first and last occurrence of the symbol $c = P[i-1]$ in the substring $L[first, last]$ by deploying the function Rank properly queried. Specifically, Rank($c, first-1$) counts how many occurrences of c occur before position *first* in L, and Rank($c, last$) counts how many occurrences of c occur up to position *last* in L. Therefore, these two values allow us to know which occurrences of c are included in $L[first, last]$, so they can be used to compute the LF-mapping of the first and the last occurrences of c in that range. Therefore Property 2 and Definition 14.1 imply the equalities deployed in Steps 5 and 6 of Algorithm 14.3, which can thus be efficiently implemented in time and space by means of a compressed data structure for Rank(c, k) (see Theorem 14.5).

For a formal proof that this mapping actually retrieves the new range of rows [*first, last*] prefixed by $P[i - 1, p]$ we refer the reader to the seminal publication [8]. Here we construct an example to convince the reader that everything works fine. Refer again to Figure 14.4 and consider, as before, the pattern $P = $ ab and the range [7, 8] of rows in $\mathcal{M}'$ prefixed by the last pattern symbol $P[2] = $ b (recall that we process P backward, hence the name *backward search*). Algorithm 14.3 picks the previous pattern symbol $P[1] = $ a, and then computes Rank($a, first - 1$) = Rank($a, 6$) = 1 and Rank(a, *last*) = Rank(a, 8) = 3, because $L[1, first - 1]$ contains one occurrence of a and $L[1, last]$ contains three occurrences of a. So Algorithm 14.3 computes the new range as: *first* = $C[a]$+Rank($a, 6$) = $2+1 = 3$, and *last* = $C[a]$+Rank($a, 8$)$- 1 = 2 + 3 - 1 = 4$, which is indeed the contiguous range [3, 4] of rows prefixed by the pattern $P = $ ab.

After the final phase (i.e. $i = 1$), *first* and *last* will delimit the rows of $\mathcal{M}'$ containing all the suffixes prefixed by P. Clearly, if *last* < *first* the pattern P does not occur in the indexed string S. The following theorem summarizes what we have sketched.

Theorem 14.6 *Given a string $S[1, n]$ drawn from an alphabet Σ, there exists a compressed index that takes $O(p \times t_{rank})$ time to support the operation Count($P[1,p]$), where t_{rank} is the time cost of a single Rank operation over the BWT of the string S (i.e. bw(S)). The space usage is bounded by $n \mathcal{H}_k(S) + o(n \log |\Sigma|)$ bits, for any $k = o(\log_{|\Sigma|} n)$.*

The interesting corollary of this result is that, by plugging the compressed data structure claimed in Theorem 14.5, we get an implementation of Count(P) that takes optimal $O(p)$ time and compressed space. However, this solution suffers some I/O inefficiency because every phase may elicit $\Theta(p)$ cache/IO misses due to the jumping around L and Rank required by Algorithm 14.3. There have been several attempts, reported in the literature, to make FM-index cache-oblivious or cache-aware, but so far we do not have an equally elegant solution for those issues.

Let us now describe the implementation of Locate(P). For a fixed parameter μ, we sample the rows i of $\mathcal{M}'$ that correspond to suffixes of the indexed string S that start at positions in S with the form $pos(i) = 1 + j\mu$, where $j = 0, 1, 2, \ldots$. Each such pair $\langle i, pos(i) \rangle$ is stored explicitly in a data structure $\mathcal{P}$ that supports membership queries in constant time (on the first *row*-component). Now, given a row index r, the position $pos(r)$ in S can be derived immediately for that row if it is sampled and thus indexed in $\mathcal{P}$; otherwise, the algorithm computes $h = LF^t(r)$, where t is the step in which h is a sampled row and thus it is found in $\mathcal{P}$. In this case, $pos(r) = pos(h) + t$ because every LF-computation moves backward in S by one single position. The sampling strategy ensures that a row in $\mathcal{P}$ is found in at most μ iterations, and thus the *occ* occurrences of the pattern P can be located via $O(\mu \times occ)$ queries to the Rank-data structure.

Theorem 14.7 *Given a string $S[1,n]$ drawn from an alphabet Σ, there exists a compressed index that takes $O(\mu\, occ)$ time and $O(\frac{n}{\mu} \log n)$ bits of space to support* Locate(P), *provided that the range [first, last] of rows prefixed by P is available.*

By fixing $\mu = \log^{1+\epsilon} n$, the solution takes polylogarithmic time per occurrence, and potentially sub-linear space (in bits) in the indexed string length n. Trade-offs are possible and literature abounds nowadays with asymptotic improvements and experimental investigations about these compressed indexes.

It is not very surprising that Count(P) can be adapted to implement the last basic operation supported by FM-index: Extract(i,j). Let r be the row of $\mathcal{M}'$ prefixed by the suffix $S[j,n]$, and assume that the value of r is known, that is the case after executing Count(P). The algorithm sets $S[j] = F[r]$, and then starts a loop which moves backward in S from $S[j-1]$ (because $S[j]$ has been found via the array F), deploying the LF-mapping (implemented via the Rank-data structure) as follows: $S[j-1-t] = L[LF^t[r]]$, for $t = 0, 1, \ldots, j-i-1$. It stops after $j-i$ steps, when we have reached $S[i]$. This approach is reminiscent of the one we took in the BWT inversion, with the difference that the array LF is not explicitly available, but its entries are generated on-the-fly via Rank computations. This guarantees still efficient time access to LF array and compressed space (thanks to Theorem 14.5).

Given the appealing asymptotic performance and structural properties of the FM-index, several authors have investigated its practical behavior by performing an extensive set of experiments [5].[9] Experiments have shown that the FM-index is compact (its space occupancy is usually not far from to the one achieved by bzip), it is fast in counting the number of pattern occurrences (a few microseconds per pattern's symbol), and the cost of their retrieval is reasonable when they are few (about 100k occurrences/sec). In addition, the FM-index allows us to trade space occupancy for search time by choosing the amount of auxiliary information stored into it (i.e. by properly setting the parameter μ and a few other parameters arising in the implementation of Rank). As a result, the FM-index combines compression and full-text

---

[9] See the Succinct Data Structure Library at https://github.com/simongog/sdsl-lite.

indexing, and like `bzip` it encapsulates a compressed version of the original file (accessible via `Extract`), and like suffix trees and suffix arrays it allows us to search for arbitrary patterns (via `Count` and `Locate`). Everything works by looking only at a small portion of the compressed file, thus avoiding its full decompression.

References

[1] Donald Adjeroh, Tim Bell, and Amar Mukherjee. *The Burrows–Wheeler Transform: Data Compression, Suffix Arrays, and Pattern Matching.* Springer, 2008.

[2] Jérémy Barbay, Meng He, J. Ian Munro, and S. Srinivasa Rao. Succinct indexes for strings, binary relations and multi-labeled trees. *Proceedings of 18th ACM–SIAM Symposium on Discrete Algorithms (SODA)*, 680–9, 2007.

[3] Jon L. Bentley, David D. Sleator, Robert E. Tarjan, and Victor K. Wei. A locally adaptive data compression scheme. *Communication of the ACM*, 29(4): 320–30, 1986.

[4] Mike Burrows and David J. Wheeler. *A Block-Sorting Lossless Data Compression Algorithm.* Technical Report 124, Digital Systems Research Center (SRC), 1994.

[5] Mark R. Nelson. Data compression with the Burrows–Wheeler transform. *Dr. Dobb's Journal of Software Tools*, 21(9): 46–50, 1996.

[6] Paolo Ferragina, Rodrigo Gonzalez, Gonzalo Navarro, and Rossano Venturini. Compressed text indexes: From theory to practice. *ACM Journal on Experimental Algorithmics*, 13: article 12, 2009.

[7] Paolo Ferragina, Raffaele Giancarlo, Giovanni Manzini, and Marinella Sciortino. Compression boosting in optimal linear time. *Journal of the ACM*, 52(4): 688–713, 2005.

[8] Paolo Ferragina and Giovanni Manzini. Indexing compressed texts. *Journal of the ACM*, 52(4): 552–81, 2005.

[9] Paolo Ferragina and Giovanni Manzini. Burrows–Wheeler transform. In Ming-Yang Kao, editor, *Encyclopedia of Algorithms*. Springer, 2008.

[10] Paolo Ferragina, Giovanni Manzini, and S. Muthukrishnan, coeditors. Theoretical Computer Science: *Special Issue on the Burrows–Wheeler Transform*. 387(3), 2007.

[11] Paolo Ferragina, Giovanni Manzini, Veli Mäkinen, and Gonzalo Navarro. Compressed representations of sequences and full-text indexes. *ACM Transactions on Algorithms*, 3: article 20, 2007.

[12] Juha Karkkainen, Dominik Kempa, and Simon J. Puglisi. Slashing the time for BWT inversion. *Proceedings of the IEEE Data Compression Conference*, 99–108, 2012.

[13] Juha Karkkainen and Simon J. Puglisi. Medium-space algorithms for inverse BWT. *Proceedings of the 18th European Symposium on Algorithms (ESA)*, Lecture Notes in Computer Science, Springer, 6346, 451–462, 2010.

[14] Juha Karkkainen and Simon J. Puglisi. Cache-friendly Burrows–Wheeler inversion. *Proceedings of the 1st International Conference on Data Compression, Communication and Processing (CCP)*, 38–42, 2011.

[15] Giovanni Manzini and Paolo Ferragina. Engineering a lightweight suffix array construction algorithm. *Algorithmica*, 40(1): 33–50, 2004.

[16] Gonzalo Navarro and Veli Mäkinen. Compressed full-text indexes. *ACM Computing Surveys*, 39(1): article 2, 2007.

[17] Simon J. Puglisi, William F. Smyth, and Andrew Turpin. A taxonomy of suffix array construction algorithms. *Proceedings of the Prague Stringology Conference*, 1–30, 2005.

[18] Julian Seward. Space–time tradeoffs in the inverse B–W transform. In *Proceedings of the IEEE Data Compression Conference*, 439–48, 2001.

[19] Julian Seward. bzip2. Available at https://www.sourceware.org/bzip2.

[20] Ian H. Witten, Alistair Moffat, and Timothy C. Bell. *Managing Gigabytes: Compressing and Indexing Documents and Images*. Morgan Kaufmann, second edition, 1999.

15 Compressed Data Structures

When Claude Shannon meets Donald E. Knuth...

In the previous chapter we presented a compressed version of suffix arrays, the FM-index. The literature nowadays offers plenty of compressed solutions for most, if not all, classic data structures for arrays, trees, and graphs [4]. In this final chapter we wish to give just an idea of these novel approaches to data structure design, and discuss the ones that we consider the most significant and fruitful, from a didactic point of view. A side effect of this discussion will be the introduction of the paradigm called *pointer-less programming*, which waives the explicit use of pointers (and thus integer offsets of four/eight bytes to index arbitrary items, such as strings, nodes, or edges) and instead uses *compressed* data structures built upon proper binary arrays that efficiently subsume the pointers, some operations over them, and even more.

In conclusion, at least from a theoretical perspective, pointer-less programming is a viable modern alternative to represent in compressed space classic pointer-based data structures, without impacting on their asymptotic performance. Having said this, and since this is a book on algorithm engineering, we must be frank in saying that pointer-less programming still needs skilled algorithm engineers to decide whether its use is effective and, if so, use it in the most fruitful way when building big-data applications.

15.1 Compressed Representation of (Binary) Arrays

Let us consider the following paradigmatic example. We are given a dictionary $\mathcal{D}$ of n strings of total length m. We map the dictionary onto a single string $T[1, m]$ (without separators between adjacent strings), and wish to support two query operations. The first is Access_string(i), which retrieves the i-th string in T; the second operation is Which_string(x), which asks to retrieve the starting position of the string in T including the symbol $T[x]$.

The classic approach to solve this problem is via an *array of pointers* $A[1, n]$ to $\mathcal{D}$'s strings, implemented by means of their offsets in $T[1, m]$, thus using $\Theta(n \log m)$ bits overall. Here, Access_string(i) boils down to returning $A[i]$, whereas Which_string(x) boils down to finding the predecessor of x in A. The first operation costs $O(1)$ time, and the second operation costs $O(\log n)$ time via binary search.

An orthogonal approach consists of adopting compressed representations for the offsets in A. In the next two subsections we will describe two approaches: one implements A's offsets via a binary array $B[1, m]$, where we set $B[i] = 1$ if and only if $T[i]$ is the first symbol of a dictionary string, enriched by a compressed data structure that supports some basic (yet useful) operations over B's bits; the other leverages the fact that A's offsets are increasing integers, and thus deploys Elias–Fano code to index them in compressed form (described in Chapter 11).

For the first solution, note that Access_string(i) requires searching for the i-th bit set to 1 in B, whereas Which_string(x) requires searching for the first bit set to 1 on the left of $B[x]$ (included) or, equivalently, counting the number k of 1s in $B[1, x]$ and then jumping to the k-th bit set to 1 in B. Nowadays, the first operation is called Select(i), whereas the counting operation is called Rank(x). Both operations could be implemented via a scan of B, but this would be costly in the worst case. The next subsection discusses a data structure that takes constant time for these two operations and occupies a space that is $o(m)$ bits in addition to B. For its space complexity, this solution is called *succinct* (because of the explicit storage of B), and turns out to be more compact in space than the pointer-based solution if $n = o(m/\log m)$.

For the second solution, we take advantage of the algorithmic properties of Elias–Fano code, which can support Access(i), to retrieve $A[i]$, in constant time, and Rank(x) in logarithmic time, taking space bounded above by $O(n \log(m/n))$ bits (see Chapter 11). We will show that this space bound is related to the entropy of array B, so this solution is called *compressed*, and turns out to be asymptotically better in space than the pointer-based solution, for all values of m and n.

15.1.1 A Succinct Solution, via Rank and Select

For achieving the goals we have stated, we introduce two new primitives and their corresponding data structures, called Rank and Select.

Definition 15.1 Let $B[1, m]$ be a binary array.

- The Rank of an index i in B relative to a bit $b \in \{0, 1\}$ represents the number of bits b occurring in $B[1, i]$. Formally, $\text{Rank}_1(i) = \sum_{j=1}^{i} B[j]$. Note that $\text{Rank}_0(i)$ can be computed in constant time as $i - \text{Rank}_1(i)$.
- Let $B[1, m]$ be a binary array. The Select of an index i in B relative to a bit $b \in \{0, 1\}$ returns the *position* of the i-th occurrence of bit b in B, and is denoted by $\text{Select}_b(i)$. Unlike Rank, Select_0 cannot be derived in constant time from Select_1, so each one needs proper data structures.

Let us consider the following binary array:

$$B = \begin{array}{|c|c|c|c|c|c|c|c|c|c|c|} \hline 0 & 0 & 1 & 0 & 1 & 0 & 0 & 1 & 0 & 1 & 0 \\ \hline \end{array}$$
$$\;\; 1 \quad 2 \quad 3 \quad 4 \quad 5 \quad 6 \quad 7 \quad 8 \quad 9 \quad 10 \quad 11$$

and consider the query $\text{Rank}_1(6)$, which is asking for the number of 1s encountered in the first six positions of B. The portion of B interested in this *counting* is the one highlighted in the following graphic, and the result is $\text{Rank}_1(6) = 2$:

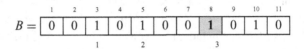

Now consider the query $\mathsf{Select}_1(3)$, which is asking for the position of the third occurrence of the bit 1 in the whole array B. The result is $\mathsf{Select}_1(3) = 8$, and the returned position is the one highlighted in the next graphic, where we also show the *rankings* of all 1s before the queried one.

$$B = \begin{array}{|c|c|c|c|c|c|c|c|c|c|c|} \hline 0 & 0 & 1 & 0 & 1 & 0 & 0 & \mathbf{1} & 0 & 1 & 0 \\ \hline \end{array}$$

Implementation of Rank. The *succinct* data structure supporting the Rank operation consists of *three levels*: in the first, we logically split the binary array B into *big blocks* of size Z each, and maintain for each some meta-information suitable to support the Rank operation; in the second level, we logically split each big block into *small blocks* of size z each, and maintain for each some other meta-information; the third level consists of a direct-access table indexed by small blocks and queried positions. The meta-information kept in the first two levels, and the table of the third level, will be proved to be *succinct* in space by occupying $o(m)$ bits overall. For simplicity of exposition we assume that z divides Z, so that the i-th *big block* is $B[Z \cdot (i - 1) + 1, Z \cdot i]$, and the j-th *small block* inside the i-th *big block* is $B[Z \cdot (i - 1) + z \cdot (j - 1) + 1, Z \cdot (i - 1) + z \cdot j]$, where $i, j \geq 1$.

The meta-information associated with the i-th big block consists of the number of 1s seen in the prefix of array B preceding this big block; it is termed *absolute rank* and denoted by r_i. The meta-information associated with the j-th small block inside the i-th big block consists of the number of 1s occurring in the prefix of that big block preceding that small block; it is termed *relative rank* and denoted by $r_{i,j}$. Figure 15.1 explains this meta-information pictorially. In particular, if r_i is by definition the number of 1s preceding (up to the beginning of B) the highlighted big block, then $r_{i+1} = r_i + 4$, because that big block includes four 1s. As for the meta-information stored for the

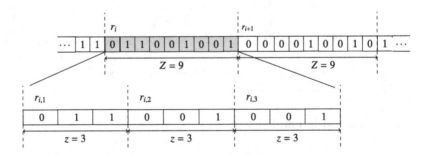

Figure 15.1 Example of meta-information stored for big blocks of size $Z = 9$ and small blocks of size $z = 3$, relative to the implementation of the Rank operation. r_i is the number of 1s from the beginning of binary array B up to the first entry of the highlighted big block (excluded), so $r_{i+1} = r_i + 4$. For the relative ranks associated at each small block, $r_{i,1} = 0, r_{i,2} = 2, r_{i,3} = 3$.

small blocks, note that $r_{i,1} = 0$, and we show it for completeness; the other two relative ranks are $r_{i,2} = 2$, since two 1s precede the second small block in the highlighted big block, and $r_{i,3} = 3$, since three 1s precede the third small block in the highlighted big block (as reported in the zoomed array depicted in Figure 15.1).

The space occupancy of all absolute ranks can be computed by multiplying the number of *big blocks* and the space needed to store one absolute rank, namely $O(\frac{m}{Z} \log m)$ bits, because each absolute rank is smaller than B's size m. By the same argument, the space needed to store all relative ranks is $O(\frac{m}{z} \log Z)$, because each relative rank is smaller than the size Z of big blocks, and thus can be stored in $O(\log Z)$ bits.

Now, let us set $Z = (\log m)^2$ and $z = \frac{1}{2} \log m$, then the total space occupancy is

$$= O\left(\frac{m}{Z} \log m + \frac{m}{z} \log Z \right)$$

$$= O\left(\frac{m}{\log^2 m} \log m + \frac{m}{\frac{1}{2} \log m} \log(\log^2 m) \right)$$

$$= O\left(\frac{m}{\log m} + \frac{m}{\log m} \log \log m \right)$$

$$= O\left(\frac{m \log \log m}{\log m} \right) = o(m).$$

It is easy to convince ourselves that we can obtain the Rank of positions at the end of each block (being either small or big) in constant time by either reading the absolute rank of the big block following the queried position, or summing the absolute rank of the big block enclosing the queried position and the relative rank of the small block following the queried position.

At this point, we know how to answer a Rank query on the last position of each (small or big) block, but what about queries on positions inside *small blocks*? The first solution we discuss is based only on the meta-information provided by absolute and relative ranks, as follows. Say $\text{Rank}_1(x)$ is formulated over an arbitrary position x in B possibly occurring inside a small block. For the sake of description, suppose $B[x]$ is included in the j-th small block, which is in turn included in the i-th big block of B, denoted by $B_{i,j}$. The answer to $\text{Rank}_1(x)$ is computed as $r_i + r_{i,j} + \text{Count}_1[B_{i,j}, x]$, where the last term counts the number of 1s occurring in the small block $B_{i,j}$ up to the bit $B[x]$ (included). Note that the indexes i and j can be computed as $i = 1 + \left\lfloor \frac{x-1}{Z} \right\rfloor$, and $j = 1 + \left\lfloor \frac{(x-1) \bmod Z}{z} \right\rfloor$, where $r_1 = 0$, $r_{i,1} = 0$, and recall that indexes are counted from 1. Having said this, the retrieval of the first two quantities takes constant time, whereas $\text{Count}_1[B_{i,j}, x]$ takes $O(z) = O(\log m)$ time in the worst case via a scan of $B_{i,j}$.

Note that if z fits in one memory word, then $\text{Count}_1[B_{i,j}, x]$ can be implemented in constant time via bit manipulation primitives, such as the `std::pop_count`[1] if z consists of a very few memory words, so that we can deploy SIMD (single instruction,

---

[1] https://en.cppreference.com/w/cpp/numeric/popcount.

R		pos	
block	1	2	3
000	0	0	0
001	0	0	1
010	0	1	1
011	0	1	2
100	1	1	1
101	1	1	2
110	1	2	2
111	1	2	3

Figure 15.2 Lookup table R of precomputed ranks for all possible small blocks of size $z = 3$ bits. Here $R[b, o]$ denotes the rank of the element in relative position o inside the block of binary configuration b.

multiple data) operations, and still be very fast; for longer z, it is still possible to achieve the constant-time optimal theoretical bound, but we need to include a third piece of meta-information consisting of a table R which tabulates the answers to all possible small-block configurations and queried positions, as shown in Figure 15.2. By means of this table, we can compute $\text{Count}_1[B_{i,j}, x]$ by accessing the corresponding entry in R, namely $R[B_{i,j}, o]$, where $o = 1 + ((x - 1) \bmod z)$ is the offset of bit $B[x]$ in the small block $B_{i,j}$. This procedure takes three memory accesses (i.e. one per r_i, one per $r_{i,j}$, and one per $R[B_{i,j}, o]$) and two additions, thus $O(1)$ time. Surprisingly enough, storing table R is not as costly as it could seem, given that we have set $z = (1/2) \log m$. In fact, R consists of 2^z rows and z columns, and each entry can be represented in $O(\log z)$ bits because it counts the number of 1s in a small block. The total space occupancy of R is therefore $2^z z \log z = O(2^{\log \sqrt{m}} (\log m) (\log \log m)) = o(m)$ bits. We conclude by observing that the last column of table R is redundant, because the information it stores is also available in $r_{i,j}$, thus it could be dropped, even if this does not change the asymptotic space occupancy of the proposed solution.

Theorem 15.1 *The space occupancy of the Rank data structure is $o(m)$ bits, and thus it is asymptotically sublinear in the size of the binary array $B[1, m]$. The Rank algorithm takes constant time in the worst case, and accesses the array B only in read-mode.*

Let us use the example shown in Figure 15.1 to visually explain the computation of $\text{Rank}_1(x)$, where we assume that $x = 17$ is the element indicated by a downward arrow in Figure 15.3. The algorithm follows the three steps already mentioned for the retrieval of the three quantities involved in the formula $r_i + r_{i,j} + R[B_{i,j}, o]$, where we recall that $i = 1 + \left\lfloor \frac{x-1}{Z} \right\rfloor$, $j = 1 + \left\lfloor \frac{(x-1) \bmod Z}{z} \right\rfloor$, and $o = 1 + ((x - 1) \bmod z)$.

1. Find the i-th big block including $B[26]$, namely $i = 1 + \left\lfloor \frac{17-1}{9} \right\rfloor = 2$, and retrieve the absolute rank r_2.

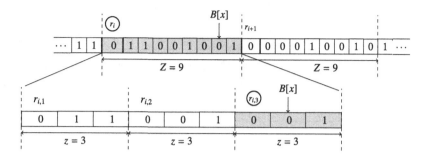

Figure 15.3 Graphic explanation of the execution of the Rank operation, where the absolute and relative ranks used in the computation are circled.

2. Find the j-th small block which contains $B[26]$, namely $j = 1 + \left\lfloor \frac{(17-1) \bmod 9}{3} \right\rfloor = 3$, and retrieve the relative rank $r_{2,3}$.
3. Find the offset position of $B[x]$ inside the small block $B_{2,3}$, namely $o = 1 + ((17 - 1) \bmod 3) = 2$, and then access the entry $R[001, 2]$, which is equal to zero in the running example (see Figure 15.2).
4. Compute the result as $\mathsf{Rank}_1(17) = r_2 + r_{2,3} + R[001, 2]$.

Implementation of `Select`. The implementation of the Select operation mainly follows the three-level design of the Rank data structure, with the algorithmic twist that here the binary array B is not split into big and small blocks of fixed length, but the splitting is driven by the number of bits set to 1.

Technically speaking, let us set $K = \log^2 m$ and use Z again to denote the size in bits of the *big blocks* that contain K bits set to 1. Clearly, Z changes among big blocks, but to keep things simple we avoid using different values of Z here and clarify things in text. By definition $Z \geq K$, hence the storage of all starting positions of big blocks takes $O(\frac{m}{K} \log m) = o(m)$ bits, and since big blocks contain exactly K bits set to 1, a simple arithmetic operation can derive the big block where the 1 searched for by the $\mathsf{Select}_1(i)$ operation occurs.

To continue the search for $\mathsf{Select}_1(i)$, we need to zoom into a big block. For time efficiency we cannot scan it, so we proceed to design the second level of the Select's data structure by splitting big blocks into *small blocks* still driven by the count of 1s. In particular, we distinguish between sparse and dense big blocks. A big block is called *sparse* if it contains "a few" 1s with respect to its size, where a "few" is quantified as $Z > K^2$. Otherwise it is called *dense*, and in this case we clearly have $Z \leq K^2$.

If a big block is sparse, then we can explicitly store the positions of its bits set to 1s, without incurring too much space occupancy. In fact, this takes $O\left(\frac{m}{K^2} K \log m\right) = O\left(\frac{m}{\log^2 m} \log m\right) = o(m)$ bits, where we have exploited the fact that the length of a sparse big block is $Z > K^2$ and $K = \log^2 m$.

On the other hand, if a big block is dense (i.e. $Z \leq K^2$), we proceed recursively by splitting that block into *small blocks* that contain $k = (\log \log m)^2$ bits set to 1 each. We

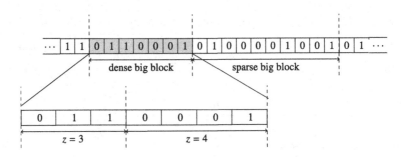

Figure 15.4 Implementation of Select. In this example, $K = 3$ and $k = 2$. Comments in text.

denote the length of a *small block* by z and observe again, as occurred for big blocks, that z may vary among small blocks, but we do not use subscripts to ease the reading. The storage of all starting positions of small blocks, relative to the beginning of their enclosing dense big block, takes $O\left(\frac{m}{k} \log K^2\right) = O\left(\frac{m}{(\log\log m)^2} \log\left(\log^4 m\right)\right) = o(m)$ bits, where we use the fact that the length of a small block is at least k and the length of its enclosing dense big block is at most K^2.

Finally, in order to keep track of the positions of the bits set to 1 in small blocks, we mimic what was done for the big blocks, and thus distinguish between *sparse* and *dense* small blocks, depending on whether the length z of a small block is larger or smaller, respectively, than $k^2 = (\log\log m)^4$ bits. As for big blocks, if the small block is sparse (i.e. $z > k^2$), we can store explicitly the positions of its 1s, but now *relative* to the beginning of the enclosing big block, thus taking $O(\frac{m}{k^2} k \log K^2) = O(\frac{m}{(\log\log m)^2} \log(\log^4 m)) = o(m)$ bits, where we use the fact that the length of a sparse small block is $z > k^2$, so their number is $O(m/k^2)$, and, moreover, z is shorter than the length of a dense big block, which is is $Z \le K^2$. We are therefore left with the storage of the 1s occurring in dense small blocks (within dense big blocks): we mimic what was done for the third level of the Rank's data structure, and thus pre-compute a table T of all answers to Select$_1$ within a dense small block, by observing that its size is $z \le k^2 = (\log\log m)^4$, and thus T occupies $O(z\, 2^z \log z) = o(m)$ bits.

In order to better understand the working of the Select$_1$ operation, let us refer to Figure 15.4, where we take for the sake of explanation $K = 3$ and $k = 2$. Note that the (highlighted) big block is dense because it contains $K = 3$ bits set to 1 and its size is $Z = 7 < 9 = K^2$, whereas the subsequent big block is sparse because it also contains $K = 3$ bits set to 1 but its size is $Z = 10 > 9 = K^2$. Moreover, the first small block of the highlighted big block is dense because it contains $k = 2$ bits set to 1 and its size is $z = 3 < 4 = k^2$, while the second small block is sparse and actually contains fewer than k bits set to 1, because k does not divide K. According to the description of the data structure for Select, the positions of the 1s of the sparse big block and of the sparse small block can be stored explicitly (the former as absolute values, the latter as relative values with respect to the beginning of their enclosing big block). Instead, the first small block of the highlighted big block contributes to the construction of the table T given that it is dense.

We are now ready to describe the implementation of $\mathsf{Select}_1(i)$, which exploits the three-level data structure, and proceeds as follows:

1. Compute the index $j = 1 + \left\lfloor \frac{i-1}{K} \right\rfloor$ of the *big block* including the i-th bit set to 1 in the binary array B. Denote this big block by B_j.
2. If B_j is sparse, the data structure has stored explicitly the result of $\mathsf{Select}_1(i)$, and we are done. Otherwise, the data structure has stored the starting position of the (dense) big block B_j, say s_j.
3. Turn $\mathsf{Select}_1(i)$ within B into a *relative* $\mathsf{Select}_1(i')$ within B_j, by computing $i' = 1 + (i - 1 \bmod K)$.
4. Compute the index $j' = 1 + \left\lfloor \frac{i'-1}{k} \right\rfloor$ of the *small block* including the i'-th bit set to 1 in B_j. Denote this small block by $B_{j,j'}$.
5. The data structure has stored the starting position of $B_{j,j'}$, relative to the beginning of B_j, say s'_j.
6. At this point, if $B_{j,j'}$ is sparse, the data structure has stored the position of the i'-th bit set to 1 in B_j, relative to the beginning of this big block, and thus we get the answer to $\mathsf{Select}_1(i)$ by summing that relative position to s_j; or, we access the precomputed table T with the binary configuration of $B_{j,j'}$ and the value $1 + (i - 1 \bmod k^2)$, and we get the answer to $\mathsf{Select}_1(i)$ by summing the retrieved T's entry to $s_j + s'_j$.

Similarly as observed for the Rank operation, since the length of dense small blocks is very short (namely, it is shorter than $(\log \log m)^4$, which is a tiny value for practical values of m), we could in practice consider scanning those small blocks, and thus drop the use of the precomputed table T.

We have therefore proved the following:

Theorem 15.2 *The space occupancy of the Select_1 data structure is $o(m)$ bits, and thus it is asymptotically sublinear in the size of the binary array $B[1, m]$. The Select_1 algorithm takes constant time in the worst case, and accesses the array B only in read-mode. The same time and space bounds hold for Select_0.*

15.1.2 A Compressed Solution, via Elias–Fano Coding

The approach we describe in this section can be directly applied to the array of (offset) pointers $A[1, n]$ to $\mathcal{D}$'s strings or to their characteristic binary vector $B[1, m]$. In fact, we can transform the latter into the former by taking the positions of the bits set to 1 in B, and thus obtain an increasing sequence of positive integers, which is the precondition of a valid input for the Elias–Fano code.

As an example, let us assume that in input we have the binary array

	1	2	3	4	5	6	7	8	9	10	11
$B =$	0	1	1	0	0	0	0	1	0	1	0

and then derive the array $A =$

1	2	3	4
2	3	8	10

. As we described in Chapter 11, the compression of A via Elias–Fano code obtains the two arrays

$L =$

1	2	3	4
10	11	00	10

and $H =$

1	2	3	4	5	6	7	8
1	1	0	0	1	1	0	0

defined over $n = 4$ items (hence four 1s in H), universe size $u = 11$, word size $b = \lceil \log_2 11 \rceil = 4$, number of bits for the least significant part $\ell = \lceil \log \frac{u}{n} \rceil = \lceil \log \frac{11}{4} \rceil = 2$, and number of bits for the most significant part $h = b - \ell = 2$.

As we anticipated in Chapter 11, the most interesting property of the Elias–Fano code is that the array H can be augmented with proper data structures and algorithms to efficiently support the following two operations:

- Access(i), which, given an index $1 \leq i \leq n$, returns $A[i]$;
- NextGEQ(x), which, given an integer $0 \leq x < u$, returns the smallest element $A[i] \geq x$.

Given these two operations on array A, it is the easy to compute $\mathrm{Select}_1(B, i)$ by means of Access(i), and compute $\mathrm{Rank}_1(B, i)$ by means of NextGEQ(i+1) $- 1$, where we assume that $A[n + 1] = \infty$ and that NextGEQ returns the position i of $A[i] \geq x$, rather than its value (to ease the explanation). We are now ready to discuss the implementation of these two operations using the terminology of Chapter 11 and by deploying an "augmentation" of H which hinges over a data structure that supports the Select_1 primitive on it.

Access(i) needs to concatenate the higher and lower bits of $A[i]$ present in L and H, respectively. The least significant bits of $A[i]$ are easily retrieved by accessing the i-th block of ℓ bits in the binary sequence L. The retrieval of the h most significant bits of $A[i]$ is a little more complicated, and boils down to determining in H the negative unary sequence referring to those bits. Since we do not know $A[i]$ but just the input i, that negative unary sequence is the one that includes the i-th bit set to 1 in H. The position of that bit (counting from 1) can be retrieved by executing $\mathrm{Select}_1(i, H)$, and then subtracting i, which returns the number of 0s preceding that position. By the properties of the Elias–Fano code, this number of 0s equals the bucket configuration that includes that bit 1; so by representing it with h bits, we get the most significant part of $A[i]$. The time complexity of this algorithm is therefore the one of the Select primitive, and thus it is constant according to Theorem 15.2; the additional space complexity required to support the Select primitive over array H is $o(|H|) = o(n)$ bits, thus it is sublinear in the number n of bits set to 1 rather than in the size m of array B.

Consider the example presented, and execute Access(3) which should return $A[3] = 8$. We retrieve the $\ell = 2$ least significant bits of $A[3]$ by accessing the third pair of bits in L, hence $L[3] = 00$. The retrieval of the remaining $h = b - \ell = 2$ most significant bits is obtained by first computing $\mathrm{Select}_1(3, H) - 3 = 5 - 3 = 2$, and by then encoding this bucket configuration in $h = 2$ bits, hence 10. By concatenating the two bit sequences we obtain the correct result: $A[3] = 10 \cdot 00 = (1000)_2 = 8$.

The other operation, NextGEQ(x), is implemented as follows. The algorithmic idea is to identify the bucket of the integer x, given its h most significant bits, and then determine the answer to NextGEQ(x) by looking at the integers of A in that bucket. More precisely, let v_h be the value of the h most significant bits of x. We search for the elements of A in the bucket of v_h by looking at its negative unary sequence in H. This negative unary sequence extends from the bit in position $p = $ Select$_0(v_h) + 1$ if $v_h > 0$, otherwise it is $p = 0$; and it terminates in position $q = $ Select$_0(v_h + 1)$. So $H[p, q] = 1^{q-p-1}0$ is that negative unary sequence, and $q - p$ is the number of integers in A that have the h most significant bits equal to v_h in value. Now, if the bit $H[p] = 0$, then the bucket is empty (i.e. $q - p = 0$), and thus no integers in A have the same h most significant bits as x. Thus, NextGEQ(x) has to return the first element of the next non-empty bucket (which surely has its h most significant bits larger than v_h). This element corresponds to the first 1 to the right of $H[p]$. We do not need its position: it is sufficient to know its rank i in A, and then execute Access(i). The rank i is $p - v_h$, because v_h is the number of bits set to 0 in $H[1, p]$. Otherwise the bucket is non-empty, its elements have the same h highest bits as x, and hence the element answering NextGEQ(x) either corresponds to a bit 1 in $H[p, q]$ or it corresponds to the first 1 to the right of $H[q]$. We distinguish between these two situations by finding the first value returned by Access(i) that is greater than or equal to x, for $i = p - v_h, \ldots, q - v_h$. The elements in a bucket are no more than $2^{\ell} = \Theta(u/n)$ (to be precise, they are no more than $\min\{n, 2^{\ell}\}$), so their scan would take $O(\min\{n, u/n\})$ time in the worst case. We can speed up this search by performing a binary search over them in $O(\min\{\log n, \log(u/n)\})$ time. The additional space complexity required to support the Select primitive over array H is $o(|H|) = o(n)$ bits.

Consider again the previous example, and execute NextGEQ(9), which should return $A[4] = 10$. Since $9 = 1001$, $\ell = 2$, and $h = 2$, we have $p = $ Select$_0(10_2) + 1 = $ Select$_0(2) + 1 = 4 + 1 = 5$ and $q = $ Select$_0(2 + 1) = 7$. Since $H[5] = 1$, the bucket is non-empty, its items in $H[5, 6]$ have the same h most significant digits as 10, and thus we could scan A between the positions $i = 5 - 2 = 3$ to $i = 7 - 2 = 5$ (not included), thus returning the value 10 because $A[3, 4] = [8, 10]$. As another example, assume we execute NextGEQ(4) (where $4 = 0100$ represented in $b = 4$ bits). We compute $p = $ Select$_0(01) + 1 = $ Select$_0(1) + 1 = 3 + 1 = 4$. Since $H[4] = 0$, the corresponding bucket is empty and thus we need to find the first element of the next non-empty bucket. This is the element of rank $i = p - v_h = 4 - 1 = 3$ in A, namely $A[3] = 8$ that we retrieve by executing Access(3).

Theorem 15.3 *Given an array $A[1, n]$ of increasing positive integers in the range $[0, m)$, there exists a compressed index for A taking $2n + n \lceil \log_2 \frac{m}{n} \rceil + o(n)$ bits, and supporting the retrieval of its elements (i.e. the Access operation) in worst-case constant time, and the retrieval of the integer greater than or equal to a given one (i.e. the NextGEQ operation) in $O(\log(m/n))$ worst-case time.*

This result can be rephrased as follows over the binary array B, interpreted as the characteristic binary vector of the array A of increasing positive integers.

Theorem 15.4 *Given a binary array* $B[1, m]$, *with n positions set to 1, there exists a compressed index for B taking* $2n + n\lceil \log_2 \frac{m}{n} \rceil + o(n)$ *bits, and supporting* $\mathsf{Rank}_1(i)$ *in* $O(\log(m/n))$ *time and* $\mathsf{Select}_1(i)$ *in* $O(1)$ *time in the worst case.*

We may observe that when n increases, the number of extra bits per element, namely $2 + \lceil \log \frac{m}{n} \rceil$, decreases and converges to 2 (plus small order terms). Vice versa, when n decreases, the number of extra bits goes to $\Theta(\log m)$, as for classic pointers. In any case, the proposed solution is no worse that the pointer-based solution, and it may turn out to be much better when B is dense. We finally notice that the term $n\log(m/n)$ relates to the information-theoretic lower bound of encoding n items in m positions, given by $\lceil \log \binom{m}{n} \rceil$ bits. This latter term can be rewritten as $\lceil \log \binom{m}{n} \rceil = n\log(em/n) - O(\log n) - \Theta(n^2/m)$, which is related to the 0-order entropy $\mathcal{H}_0$ of a bit string of length m with n bits set to 1, in fact $\lceil \log \binom{m}{n} \rceil = m\mathcal{H}_0 - O(\log m)$ (see section 2.3.1 in [4]). Hence, we can conclude that the proposed approach is close to the optimal space complexity, except for the additive two bits per element, provided that no further information about the distribution of the 1s is available and can thus be deployed.

15.2   Succinct Representation of Trees

In this section we address the problem of storing a tree in compressed form while still being able to perform some operations over its structure efficiently in time.

15.2.1   Binary Trees

The classic approach to representing a binary tree consists of storing two pointers per node (either an internal or a leaf node) so that navigational operations to *left* or *right* children can be implemented in constant time by following the corresponding pointer. If a child is missing, or we are at a leaf, pointers are set to NULL. This tree representation takes $\Theta(n\log n)$ bits, where n is the total number of nodes and leaves of the tree. Additional space is needed to answer more sophisticated queries, such as *parent* queries, or *subtree size* queries. In the former case, we need additional $\Theta(n\log n)$ bits for storing the pointer to the node's parent; in the latter case, we still need additional $\Theta(n\log n)$ bits for storing the subtree size.

The question is whether this amount of bits is necessary to support constant-time navigational operations, or whether it can be improved. It is known that a lower bound to the storage complexity of a binary tree is $2n$ bits, because there are asymptotically 2^{2n} distinct binary trees on n nodes,[2] and thus we need that amount of bits to dis-

---

[2] This result comes from the fact that we can explore a binary tree transforming it into a balanced sequence of opening (and closed) parentheses. An open parenthesis is printed when a node is visited, and a closed parenthesis is printed as soon as that node (and its subtree) has been fully visited in a pre-order traversal of the tree. Each binary tree of n nodes is now identified by a sequence of n pairs of parentheses that are correctly matched. Such configurations are $C_{n-1} = \frac{1}{n}\binom{2(n-1)}{n-1} \approx \frac{4^{n-1}}{(n-1)^{\frac{3}{2}}\sqrt{\pi}}$, called *Catalan numbers*, that are $\Theta(2^{2n})$ asymptotically.

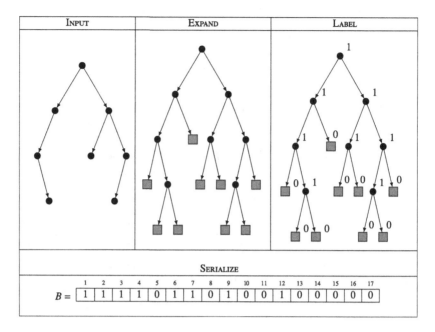

| | | | INPUT | | | EXPAND | | | LABEL | |

Figure 15.5 Construction of the binary array B from the binary tree T, where the added *dummy* leaves are represented as gray squares. The input binary tree consists of $n = 8$ nodes (including its leaves). The first step creates the expanded binary tree $\widehat{T}$ of $2n + 1 = 17$ total nodes (including dummy leaves), which are then labeled with 0 (dummy leaves) and 1 (original nodes). The final step consists of serializing the labeled nodes of $\widehat{T}$ into a binary array B of 17 bits.

tinguish one tree from another one. In this section we describe a brilliant idea dating back to 1989 [3], and due to Guy Jacobson, which matches this space lower bound (up to lower-order terms) by turning constant-time navigational queries over binary trees into constant-time Rank and Select operations over binary arrays suitably derived from those binary trees. A win–win situation, indeed.

In describing this transformation we refer the reader to Figure 15.5, which shows a running example for a binary tree T of $n = 8$ nodes (including leaves). The transformation generates a binary array B in three main steps:

1. **Expand:** Complete all nonbinary nodes and leaves in T with some special nodes, called *dummy* leaves, thus forming the *expanded* binary tree $\widehat{T}$;
2. **Label with one bit:** Label dummy leaves in $\widehat{T}$ with bit 0, and all other nodes of $\widehat{T}$ that were present in the original tree T with bit 1;
3. **Serialize:** Visit $\widehat{T}$ per levels, from left to right, and write down in an array B the binary labels encountered in the visit.

It is easy to show that the expanded binary tree $\widehat{T}$ consists of $2n+1$ nodes (including the dummy leaves), and thus the output binary array B consists of $2n+1$ bits. The proof may be addressed by induction, and this is left to the reader.

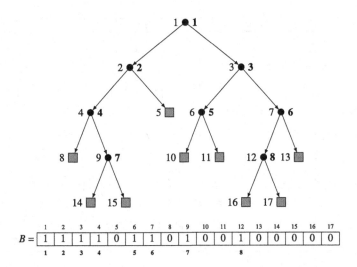

Figure 15.6 Example of the two (plain and bold) logical labelings computed over the expanded tree $\widehat{T}$ and the corresponding binary array B. The indexes above B refer to the plain labeling (i.e. BFS numbering) of $\widehat{T}$'s nodes, whereas the indexes below B represent the bold labeling (i.e. BFS numbering) of T's nodes.

As far as the navigational queries are concerned, we label *logically* (i.e. the labels are not stored, but used to perform the algorithms) each node of the expanded tree $\widehat{T}$ with two integers that, for the sake of discussion and illustration, are denoted in **bold** and plain. The **bold** labels are integers from 1 to n, they are attached to the nodes of the input tree T, and correspond to a *BFS (breadth-first search) numbering* of T. The plain labels are integers from 1 to $2n + 1$, they are attached to the nodes of the expanded tree $\widehat{T}$, and correspond to a *BFS numbering* of $\widehat{T}$. This labeling of $\widehat{T}$'s nodes naturally maps onto a labeling of B's bits that is a *logical labeling* (shown in Figure 15.6 only for illustrative purposes), since we don't actually store those numbers.

We then enrich the binary array $B[1, 2n+1]$ with the two data structures that support Rank_1 and Select_1, and take $o(n)$ bits in addition to the space occupancy of B (according to Theorem 15.2). The key tool to implement the navigational operations over T is a bijection from bold labels to plain ones, and vice versa, thanks to Select and Rank operations respectively. More precisely, the plain label j can be derived from the bold label $\mathbf{i}$ of a node in $\widehat{T}$ via the computation $j = \mathsf{Select}_1(\mathbf{i})$; vice versa, the bold label $\mathbf{i}$ can be derived from the plain label j of a node in $\widehat{T}$ via the computation $\mathbf{i} = \mathsf{Rank}_1(j)$. The former comes from the fact that the 1s are assigned to the nodes of the input tree T, included in $\widehat{T}$, so that $\mathsf{Select}_1(\mathbf{i})$ gives the position of that node in B jumping the zeros due to the added dummy leaves. The reverse, that is, $\mathbf{i} = \mathsf{Rank}_1(j)$, comes from the complementarity of Rank and Select operations. As an illustrative example, referring to Figure 15.6, we may check that the node of $\widehat{T}$ at the second level and the farthest right has plain label $j = 7$ and bold label $\mathbf{i} = \mathbf{6}$: and in fact the reader can check on the array B that $7 = \mathsf{Select}_1(\mathbf{6})$ and, vice versa, $\mathbf{6} = \mathsf{Rank}_1(7)$.

Now we are ready to implement the three navigational operations mentioned at the beginning of this section, by noting that in the expanded binary tree $\widehat{T}$ an *internal* node with bold number $\mathbf{x}$ has left child with plain number $2x$ and right child with plain number $2x + 1$; this is the same numbering rule of binary heaps, here applied to the *complete* binary tree $\widehat{T}$, as the reader can easily check in Figure 15.6. Another important observation is that one can check if a node in $\widehat{T}$ is an internal (original) node or a dummy leaf just by checking its corresponding bit $B[i] = 1$ or 0, respectively, where i is the plain label of that node. Again referring to Figure 15.6 and the node with plain label 7 and bold label $\mathbf{6}$, the left child has plain label $2 \cdot \mathbf{6} = 12$ and right child has plain label $2 \cdot \mathbf{6} + 1 = 13$; moreover, it is an internal node of $\widehat{T}$, and its bit $B[7] = 1$, its left child is also internal, and in fact its bit $B[12] = 1$, whereas its right child is a dummy leaf, and its bit $B[13] = 0$.

We now have all the algorithmic ingredients to implement the three main navigational operations over the nodes of the input tree T, in constant time:

1. LEFT CHILD: Given a node of the input tree T, represented by its (bold) number $\mathbf{x}$, we use the formula above and compute first the plain labeling of its left child, namely $2 \cdot \mathbf{x}$, and then turn it into its corresponding bold labeling via the computation `left_child(x)` $= \mathsf{Rank}_1(2\,\mathbf{x})$.
2. RIGHT CHILD: Similarly, the bold label for the right child is `right_child(x)` $= \mathsf{Rank}_1(2\,\mathbf{x} + 1)$.
3. PARENT: By inverting the reasoning behind the computation of the right and left children, we have that the bold label of the parent is `parent(x)` $= \lfloor \mathsf{Select}_1(\mathbf{x})/2 \rfloor$.

As we have observed, the algorithm has to check whether $B[2\,\mathbf{x}] = 0$ or $B[2\,\mathbf{x}+1] = 0$, in which cases the retrieved child is NULL. The parent is NULL if the query is executed over the root of T, hence the node with bold label $\mathbf{1}$. We have therefore proved the following:

Theorem 15.5 *A binary tree of n nodes can be represented in $2n + 1 + o(n)$ bits, and supports queries for* `parent`, `left_child` *and* `right_child`, *in constant time.*

Note that this *succinct* representation achieves the same query performance as the pointer-based representation, but with an improvement of a factor $\Theta(\log n)$ in its space occupancy. Actually, if we need to move downwards in T, we only have to build the data structure for Rank_1; in fact Select_1 is only needed for the parent computation. Finally, we note that this succinct tree representation can still be enriched with auxiliary data attached to the nodes of T. It is enough to store an array $A[1, n]$ that keeps in $A[i]$ the auxiliary information associated to the node with bold labeling $\mathbf{i}$ in T. A similar argument can be followed to manage auxiliary information attached to the edges of T, by using the destination node as their indexing handle.

We conclude this section with a running example for the three navigational operations we have described, executed on the binary tree of Figure 15.6. We start by computing the left child of the node with bold label **6** in $\widehat{T}$: `left_child(6)` = $\mathsf{Rank}_1(2 \times 6) = \mathsf{Rank}_1(12) = 8$; but now we discover that this child exists, because $B[12] = 1$. Pictorially, the computation is as follows:

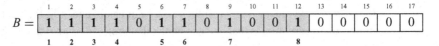

Let us now compute the right child of the same node: `right_child(6)` = $\mathsf{Rank}_1(2 \times 6 + 1) = \mathsf{Rank}_1(13) = 6$; but now we discover that this child does not exist, because $B[13] = 0$. Pictorially, the computation is as follows:

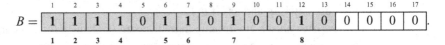

Finally, let us compute the parent of that node: it is `parent(6)` = $\lfloor \mathsf{Select}_1(6)/2 \rfloor = \lfloor \frac{7}{2} \rfloor = \mathbf{3}$; we can conclude that the parent exists because its index is larger than 0. Pictorially, the computation is as follows:

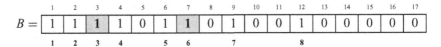

15.2.2 Arbitrary Trees

We now explore another implementation of trees, which is powerful enough to manage ordered trees of arbitrary degree and perform a larger set of queries in constant time, such as parent, first child (from the left), next sibling (on the right), and the node's degree. The *ordering* property is necessary in order for us to refer to the first and next child. The solution is called LOUDS, which stands for **Level Order Unary Degree Sequence**. This approach is based on the intuition that a tree is uniquely determined by its degree sequence written in BFS order, and works as follows:

1. **Expand:** Append a "dummy root" of degree 1.
2. **Label with node's degree:** Label every tree node with its degree.
3. **Serialize:** Visit the tree level-wise and from left to right (i.e. BFS order), encode the sequence of the nodes' degrees in unary, and store them in a binary array B.

A running example of LOUDS for a tree of degree at most three is provided in Figure 15.7. This figure allows us to first derive a bound on the space occupancy of this tree representation (hence array B), and then infer two properties of B upon which hinge the implementation of the four navigational operations supported by LOUDS.

LOUDS takes $2n + 1$ bits to encode the tree's structure, like the Jacobson's representation of the previous section. The proof follows by a simple counting argument: the number of bits 0 in B is n, because the unary encoding associates a bit 0 to every child of a node in the expanded tree (and thus, to all its nodes except the dummy root);

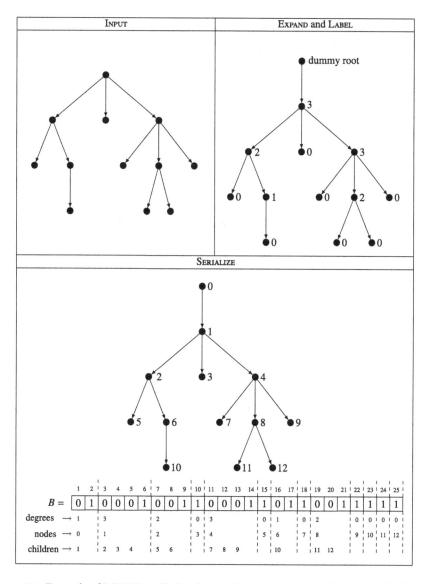

Figure 15.7 Example of LOUDS applied to the tree shown at the upper-left corner of the figure. The result of steps EXPAND and LABEL is shown on the same tree at the upper-right corner of the picture, where each node reports its degree on the right. The result of the final step SERIALIZE is shown in the tree, above, which reports the BFS numbering for each node, and, below, the binary array B, which consists of the sequence of unary representations of the degrees for each node (see text). For the sake of illustration (and thus not stored), the values above B represent the array indexes, while below B we show three lists: the first is denoted as "degrees" and reports the nodes' degrees encoded in unary in the array B; the second list is denoted as "nodes" and reports the BFS numbering of the nodes in T whose degree is indicated in the list above; while the third list represents, for each 0 entry in B, the child(ren) of the corresponding node reported in the list "nodes."

the number of bits 1 in B is $n + 1$, because every node (including the dummy root) generates a unary encoding that is ended by a 1.

From the BFS numbering of the tree nodes and the BFS-ordered serialization of the unary encoding of their degrees, it is not difficult to get an intuition of the correctness of the following two properties relating B's bits and tree nodes:

Property 1. The node numbered k, according to the BFS visit, corresponds to the k-th bit 0 in B.

Property 2. The children of the node numbered k correspond to the maximal sequence of 0s following the k-th bit 1 in B.

Given these two properties, the four navigational operations – parent, left child, next sibling, degree – can be easily implemented in constant time as follows (refer to Figure 15.7 for the running examples, and recall that the BFS numbering of a node equals the position in B of its corresponding bit 0):

DEGREE: Given a node with BFS number x, its degree can be derived as $\deg(x) = \mathsf{Select}_1(x+1) - (\mathsf{Select}_1(x) + 1)$ (here we use Property 2). As an example, $\deg(4) = \mathsf{Select}_1(5) - (\mathsf{Select}_1(4) + 1) = 14 - (10 + 1) = 3$, since

	1	2	3	4	5	6	7	8	9	10	11	12	13	14	15	16	17	18	19	20	21	22	23	24	25
$B =$	0	1	0	0	0	0	1	0	0	1	**1**	0	0	0	**1**	1	0	1	1	0	0	1	1	1	1

PARENT: Given a node with BFS number x, the BFS numbering of its parent can be derived as $\mathtt{parent}(x) = \mathsf{Rank}_1(\mathsf{Select}_0(x)) = \mathsf{Select}_0(x) - x$ (here we use first Property 1 and then Property 2). As an example, $\mathtt{parent}(5) = \mathsf{Select}_0(5) - 5 = 7 - 5 = 2$, since

	1	2	3	4	5	6	7	8	9	10	11	12	13	14	15	16	17	18	19	20	21	22	23	24	25
$B =$	0	1	0	0	0	1	**0**	0	1	1	0	0	0	1	1	0	1	1	0	0	1	1	1	1	

FIRST CHILD: From the computation of $\deg(x)$ we know that the degree of a node with BFS number x is located between the positions $\mathsf{Select}_1(x)+1$ and $\mathsf{Select}_1(x+1)$. So if $\deg(x) = 0$, we return NULL; otherwise, we jump to the first 0 of that unary-degree sequence, which is located at position $\mathsf{Select}_1(x) + 1$ in B, and then return the BFS numbering of its corresponding node by executing Rank_1 (here we use Property 2). Note that $\mathsf{Rank}_0(\mathsf{Select}_1(x) + 1) = \mathsf{Select}_1(x) + 1 - x$. Thus we have proved the following:

$$\mathtt{first\_child}(x) = \begin{cases} \text{NULL} & \text{if } \deg(x) = 0 \\ \mathsf{Select}_1(x) + 1 - x & \text{otherwise} \end{cases}$$

Here we consider two examples, for the two possible cases. As for $\mathtt{first\_child}(9)$, since $\deg(9) = \mathsf{Select}_1(9+1) - \mathsf{Select}_1(9) - 1 = 22 - 21 - 1 = 0$, the answer is NULL:

	1	2	3	4	5	6	7	8	9	10	11	12	13	14	15	16	17	18	19	20	21	22	23	24	25
$B =$	0	1	0	0	0	0	1	0	0	1	1	0	0	0	1	1	0	1	1	0	0	**1**	**1**	1	1

As for `first_child(8)`, since $\deg(8) = \mathsf{Select}_1(8+1) - \mathsf{Select}_1(8) - 1 = 21 - 18 - 1 = 2$, the first child of the node whose BFS numbering is 8 does exist, and its BFS numbering can be computed by $\mathsf{first\_child}(8) = \mathsf{Select}_1(8) + 1 - 8 = 18 + 1 - 8 = 11$:

1	2	3	4	5	6	7	8	9	10	11	12	13	14	15	16	17	18	19	20	21	22	23	24	25
0	1	0	0	0	1	0	0	1	1	0	0	0	1	1	0	1	**1**	0	0	**1**	1	1	1	1

$B =$

NEXT SIBLING: Let us consider a node with BFS numbering x, and compute $y = \mathsf{Select}_0(x)$ as its corresponding null bit in B (according to Property 1). Hence its sibling gets the next BFS number, that is, $x + 1$, if the next bit $B[y + 1]$ is 0, otherwise the requested sibling does not exist. Formally,

$$\mathtt{next\_sibling}(x) = \begin{cases} x+1 & \text{if } B[\mathtt{Select\_0}(x)+1] = 0 \\ \text{NULL} & \text{otherwise} \end{cases}$$

We consider again two examples, for the two possible cases. For `next_sibling(12)`, we first compute $y = \mathsf{Select}_0(12) = 20$, and since $B[y+1] = B[21] = 1$, the answer is NULL because the sibling does not exist:

1	2	3	4	5	6	7	8	9	10	11	12	13	14	15	16	17	18	19	20	21	22	23	24	25
0	1	0	0	0	1	0	0	1	1	0	0	0	1	1	0	1	1	0	**0**	**1**	1	1	1	1

$B =$

For `next_sibling(11)`, we first compute $y = \mathsf{Select}_0(11) = 19$, and since $B[19+1] = B[20] = 0$ the requested sibling has BFS numbering $11 + 1 = 12$:

1	2	3	4	5	6	7	8	9	10	11	12	13	14	15	16	17	18	19	20	21	22	23	24	25
0	1	0	0	0	1	0	0	1	1	0	0	0	1	1	0	1	1	**1**	**0**	0	1	1	1	1

$B =$

15.3   Succinct Representation of Graphs

We have eventually arrived at the final topic of this book, which is probably one of the most challenging of all topics investigated in current years, because of the advent of graph databases, social networks, and knowledge graphs. We are being flooded with data and most of the time they are related, which can be fruitfully modeled via a *graph* data structure. In this section, we aim to design succinct graph representations that efficiently support some graph traversals directly over them. The case of satellite information associated to graph nodes or edges, so-called *labeled graphs*, can be dealt with by adopting additional data structures, as was the case for labeled trees discussed in the previous section.

We will consider three orthogonal approaches to the succinct representation of graphs: one leverages the power of the Elias–Fano code in the compressed indexing of increasing integer sequences, such as the ones describing the adjacency lists of nodes; another exploits the specialities of Web graphs to derive highly compressible binary sequences; and the third adopts a sophisticated compressed indexing approach based on k^2-trees and a regular decomposition of the adjacency (binary) matrix in (binary) submatrices.

Let us start by introducing some useful notation and terminology. The input graph is denoted by $G = (V, E)$, where V is a set of n graph nodes and E is a set of m graph

Node	Outdegree	Adjacency lists
. . .	. . .	. . .
15	9	13, 15, 16, 17, 18, 19, 23, 24, 203
16	10	15, 16, 17, 22, 23, 24, 316, 317, 3041
17	0	
18	5	13, 15, 16, 17, 50
. . .	. . .	. . .

Figure 15.8 Naïve representation of graphs by adjacency lists.

edges. For the sake of presentation, we assume that nodes are identified by means of positive integers from 1 to n, and we overload the symbol E to denote also the adjacency matrix of the graph, so that $E[u, v] = 1$ if and only if (u, v) is an edge of G. For a given node $u \in V$, the nodes v connected to u by means of a graph edge (i.e. $E[u, v] = 1$) are called *adjacent nodes* of u, and if we sort them in *increasing order* by their integer label, we get the *adjacency list* of u. The classic and naïve representation of G consists of encoding nodes in adjacency lists with $\Theta(\log n)$ bits each, thus taking overall $\Theta(m \log n)$ bits for storing the entire graph.

An illustrative example of a graph representation via its adjacency lists is provided in Figure 15.8. It is pretty much obvious from the picture how to deploy the Elias–Fano code to compress and efficiently access the adjacency lists of G, because of their increasing order, as discussed in Chapter 11. This is surely a well-justified approach to apply whenever no special properties can be proved over the distribution of the integers (i.e. node IDs) in the adjacency lists. In this case, the space occupancy could be evaluated as $O(m (2 + \log \frac{n^2}{m}))$ bits, by observing that we have m bits set to 1 over n^2 possible entries of E.

The next two subsections investigate the case of some special graphs, in which *specially designed* approaches to their succinct representation can be exploited to get further space savings with respect to the Elias–Fano encoding described in the previous paragraph.

15.3.1   The Case of Web Graphs

A Web graph is a directed graph in which nodes are Web pages and edges are the hyperlinks between them. Web pages are identified by means of their URLs, which can be turned into integers (and thus, nodeIDs) by taking their ranking in the alphabetical order of their *reversed* URLs, namely URLs in which the host has been reversed.[3]

As shown in [1], Web graphs satisfy two interesting properties, *locality* and *similarity*: the first means that most outgoing links from a page point to pages in the same

---

[3] This means that the URL string www.corriere.it/esteri/page.html is *reversed* as it.corriere.www/esteri/page.html, and then alphabetically ordered. This order tends to cluster URLs coming from the same host.

host; the second means that two pages coming from the same host share many outgoing links. Interpreting these two properties in terms of nodeIDs, we can deduce that, by *locality*, a node u often points to nodes v such that $|u - v|$ is small, and furthermore, that the difference between nodes in the same adjacency list is often small, because they may come from the same host; and, by *similarity*, we can deduce that u's and v's adjacency lists share many elements provided that $|u - v|$ is small.

The *locality* property therefore suggests that adjacency lists of nodes from the same host occur close to each other in the reversed-URL ordering, and they show the presence of *clustered* integers, possibly forming *contiguous increasing runs*. We know from Chapter 11 that the Elias–Fano code does not best exploit this type of integers distribution rather, the simpler γ- or δ-codes do, and even better in terms of space occupancy is the interpolative code, which, however, does not support the efficient access to the individual elements of those compressed lists. Therefore, unless graph backups are mandatory, the γ- and δ-codes are a good choice given their interesting storage-versus-access trade-off. And, indeed, they may be used in the following algorithm as an *escape* compression strategy, whenever no special property about an increasing sequence of nodeIDs can be proved.

If we also take into account the *similarity* property, then a more effective storage of Web graphs is possible [1]. The key idea is to represent the adjacency list $L[x]$ of a node x as the "modified" version of some previous, but close, list $L[y]$, called the *reference list*. The difference $x - y = r > 0$ is called the *reference number*. We use $r = 0$ to mean that $L[x]$ is encoded as is, without applying the reference compression with respect to any previous $L[y]$: here, we may just use an integer coder (such as γ- or δ-codes) over the differences between consecutive nodeIDs. The choice of r is critical, and occurs within a *window* of size W. The larger W is, the better the compression ratio, but the slower and more memory-consuming the compression phase turns out to be. In fact, the value of W impacts on the number of reference lists examined to find the one that compresses $L[x]$ best. Of course, the list $L[y]$ can in turn be compressed as the "modified" version of some previous list $L[z]$, with $z < y$ and $y - z < W$, and so on, thus creating *reference chains* whose length might be arbitrarily long. This impacts on the decompression efficiency of this compressed storage approach. In order to trade space occupancy with decompression efficiency, the authors of [1] have introduced another parameter, denoted by R and called *maximum reference count*, that limits the set of reference lists to the ones in the window W that do not produce reference chains longer than R. A small value for R is likely to produce worse compression, but shorter (random) access times.[4]

---

[4] For a principled management of reference lists and chains, offering good compression ratios together with fast and flexible access to compressed adjacency lists (without incurring complete decompression of the entire graph), we refer the reader to *Zuckerli* [6]. Zuckerli is a scalable compression system meant for large real-world graphs, experimented over billions of nodes and edges. Compared to WebGraph, Zuckerli leverages advanced compression techniques and novel heuristic graph algorithms that can achieve up to 30 percent space reduction with a resource usage for decompression comparable to that of WebGraph.

Node	Outd	Ref	Copy list	Extra nodes
...	...	...	...	...
15	9	0	-	13, 15, 16, 17, 18, 19, 23, 24, 203
16	10	1	011100110	22, 316, 317, 3041
17	0		-	-
18	5	3	111100000	50
...	...	...	...	...

Figure 15.9 Representation of adjacency lists in Figure 15.8 by means of *copy lists*. Node 15 is not subject to reference compression (in fact, its "Ref" field is 0), whereas nodes 16 and 18 have their adjacency lists compressed with respect to the reference list $L[15]$.

Now, in order to differentially compress $L[x]$ in terms of its reference list $L[y]$, we build a binary sequence $B[x]$ of $|L[y]|$ bits, each one indicating whether the corresponding element of $L[y]$ is or is not also an element of $L[x]$: in the former case that bit is set to 1, in the latter case it is set to 0. Bit sequence $B[x]$ is called the *copy list* of $L[y]$. From the *similarity* property and the fact that r is small, we expect that $L[x] \cap L[y]$ is large, so many items of $L[x]$ are represented via just one bit (set to 1) in $B[x]$; moreover, we expect that $L[x] \setminus L[y]$ is small and thus its nodes, called the *extra nodes*, are stored explicitly or compressed via some integer coder (such as γ- or δ-codes) applied over the differences between consecutive nodeIDs. In order to reconstruct the original adjacency list $L[x]$, a merge operation is performed between the list of extra nodes and the referred adjacency list $L[y]$ limited to the elements set to 1 in $B[x]$. An example of differential compression is shown in Figure 15.9.

An attentive reader may have noticed that the copy lists are an alternating sequence of maximal runs composed either of 1s or of 0s. Hence, they can be encoded via the following scheme: first, we store the initial bit of the copy list, and then we encode with a suitable integer compressor the length ℓ of each run. The type of run (whether it is a run of 1s or 0s) has not to be stored because runs are alternating and we know the type of the first one, since its bit value is stored in the front of the compressed bit sequence. The resulting binary sequence is called a *copy block*. An additional space saving is obtained by dropping the encoding of the length of the last run from the *copy blocks*, because it can be easily derived from the other available information (e.g. $|L[y]|$) stored in Outd, and the length of the other runs available in copy blocks; see Figure 15.9 and the seminal paper [1] for other succinctly encoding tricks.

As illustrated in Figure 15.10, the adjacency list $L[18]$ has a copy list which starts with a run of 1s (because of the content of the field "First bit") of length 4 (because the first encoded integer is 4), and with a second run of 0s having length $|L[15]| - 4 = 9 - 4 = 5$, which is correct, as the reader can verify by looking at the copy list of $L[18]$ in Figure 15.9. For completeness, we look at the adjacency list $L[16]$: its copy blocks are 5, the first one is a run of 0s (because of the content of the field "First bit"), and the last one not stored is a 0-run again (because of the alternation of the $4 + 1$ runs) having length $|L[15]| - 8 = 9 - 8 = 1$.

Node	Outd	Ref	First bit	Copy blocks	Extra nodes
...	...	...	...	...	...
15	9	0	-	-	13, 15, 16, 17, 18, 19, 23, 24, 203
16	10	1	0	1, 3, 2, 2	22, 316, 317, 3041
17	0	-	-	-	-
18	5	3	1	4	50
...	...	...	...	...	...

Figure 15.10 Representation of adjacency lists by means of *copy blocks*. For the sake of illustration, we use commas to separate the lengths of the maximal runs of 1s or 0s.

Experiments have shown that the extra nodes often form increasing sequences of consecutive integers, called *intervals*. Two types of compression can be applied to squeeze them: if an interval is longer than some predefined threshold, it is encoded via its left extreme and its length, properly encoded in a succinct way; otherwise, its integers can be encoded by taking into account the preceding intervals or nodeIDs in order to squeeze the used bits. Details about these special encoding steps can be found in the original publication [1], where it is also shown that Web graphs can be compressed by up to three bits per edge.

15.3.2 The Case of Generic Graphs

The final compression scheme for graphs that we consider exploits the sparsity of their adjacency matrices and a form of *clustering* of their 1-entries, which typically occur in generic graphs, in order to obtain a compressed and efficiently navigable representation [2, 4]. The proposed scheme hinges upon a k^2-ary tree (aka k^2-tree) built upon the adjacency matrix E of the input graph, as follows.

For the sake of presentation, let us assume that the graph consists of n nodes and m edges, so its adjacency matrix E has size $n \times n$ of which only m entries are set to 1. We assume that $n = k^h$, otherwise we pad the matrix in its bottom and right part, in order to make it have the width of the smallest power of k bigger than n. The size of E is then such that it consists of $n^2 = k^{2h}$ binary entries.

The original matrix E is *logically assigned* to the root of the k^2-tree. Then we split E in exactly k^2 square submatrices $E_{1,1}, \ldots, E_{k,k}$, and each one is *logically assigned* to a child of the root, which therefore has k^2 children. These children are labeled with 1 if the corresponding submatrix contains at least one bit set to 1, otherwise they are labeled with 0. The nodes labeled with 0 are the leaves of the k^2-tree, whereas the nodes labeled with 1 are decomposed recursively in k^2 further submatrices, which will constitute the children of the decomposed nodes. This decomposition process stops as soon as it reaches a submatrix size equal to 1. See Figure 15.11 for a running example.

Given this decomposition strategy, the k^2-tree has height $h = \Theta(\log_k n)$, and consists of at most n^2 leaves. The k^2-tree is fully balanced and complete if E is full of 1s; conversely, the sparser and the more clustered the 1s in E are, the smaller the k^2-tree, which, regardless, contains as many paths of length h as 1s in E, which are m. Thus

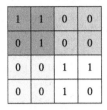
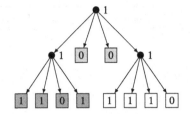

Figure 15.11 Example of k^2-tree over a 4×4 adjacency matrix, here $k = 2$. The tree has height 2, and its leaves are represented by squares whereas its internal nodes are represented by dots. Internal nodes are labeled with 1, whereas leaves are labeled with 0 if they represent *null* submatrices, or with 1 if they correspond to a submatrix of a singleton bit set to 1.

the total number of nodes is upper-bounded by mhk^2, because any node on such paths has k^2 children.[5] It goes without saying that the larger k is, the shallower the tree is, but the larger its branching factor is. This trade-off impacts on the space occupancy and the performance of the navigational operations over the k^2-tree, and it is driven by the composition of E.

It is easy to check the existence of a graph edge (u, v) by navigating the k^2-tree: start from the root and go to the child $E_{i,j}$ such that $i = \lceil (u\,k)/n \rceil$ and $j = \lceil (v\,k)/n \rceil$; then set the new u and v as $1+((u-1) \bmod (n/k))$ and $1+((v-1) \bmod (n/k))$, respectively, and repeat that computation recursively (with the new n being n/k) relative to the currently visited node until a leaf is reached; its label will provide the answer to the existence of the queried edge. The time complexity is therefore $O(h)$ in the worst case.

Retrieving a row or a column of the compressed matrix is a little more complicated, but it allows us to navigate the graph via its *forward* and *backward* edges. This is a feature not supported by the graph representations described in the previous sections, unless one represented with them both the adjacency matrix and its *transpose*, thus duplicating the space occupancy. The intuition behind a *row retrieval* (column retrieval is similar) by means of a k^2-tree extends the one behind the retrieval of a single matrix entry, with the additional trick that a row can span several nodes at different levels, so many paths have to be traversed, with the consequence that the retrieved row has to *recombine* the answers coming from all those paths (i.e. all reached leaves). Figure 15.12 shows the case of retrieving the row 15 from the adjacency matrix of a graph with $n = 16$ nodes and having set $k = 2$. Null submatrices are delimited by bold segments, and we visualize the part of the adjacency matrix that is explored by the algorithm. Note that the first half of the queried row is available in the child $E_{2,1}$ because it is fully null; to retrieve the other entries we have to traverse paths at different depths, and thus referring to submatrices of different sizes. In the figure, the parameter p_i denotes the row queried at every recursive level, starting with $p_0 = 15$.

---

[5] Actually, a better upper bound on the number of nodes can be derived by observing that, at the top of the k^2-tree, many nodes are shared by the m paths mentioned in the text. The upper bound can thus be refined as $mk^2(\log_{k^2} \frac{n^2}{m} + O(1))$ bits.

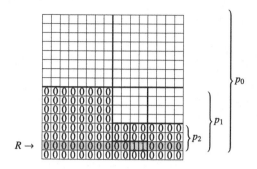

Figure 15.12 An example where $n = 16$ and $k = 2$. In this case $p_0 = 15, p_1 = 7, p_2 = 3$, $p_3 = 1, p_4 = 1$. Counting the children in BFS order, as $\{1, 2, 3, 4\}$, we note that: at the first level we visit two children (submatrices) of the root, that is, third and fourth, the former being fully null; at the second level we visit two children of the latter fourth child, that is, third and fourth, the latter being fully null; at the third level we visit again two children of the former, that is, third and fourth, the former being fully null; and then we finally visit two children of the latter, which turns out to be labeled 1.

The nice idea behind the use of k^2-trees is that they may be efficiently stored using a variant of the LOUDS representation (see Section 15.2.2) that makes use of two arrays: T is a bit array that stores the labels of all internal nodes of the k^2-tree serialized in BFS order, and L is another bit array that stores the labels of the lowest level in rightward order. Finally, Rank_1 and Select_1 data structures are built over T, in order to support an efficient tree navigation. The array L is not indexed because leaves have no children, and thus the navigation surely stops at them.

In the running example of Figure 15.11, the arrays T and L are the following ones:

$$T = \begin{array}{|c|c|c|c|} \hline 1 & 0 & 0 & 1 \\ \hline \end{array} \quad \text{and} \quad L = \begin{array}{|c|c|c|c|c|c|c|c|} \hline 1 & 1 & 0 & 1 & 1 & 1 & 1 & 0 \\ \hline \end{array}$$

We observe that, given an entry $T[i] = 1$ corresponding to an internal node of the k^2-tree, the position (according to the BFS numbering) of its j-th child (as internal node) is $\mathsf{Rank}_1(T, i) \times k^2 + j$, because we need to take into account all the k^2 children of nodes to the left (according to the BFS numbering) of $T[i]$ and then add the queried child-offset. As for the asymptotic time and space performance of the k^2-tree-based solution, we note that the worst-case time complexity of retrieving a row (full of 1s) of the adjacency matrix is $O(n)$, since Rank_1 takes constant time and, at level ℓ, in the pathological case, we may need to explore all k^ℓ submatrices covering that queried row, until we reach the last level, where we visit the submatrices of size 1×1 set to 1. On average, the time complexity may be proved to be $O(\sqrt{m})$ [2]. This means that the sparser the matrix (hence, the graph) is, the faster the decoding of one row is, and thus the retrieval of the adjacency list of a node of the indexed graph is also faster. Moreover, since the total k^2-tree size has been estimated to be upper-bounded by $m h k^2 = m k^2 \log_k n$, this is the number of bits (up to lower-order terms) taken by the succinct solution with the use of Rank and Select data structures built over the binary arrays T and L. More details can be found in the literature, such as [2, 4].

References

[1] Paolo Boldi and Sebastiano Vigna. The Webgraph framework I: Compression techniques. In *Proceedings of the 13th International Conference on World Wide Web (WWW)*, 595–02, 2004.

[2] Nieves R. Brisaboa, Susana Ladra, and Gonzalo Navarro. k^2-trees for compact web graph representation. In *Proceedings of the 16th International Symposium on String Processing and Information Retrieval (SPIRE)*, 8–30, 2009.

[3] Guy Jacobson. Space-efficient static trees and graphs. In *Proceedings of the 30th Annual Symposium on Foundations of Computer Science (FOCS)*, 549–54, 1989.

[4] Gonzalo Navarro. *Compact Data Structures: A Practical Approach*. Cambridge University Press, 2016.

[5] Luca Versari, Iulia-Maria Comsa, Alessio Conte, and Roberto Grossi. Zuckerli: A new compressed representation for graphs. *IEEE Access*, 8, 219233–43, 2020.

16 Conclusion

*In the end we retain from our studies only
that which we practically apply.*
Attributed to Johann Wolfgang Von Goethe

Arriving at the end of this book, you might ask, "What's next ?" And indeed, although the previous fiftheen chapters have just scratched the surface of algorithmics, I hope they have increased your interest in this field and had positive impact on your academic or professional approach to problem solving. Moreover, I hope that after reading these pages you agree with the phrase at the beginning of this book: "Programming is still an art, but you need good tools to express it at the highest level of beauty."

That said, let me dig into the question of the "next" algorithmic tools and computing infrastructures that algorithm engineers will need to study, design, and practice with in the coming years.

In this book we have commented at length on the evolution of computer memories, and their increased complexity, type, and number. These features have driven us to introduce the *simplified* two-level memory model that allowed us to analyze the performance of the proposed algorithmic solutions with simplicity and obtain a much better approximation than the classical RAM model. However, the algorithms optimized over this model of computation will probably become less effective in the years to come, because of the evolution of ICT infrastructures and the demanding challenges posed by new data-intensive workloads. In fact, data is the core resource in our present digital economy era, and companies will be able to successfully deal with digital transformation if they can develop customer-centric and data-driven digital services that increasingly offer real-time responses by means of a digital infrastructure platform centered on big data. Add to this complex industrial scenario the eager requests of researchers, engineers, and analysts to digitalize larger and larger amounts of data and have available more and more computing power that should accelerate their "time to results" in several processing-power- and data-demanding applications, such as autonomous driving, biological and medical sciences, energy, economics and financials, and advanced scientific and engineering research, just to mention a few.

It goes without saying that storage devices will continue to play a critical role in driving these innovations, because are a key component of HPC (high-performance computing) infrastructures. In particular, physically distributed, globally shared memory will become more and more important to cope with those data-intensive workloads, especially the ones that elicit nonpatterned memory access, such as graph analytics. Moreover, as the next-generation cloud architectures become ubiquitous, applications will need more and more capability to move computing workflows through multiple containers, each provided dynamically with appropriate hardware and software resources, possibly enriched with some embedded intelligence. But, although recent years have seen impressive progress in the rollout of advanced computing and storage infrastructures, and more will surely come in the near future, we are perfectly aware that those hardware solutions will not be enough to ensure that storage and computing resources will be available *where and when* they will be needed.

As a result, the design of algorithms and data structures will play an even more crucial role than before, because they may guarantee advancements that go far beyond Moore's law.[1] But these "advancements" will be possible only if algorithm engineers will enrich their "algorithmic toolbox" with knowledge and competence that can build upon the topics discussed in the previous pages by adding, first and foremost, methods and techniques from the fields of artificial intelligence (AI) and machine learning (ML), optimization, and cryptography. This should be driven by the same spirit that moved designers and engineers in the recent past toward the introduction in their algorithmic solutions of database concepts (generating I/O-efficient data structures), bioinformatics challenges (generating genome search engines), and, more recently, information theory (which drove the design of the compressed indexes of Chapter 15). And indeed, it is not surprising that in the recent years we have witnessed an upsurge in interest in data structures and algorithms building upon AI/ML tools (the *learned indexes*, or *algorithms with predictions*) to exploit data distribution or GPU/TPU hardware to improve their performance, or to optimize computational resources with respect to *multiple criteria* (hence, not just time and/or space taken individually), or, finally, to deal with cloud computing and storage by offering *robustness* against malicious leaking (by internal or external parties) of various types of information using increasingly sophisticated cryptographic techniques. In the latter scenario, the key issue is to support secure and efficient searches and mining operations over sensitive data, such as genomic and medical data, which have been encrypted and indexed in a way that there can not be leak of query access patterns, their responses, and, of course, the underlying indexed data. In order to perform *private and secure real-time computations*, researchers and professionals are investigating how to combine cryptographic and data-structure methodologies in novel and efficient ways that aim at achieving guarantees of privacy and security, not only in theory but also with practically efficient performance. Last, but not least, AI/ML and multi-criteria optimization will also play a crucial role in the data compression field, where the goal is to increase the performance of HPC infrastructures by automatically, dynamically, and efficiently determining the best compression approaches that satisfy the computational-resource

---

[1] Moore's law (1965) predicted that the number of transistors in a microchip would double about every 18 months: see https://en.wikipedia.org/wiki/Moore%27s_law.

constraints imposed by modern customer-centric applications. This will require the design of novel encoding schemes which exploit not only the (classic) repetitions in the input data, but also some novel forms of *regularities* that are not captured by current compressors, and that can be identified by properly designed and trained ML models. These new encoding schemes will also be required to compress *structured data*, such as matrices and labeled graphs (namely the ones generated by AI/ML applications, knowledge graphs, and graph databases), in a way that will eventually allow them to support arithmetic/query operations directly on their compressed versions.

No doubt, the coming years will be full of striking challenges for algorithm designers and engineers.

Index

Printed in the United States
by Baker & Taylor Publisher Services